The World Sunday School Movement

THE WORLD
SUNDAY SCHOOL MOVEMENT

The Story of a Broadening Mission

GERALD E. KNOFF

A Crossroad Book
THE SEABURY PRESS · NEW YORK

1979
The Seabury Press
815 Second Avenue
New York, N.Y. 10017

Library of Congress Cataloging in Publication Data
Knoff, Gerald E   The world Sunday school movement.
"A Crossroad book."
Bibliography: p. 269
1. Sunday—Schools—History. I. Title.
BV1515.K58   268'.09   78-26096   ISBN 0-8164-0416-X

In the year 1780,
ROBERT RAIKES
established his first Sunday school
in Sooty Alley, Gloucester, England.
In the year 1880, just a century later,
LUTHER ALLAN WEIGLE
was born.

This book,
concerned with the history
of the movement they served so well,
is dedicated
to the memory of these two able and consecrated men.

The author hopes
it may serve as an early
centennial and bicentennial thank offering.

"True progress never despises the past. Reform always tries to comprehend the existing system and to understand how it has come to be what it is."

—The Rev. Dr. J. A. MacFadyyen, Manchester, England, Minister of the Chorlton Road Congregational Church, at the First World Sunday School Convention, London, 1889

Contents

2. Organization and Program Emerge, 1907–1924
page 48

3. A Federation of Autonomous Units, 1924–1939
page 98

6. _Common Ecumenical Study and Progress Toward Merger,_
_1965–1971_
page 213

Foreword

THE PUBLICATION of this informative volume serves to remind us of the forthcoming bicentennial of the Sunday school in 1980. Two hundred years ago (more or less) Robert Raikes of Gloucester, England launched a modest school on Sunday for the street children of his city. It did not take long for the news about Raikes' effort at literacy education to spread throughout England and across the ocean to the new United States. In due course this institution became one of the universal marks of Protestant congregations on either side of the Atlantic. Along with the Sunday service and the prayer meeting, the Sunday school served as the incubator of conversion and the nursery of piety. Toward the end of the nineteenth century the "Sunday school movement," as it was so affectionately called in those days, spread well beyond England and America to other countries around the globe. The story of its transformation into a worldwide institution is intertwined with the saga of the missionary movement and the expansion of Anglo-American influence. Like the British empire of the early twentieth century, "the sun never set" on the Sunday school.

For a variety of reasons almost all students of church history have neglected the significance of this complex and intriguing tale. "As a church historian," Professor Martin E. Marty of the University of Chicago wrote in 1975, "I have always been amazed to see how little attention has been given this basic institution by historians and scholars." While several historical studies of the Sunday school have appeared in recent years (and more are slated to be published in the near future), this subject still remains a largely unknown territory.

In future years the scholarly explorers of this terrain will be grateful to Dr. Gerald E. Knoff for his persistence in ferreting out the material which is presented in this work. This carefully documented study represents several "firsts." Dr. Knoff is the first chronicler of the history of the various organizational efforts to support the worldwide development of the Sunday school.

xi

He is also the first interpreter to do justice to the contribution of the Sunday school movement to the cause of ecumenism. As a veteran Christian educator and distinguished church leader during the last twenty years, Dr. Knoff has long demonstrated a judicious and thoughtful concern for the educational ministry of the church. Those qualities of mind and spirit are happily manifest in this book.

—Robert Wood Lynn

Acknowledgments

THE DESIRE TO recount the history of the world Sunday school movement emerged in the early months of 1970, during some of the later sessions of the committee proposing a merger of the World Council of Christian Education and the World Council of Churches. *The Big Little School* by Robert W. Lynn and Elliott Wright was the first book to tell the story of this movement. This is the second. It is hoped there will be others, dealing with the historical developments in several areas of the world.

The list of persons who have helped me in this endeavor is a long one. First among them is Robert Lynn himself, then dean of the Auburn Seminary program and professor at Union Theological Seminary in New York City. He first proposed that I begin this undertaking and he has been, since then, my encouraging guide and friend.

Former staff members of the World Council of Christian Education and Sunday School Association have shared generously with me their personal collections and reminiscences: Forrest L. Knapp, Everett M. Stowe, Nelson Chappel, Loren Walters, Ralph N. Mould, H. A. Hamilton, and Andrew Wright. Messrs. Knapp, Chappel, and Mould read the entire manuscript. A. W. Andrews of the National Christian Education Council of England and Wales put at my disposal, in his office, a valuable collection of archives.

The staff of the Union Seminary library and that of the Disciples of Christ Historical Society in Nashville, Tennessee, met my every need.

In the Sterling Memorial Library of Yale University there are nearly seventy boxes of the personal papers of Luther A. Weigle, chairman of the association-council for forty years. In the late summer of 1977 these boxes were not completely sorted or described. I have worked through some of this material, but a complete account of the relation of Dr. Weigle to the World's Sunday School Association will have to await a careful examination of these documents by another researcher. In this place Patricia Bodak and Lawrence Dowler helped me.

My special thanks go to Ans Van der Bent, librarian of the World Council of Churches, in the Ecumenical Centre, Geneva, and to those of the staff, for their patience and helpfulness during concentrated research in the autumn of 1975.

During my stay in Geneva, two staff members of the Office of Education were of the greatest assistance: Gerson Meyer put me in touch with valuable documentary material. William B. Kennedy not only encouraged me in every way, but also took me into his home for an extended stay. He and his wife, Frances, made my visit in a Swiss-French culture warm with "deep South" hospitality. Dr. Kennedy also read the manuscript in an earlier draft.

Roland H. Bainton, inspiring teacher of earlier years, has helped in suggesting sources to be explored. I record my appreciation to all those who made possible much of the gathering of primary data for this study in libraries in New Haven, New York, Nashville, Philadelphia, Princeton, Geneva, London, and other cities.

Harriet M. Ranck was the faithful and efficient typist who brought order out of the marked-up pages. My wife, Dorothy, helped with proofreading and provided constant and often-needed encouragement. Coleman Burke and Constable MacCracken helped with publishing arrangements. My thanks to them.

In late February 1949 the British committee of the World Council of Christian Education expressed a desire to have written a history of the association-council, and sent its desire to the Board of Managers. It was voted ". . . that the chairman and the two general secretaries be responsible for planning such a history and gathering material for it."

As is often the way with administrative bodies, the Board made no provisions for lightening the loads of the two general secretaries to make the preparation of such a history possible.

It remained for me, a later member of the Board of Managers, to discharge this responsibility as best I was able, regarding the task as a debt of honor to the agency which had given me so many rich experiences and friendships, and, from beginning to end, as a pleasant labor of love.

Gerald E. Knoff
East Sandwich, Massachusetts

The World Sunday School Movement

1

"Fellowship, Inspiration, and Edification" 1889-1907

Gloucester to the Pacific

AS THE NINETEENTH CENTURY drew to a close, there was every reason for the Protestant, evangelical Sunday school forces in English-speaking countries to believe that the way ahead would always be an upward path.

In the Great Britain of the late 1880s, European tranquility seemed assured with the first Mediterranean agreement involving England, Italy, Austria, and Spain and encouraged by Germany. Germany, Austria, and Italy had concluded the Triple Alliance, with renewals to take place at five-year intervals. A second Mediterranean agreement followed the first, this time without the support of Bismark. European affairs, and by extension the peace of the world, seemed fairly stable to both the statesman and the ordinary subject of the aging Queen Victoria.

Canada shared in the imperial peace, and at home conditions were, for the most part, placid and forward-looking. The Northwest Rebellion had been quickly put down, partly because the newly completed Canadian Pacific Railway was able to transport troops and munitions to and from all provinces. Disputes with the United States over fishing rights in the Bering Sea were settled in favor of Canada. A depression caused by the McKinley Tariff elicited two solutions: the Imperial Federation League urged preferential trade with Britain, while the liberals urged unrestricted reciprocity in international trade.

The social situation in the United States about this time had engendered considerable turbulence. There had been widespread railroad strikes in 1877; the Haymarket killings in Chicago in 1886; the Carnegie Steel battles took place six years later in Homestead, Pennsylvania, with ten killed and sixty wounded. In 1892 the Pullman strike in Illinois prompted President Cleveland to call out two thousand federal troops to put matters to right.

In the face of this era of violence, there is little if any social awareness or criticism in the records of the Sunday school movement of the late 1880s, but there is not much either to be found in the church life of the American nation. The rise of the "social gospel" was just beginning, and its beginnings were not spectacular. On the whole the 1880s were not a period of critical protest, either in church or state. Henry Steele Commager in *The American Mind* observed that: "during the nineteenth century and well into the twentieth, religion prospered while theology went slowly bankrupt." [2]

To be sure, there were as early as 1889, in the proceedings of the first World Convention, some criticisms of the life and culture of the day both in Britain and in America. The issues, however, were those of conventional, personal morality and of churchly traditions. The comments of Sidney Mead on an earlier period could have been extended to the end of the century as well: "One cannot say . . . that these leaders (1783–1850) gave no thought to 'social renovation'—but rather believing as they did that it would automatically follow upon the dissemination of 'scriptural holiness,' they took a great deal for granted." And Professor Mead wryly added: "Time has not borne out their optimism." [3]

Meanwhile, the Sunday school movement, begun by Robert Raikes on behalf of the ragged children of Gloucester, had grown and flourished. The early opposition of such leaders as the late eighteenth-century bishop of Rochester and the archbishop of Canterbury had given way to support, as Raikes' schools themselves changed from "ragged schools" to Bible schools for children, and then to religious schools for persons of all ages.

In the 1880s, the memory of Robert Raikes was still warm and influential and, especially among the evangelical churches, the number of Sunday schools was growing, and the number of "scholars" increasing.[4]

In the United States there was reassurance in the presence of many tested leaders. True, some of the older statesmen had died, but others in the prime of life were devoted to the Sunday school movement. In the year 1889, John H. Vincent, founder with B. F. Jacobs of the International Uniform Lesson System (of which more later), had been a Methodist bishop for seventeen years. He would live until 1920. B. F. Jacobs, his energetic colleague, was fifty-five. H. J. Heinz, the Pittsburgh merchant, would be active until his death in 1919. In Philadelphia, John Wanamaker had been superintendent of the Bethany Presbyterian Sunday school for thirty-eight years. It was the largest in America and reputedly the second largest in the world. He outlived his friend, Heinz, by three years.

In Britain there were comparable lay and clerical leaders. F. F. Belsey of London was to become the first president of the world organization whose story we relate. He had been a member of the English section of the International Lesson Committee. This unusual association of lay leaders was drawn together in two nations by a common evangelistic concern: enthusiasm for the Sunday school and a love of children.

A centenary of the work of Robert Raikes had been observed and a statue of the Gloucester layman had been erected on the Thames embankment. The London Sunday School Union was approaching its own centenary year (1903). *The Sunday School Chronicle* had been founded fifteen years before, providing notes and general religious news. The headquarters of the Union at 56, Old Bailey, had become a recognized center for all of Britain. Two related movements were beginning—the International Bible Reading Association and Christian Endeavor. The latter movement was founded in Portland, Maine. Both were fostered in Britain by the Sunday School Union.[5]

In addition to the presence of those trusted leaders, there was the momentum of the past successful years of the Sunday school effort. In the United States, the Sunday school had been extended through the pioneer missionary work of the American Sunday School Union. As a result of the several national (later international) Sunday school conventions, beginning in 1832, cooperative Sunday school associations had multiplied to a point that E. Payson Porter reported in 1889:

> It would be perfectly safe to say that in the United States of America we have 10,000,000 connected with our Sunday schools. We claim in the United States, 60,000,000 of population, and this would give us about 15% of the population attending the Sunday schools.

Connecticut, Pennsylvania, and Maryland were doing better, their ratio being twenty-four percent. Among the big cities, twelve and a half percent of New York City's population were said to be attending Sunday school, in Philadelphia eighteen percent, in Chicago eleven percent, and in Brooklyn thirteen and a quarter percent.[6]

Even discounting the figures because of the notorious unreliability of church statistics, and after making allowance for a certain human element of boosterism, the Sunday school movement in the United States was clearly a development of considerable magnitude and strength.

In North America, as a result of the Fifth National Convention (Indianapolis, 1872), the Uniform Lesson Committee, newly created there, had from the beginning two Canadian members. It was only natural that the next convention (Baltimore, 1875) should be called the Sixth National, the First International Convention, a designation establishing a series which continued until the last, held in San Francisco in 1960.

In earlier years, along the Atlantic seaboard, Sunday schools lifted their voices in song:

> *Far out upon the prairie*
> *There many children dwell,*
> *Who never read the Bible*
> *Nor hear the Sabbath bell.*[7]

At the end of the nineteenth century, evangelistic fervor was thriving, and the geographical reference was greatly extended. As we shall see, the "prairie" by then was overseas.

The growth of the Sunday school in the United States, in Canada, and in Great Britain was accompanied, though not paralleled, by growth in other nations. Sunday schools were begun in India as early as 1803. By the middle of the nineteenth century Sunday schools were found in the Netherlands, France, Italy, Switzerland, Germany, Denmark, and Belgium. In Sweden, Bohemia, Russia, Bulgaria, and Finland Sunday schools were operating in the latter half of the 1900s.[8]

In many of these nations the beginnings were small indeed and beset with difficulties and handicaps born of religious bigotry. But the beginnings were there upon which might be built Christian international understanding and, in time, cooperation.

Out of the successful international (three nations, including Canada) experience, a sense of need for wider cooperation grew. The feeling was reciprocated in Britain and in this fraternal [9] atmosphere the groundwork was laid for the calling of a "world" convention.

The leaders were available. The movement had succeeded in the three Anglo-Saxon nations. In addition, the climate of the churches in the last decade of the nineteenth century was, on the whole, optimistic and ebullient. And this on both sides of the Atlantic:

> The fifteen years comprised between 1848 and 1863, or thereabouts were characterised, at least in this country [Britain], by a new and vigorous development of Sunday-school ideas, in the direction of organization and methods. The Senior Department on the one side, and the Infant or Primary Department on the other, were added to the school and speedily incorporated with it; while the earliest efforts to provide recreative engagements for scholars on week evenings belong to the same period of revival.[10]

The quarter-century following Mr. W. H. Grosser's observation was characterized by a similar self-confidence.

During this same period the foreign missions movement reached a new high. Dwight L. Moody, John R. Mott, Luther Wishard, and others brought new zeal to the denominational boards of Foreign Missions which had been established in the early years of the nineteenth century. Sydney Ahlstrom observes that "evangelism was made the task of the denomination as a whole, every member thus being at least theoretically a participant." [11] In Britain, also, a new foreign missionary endeavor followed the pioneer work of William Cary.

Even though the instruction of children, young people and adults in the basic elements of the Christian faith was part of this outreach, Sunday school leaders in both America and Britain felt a specialized agency was needed.

The instrument for a proposed world Sunday school gathering was available in the International Sunday School Association. A short description of this body and its antecedents may be helpful in understanding relationships.

The international conventions [12] came to be composed of delegates from state and provincial Sunday school associations, and in these regions conventions composed in turn of delegates from county and city Sunday school associations flourished. At the Chicago International Convention of 1887, just two years before the convening of the First World Convention, 797 persons were registered from forty states and territories, and three Canadian provinces.

Canada, at this time, had its Sunday schools organized into at least seven provincial councils of which three sent representatives to the Chicago gathering. It was reported that in 1887 there were in Canada 418,243 Sunday school scholars with 50,956 teachers and officers, listed in the seven provinces. [13] Impressive organizations had been established. A generally harmonious and encouraging outlook enveloped them. Therefore, it seemed only natural that closer relationships should be established between the two Sunday school agencies, operating in the three countries on both sides of the Atlantic.

Unifying the Individual Efforts

That beginning came in 1886. The Fourth International Convention, meeting in Louisville in 1884, had appointed, as was customary, an *ad interim* executive committee to carry on its concerns, chiefly to plan for the next triennial gathering. This executive committee met at Lake Chautauqua, New York, in 1886, and there B. F. Jacobs urged the calling of a world convention to be held in London. Others agreed and the Louisville convention proposed that there should be held an "International Sunday-school Convention to include all lands, to be held in Europe at such time and place as may be decided upon by the new Executive Committee in correspondence with workers abroad." [14] The Fifth International Convention met in Chicago in 1887 and the "Chautauqua" resolution was put before it, "with a view to unifying the individual Sunday school efforts of the world." [15]

Edward Towers, one of the honorary secretaries of the London Sunday-School Union, was present at the convention and he secured the cooperation of his organization. European workers expressed their "concurrence in the plan" and enabling actions were thus completed. [16]

It was probably the London Sunday-School Union which decided that the meeting was to be in London, and announcements were mailed to Sunday school workers and organizations in many countries. A heavy reliance was placed upon North American attendance, a reliance which proved to be well-founded.[17]

Of the American delegation, it was reported that seventy-seven were Baptists, fifty-eight Methodists, forty-seven Congregationalists, forty-five Presbyterians, "and the rest scattering." The predominantly lay composition of the United States delegation is illustrated by the reporting of fifty-four United States ministers among the 400 delegates and many of these ministers were on the program.

The shaping of the program seems to have rested largely with the London union, and from then on either the American branch or the British branch assumed almost complete responsibility for a convention program. It was a convenient sharing, made almost necessary by the distance between the two nations. Nevertheless, the division of labor proved to be a source of irritation even as late as 1950.

A Sunday School Institute. . . 3,000 Miles Long!

Long before the gavel fell in City Temple, London, the convention had actually begun aboard ship for the United States and many of the Canadian delegates. The SS. *Bothnia* of the Cunard Line had been chosen by 243 of the North American delegates, though there were others with reservations on other ships and other lines. Two hundred of these persons met the night before the sailing, June 16, 1889, at the Metropolitan Hotel in New York. The next day, after passing Sandy Hook, New Jersey, B. F. Jacobs called the delegates on the *Bothnia* to order, and committees were appointed for the voyage. Song books and a reed organ were available. An executive committee meeting of the international convention was held as soon as it was discovered there was a quorum at hand.

A teachers' meeting, held on the first Saturday morning at sea, prepared the teachers for the Sunday school scheduled for the next day, utilizing, undoubtedly, the Uniform Lessons. The Sunday school session was held on Sunday afternoon, with fourteen officers, ten teachers, and 219 scholars present, plus two teachers and eight scholars in the primary school, and two teachers and twenty-eight scholars in steerage. Total: 283!

There had been an Anglican service in the morning, perhaps led by the captain of the *Bothnia,* according to Church of England usage and Cunard Line practice. A Vesper service in the afternoon was held and a preaching service at night. In addition there had been held "a rousing Salvation Army meeting in the fore-part of the ship." Contemporary comments on the busy day were approving, and in one case, lyrical: "Thus passed one of the sweetest Sabbaths of life, a Sabbath that will be remembered with joy when we shall have reached the land 'where congregations ne'er break up, and

Sabbaths have no end.' '' The voyage was described as ''. . . a Sunday school institute, gospel service, Bible reading, sermon, song, social converse and Christian work all in one and 3,000 miles long!''

One passenger-delegate, recalling bitter-sweet memories of the crossing, chose verse for her recollections:

> *How bright, how glad to me the day*
> *When out upon my ocean way*
> > *Standing on deck of Bothnia grand,*
> > *I gazed on fast receding land. . . .*
>
> *Now swiftly pass the hours along,*
> *In converse sweet or sacred song,*
> > *And morn and noon, and even and night*
> > *Made up one round of pure delight. . . .*

Not *unalloyed* pleasure, however, for the poet continued:

> *It matters little now to me*
> *That I was sick, so sick at sea;*
> > *For friends were kind and ever near*
> > *With hands to help and words to cheer. . . .*
>
> *Long! long! may this glad picture stay*
> *To grow more bright, from day to day;*
> > *And may we when life's voyage ends*
> > *In heaven greet all our Bothnia friends.*[18]

This full schedule of study and worship was not confined to the 1889 crossing of the *Bothnia*. That trip proved to be a pattern for later voyages to World Sunday School Conventions.

When the Americans journeyed to the third convention, also held in London, even more dramatic developments marked the voyage.

In the summer of 1898, the vessel was the SS. *Catalonia,* again of the Cunard Line. It sailed from Boston on June 29, at five in the morning. Devotional services were held twice a day. Evening services had been started but were discontinued when gospel meetings on the steerage deck were begun. In these gospel meetings several people were brought under conviction, one backslider was reclaimed, and ''a widow returning to Ireland was converted.'' Several meetings on Sunday school work were held, including four conferences on primary work. On July 3, the Catalonia Sunday School was organized.

In 1898 the turbulent North Atlantic was as unkind to a delegate, Miss H. L. Shoemaker, as it had been to one of the voyagers to the first convention. She managed a wan remembrance of the Fourth of July in her distress:

My country 'tis of thee,
Steaming along at sea,
For thee I sigh!
Land of the solid ground,
Land where no smells abound,
Land where no fog-horns sound,
For thee I die!

How can the cheerful smile?
How can they time beguile?
Would I were home!
What are their joys to me?
Steaming along at sea,
Woeful as I can be,
Why did I come? [19]

In the midst of all the busy, evangelistic activity, a fire broke out at sea on July sixth, and five hours were required to subdue the blaze discovered in a store of cotton in the hold. After an anchorage at Queenstown, the ship continued to Liverpool where the delegates spent Sunday and continued on their way to London by train on Monday morning.[20]

En route to the Fourth World Convention to be held in Jerusalem, 817 Americans sailed on the *Grosser Kurfurst* from New York City, and 485 other delegates on the *Victoria Augusta* from Marseilles. "Records of the passages of both of these vessels show the fine spirit of fellowship, the free exchange of experiences, and the valuable group meetings and services which helped to fill up days of close personal contacts." [21]

The passengers on the *Grosser Kurfurst* were busily occupied with meetings and with two simultaneous services on Sunday morning and two simultaneous Sunday schools in the afternoon. So many meetings were held that one passenger posted a notice that "There will be a meeting, held *sometime,* of all those who are in favor of holding fewer meetings. Called by the fellow who tried to attend all the meetings." [22]

Perhaps he and others were invigorated by the hearty yell of the members of the Ohio delegation as they made their way from deck to deck and from salon to salon:

Hi oh, O-hi-o,
We make music where we go!
Never sulk, never sour,
Jerusalem, Jerusalem, Nineteen Four!
OHIO [23]

The *Grosser Kurfurst* stopped at Funchal, Madeira, Gibraltar, Algiers, Malta, Athens, Constantinople, Ephesus, and Beirut. Then a company visited Baalbeck and thence (for forty persons) by horse to Jerusalem. On the return trip the pilgrims visited Cairo and Naples. As a result of these many stops, visits which included contacts with mission stations, more than $3900 was collected for eight missionary ventures. [24]

As delegates prepared to cross the Atlantic in 1907 for the fifth convention scheduled for Rome, it was decided that there should be a two-day preliminary meeting in Boston on April 25 and 26. More than 300 gathered for this affair which the *Boston Globe* described as "an exhibition of that enthusiastic and tactful hospitality with which Boston delights to welcome visitors who come for a special purpose." A reception was given by the lieutenant governor of Massachusetts, an automobile tour of Boston and environs was organized, and a reception at the home of W. N. Hartshorne, one of the leaders of the International and the World Convention, was held. The program was over-loaded: "After-dinner speeches were 'limited to five minutes' as per announcement, but the bottled-up eloquence could not escape fast enough to give the ten men on the program time, and five of them had to content themselves with applauding the others."

The reception and speeches finally concluding, the guests and delegates made their way to the Tremont Temple for an eight o'clock rally, where a large audience had assembled. The testimonies were eloquent. The Honorable Samuel B. Capen declared: "Blot out the work which these gentlemen are doing, and what has been done during the past twenty-five years, and you have put back the coming of the Kingdom by a century." [25]

No doubt, Mr. Capen's estimate of the importance of the work was shared by the delegates and the congregation in Tremont Temple, as they made their way home from the church to their homes and hotels. It had been a busy day and the SS. *Romanic* of the White Star Line was to sail the next day.

It did, and with 999 souls aboard. The crew numbered 246. Three hundred thirty-five delegates were in first class, and 418 in steerage. All physical barriers between first and second class had been removed. On the day after the sailing (Sunday, April 28), a church service was held at ten, Sunday school at three, and a song-and-praise service at eight in the evening. There was a forty-five minute song-and-praise service daily at ten, and "several instructive lectures" from time to time. Stops were made along the way: Ponta Delgada and Funchal in the Azores, Gibraltar, Algiers, Naples, Genoa, and then a train down to Rome.

Not all the American delegates were on the *Romanic*. Others chose the *Neckar* of the North German Lloyd Line, and on it similar programs of Sunday school instruction, divine worship, praise services, addresses, and lectures were quickly inaugurated. Individual evangelistic work was carried on with members of the crew. Some of the same stops in the Azores and in North Africa were made. The trip apparently ended in Naples. [26]

The voyage on the *Romanic* produced significant financial assistance for the foreign missionary efforts of the churches. Missionary meetings had been held on board. As a result of these services, and of field excursions at some of the stops, $100 was raised for work in Gibraltar, $5,100 for efforts in Algeria, and $800 for work on behalf of women in that country. Methodists raised in all nearly $50,000 for Algerian work. For international Sunday school work, $11,000 was raised before disembarkation. By any standard, it was an impressive endeavor. [27] Worship, Christian education, evangelism, mission, stewardship, ecumenism—all were a part of the spiritual cargo of the *Romanic* and the *Neckar*.

Characteristics of Early Conventions

The early conventions had common characteristics and were motivated by similar impulses. No significant differences can be discerned between those in Britain and those in America or Canada. They shared a common evangelical background, a common language, and a common outlook of mind and spirit.

"It is Daybreak Everywhere"

First of all, a hearty and unquenchable optimism is characteristic of these conventions, more accurately, of the people who composed them. In large measure, the optimism about the Christian situation in Britain and the United States supported this convention *élan*. Let two Sunday school missionaries of the Midwest make their testimony.

Boston W. Smith tells his convention audience:

> I began my voluntary missionary work in Illinois. Mr. Jacobs came to a Convention, and said "They're all dead in Madison County; they don't do anything for Sunday schools down there." I had a young fellow with me there, and when we went away we went to our employers and said we wanted a week off. We got it, and went off on the Monday morning early, and travelled all over the county, and visited every township, and at the next Convention we came up as a banner county for Illinois.[28]

Mr. Smith went to Minnesota in 1880 and discovered that of 154 Baptist chapels there were only sixty-six Sunday schools, and he marked on a map such deficiencies. He continued:

> We put sixty-six crimson spots on the map I showed you, [marking chapels with Sunday schools] and I put a fresh one for every new school. Now instead of the sixty-six schools, we have 201 Baptist Sunday schools and in these schools there are gathered every Sunday 16,500 scholars for the study of God's Word. That is not the best of it. The other denominations would bear just the same record if they would speak. The Presbyterians have a Sunday school missionary, and the Congregationalists have theirs, and we work together, and meet in blessed conventions, sometimes at one church and sometimes at another.[29]

In like manner, R. Cowden of Gallion, Ohio, recalled in London the zeal for Sunday school reporting and extension. A secretary of the county Sunday School Union had difficulty in obtaining reports from the schools:

> So he went to the president of the union and stated his case. Said the president, "Have you a horse?" "Yes" was the reply "I have!" "Can you ride?" "Yes, sir!" "Then I advise you to saddle that horse, mount him, and go for them." And he did just that thing. For a week or ten days he visited every school in the county, and collected statistics in the only way possible. Thus was laid the foundation of the county Sunday School conventions which have been flourishing ever since.[30]

Mr. Cowan's concluding metaphor may have been mixed, but his devotion shines through. Buoyant optimism exhibited again! This sanguine spirit was not just an American phenomenon, for the British, too, were of a like disposition:

> The very atmosphere of success is charged with a sacred discontent— discontent with things that were and things that are, combined with the strong conviction that perfection is yet before us, that there is always something better, grander, within our reach.[31]

In similar a vein, Constance Parker, a British worker, set forth a characteristic affirmation:

> The ministry of the Sunday School Union is a powerful and supremely blessed ministry to the men of tomorrow. The work already done is a joyous prophecy. The world is not growing worse; it was never as good as it is today. This is not the devil's world. The Hand pierced on Calvary's Cross is on the helm of the universe.[32]

This confidence was radiated also by those at work in the "foreign field." R. Burges affirmed that "The evangelisation of India in this generation is by no means an impossible task to the Sunday schools of Christendom." [33] The third convention also heard from Japan: "I am fully convinced that if we seize the 10,000,000 of boys and girls in Japan today and give them a sword of the Spirit they will tomorrow conquer that nation in the name of our King Jesus Christ." [34] In cadences which strangely resemble a passage in John F. Kennedy's 1961 inaugural address, B. F. Jacobs declared: "But no price is too great to pay; no sacrifice too great to make, no trial too heavy to endure, if we may attain the highest aim of life, the supreme blessing of mankind through the Gospel of Jesus Christ." [35]

Earlier in the same city at the close of the first convention, Mr. Jacobs looked forward eleven years to the close of the century and in solemnity reminded his hearers that:

We are in His tremendous presence, under His omniscient eye, in the grasp of His infinite power, in the gracious sphere of His healing love. Let us here decide if the Lord tarries, and we live, the coming year shall witness that our gathering in this Convention was of Him, and for Him, and, if, during this year Jesus shall come, blessed will that servant be who is found waiting, and watching, and working for his Lord.

Brethren, "Let us rise and go to our work, tomorrow we shall rise and go to our reward." [Loud cheers] [36]

That this optimism continued into the next century is shown by a confident assertion of Chairman Bailey: "From the Sunday-school standpoint, it is daybreak everywhere." [37]

CONFIDENCE IN ORGANIZATIONAL EFFORT

Not only did the Sunday school leaders of the period have confidence that the daybreak of the movement was on the eastern horizon, they had also an unbounded confidence in the efficacy of organized efforts. Such endeavors had succeeded in the United States, in Canada, and in the United Kingdom. Success in other places and throughout the wide, wide world seemed only natural to expect. The methods had already been tested. What worked in Minnesota would no doubt work in Africa, so let us get on with the job of bringing the Gospel through the Sunday school movement to every person. A delegate from Indiana at the third convention recalled that he had ". . . always heard that the sun never sets on British soil. That is a proud boast. All we want is that the sun should never set on the British Interdenominational Sunday School Association. Organize the world for the saving of the world." [38]

What had been accomplished in the Anglo-Saxon countries could be done elsewhere. Principal D. L. Ritchie of Nottingham was certain of this in 1913, using a logical sequence characteristic of the period before 1907:

Look then at these two, in my judgment, invulnerable positions:
  i   This vision of the Sunday-school's conquest of the world is true and reasonable in the nature of the things with which it works.
  ii   This vision of the Sunday-school's conquest of the world is true and reasonable because what has been accomplished is a guarantee of future victory.[39]

This confidence in organizational effectiveness was justified at least in Germany as Count Bernstorff attested:

When the Sunday school movement began there were in Berlin only four children's services. In all the other churches there was nothing done for the children. Now there is not one church without a Sunday school, and in most parishes there are a great many more than one, because, besides the Sunday schools held in the churches, we have those conducted by City missions and by other agents of home mission work.[40]

In Europe, the organized Sunday school movement was seen as a means of lifting the established churches out of their spiritual lethargy and complacency:

The Protestant churches . . . for long years were supine and indifferent, lost in the darkness of rationalism, or overborne by spiritual lethargy and death. And though, in many cases, they had their catechumen classes as a kind of heritage from the great Reformers, yet these had in large measure become so formal and lifeless as to possess no spiritually vitalizing power whatever. . . . The great question, therefore, has often presented itself to the earnest Christian element in those lands. . . . "How is this sad state of things to be met?" Looking to England and America they see what a blessing the Sunday-school has been among us, and they say: "Surely what this institution has accomplished in those great countries it can do for us!" [41]

If there had been any doubt about the effectiveness of the Sunday school movement and the nature of the American leaders who were involved in it, those uncertainties were dispelled by the success of the Jerusalem convention in 1904. The editor of the *Sunday School Times* asserted with pride:

The Jerusalem Sunday-school convention showed the world that Sunday-school people are men and women who do things, who do them on a big scale. There are three American business men whose names are known throughout the world as leading the world in their respective lines of business. Each of the three is a Sunday-school man to the core; each is more deeply interested in Sunday-school work than in his multi-million-dollar business, if he had to choose between the two; and one of these three is one of the men who made the Jerusalem Sunday-school convention a reality. Here is a fact for the world to ponder.[42]

This expectation of uninterrupted progress seemed clearly reasonable as the results of the first convention were observed in Britain. F. F. Belsey, president of the Second World's Convention, reported:

. . . you will be very glad to know that we have now arranged in England for holding, triennially, a great international convention of our own. [Cheers] That convention will meet in October at Birmingham. It met three years ago at Nottingham. We are also arranging for holding district conventions annually. We try to wake up the eastern counties first. We had a splendid convention at Ipswich, had another at Bristol, and next year we are going to avail ourselves of all the latent fire and enthusiasm of Yorkshire. [Applause] This has been, I think, one effect that may be chiefly traced to the gathering of 1889.[43]

"SANCTIFIED COMMON SENSE, AND WARM-HEARTED ENERGY, AND DEVOTION"

It would be inaccurate to assume that this confidence in organizational efforts was an end in itself. It is true that some extravagant language of the time might give that impression, but underneath there was a deep conviction that God had called the Sunday school and the organized Sunday school movement into being as instruments of His divine will in winning the nations to His love and purpose, as revealed in His Son, Jesus Christ, Lord and Savior of mankind. That conviction had sent Boston Smith to the prairies of Illinois and Minnesota; it sent the delegates to the steerage quarters of the SS. *Catalonia;* and it impelled the missionary offerings on board trans-Atlantic ships and at the convention sessions themselves.

Councillor Mellors of Nottingham, England, raised a basic question at the first convention and proceeded at once to advance his answer:

> When will the church realize that the masses are to be laid hold of for Christ, if not for churches, and that the present indifference among Christian workers, the class distinctions, the pew rent exclusiveness, the sectarian bitterness, the set forms of service, and other similar impediments are rightly or wrongly through prejudice or otherwise, the means that occasion the alienation of the masses from the Gospel. The people may be won, and all that is required is sanctified common sense, and warm-hearted energy and devotion.[44]

Four years later, Dr. J. L. Phillips recalled that:

> The first world's convention gave birth to the India Sunday-school mission; let the second world's Sunday-school convention give birth to another. Let it be a Sunday-school mission, if you please to Japan, called the America of the East, now not only open but ready for teaching such as you can give.[45]

With such common convictions it is not at all surprising to read that Professor H. M. Hamill of Tennessee declared at the third convention that evangelism, not education, is the primary aim of the Sunday school.

> . . . it must be remembered that after all the primary aim of the Sunday school is not so much educational as it is evangelistic. [Cheers] God permits us to encompass the child with the great forces that centre in and about the Sabbath school in order that we may win the souls of the children. What are these forces? In the first place there is the Word of God, then there is that holy place, the temple of our Lord; and finally there is the personality of the godly man or woman incarnating God's word. These are the forces that come together for the saving of our children.[46]

The evangelistic concern was succinctly summed up in the motto for the third convention: "With one mind striving together for the faith of the Gospel. Uniting, ingathering, upbuilding." [47]

This evangelistic concern was placed not only in the center of the Sunday school gatherings. It was also urged that it be in the very heart of every Christian present. Every individual must "rise to the very highest planes of intelligence and spirituality to do what God has entrusted to us . . ." and:

> if there is one thought beyond all others that we must not omit to carry away with us, it is that of responsibility. Responsibility God has cast upon each one of us; we may lose health and wealth and position, but no man can ever shake from him the responsibility that God has placed upon his shoulders.[48]

With this intensity of evangelistic and missionary commitment expressed, it is not strange that the early conventions accepted for themselves responsibilities for appointing and supporting missionaries for the extension of Sunday school work. By 1898 (the third convention) Richard Burges had been appointed for India, and T. C. Ikehara for Japan. At the 1889 convention, an offering had been taken to send Dr. James Phillips to India as the first Sunday school missionary to that country. These efforts were seen only as a beginning. There were China and China's children on the horizon. Looking to the Far East there came this stirring call:

> But what about China? We have heard much of an open door for commerce, brethren, can we not discern the signs of the times? See, God has set before us an open door. Has not the time come for sending a Sunday school missionary to do for China's children what we are doing for the little ones of India? Let the World's Third Sunday school convention find our brethren of Canada and the United States returning home resolved to organize Bible reading among their own children, and by means of small subscriptions send a missionary to organize Sunday schools in China. The hope of that great and interesting country is her children.[49]

In a similar spirit, at the Jerusalem convention, in 1904, the Palestine Sunday-school Association was formed, officers chosen, and over $100 raised for its support.[50]

This evangelistic and missionary imperative, so evident in the Sunday school conventions, was an integral part of the common revivalistic emphasis of the British and North American evangelical Protestantism of the period.

The "Great Awakening" of the 1730s and 1740s and the "Second Awakening" coming toward the close of the eighteenth century were over. There were, however, new shoots growing from these old stumps as Baptist, Disciple, Methodist and Presbyterian missionaries found itinerant preachers and revivalistic methods the most effective means of reaching the unchurched frontiers beyond the Appalachians.

In time new evangelists appeared to take the place of the earlier leaders: Solomon Stoddard, Jonathan Edwards, George Whitefield, and Timothy Dwight; and new preachers such as Charles Finney, Charles Spurgeon, Dwight L. Moody, and Reuben A. Torrey. "Revivalism had been born in the marriage of Calvinism and the American frontier, introduced to the city by Finney, and nourished to gigantic growth by Moody." [51]

In Britain, William Wilberforce, Lord Shaftesbury, and others had laid the foundations for British evangelicalism, both within and without the Church of England, and the movement was strong among all British classes:

> It is important not to underestimate the persuasive powers of the Evangelicals themselves . . . it is not difficult to appreciate the influence that Evangelical nursemaids could have upon their young charges, nor in their very different

way that the young women who taught in Sunday schools and ragged schools could gain over the roughest of their pupils.[52]

And when these nursemaids and their mistresses went to the Sunday school conventions they found others of like persuasion to deepen their resolve both to "be like Jesus" and to win others to Him.

COOPERATION ACROSS DENOMINATIONAL LINES AND . . .

It would not be accurate to use the wording "denominational cooperation" for this subsection. The denominations were not yet ready to cooperate officially as national bodies. It was an unofficial cooperation which led to the foundations of the county, state, and then the international association, and now was influencing the formative years of what became the World's Sunday School Association. This voluntary Sunday school cooperation became one of the inheritances in the establishment of city, state, provincial, and national councils of churches in the twentieth century, in many instances the oldest such tradition. The movement was not anti-denominational. Boston W. Smith, the Midwestern Sunday school organizer of whom we have heard before, declared:

> . . . though I am engaged in Sunday school work, I defy you to find a man, woman, or child, who has heard me say a word against any other denomination. We can work together on denominational lines, and I believe the time is coming when we must work on these lines.[53]

Furthermore, this common joining of endeavor was seen as bearing fruit:

> I can remember very well when the walls between the denominations of the churches were so high in the little town I lived in, that there wasn't a ladder in the whole neighborhood high enough to climb to the top of the wall and look down. But, thank God, the walls are so low now that we can walk up and look over, and can say, "God bless you, brother; how is the Sunday school getting on? Did you come to the Convention? Anything we can do to help you?" "Oh yes, I was at your convention. Wasn't it splendid?" It is bringing down the walls, and we feel more like brother and sister than before.[54]

. . . AND DENOMINATIONAL OPPOSITION AND BITTERNESS

The walls may have been lowered in the United States, Canada, and Great Britain, but as delegates from those countries were soon to learn, that was not necessarily characteristic of other nations, not even of all the countries of "Christian Europe." In kingdoms where there was a Roman Catholic majority, in lands where there was a Protestant establishment, the outlook was not all sunshine and roses. There was more notice taken of European church opposition in the next period, but even in these earlier conventions, before the movement had spread very much in Europe, there were indications of opposition to the new movement of organized Sunday school work.

In Scotland where the Sunday school work had begun as early as 1788, where a society to manage Sunday schools had been organized in Glasgow, and where one of the first, if not the first Sunday school union in Scotland had been formed in 1797, such efforts were not always appreciated. At times sheriffs considered such meetings illegal and summoned teachers before the magistrate.[55]

In England the trouble seemed not to be so much opposition as indifference. Giving some credit to the Church of England Sunday School Institute, Benjamin Clarke, editor of the *Sunday School Chronicle,* regretted that the Sunday school had taken so feeble a hold in the Church of England, and that her ministers had been so slow in realizing its possibilities.[56] A partial reason for the lag was the establishment of Anglican day schools.

On the continent, the Sunday school movement faced formidable obstacles. In Germany, the free churches received harsh treatment at the hands of the pastors of the established Lutheran and Reformed churches. Persons in England and the United States must have found it difficult to understand why evangelical ministers were obliged to labor under such difficulties. The schools in Germany were under the control of narrow-minded state clergymen. This disability was particularly, but not exclusively, true in Saxony, the land of Luther.[57]

Count Bernstorff, a friend of the Sunday school movement, confirmed the complaint, indicating that both the pastors and the schoolmasters were jealous of the movement because they thought it to be in opposition to their work.[58]

In describing the situation in Sweden, a stronger word was used—"persecution"—instigated by the priests of the Church of Sweden: "Many workers have both privately and officially been interdicted, and pointed out as straying and perilous men, and it has happened that some have been imprisoned and fined because they have kept Sunday school." [59]

In Catholic countries of Europe the opposition was much more determined and relentless. Sanctions made Sunday school promoters more vulnerable than in other lands. A speaker at the third Convention told of fathers who were dismissed from their work, and of families turned out of their homes because the children were known to attend Sunday schools.[60]

This opposition was not a temporary excess. Reports of similar incidents in many European countries persisted well into the next period of the world Sunday school movement after 1907, even to the beginning of World War I. The accounts are too varied, too numerous, too vivid, to be the products solely of anti-Catholicism. If the Protestant Sunday school movement of the time had a strain of anti-Catholicism in it, and as we shall shortly see that it did, there was a hard core of experience at its center.

Having said this, it is also true that the protagonists of the Sunday school movement in Europe were naïve in thinking that their vigorous promotion could cause anything but resentment and opposition among Catholic and Lutheran churches whose traditions of pastoral care, child nurture, and a settled liturgy were at such variance with the evangelistic, nonchurchly, revivalistic spirit of the Sunday school. In addition there was the national factor. The Sunday school was seen as a British, or worse yet, an American import. Not surprisingly, among Roman Catholics such foreign influence was unwelcome, and in addition the great gulf between Protestants and Catholics was wide, deep, and seething with suspicion. And so the religious strife continued, with the Sunday school sometimes unwittingly playing a divisive role well into the twentieth century.

A SOCIAL CLASS MOVEMENT

The efforts of Robert Raikes were those of a benevolently minded man who set out to raise the living conditions and the degraded social circumstances of the poor children of Gloucester. Ann Boylan, in an unpublished dissertation, reported that racial segregation was common in America as black children were placed in separate classes while attending white Sunday schools. Separate schools were often held for "church children" and for "lower classes." However, by the third decade of the nineteenth century, the class distinctions began to disappear in most American Sunday schools. In these schools the claim was made that "rich and poor meet together." [61]

Little in the world convention proceedings of 1889–1907 suggest that class distinctions were a problem in the American Sunday schools. To be sure, an American Methodist clergyman in New York did observe that in his congregation there were both "some very cultivated and intelligent people" as well as "a great number of female servants" who were "among the best attendants, the devoutest worshippers and the largest contributors for their means."

There is testimony that Sunday schools in Wales were usually all-inclusive. They were cited as "the only schools known to me that come up to the idea that has been put into words again and again at this Convention, namely that the whole church may so instruct its members that all may work together in unity and to the edification of one another." [62]

Convention testimony about class distinctions in Australia is not completely consistent. G. M. Hitchcock of Geelong, Victoria, evidently struck a popular note when he declared that his country made two mistakes in copying English patterns:

First, the mistake that the schools were for the poor. [Hear, hear]—and then the other mistake that they were only for children. [Hear, hear] Now, it has taken a good deal of hard work to knock down these two mistakes. It was comparatively easy to knock down the first, for this reason, we are an essentially democratic community—[Hear, hear]—and so long as children are clean and tidy, and come to school, it does not matter whether the father or mother is worth £50 or £50,000. But the other matter is not quite so easily got rid of.[63]

While Mr. Hitchcock presented a favorable picture, a few years later there came a statement, intended to be encouraging, which revealed that class distinctions were not altogether strange in the Australian Sunday school:

There is a road in my parish (in Australia) called the G. H. road, where there is a villa and in the villa are four sitting rooms . . . and on Sunday afternoon every one of those rooms is full of the children of the gentry. Many of these have parents who would not send their children to the Sunday school.[64]

Ireland, too, was commended as a nation where "the children of the gentry sit side by side with the children of the peasantry." [65]

In contrast to Wales, Ireland, possibly Australia, and, for the most part, the United States, Denmark struggled with the problem of class distinction in the carrying on of its Sunday school work: "We have in Copenhagen special Sunday schools for the higher classes. We are able to have a hall nearly as large as this filled with children of the higher classes coming on Sunday to have their Sunday school instruction, especially in the winter." [66]

A Dr. Fulton regretted that in France and Italy few of the "upper classes" were being reached with instruction in God's Word, nor were many efforts being made to reach them.[67]

Of all the nations represented at the earlier conventions, it is England which seemed most aware of class distinctions, their effect upon the Sunday schools of the time, and the not very successful efforts to overcome these social distinctions. Constance Parker described the general contrasts which prevailed throughout the nineteenth century:

There was . . . the contrast between rich and poor, accepted, by the rich at any rate, as part of the plan of providence. "The mind of the teacher and student is driven to admit, though it be awestruck by apparent injustice, that the inequality is the work of God," said Trollope. The poor could and should be relieved by private charity, which was described, again by the giver, as "the beautiful feeling which connects the superior with the inferior and binds the interests and pleasures of both into one." [68]

In the First World Convention both the Lord Mayor of London and the president of the convention admired the American practice of inclusive Sunday schools, while decrying the situation in their own country. For the most part English Sunday schools were for the "poorer classes in Mission districts." In the first and second conventions, C. H. Kelly of the Wesleyan Methodist Sunday School Union, Dr. J. H. Gladstone (admitting distinctions were not so severe "in the North"), W. H. Graser, F. F. Belsey, Lord

Aberdeen, Edward Towers, and others deplored identification of Sunday school with the poor, and expressed their regret that the movement was not reaching the middle and upper economic groups. Lord Aberdeen cited a London effort to reach the privileged children: ". . . in the parish of Kensington . . . the vicar, Mr. Carr-Glyn has for some time had a Sunday school to which only the children of the upper classes are admitted, and it has been carried on with great success, and great appreciation in regard to the parents." [69]

It is to the credit of English Sunday school workers that they realized the formidable obstacle they confronted in combatting the entrenched social stratification of the time. Sunday school was usually for the "downstairs people" not those who lived "upstairs" on Eaton Place, to recall the popular television series of the late 1970s.

Two Flags over Two Shoulders

Not all of the preceding five characteristics will prevail with the same strength into the next periods of the world Sunday school gatherings. We come now to one which will endure, sometimes for the strength of the movement, sometimes for its weakness. It is the dominance of the organization by its Anglo-American members: British, Canadian, and American.

This dominance was, of course, a more or less inevitable consequence of the convening of the First World Convention and those which followed it. Before the incorporation in 1907, there was no continuing structure save for successive continuation committees. Effective sponsorship was in the hands of the two agencies on opposite shores of the Atlantic, the International Sunday School Association and the London Sunday School Union.

Again, the number of delegates at the early conventions from these three countries set the stage for this kind of unintended imperialism. At the first convention, for example, of the 871 delegates, Canada, Great Britain, and the United States furnished all but thirty-five. With nine from Australia, the Anglo-Saxons almost *were* the convention. It was a world gathering only in name. [70]

Subsequent statistics did not substantially alter the dominant position of English-speaking delegates. At St. Louis in 1893, there was only one delegate from nations other than Great Britain, Canada, and the United States out of a total of 881. This in spite of the fact that the call to the meeting had been for a "convention for all lands." [71]

The Jerusalem convention of 1904 drew from a greater number of nations—twenty-six. Even so, two-thirds of the 1526 delegates came from Canada, Great Britain, and the United States. [72]

At the opening session of that convention, the variety of faces and attire so impressed one American delegate that he described the scene in words similar to those used many years later by persons attending the assemblies of the

World Council of Churches as they reported their new and strange ecumenical contacts:

> Alongside the familiar faces of Warren and Hartshorn and McCrillis and Potts and Clark and Belsey were other faces never before seen in a Sunday-school convention. Franciscan monks rubbed elbows with Past Patriarchs of the Greek Church. Near the Superintendent of Public Instruction and Press Censor of Palestine for the Sultan sat the kindly-faced Samaritan High Priest and his son. Black pointed cowls were there, and brown robes held at the waist by loosely knotted cords. The fez and turban of the East contrasted with the bared heads of the West. Muhammedans, Copts, Greek Catholics, Roman Catholics, Armenians, members of the Syriac Church, mingled with Christian Jews, Polish Jews, Aleppo Jews, and Spanish Jews, while Christian missionaries fresh from their fields of work marveled and rejoiced at the compelling interest of this new factor in the Kingdom.[73]

Not only were the conventions dominated by the English-speaking nations (Canada, Great Britain, and the United States), but the officers came from these three countries. It was not until 1958 that a person from another national culture was chosen as president—Bishop Shot K. Mondol of India—to be succeeded four years later by Sir Francis Ibiam of Nigeria. Even so, these elections were something short of revolutionary, for Bishop Mondol was an episcopal leader of the Methodist Church of the United States, and Sir Francis had been educated in part in Britain, and grew up in a nation of the British Commonwealth.[74]

Of twenty-three officers elected at the second convention (1893), seven were from Great Britain, ten from the United States and three from Canada, with three from as many other nations. This slate of officers had been proposed by a nominating committee consisting of four from the United States two from England, and one from Germany.[75]

An effort to broaden the base seems to have been made by the time of the third convention (1898), for among the fifty-six officials of the convention, eleven nations were represented. Still Canada, Britain, and the United States were in control, holding thirty-eight out of the total. This brief expansion did not endure. The officers of the fourth convention (1904), had forty-three from the "Big Three," and one each from four other nations. A wider spread was revealed at Rome in 1907, thirty-four out of forty-seven.

It was not only by numbers or the proportion of officers that certain nations came to dominate the international and world gatherings. The ascendency came about also through methods of working, in manners of thinking, in basic presuppositions. Martin Carnoy in his *Education as Cultural Imperialism* points out how the schools, colleges, and universities established by the American missionary movement were dominated by Western, indeed American, ways of thinking, working, and expression:

The institutions that were formed were American, built with American money, staffed with American teachers, using American programs, methods and standards. Only the students were foreign, and the best of these were selected for further training in the United States. It was this early flow of selected foreign students to selected American colleges, usually Presbyterian, Baptist, or Methodist, that set a pattern which still dominates much of our thinking about foreign students.[76]

It is not difficult to understand why this dominance came to be. Great Britain and the United States were characterized by the number of their voluntary societies more than other nations of the late nineteenth century. Ian Bradley reported that there were representatives of nearly 500 voluntary societies who attended the funeral service of Lord Shaftesbury in Westminster Abbey, most of them having been established during his own lifetime.[77] The United States, too, was a land in which the principle of ''voluntaryism'' found supportive soil. Alexis de Tocqueville, as long ago as 1835, observed the American fondness for organized groups:

Americans of all ages, all conditions, and all dispositions constantly form associations. . . . The Americans make associations to give entertainments, to found seminaries, to build inns, to construct churches, to diffuse books, to send missionaries to the Antipodes; in this manner they found hospitals, prisons, and schools. . . . Wherever at the head of some new undertaking you see the government in France, or a man of rank in England, in the United States you will be sure to find an association.[78]

The astute French observer might have added Sunday schools and Sunday school organizations to his list.

This Anglo-Saxon dominance was not established without protest, even in the first convention. A delegate from France rose to point out to the predominantly British and American meeting that:

There is more difficulty than you Anglo-Saxons are apt to think between what does for you and what will do for France. The reason is historical. You have spread so far over the world that you are apt to think that what suits Anglo-Saxons is necessarily international. Yet there are differences and that is why it is useful to have in a Convention like this representatives from such comparatively small bodies of Sunday school workers as that to which I belong.[79]

At the same convention, protests were voiced from Denmark about the selection of hymn and tune books [80] and about the references to Continental missions as if they were similar to China and India missions ending with the jibe that ''Of course we have some people not much better than heathens but you have some, too. [Hear, hear]'' [81]

Some oratory at the first convention verged on the sentimental. American and Canadian speakers were frequently overcome by the experience of discovering the roots of their religious, national, and cultural past in the city of

London. A Canadian speaker was interrupted twice by cheers as he spoke of his pleasure of seeing a bust of Longfellow alongside that of Chaucer in Westminster Abbey, and expressed his delight in seeing "the two countries so associated, so bound together, by bonds of love, as they ought always to be, in the march onward for the glory of the world and the glory of our Lord Jesus Christ. [Cheers]." [82]

In the second session of the first day of the first convention, six members from Great Britain, five from the United States, and one from Canada were nominated for an executive committee. This membership for a world convention seemed narrowly limited to a delegate who, after conversing with some friends from the Continent, proposed that some Continental delegates be added. President F. F. Belsey agreed, soliciting suitable names from different countries.[83]

Sometimes a strain of something deeper and less lovely than sentimental affection arose among the three countries. One speaker from New York seemed to have forgotten both that he was in a supposedly world Christian gathering and, as well, a sizeable portion of the New Testament:

> The city of New York, which I represent at present, is made up very largely of those who come not from England alone, but from every portion of the world. We would be glad if a great many more came from England than from other parts, because we have a great many with us whom we cannot call brethren.[84]

In time, of course, stringent immigration quotas would take care of Mr. Porter's complaint.

In 1889, the Fourth of July fell in the midst of this ethnocentrism. President F. F. Belsey (British) proposed that while the convention not be interfered with, there would be an afternoon celebration in the church basement, taking "quiet tea together in a very modest manner, and strictly in accordance with Sunday school delegate lines." [85] The next day, and the friends of American independence assembled, the president of the world convention, a loyal subject of Queen Victoria, moved a resolution:

> The English and Colonial delegates at this Convention congratulate very heartily the American brothers and sisters on this auspicious day, and trust that the anniversary spent in this country and under these happy circumstances, may be fraught with many happy reminiscences.[86]

Flags for the occasion had been mounted on either side of the meeting room, and two verses of *America* were sung, followed by a verse of *God Save the Queen.* Cheers were then given for the queen and the president of the United States.

During the course of the St. Louis convention in 1893, and the Third World Convention in 1898, the same assumption appeared that somehow both the political hopes of the world and the future of the Christian enterprise depended upon the continuing progress of the two nations—Great Britain and the United States. Patriotism was to be taught in the Sunday school, according to P. H. Barstow of Washington, D.C. Speaking of his own Sunday school, he reported:

> I seized the opportunity of teaching, by illustration, how much, in my judgment, the world is looking to the two countries, the one under the Stars and Stripes and the other under the Union Jack, for the carrying of the teaching of God's word into all its parts. So from the pulpit platform to the topmost pipe of the great organ in a church but little smaller than this one in which we meet, I festooned our own starry banner. But in the very centre, against the balcony which surrounds the organ, I crossed two beautiful silk banners, the Union Jack and the Stars and Stripes. But over them, and floating out between them, fluttered another banner, representing more than either of these—the white flag of the gospel of peace to all mankind. But the two flags of colour were the wings which shall carry the peace banner to the uttermost parts of the earth and to the islands of the sea. . . . More than fifteen hundred men, women, and children looked on that scene that day and sang the mingled songs of patriotism and Christianity and good fellowship and national fraternity, and do you think they will ever forget? [87]

The answer to Mr. Barstow's rhetorical question proved to be, "No." American Protestantism sang for a long time the "mingled songs of patriotism and Christianity and good fellowship and national fraternity" down to but not ending with Irving Berlin and "God Bless America, land that I love."

Earlier, in the second convention, immediately after the call to order by President B. F. Jacobs, Professor Lindsay, the song leader, signaled the organist and the strains of *God Save the Queen* poured forth. Then Professor Lindsay unrolled a large Union Jack and, throwing it over his right shoulder, led the choir and convention in singing the British national hymn. Then as the same tune was used with the words of *My Country, 'tis of Thee,* Professor Lindsay unfurled the American flag and threw it over his left shoulder, and immediately after the audience joined in singing *Blest be the Tie That Binds:* "the vast audience singing with gladsome voice this blessed hymn of a universal [sic] Christian brotherhood." [88]

It will be remembered that at the St. Louis convention there was only one person registered from outside the boundaries of Canada, Britain, and the United States.[89] So this touching display of civil religion could not have offended many. Evidently the "flag ceremony" was memorable, for it was repeated seventeen years later with an appearance of spontaneity.

Between the first and the second conventions (1889 and 1893), Britain and America had settled a dispute over fishing rights in the Bering Sea, and its settlement by arbitration, though denying American claims, proved encouraging. F. F. Belsey alluded, in a gentlemanly and oblique manner, to it in bringing greetings to the St. Louis convention.[90] Other speakers grew more fervent in St. Louis. Dr. John Potts thanked God for the Sunday school work "being carried on in the very center of the world, Old England." [91] And Dr. J. L. Phillips elicited enthusiastic applause as he raised the question:

> What would our work be worth, what would our lives be worth were it not for the glorious Union Jack under which I was born in India. [Cheers.] God bless Queen Victoria, Empress of India. [Cheers.] In many a home in England, Wales, Ireland, Scotland, and India I have heard many earnest prayers offered for the President of the United States, coupled with prayers for the Queen and Empress. God bless our Christian rulers and grant during their reign the world may be evangelized and the Sunday-school workers see and seize our opportunities for reaching the childhood of the present generation.[92]

In the farewell meeting of the first convention, B. F. Jacobs stated his belief that even if the flood and full tide of ruin, sin, and disaster should come down, the "strong faith and strong government of England" together with the "strong faith and united hearts of America" would do much to stem the tide. "More than any other government on the face of the earth, England had conserved and preserved the Christian liberties they enjoyed." Victoria, "that blessed and honorable woman," forever during her life had stretched up and out her hand in favour of freedom throughout the earth.[93]

This bond of fraternal good feeling was especially strong between Canada and the United States, declared Aquila Lucas of New Brunswick at the third Convention:

> We are scarcely two people in that great country, at least on Sunday school lines. We in Canada fully understand that the beloved sister went out from the home when father was severe in his government, and mother love did not influence the home household as much as it does today [laughter]. In this great international work you of Great Britain cannot understand as we do the kinship and interests along the long line linking the entire continent together.[94]

In this chorus of mutual British and American esteem there have been discovered only two notes of warning, two illustrations of a wider outlook. One came from a German count, one from the pastor of London's City Temple. Both were voiced in 1898.

Count Bernstorff, in the closing meeting in 1898, looked ahead and sensed intimations of 1914:

> You understand that with these feelings that I have for your country it is quite natural that I should find an estrangement between Great Britain and Germany something entirely unnatural—a thing, according to my idea, which can never be permanent—but which should not be even for a time. We have too many things which bind us together, and especially not only the race, but also our common Protestantism.[95]

Joseph Parker, pastor of London's City Temple, brought a wider view, which, while it falls short of late twentieth-century ecumenism, yet transcended those genial Anglo-American expressions of brotherhood. After testifying to his impeccable British credentials, Dr. Parker called the third convention to an awareness of a "larger race, the human race":

> We have here today, and every day in this church, people from France, and Germany, and Sweden, and Africa, and many other places that are not usually regarded as representing the Anglo-Saxon race. If the Anglo-Saxon is going to work for peace, I am with it. If the Anglo-Saxon is going to be for the world, I am with it; if against the world, I am not with it. "God hath made of one blood," and I would like to trace God's action among the nations, because Luther was not what I should call an Englishman. I am almost sure he was not an American, and I believe the Australians could not honestly claim him. And Calvin, and the great leaders of thought all over Europe, I am with them, because my cry is not "The Anglo-Saxon race." My cry is Christian Protestantism for the world. [Loud cheers.] [96]

Dr. Parker raised the only recorded voice in these early conventions on behalf of a wider fellowship, and protested, at least by implication, the cozy North Atlantic confraternity.

"A CHRISTIAN FLAG THAT WAVES AT MANILA"

Closely allied with this strong, fraternal association existing among Canada, Britain, and America was an uncritical assumption that the march of empire was the facilitator of the spread of the Gospel. It would be too much to say that the spread of geographical dominion was taken to be the gradual advent of the Kingdom of God. That would be inaccurate caricature. There are many expressions in the early conventions, however, that display to our more critical eyes deplorable confusion between Caesar's reign and that of the Gospel. Christian hearts and minds had not yet become aware of the insidious blurring of patriotic sentiment and religious zeal. "The mingled songs of patriotism and Christianity" sung in London in 1898 proved to be tunes both seductive and perduring.

In the third convention (1898), this confusion was especially tempting for the American delegates because of the conclusion of the Spanish-American war. This conflict and the decisions which followed it were not without their strong religious overtones. President McKinley had hesitated about taking the Philippines, but at last confided to a Methodist delegation his decision to "take them all and educate the Filipinos, and uplift and civilize and Christianize them." This annexation, Professor Samuel E. Morison declares, was a major turning point in American history.[97]

Aware of this kind of religious talk coming from their president, the American delegates to the 1898 convention saw some association of the westward march of empire, of "Manifest Destiny," with the Great Commandment of their Lord. B. F. Jacobs was especially eloquent:

> Cuba will soon be a part of our field and will need our help. As the Bible distributor's cart entered Rome with Garibaldi's victorious soldiers, so the Bible and the Sunday School should enter Cuba with the American flag. And as the work is extended to Cuba, it should also be carried to the other West India Islands and to Central and South America. The International Sunday School field should include the entire Western Hemisphere. This is our work, and we cannot avoid responsibility. We must advance beyond all others, for we are "The heirs of all the ages in the foremost files of time." [98]

Bishop Thoburn, one of the great missionary leaders of the Methodist Episcopal Church, was even more explicit in his geographical reference:

> There is a Christian flag that waves at Manila this morning. Christian Sunday schools must soon be planted upon these rich and promising islands, and I think I give expression to the 40,000,000 or 50,000,000 of people on the other side of the Atlantic when I say that the flag which now protects the Christian preacher and teacher will wave as long as there is a Christian nation called America. [Loud applause.] [99]

There was a moment in the third convention when, at the suggestion of a Rhode Island delegate, the Rev. Dr. Spalding prayed that America might be made equal to and discharge worthily her new responsibilities created by the Spanish-American war.[100] A resolution hailed with satisfaction evidences that the war was coming to a close, praying that the outcome might be not only the political enfranchisement of peoples but also the "enlargement of the life-giving Word of God and the spread of religious liberty." [101]

This awareness of the virtually unlimited and happy future was not confined to people from the United States. Canadians—influenced similarly by many of the same geographic, economic, and cultural factors—shared in it as well. The tides of emigration were washing the shores of Quebec and Ontario just as they were engulfing Ellis Island. The Rev. Aquila Lucas of New Brunswick saw in this influx a mighty portent for the future of his country, and a new Canada emerging:

> In the future generations these emigrants or their offspring will neither be Russians, nor Germans, nor Scandinavians, nor any other named country from which their fathers came, but they will be Canadians, and they will be worth more to us, and to the State in proportion to the aggressive Sunday school work which is carried on. And so this organized Sunday school work of Canada from the east to the extreme west is being done by the help of the Spirit of God in obedience to the fundamental principles of the Word, and with a full faith in the certainty of the greatness of that land in the future.[102]

Among the voices of fulsome praise for the role of America during and beyond the Spanish-American War there was only one voice raised in a word of understanding for the vanquished and humiliated Spanish forces. That voice again was that of Dr. Joseph Parker:

> . . . I think it was a thousand pities that, when Spain offered to evacuate a certain place—if it could retain side-arms—the occasion was not eagerly seized and embraced. I will say here that I have never been an admirer of Spain. I remember its Inquisition and its bull-baiting, and its inconceivably rotten and terrorizing Papacy; but I will be just, and acknowledge that in this ever-to-be-deplored conflict the Spaniards have shown themselves to be anything but cowards. Let us be just even to the opposition. They have fought splendidly, according to their ability and resources. They have justified their title to a high military place in Europe, and this tribute has been so ungrudgingly conceded by Americans that I am thankful that this noble trait in their character has been so displayed. . . . America touched the highest point in her history when she was gentle to her Spanish opponents, when she took them on board her own ships and received the great Spanish admiral as being every inch a seaman and every inch a soldier. I do not believe in a God who classifies nations invidiously, but the God in whom I do believe classifies nations generously, justly giving to each nation a portion in due season and charging each nation with its own special responsibility. I do not ask you to take up any party cry, but I ask you to adopt the cry of Christian Protestantism for the world, the enemy of Rome and the friend of man.[103]

Again, we must deplore the anti-Catholicism in Dr. Parker's exhortation. At the same time we can admire his plea for fairness in the discussion of the progress of the war. One wonders how this even-handedness appeared to the American delegates, many of whom seem to have succumbed to the patriotic fervor of the 1890s.

What can be said by way of summary and comment about the frequent invocations of British-American friendship, and the near identification of national destiny with the prospects of the Gospel? From our perspective, sensitive to the perils of confusing the claims of Christ and those of Caesar, it is clear that there was too much of both. Those who followed the God of all the nations, revealed in the life, ministry, and death of One who found himself so frequently at variance with his own nation and culture, could have been more cautious and reserved in identifying the worldwide empire of the good queen and the burgeoning empire of America with the progress of Christ's Kingdom.

We must remember, however, that there is an immense generation gap between them and us, a span of nearly a century. Our judgments should be tempered with understanding. These leaders were men of their own time, not of ours. Sunday school leaders and parsons pretty accurately reflected the spirit of their own eras. It ought to humble us more than a little to remember that no doubt the chroniclers of a century from now will find many defective and incomplete aspects of our own witness and ministry in the twentieth century. God used these ministers and laymen for the accomplishment of his holy purposes. Because of them, we are able to serve our own day.

INDIFFERENCE TO CHURCH UNITY

The world Sunday school conventions were based upon the two support-ing associations, of Great Britain on the one hand and of the United States and Canada on the other. While the movements were not lay movements as has been often asserted (ministers composed a significant proportion of their leadership), neither were they official "church" movements, that is, au-thorized and validated by official actions of the denominations themselves. The national organization in the United States was based upon state conven-tions, these bodies were based upon county conventions, and they, in turn, upon local conventions or associations. All of this structure was without official denominational authorizations or connections. The Sunday school movement was an independent, self-constituting development, existing to support the work of the churches, in this respect not unlike the nature of the early Y.M.C.A. movement.

The 1890s came before there was any widespread interest in organic church unity. The day of ecumenical interest had not yet dawned. Did these cooperating Sunday school leaders sense the coming interest in church union? Only dimly, and not very often. Theodore S. Cuyler of the Lafayette Avenue Presbyterian Church in Brooklyn advocated involvement in practi-cal affairs:

> In such a work as this in which we are engaged, denominationalism is of no more account than the colour of your eye or the height of your stature. What is the good of talking everlastingly about unity? There is an immense amount of breath wasted in talk of that kind. The only way to get at unity is just to practice it in Christian work. Horses unharnessed will soon fall to biting and kicking one another. Harnessed, and with a good load to pull, they will pull together.[104]

In a similar vein, Dr. Potts, then chairman of the International Lesson Committee, compared the church to an army, divided as an army is into companies, regiments, battalions, and brigades. He voiced a favorite cliché—"Unity, not uniformity, is the desirable object to be attained"—and then dropping his military metaphor asserted that "We may be as distinct as the billows but one as the sea." [105]

There were voices raised in the early conventions, however, who saw the waste and frustration in the fragmented Protestantism of the day. At the second convention (1893) held in St. Louis, M. Greenwood, Jr., deplored the spectacle of eleven Protestant church buildings within four blocks. He esti-mated that if some kind of unification could be achieved, 50,000 preachers would be spared for missionary endeavor and 50,000,000 dollars available for nations sitting in darkness.[106]

By the time the fifth convention (1907) met in Rome, there was one voice at least which went beyond the popular assumption that fraternal love and practical involvement were all that were needed. F. B. Meyer asserted that some grave mistakes had been made:

> We have been antagonizing the Roman Catholic; we have been antagonizing the Greek Christian; antagonizing those who don't agree with us, instead of believing that there was a common unity between us, and trying to discover the points of agreement rather than those of discord. . . . And remember when you sing the glory and the unity and blessing of other denominations than your own, and of other churches than your own, you are most certain to get blessing for yourselves. . . . I have found in my own ministry that supposing I pray for my own little flock, God bless me, God fill my pews, God send me a revival, I miss the blessing, but as I pray for my big brother, Mr. Spurgeon, on the right hand side of my church, God bless him, or my other big brother, Campbell Morgan, on the other side of my church, God bless him, I'm sure to get a blessing without praying for it, for the overflow of their cups fills my little bucket.[107]

The Rome convention heard two national statements which were of unusual interest. The French Sunday School Union reported that there were three separate Protestant synods in that country, ranging from conservative evangelicals to near Unitarianism, and that the union represented them all, the only one in the world, he believed, which united all the Protestant denominations of a nation.[108] From Turkey came the report that nearly every one of the churches in the Levant grew out of an earlier established Sunday school.[109]

The early conventions came before the historic ecumenical conferences of Edinburgh (1910), Stockholm (1925), and Lausanne (1927). The leadership of Mott, Brent, Temple, Soderblom, and the other early ecumenical giants was still to come. The early Sunday school people gave voice to the best they knew: fraternity, forbearance with one another, Christian affection, and cooperation in good works. These attributes, so frequently displayed in the records of these sessions, were also, we may believe, works of the Spirit.

And perhaps, so far as America was concerned, there was another reason why the cause of corporate Church unity did not appear in these early days. The ecumenical concerns of the twentieth century have been undergirded and carried along by deep theological motivations. It has not at all been just a practical concern. That motivation was in short supply in American Protestantism at the close of the century, if Kenneth Scott Latourette is correct in saying that "no theologian or theology of first rank issued from the nineteenth century Christianity of the United States." [110]

The Sunday school conventions, however, did find it possible to hold a sacramental service from time to time. In 1904 a union observance of the

Lord's Supper was held on the opening day, a Sunday afternoon. It was estimated that there were 800 communicants, with thirty ministers of different denominations participating.[111] Later interchurch gatherings found it difficult, often impossible, to hold such communion services.

CHURCH AND SUNDAY SCHOOL RELATIONS

Because of the circumstances of its beginnings and the nature of its development in Britain and in the United States, the Sunday school movement was associated with the church, but was not yet an integral part of its life and concern. It existed, for the most part, alongside the church.

By the end of the century, however, this "fraternal relationship" was beginning to be transcended. The senior secretary of the London Sunday School Union declared to the First World Convention that the Sunday school is a church institution with teachers to be appointed by the church, facilities to be arranged by it, and officers of the school authorized by official church action and the school reporting back to the church in its quarterly meetings.[112] Secretary Hartley was supported in this position by B. L. Green of Manchester, who expressed equal concern that many ministers did not interest themselves very much in Sunday school work. Were they to evince such an interest, "We question whether the benefits would be all on one side." [113] A gentle jibe.

The assumption of the tasks of the Sunday school movement as legitimate and official responsibilities of the churches themselves came slowly. As early as 1844, the bishops of the Methodist Episcopal Church declared that this work was "one of the most effective auxiliaries" for spreading scriptural truth.[114] By the middle of the century, denominational boards for Sunday school work were being organized, and by the beginning of the twentieth century most denominations had such structures.

In the United States and Canada considerable tension developed in time because of the developing dual structures; the city and county Sunday school associations forming the state and provincial associations, these bodies in turn forming the substructure of the international association, and, at the top of the pyramid, the World's Sunday School Association was composed of national bodies as member units. In 1922 the Canadian and American churches resolved this tension by creating the International Council of Religious Education, a body which until its absorption into the National Council of Churches in 1950 had a dual organizational membership base: denominational boards of Christian education and state councils of churches or Christian education.

In Britain J. Kenneth Meir recounts a longer separation of concerns:

For long years in her [the Sunday school] early history she was independent of the local church, and even sometimes in complete isolation from it. Unthinkingly we perpetuate this unhappy tradition every time we hold a Sunday School Anniversary as well as a Church Anniversary.[115]

Maintaining this close association with the churches and, indeed, a growth toward incorporating the teaching enterprise with the total mission of the church, the World Sunday School Association, when it was formed in 1907, restricted membership to persons holding "what is commonly known as the 'Evangelical Faith.' " Never adequately or specifically defined, this formula seems to have been generally understood as meaning a Trinitarian confession. Certainly it did not mean "free church," for from the beginning persons from liturgical churches, Lutherans, Anglicans, and others were active in the association's and the conventions' affairs.

BIBLE READING AND TEACHING

It is rather surprising that there is so little recorded directly about the Bible and ways of teaching of it. One gets the impression that the importance of the Bible was simply taken for granted, and that the Sunday school forces of the world had already discovered what they believed to be as effective a manner of presenting the Scriptures to children, youth, and adults as was likely to be discovered.

There are frequent references to the International Bible Reading Association and appeals to adopt its program in Sunday schools and in congregations. It had begun in Britain in 1882, seven years before the convening of the first Convention. By 1898 it had an English membership of 620,000. Its recommendations for daily Bible reading had been translated into twenty-nine languages other than English.[116] It was widely used in the countries of the empire.

The English Revised Version of the Bible had appeared in 1881, the first substantial revision since the King James Version of 1611, done by a company of scholars who were themselves deeply influenced by the new, scholarly currents about the origins and meaning of the Scriptures. In the third convention of 1898, W. T. Davison, of the Wesleyan College in Handsworth, Birmingham, England, recommended use of this contemporary version.[117]

In the same convention, Mr. Davison counseled the delegates not to shun nor be afraid of the processes of the literary and historical criticism of the Bible:

> The Bible requires to be studied like any other book, with all our reasoning powers. This brings us to the much discussed subject of modern Biblical criticism. What has the Sunday school teacher to do with it? Speaking generally, I think, very little; but every teacher may understand what is meant by it—learn not to be afraid of it, leave the work itself to those whom it chiefly concerns, and then acquaint himself with the best results of the science when these are fairly and firmly established. Criticism means inquiry and judgment. Biblical

criticism means investigation into the books of the Bible on their literary side, inquiring as to the text, date, authorship, contents, and composition of the books, and forming a judgment according to the best light available. No Christian, at least no Protestant, should be afraid of such inquiry, even if from time to time it should be found needful to modify opinions held concerning some books, their date, structure, or meaning.[118]

This reasoned appeal was seconded by the Rev. George Parkin of Manchester, asserting that the biblical scholars seeking for truth studied, figuratively, on their knees, a proper attitude for those who would enter into the Kingdom of Truth, such persons to be "humble, inquiring, and willing to be taught." [119]

The reassurances of Davison and Parkin came at a time when British and American biblical scholarship was making constructive use of earlier German contributions. Julius Wellhausen had carried on his great studies of Old Testament origins and Adolf Harnack had performed a similar service for the New Testament and other early Christian writings.

In England, Bishops Lightfoot and Westcott and F. J. Hort led the way in New Testament studies, along with Professors S. R. Driver and George Adam Smith in Old Testament scholarship. For the most part, the new historical approach to the Scriptures was rather calmly accepted by British Christians, even though William Robertson Smith was deposed from his Old Testament chair at the Free Church of Scotland College at Aberdeen, and evangelist Charles H. Spurgeon and pastor Joseph Parker opposed and derided the new historical and literary criticism.

Except for the instance cited above, there is no evidence that many of the leaders nor any of the rank-and-file Sunday school convention delegates were greatly troubled by these new winds of scholarly inquiry, indeed no evidence that they knew such existed. No record of any extended discussion of these issues exists. Davison and Parkin were English. No American speaker or leader appears to have discussed at all the new biblical scholarship which was to prove so enormously influential in the new century.[120]

Far more attention was given to discussing the usefulness of the International Uniform Lessons than to considering the program of the International Bible Reading Association or the progress of the higher and lower criticism. In the first three conventions many speakers rose to discuss the advantages of the series, and what is more surprising, in view of its usage throughout the world, others spoke about its unsuitability for the Sunday schools they knew best.

The uniform lessons had originated with dissatisfaction with the chaotic Sunday school curriculum of the United States. There was established a "uniform lesson"—one Bible passage each Sunday—for all ages, from the very youngest members in the primary classes to the oldest men and women in the adult classes. Originated by Dr. John H. Vincent and popularized by the indefatigable B. F. Jacobs, the uniform lessons profoundly affected curriculum practices, teacher-training enterprises, and church architecture. "Uniform" for age-groups soon became expanded to "uniform" for all countries of the world, and the idea of one lesson for each Sunday, for persons of all ages, throughout the whole Protestant world became an irresistible vision of delight for many.

But not for all. During the First World Convention, querulous voices were raised about the validity of the assumptions of the promoters of the uniform lessons. The Rev. Dr. Peloubet (the originator of a series of lesson helps which today still bears his name) asserted that the series was winning its way because of its intrinsic excellence. Benjamin Clarke of Great Britain attacked the quality of the series. He failed to see any positive qualities other than that they came from the pens of eminent American ministers.[121] Specifically, he was critical of the lack of continuity, neglect of the teachings of the prophets, neglect of doctrines and denominational beliefs, ignoring of temperance and church festivals, unsuitability for little children ("from the same joint we find meat for the man, and broth for the babe"), sacrificing utility to mere sentiment, and unsystematic and unsatisfactory treatment of the epistles.[122]

One British speaker in the third convention (London, 1898) pointed out that if a student entered the series late, it would be two and a half years before he would begin to learn about the life and ministry of Jesus.[123] Alternate lessons for young children were requested at the third convention, but nothing was done about the expressed need.

Other objections came from specific countries. Pastor Matthieu Lelievre of France was not ready to buy goods with a British or American label:

> I am disposed to admit it with a single restriction, that it (the Uniform Series) is perfect for English-speaking peoples. The coat is perfect, and made by the best workmen in the world, as we have been told; but it has, at least from our point of view, a radical defect—it does not fit us.[124]

Pastor Lelievre reported that France, after twelve years of use, had rejected the Uniform Lesson Plan and that in Switzerland opinion was divided about its merits. Something of the same attitude seemed current in Belgium and Italy.[125]

Pastor Charles Jaulmes joined his French colleague by voicing two chief criticisms. Swiss Sunday schools were not ready for the uniform lessons, and because of the short age span in his country (eight to thirteen), and because of catechumen classes, the uniform lessons did not meet Swiss needs. But if the uniform lessons were to be continued he hoped that fewer dogmatic and abstract subjects be treated, that yearly changes from Testament to Testament be employed, not switches at six-month intervals, and that a shortened cycle of four to five years be employed. He asked for a commission to be appointed to review the 1889 situation, ending with a plea:

When a big brother goes out for a walk with a little one, the latter may get tired in trying to keep up with the former, but still he does not want to let go his brother's hand. Should he, then, hesitate to ask his big brother just to walk a little slower for his younger brother's sake? [126]

Even from Britain, where a section of the Uniform Lesson Committee had been established, came objections. An alternate proposal emerged which would safeguard the admitted advantage of a common lesson throughout the single school:

. . . the question is whether the advantage of graded lessons could not be gained without that great disadvantage, by having all the classes studying the same great thing. But they might be studying it with different passages of Scripture attached to it, and then the literature would unfold the great subject, and it would be of use, the literature that was provided for the senior class would be of use even to the junior teacher.[127]

Count Bernstorff reported in 1898 that the lessons had lost ground in Europe because they ignored the Ecclesiastical year, with its observance of Christmas, Easter, and Pentecost.[128] And at the 1907 convention in Rome, it was asserted that though there was use of the uniform series in China at the time, there was considerable criticism of its being unsuited to the needs of the Chinese and the churches.[129]

To these complaints, the supporters of the series pointed out that there was no satisfactory extant substitute for the Uniform Lessons Plan and that no one wanted to return to the chaos of the days before 1872. Patience was needed and in time improvements would be made.

In 1893 it was reported that the French-speaking cantons of Switzerland did not use the international lessons and that an intercantonal committee representing Geneva, Vaud, and Neuchatel were preparing another, more systematic series.[130]

The successive conventions of the early period, lacking any effective interim machinery for dealing with educational proposals, were unable to respond to such suggestions. No doubt the comments received the attention and scrutiny of the International Lesson Committee which by this time was meeting in two sections: an American and a British subgroup. The formal organization of the World's Sunday School Association in 1907 only partially met the need, for substantial and diversified curriculum assistance was to come only after two world wars. The international committee did, from time to time, make improvements and modifications in its outlines, but the basic plan continued.

The International Uniform Lessons in spite of much criticism continued. In Indianapolis, the city in which they were authorized a century earlier, their centennial was observed in 1972. Few ecclesiastical programs have lasted so long, and reached so many.

Educational Concerns of the Conventions

The programs of the successive conventions were uniformly arranged for speeches, lectures, and addresses, and the delegates apparently were expected to sit and listen for the three or more sessions a day.

The program of the 1889 meeting ran into an unexpected protest as a "Scotch" [sic] delegate, after hearing a number of speeches, rose to ask if there were to be no remarks on the presentations. The chairman of the meeting was courteous, but he doubted that it could be done. The delegate persisted, citing his dissatisfaction with some of the statistics. The matter was referred to the executive committee. That committee seriously considered the matter, and reported back to the convention through B. F. Jacobs, who indicated that an attempt would be made to find time for some discussion. At the same time he pointed out that the effort would not be easy because: "It is very difficult to determine exactly the limits to which any man will go when he is once allowed to be on the platform. [Laughter]" It was next proposed that the time for the papers be limited, and at a later session Mr. Jacobs brought a recommendation that the time for the papers be shortened, and time for discussion on them provided. The delegate from Scotland was pleased.[131]

The reform did not seem to be permanent. The second, third, and later conventions all followed the same format: speeches, speeches, speeches! It was a convention pattern which had not entirely disappeared from ecumenical and interchurch gatherings by the last quarter of this century.

CONCERN FOR CHILDREN

Concern for the religious nurture of children was a primary interest of the conventions. Children had been the object of Robert Raikes' solicitude in Gloucester, and British Sunday schools were largely preoccupied with ministering to them.

American Sunday schools developed an interest in serving both youth and adults. In 1904, an American commented on an address by the archdeacon of London that he spoke from the standpoint of the English Sunday school as being an agency for the instruction of children, "as contrasted with the broader fact of the Sunday-school as the teaching service of the church, embracing the entire church, parents and children alike." [132] This tension persisted long after the Jerusalem convention, and indeed proved to be a constant strain through the life of the continuing body.

The influence of Horace Bushnell (1802–1876) was felt in St. Louis at the second convention as Annie S. Harlow averred that "the natural time to become Christians is in childhood."

> We need the positive conviction that the Holy Ghost does move mightily in the hearts of little people: and then we need one more solid conviction that the

Word of God, when it is implanted in the heart, will not return void to him who gave it.[133]

In similar fashion the influence of F. W. A. Froebel, the founder of the kindergarten movement (1782–1852), was manifested in an address by Mrs. Wilbur F. Crafts, one of the very few women speakers of this period (unidentified in the record). Mrs. Crafts asserted that Froebel had much to give the teacher of young children because: he would make nature the starting point in learning; he believed in Bible lessons for children; he stressed the "imitative instinct"; he minimized the abstract; he sought types and symbols in the concrete world; and he stressed Christian action before Christian dogma. Mrs. Crafts urged Christian workers to adapt (not adopt) the kindergarten method in their teaching, though she admitted that the "character of many of the exercises, such as sewing, weaving, molding, games, etc. are not suited to the Sabbath day." But the elements of the kindergarten could be used, Mrs. Crafts asserted. In the adaptation it will not be necessary to abandon belief in spiritual regeneration, and she quoted Froebel on the point: "the Christian religion has power to transform the children of vicious parents, and that if it were not so, the Christian idea would have no significance." [134]

In England a child-centered philosophy of education was beginning to be heard as the nineteenth century came to a close. Chairman Edward Towers quoted Edward Ranken in the third convention:

> We are beginning to study the child, and to acknowledge that he is the master of the situation. Instead of making education conform to the views of the educator we are endeavoring to make the educator conform his views to the nature and capabilities of the child. We are trying to study the child, to find out what he really is, to do our best for him. He is treated as a living organism that allows of growth peculiar to himself, which must be known and followed before the perfecting of the growth can be attained. He is no longer treated as clay in the hands of the potter, to be molded into any shape we wish. The most powerful signs of the times educationally are the scientific interest taken in their work by the tutors, and the lofty anxiety for the welfare of the children shown by all classes in it.[135]

Teaching must support, not run counter to, the natural growth processes of the child. Mrs. J. W. Barnes expressed a philosophy of Christian growth gaining in popularity among children's workers:

> Our part is to fit our processes of education to the stages of the unfolding of the child. If we leave the little rose-bud on the bush to itself, Nature takes care of it and unfolds it in the right way. If we go and keep opening it, it will be blighted: but if we leave Nature to work in its own way, we shall see the flower developed. It is so with regard to our teaching. We want to have our material and our methods of work alongside of the development that God has placed in the child itself.[136]

Here were overtones of developmental psychology and of what came to be called "progressive education." Here was criticism, implied but clear, of the traditional didactic approach to the education of the child. These fresh currents of educational philosophy were being felt partly as a result of a new interest in child learning, and, in the United States, by the formation of an organization concerned for childhood religious education.

The first primary teachers' class began in Newark, New Jersey. It spread to the larger cities of the East, and in 1884 the National Union of Primary Teachers was formed. Three years later the name was changed to the International Union of Primary Sunday-school Teachers of the United States and British American Provinces [Canada]. By 1898 250 unions had been organized in the two countries. These unions had five special lines of activity: child study, blackboard classes, normal classes, home cooperation, and superintendent's help.[137]

This emphasis upon new skills in working with children seems to have been the wedge opening a more diversified agenda for world conventions. To be sure, addresses remained the principal feature of the programs, but other types of presentations began to appear. At the third convention, a Miss Keysworth taught a demonstration class of twenty children, ages 4 or 5 up to 10 or 11, using the International Lesson on Elijah on Mt. Carmel, I Kings 18:30–39: ". . . she kept the close attention of the class and of the audience, and brought out the lesson that the side upon which Elijah had placed himself was the strongest, and that it is to God we must trust and to no other." [138]

YOUTH WORK

There is virtually no evidence that the early conventions were interested in the Christian education of adolescents, much less in encouraging youth movements. The story of that development, and it is a rich and full account, does not begin until well into the twentieth century. The 1928 convention in Los Angeles and the 1932 Rio de Janeiro convention were the precursors of interest in youth work, championed especially by the American section of the organization. There is a reference in the first convention to the problem of retaining older students in the Sunday school and church, but that is all.

It may be that the adult classes claimed young people at an early age, as is suggested below. It may be that the rapid rise of the Christian Endeavor Movement, begun in 1881 in Portland, Maine, provided an agency for young people which led to the comparative silence in Sunday school conventions about educational work with youth.

THE TEACHING OF ADULTS

The place of adults in the Sunday school program was of considerable interest to the delegates of the 1889 convention. There is some evidence that the teaching of adults was looked upon as a separate venture, and was to be structured separately from the nurture of children and young people. Councillor Pitt of West Bromwich, England, indicated that many thought of adult Bible classes in this way, that they were usually held in separate buildings, and that they were sometimes looked upon as antagonistic to the ordinary Sunday school. All of this was mistaken, even though the pattern of a separate structure is revealed:

> The Sunday school takes the child when it is about six years old, and retains it till it has grown up to about seventeen, or eighteen years of age. It is at this age our adult classes step in and say, "Now hand over to us your senior scholars of both sexes, and we will provide for them in every possible way." [139]

To judge from the accounts, the adults being reached by the Sunday schools were male adults and the social structures in which these men lived and worked were accepted without question. Echoes of the class structure of England were heard in the protestations of the same speaker to the effect that it was a mistaken conception to assume that the working men of England were opposed to the Gospel of Christ. Such a statement was a libel upon their character: "We find a great number of them love their Bible, and can and do, worship Christ as their Saviour. Working men like a religion of sympathy, which is the essence of the Gospel of our blessed Lord." [140]

Councillor Pitt's presentation echoed another, that of Robert Raikes himself, in his "social uplift" attempt, this time directed to adults of the working classes:

> We have seen men come to us poorly clad, with big mufflers around their necks, and almost afraid to sit in Chapel. In about a fortnight the muffler has given place to a neat tie and a clean collar. In about another month the old garments have disappeared altogether to make way for a new suit. And we venture to think that, if our classes become the means of making men more respectable, they not only confer a great commercial benefit, but also a great social and moral good upon society. [141]

The progress of the Gospel and the rise of social respectability were often linked together. B. F. Jacobs in the two early conventions held in London, saw in the Sunday school movement an opportunity for masculine Christian service and possible balance to the usual feminization of the Sunday school.

Men of outstanding character and intellectual traits were engaged in Sunday school work: "There are at this hour engaged in this work men of equal brain power, equal heart power, of equal influence in the pulpit and in business circles, of equal purity of life and breadth of character with any other men that tread the planet on which we live. [Cheers.]" [142]

More men were needed as teachers and officers, especially men of ability and influence. B. F. Jacobs admitted the value of women as teachers *"and in some cases as officers,*" [143] but it was men who were needed in the greatest of all professions, the teaching of the Word of God. Mr. Jacobs exhorted his listeners: "Some of the great men of America and England are now engaged in Sunday school work, and other men may learn the value that such service will be to themselves and to others whose lives they may influence for good." [144]

Mr. Jacobs was not content to let his appeal contain only generalities. He held up by name two renowned Americans as examples of the type of persons he wanted active as Sunday school teachers. One was William Rainey Harper, professor of Hebrew at "Yale College in Newhaven" [145] and later the energetic president of the University of Chicago. The other example was George W. Cabel of Boston whose name, he assumed, had crossed the Atlantic. Mr. Cabel was reported to be teaching a class of more than 2,000 men and women coming together on Saturday afternoons from seventy-three towns and cities in the vicinity. "It is dignified work teaching in the Sunday school" declared Mr. Jacobs in the closing meeting of the Convention. [146]

CURRICULUM

The early, and indeed the later, conventions seem not to have been interested in teaching methods. To be sure, there had been that demonstration class at the third convention, and earlier a brief reference in the first convention, urged that teaching methods and procedures should vary according to the needs and interests of age groups, otherwise waste of conscientious, earnest labor would occur, and opportunities were so small and precious that the risk of such waste must not be run. [147]

The impetus given to Christian unity by the uniform lessons was frequently mentioned.

> Christian union cannot be brought about by the resolutions of popular assemblies. Nor can it be entirely assured by united Christian work. As we come to a better understanding of the great charter of our common faith, our hearts will be knit together and our eyes will see alike. If we are ever to be in outward appearance what we know we are in heart, "One in Christ," it must come through the study of the Bible. Hail, then, O glorious day, for on the mountain tops we already see the tokens of thy coming. [148]

The grading of the Sunday school according to ages or age groups seems to have been an accepted practice by the turn of the century, and one description portrayed a school with six departments: kindergarten, children two to five years; primary, five years and first and second grades; intermediate, fourth, fifth, and sixth grades; junior, seventh and eighth grades; and high school, adult, and home department. This school had over 2,000 scholars and teachers, including 700 to 800 in the adult department. [149]

In all of this nondenominational activity, official denominational involvement was minimal. In 1889, only one denominational publication was issuing lesson helps, and even this was deplored by the editor of the *Sunday School Chronicle*. He declared that "the Sunday School is no place for denominational teaching, at all events among the younger scholars." [150]

Teacher training began in Great Britain at about the middle of the century. In 1849, a group met weekly at the Sunday School Union building, 60, Paternoster Row, focusing its attention on the study of the next Sunday's lesson. In 1856, in Pimlico (S.W. London), teaching demonstrations were arranged with the help of nearby Westminster Training College. Later the two efforts were united, and the venture was in operation at the time of the first convention.

Teacher training spread to America by way of the New York Sunday School Union. In the 1860s, both in Great Britain and in the United States, normal classes were established to prepare senior Sunday school scholars for teaching before they began their teaching efforts. The venture did not prove popular and there was substituted for it private study in reading courses with correspondence questions and answers, including correspondence courses in Greek and Hebrew.[151] (Lake Chautauqua, New York, became a popular and effective center for such programs.) Meanwhile the members of the International Lesson Committee were trying to make their series of maximum usefulness, and welcomed reasoned criticism of their efforts.[152]

We welcome friendly criticism. We have profited by some criticism which seemed unfriendly. We have listened occasionally to some which seemed to be based on lack of information and which demanded of us tasks which we were not appointed to perform. We have neither sought nor received any other reward than the consciousness of having done, to the best of our ability, the work to which we were called . . .[153]

ASSOCIATED ACTIVITIES

In the 1890s, the Sunday school had already gathered around itself some associated activities for children and young people. Music was a frequent concern. At the first convention, Alfred H. Miles of London deplored the character of the hymns and tunes in common use, songs which he termed "frivolous and unworthy," some of which had been taken from music played on merry-go-round organs at country fairs. He thought that other instruments ought to be used and orchestras and choirs formed, along with regular provisions for practice. He also thought that songs should be written "from a youthful standpoint." [154]

Perhaps as a result of this plea or for other reasons, over 5,000 Sunday school children sang at the third convention, and later that same afternoon in London's Crystal Palace 4,000 senior scholars and adults sang, accompanied by the Crystal Palace and the London Sunday School Choir Orchestra.[155]

A number of other activities were reported as being supportive to the British Sunday schools such as recreational evening classes: Christian endeavor societies, adult classes, pleasant Sunday afternoons, home reading circles, boys' brigades, bands of hope, and drawing room classes.[156] Professor Charles F. Bradley of Evanston, Illinois, listed a similar number of attractions for American boys and girls.[157] All of them were results of the British and American genius for organization. All of them were independent of official church sponsorship. Most of them were also independent of the Sunday school, though supportive of it.

Social and Ethical Issues

In two previous sections we discussed the commonality of interests among the three Anglo-Saxon nations, and the blurring of the distinctions between the progress of the Gospel and the onward march of political empires. The reader might infer from the two treatments that the Sunday school convention delegates lacked insight into social and ethical issues, or were insensitive to them.

That was not wholly true. The ethical issues felt by these conventioneers were, of course, those of their own day. The concerns which the delegates did identify were seldom thoroughly and critically dealt with. The first observation is only to say that these people dealt with their own problems, not with ours. The second reminds us that these Christian people were in a convention, not in a "think-tank process," and conventions of any kind, in any era, are not noted for in-depth analyses. The concern was of the church for the world seen by one speaker as part of the Christian heritage of Sunday school people: "The Evangelical revival of the 18th century pressed home upon the consciences of Englishmen the great question of the Relation of the Church of Christ to the World around it, with a force and directness which could not be evaded . . ." [158]

What were these issues and what was said about them?

SABBATH OBSERVANCE

The issue of Sabbath observance was often referred to in the years before 1907. One missionary, on returning to America from his post, was dismayed to see a decided falling-off in Sunday observance. As he was coming home from church one Sunday noon, he saw a group of people in tennis clothes playing on the courts, a sight that public opinion would not have tolerated in 1879. Attempts were being made to open art galleries and museums on the Lord's Day, efforts which he saw as the thin end of a wedge.[159] Matters were no better in France, Germany, and other places, regretted another speaker. In Australia, Christian people and Christian workers were grievously sinning by using railways and tram cars on the Lord's Day, and convention delegates were urged to refrain from unnecessary work on Sunday.[160] In 1898 the bicycle craze was seen as a threat to strict Sunday observance and Sunday school teachers were urged to combat this temptation.

TEMPERANCE

In Australia it was reported some progress had been made about the selling of liquor on Sunday: "No publican is allowed to sell any liquor except to anyone who proves that he has travelled ten miles or more on that day. Otherwise the bar is locked, and it is illegal to unlock that bar." [161]

We are told that a little later in Britain a popular election song of the Liberal Party (traditionally nonconformist) in 1905 went: "The Churchman and the Brewer we will drive them from the land, For the Nonconformist children are marching hand in hand." [162]

As the first convention came to its close, three resolutions were passed on the temperance question: one urged intensification of Sunday school efforts toward that end, another favored "temperance, piety and personal purity in the home," and a third urged prohibition of liquor shipments to Africa.[163] In a separate resolution the crowned heads of Europe were requested to initiate efforts on behalf of the Lord's Day observance.

PROBLEMS OF INDUSTRIALIZATION AND URBANIZATION

It is interesting to observe that the references to the growing problems of industrialization and urbanization in the early Sunday school conventions come from British speakers. There is nothing heard about these issues from American Sunday school leaders in the first years of the world movement. Mr. Flower, secretary of the Recreative Evening Schools Association, was reported as saying that:

> Vast numbers of our youth are growing up year by year to swell the ranks of the unemployed, because unskilled; while, at the same time, the demand for un-skilled labour is year by year decreasing. These are facts of serious import. They are the raw material of revolutions. They constitute a social and political danger of the first magnitude.[164]

In the same convention, the Countess of Aberdeen was more vivid:

> We are constantly saddened and distressed by hearing of the many miseries, of the terrible poverty of a certain class of people, of those who suffer under the sweating system, of those whom the Poor Law fails to reach, of those who are out of work; and whatever investigations are made into these matters, you always find the same thing, that the vast majority of those who are thus suffer-ing are the unskilled, the untrained, the incompetent. . . . It is the untrained and the incompetent who have to submit to those terrible hours, and who have to take the wretched pay which must grind all the spiritual life out of them, and which must prevent the soul awakening to a sense of its high destiny.[165]

F. F. Belsey, four years later, took notice of the departure of young people from the villages and towns to the great cities, and proposed the strengthening of the village Sunday schools as the best antidote against the temptations of the great urban hives of industry.[166]

It is difficult to account for the American silence. True, the great reform and progressive movements of the early part of the twentieth century had not yet gathered momentum. Yet the beginnings of the progressive movement were discernible by 1907. Ida M. Tarbell had already begun her reporting on the Standard Oil Company by 1902. Upton Sinclair in *The Jungle* had reported on the horrors of the Chicago stockyards. In 1905 Ray Stannard Baker had written an article in *McClures* on the condition of the Negro. There were other forthright reporters, some of whom were denounced by Theodore Roosevelt as "muckrakers." All of this appeared to be ignored by the American leaders of the Sunday school movement. Their silence in the early conventions was prophetic, for there is little voice given in the next period to any of the gigantic problems engendered by industrialization and urbanization.

ATTITUDES AND PRACTICES TOWARD BLACKS

Separation and paternalism best describe the attitudes of white conventioneers toward Negro Sunday school work (to use the terminology of the time). At the first convention there was an interdenominational effort to promote and administer Sunday schools among blacks in the United States. A special secretary had been employed for that purpose and he reported to the convention that the idea of establishing interdenominational Sunday schools was not, at first, very well received by leaders of black denominations. They, very naturally, saw the efforts as threats to denominational autonomy. But open opposition gave way to respectful submission, and that to "a sort of open-shut-approbation." He reported later that: "Gradually the idea of broader Christian fellowship is surging upon us, and the day of interdenominational fellowship and cooperation is dawning." [167]

The cooperative Sunday school movement among the blacks had been carried into nine states, though only four had anything like permanent interdenominational state organizations: Georgia, Florida, Alabama, and South Carolina. Of these, Georgia was the best organized, with sixty-nine county Sunday school associations out of the state's 139 counties.

Segregation of effort was not questioned. There is no evidence, however, that segregation was practiced in the conventions themselves, and almost fifty years later an American secretary of the association faced the issue and insisted that a segregation-minded local committee modify its rigid demand and allow an unsegregated convention to be held in Durban.[168]

This section on social and ethical issues is brief because the evidence is so scarce. It may be that one of the reasons for the scanty references is that societies dealing with specialized social concerns were growing rapidly on both sides of the North Atlantic. Ian Bradley illustrates the situation in Britain:

> Most of the famous humanitarian ventures of the nineteenth century had Evangelical inspiration and leadership: Elizabeth Fry's work in prisons; Josephine Butler's crusade on behalf of prostitutes; Dr. Barnardo's mission to deprived children; Edward Rudolf's establishment of the Church of England's Children's Society for Waifs and Strays; and the movements which Shaftesbury himself led to reform the factory system, humanize the laws relating to lunatics and establish decent housing for the working classes.[169]

It would be interesting to discover to what extent the several leaders of the British Sunday school movement were active in these social and philanthropic endeavors. That attempt, however, cannot be made in this volume.

Meeting the Needs of the Continents

In the early conventions, reports were given from time to time on the progress of Sunday school work in the United States, Great Britain, and Canada. The interest of the conventions, however, did not stay focused only on these three familiar nations. The needs of the mission fields were more burning and more clamant than those of the North Atlantic nations. Reports were similarly given of work in the European nations, but again their needs did not receive the attention given to the expansion of the Christian enterprise in Asia. Africa and South America were discussed in later periods.

EUROPE

In Sweden, the clergy, joined by the schools and the church councils, had resisted the Sunday school movement. An anecdote in this connection was told of the introduction of Christianity to Sweden, a tale not without its application to every land and every time.

A missionary in the early centuries of the Christian era had told the Gospel story in Sweden, and in time was allowed to relate the story of the Savior to the king. Whereupon:

> A chief, noticing the attention of the king, and fearing some new ideas might be introduced and so spoil the people, arose and said, 'I fear that the introduction of new ideas among us will not work for good, and, as for a new God, we need none; but, if the people must make a change, I propose that we adopt a native Swede.' [170]

It might have appeared that the British and American type of Sunday school did not resemble closely enough "a native Swede."

Since most of the directors and missionaries of the Sunday school movement in Sweden were Baptists, early progress was primarily centered in that denomination. Only later did the clergy of the established Lutheran church begin to have children's services, partly in self-defense, a development, however, which received the blessing and encouragement of one of the Sunday school protagonists.[171]

The early conventions coincided with the great Swedish emigrations to America. Between 1870 and 1914 nearly 1,500,000 Swedes came to the United States, most of them settling in the upper Mississippi Valley— Illinois, Wisconsin, Minnesota, Iowa, and the Dakotas. So great was this emigration that even the Sunday school work in the mother country was handicapped. In 1889 it was regretfully stated that "Thus, the missionaries very often report, 'The Sunday school in the place had ceased to exist, because the teacher had gone to America, and there is none in the neighborhood to fill his place.' " [172] This difficult situation persisted as more and more Swedes left for the north central states of the United States, and in 1893 a plea was made for reciprocal assistance:

> When we often sacrifice the best of our teachers and preachers to America, it seems but fair that we in return not only ask, but should receive abundant support from that great country, and we are certain that it will be of great benefit for America as well as for Sweden. Send us means and we will send a so much better people to America.[173]

Denmark shared in this "emigration drain" to the same American states, but with lesser numbers involved. Even so, in 1889, the Danes reported about 35,000 scholars and 2,000 teachers in Sunday schools, about four times as many as reported nine years before.[174]

In Germany, Sunday school work had begun in 1826. The first German Sunday School Union had been formed in Hamburg, again among dissenting churches. Another was established in Berlin in 1886, and later, the two united under the name: the Sunday-school Union of the Dissenting Churches of Germany.[175]

ASIA

The Sunday school movement had spread to India, carried by American and British missionaries. It was reported that there were 553 schools, enrolling 257,671 scholars and teachers. In the schools, the International Uniform Series was firmly rooted.[176]

Realization of this dependency upon foreign leaders and programs, and its consequent limitations, finally provoked an awareness of a need for the use of a native heritage. This was felt as early as the first convention. Specifically, indigenous religious art was needed. But unfortunately the lack of it persisted into the middle of the next century:

> More artists are wanted for India, who will delight the young people with pretty pictures of the common life of their own country, and give them charming

views of the scenery of their own land, and conceive for them the characters of the Bible in truly Oriental appearance. As yet the Sunday school children of India have been shown mainly western pictures.[177]

As a counterpoint to the frequently patronizing attitudes expressed by Western Sunday school leaders, a Connecticut speaker made a plea for the indigenization of the Christian faith which went far beyond the use of indigenous art in Christian teaching:

> . . . if there existed in these nations a large, important, influential body of native Christians, engaged in voluntary Christian work, who could say to their fellow natives, "Look at us. We are of the same flesh and blood as you are. We have not ceased to be patriots because we have become Christians. We are not foreigners. We owe no foreign allegiance. We have no foreign interests. This Christianity is not foreign. It is from the one and only God who made us all. It is from outside only because it is from above. Do not identify it with any nation. It is ours as truly as theirs. . . ."—What an incalculable influence and power upon their fellow natives would such a body of men by their testimony exert for Christ and His cause. . . . Christ would present Himself to the human heart free from the entangling alliances of his professed followers with the opium of Old England or the rum of New England.[178]

It would be a long time before the full import of this exhortation would be understood and acted upon.

In Japan, unlike India, only a small percentage of the schools used the international plan, the rest using independently produced curricula. In 1898, Japan reported 901 schools, including about one hundred in Tokyo alone, and more than 35,000 scholars. This was a year's gain of sixty-four schools and 4,409 scholars. Some schools had only a half-dozen scholars, while a few had two or three hundred each. Attendance was extremely irregular "due to the fact that a large portion of the scholars are children of the lower classes who attend from curiosity, and in many cases they come without their parents' knowledge." [179]

After the adjournment of the Jerusalem convention in 1904, it became apparent to many that these informal gatherings of Christian workers, with an *ad interim* or some other continuing body appointed toward the close of the meetings, needed a more adequate and continuing organization. Administrative responsibility had been delegated to one or the other of the Sunday school associations in Great Britain or the United States, but it became clear that a more formal structure was imperative.

The fifth convention in Rome was a historic turning point for the Sunday school associations. Evangelistic and missionary concerns would continue into the next period along with occasional confusion of national and religious goals. The British-American-Canadian dominance would continue, although other nations, notably Japan and those of Europe, would become more influential. It is to this more structured period, dating from 1907, that we now turn.

CHAPTER

2

———— ◆ ————

Organization and Program Emerge
1907-1924

THIS PERIOD begins in 1907 with the convention in Rome and terminates in 1924. In 1924, two new leaders appeared on the scene. They were the principal elected officers of the association-council. They became close friends and their leadership continued, one for nearly forty, the other for exactly forty years.

Life does not, however, consist of sharp breaks with the past. Certainly organizational life does not. During the early years of this second period we shall find many continuities with the earlier period. This chapter will, therefore, utilize some of the framework of the first, and if the reader is interested in an uninterrupted narrative, the related subdivisions in Chapters One and Two could be read in sequence. The same continuity will not prevail into Chapter Three and later chapters, for in those years different world situations will have evolved, different issues will have emerged, and organizational responses will not be the same.

Trans-Oceanic Voyages

For the eighth convention in Tokyo in 1920, two ships had been chartered to sail from the Pacific coast—the SS. *Siberia Maru* from San Francisco and the *Monteagle* from Vancouver. Tours were planned for Japan, the Philippines, China, and Korea before and after the convention. One party went on to India, Palestine, and Egypt and thus around the world.

Unfortunately, the SS. *Monteagle* was delayed by storms and was not able to reach Yokohama until October 9. The convention had begun on schedule October 5th. The delayed but ingenious delegates organized a "Tokyo convention" on board ship utilizing those four days. A chorus of one hundred voices was organized and, using the printed convention program as an outline, various members on the ship gave addresses.[1]

On Friday evening, June 6, 1924, 450 American delegates to the Glasgow convention met at the Prince George Hotel in New York for an "acquaintance reception" for those sailing on the SS. *Cameronia.*[2] Hardly had the ship sailed the next noon when, following the pattern set on the *Bothnia* thirty years before, the delegates set to drafting the needed talent for addresses, meetings, and conferences of all sorts. Old timers must have found it a very comfortable pattern. Even at sea the world was not entirely forgotten, for the message came of Calvin Coolidge's nomination as Republican candidate for president.

On this voyage a new name appears for the first time, one which was to be the most influential name in the later history of the movement, now about to become an organization:

> A stirring glimpse of the need, the possibilities, and the method of the new plans for religious education was given by Prof. L. A. Weigle of Yale University, in his morning addresses on "Jesus' Way of Teaching," "The New Outlook on Sunday school work" and on "Prayer."

On Sunday, June 15, Dr. Weigle preached at Divine Worship ("New Outlook," a new leader; "Religious Education," a new term). And there were more new insights to come because this Yale professor had come on board, not only the *Cameronia,* but aboard the world Sunday school movement. From this time on the intensity of earlier evangelistic efforts will diminish, the missionary impulse will remain though changed, and a new sophisticated educational interest will increase.

On the SS. *Marloch,* sailing from Montreal and Quebec, there were also held on the first Sunday, preaching, Sunday school and missionary addresses, with a similar program held on the second Sunday.[3]

Characteristics of the Conventions from Rome to Glasgow

EVANGELISTIC AND MISSIONARY EFFORTS

Much of the unbounded optimism and the confidence in organizational effort, described in Chapter One, carried over into this period, though expressions of these attitudes were more subdued. The evangelistic and missionary imperatives can still be discerned, but with a growing emphasis upon the established missionary operations and structures of the churches. Spontaneous, evangelistic efforts become less noticeable.

During the Rome convention, it was proposed that a Sunday school missionary tour around the world be organized for the year 1909. Its title would be ''World's Sunday School Visitation.'' Its object: to confer and cooperate with Sunday school workers in Japan, India, and China. It was to be composed of practical Sunday school workers willing to bear their own expenses.[4]

The sixth convention (1910), recognizing the affinity of the work of the Sunday schools with that of the Foreign Mission Boards, addressed a message to the Mission Boards of Protestant Christians. It stated that Robert Raikes and William Cary (a founder of the Western foreign missionary movement) were contemporaries. The Sunday schools, growing so rapidly in numbers and importance, could be helped by the mission boards. For example, the boards could study the potential of the Sunday schools in general and in particular. Missionary training institutions could be of assistance. Missionaries on the field should cooperate with interdenominational Sunday school movements. Boards could give financial support to missionaries for Sunday school equipment.[5]

At this sixth convention, $60,000 was raised at one session for the triennium (1910–1913). Two days later $15,000 more was raised. In addition, $5,000 was given for intermediate work. In all—$80,000 [6]—an impressive sum raised by an agency dependent upon voluntary leadership.

One reporter saw, as the chief contribution of the Washington convention, its self-awareness as an innovative development of the world missionary movement:

> The missionary note, which fairly dominated it, was the chief factor in the convention's cosmopolitanism. It seems that the Sunday-school is to take its place as a great missionary agency. This is the most significant fact about the convention. Not as an additional method, but as one of its master motives, the Sunday-school is to take on responsibility for world evangelization. This will probably not become as spectacular as some other missionary movements; but what can mean more than the imparting of a sense of world-responsibility to the whole body of the youth of the churches? [7]

E. K. Warren, a Michigan Sunday school leader, affirmed that in the assumption of this missionary responsibility, no time was to be lost, and he and others acted accordingly:

> Just one week after the close of the Washington convention, the American section of our Central Committee met together in the city of Chicago to plan an aggressive campaign for the world's field without loss of time. The main point attained was the decision to begin an investigation of the conditions in South America.

> Less than three weeks later, the committee was again called to meet at Winona Lake, Indiana, and since that date there have been called twelve meetings of our Central Committee and five meetings of our Zurich Program Committee. All of these gatherings have been well attended, and we feel that the results attained have more than repaid us for any sacrifice of time, strength, and

money which may have been necessary. A conservative estimate would indicate to the travelling of nearly 250,000 miles and the report of the work accomplished by the American section may well be duplicated by the faithful workers of the European section.[8]

DENOMINATIONAL OPPOSITION

Denominational opposition and bitterness continued to be a problem in Europe. Sometimes the trouble came from lands predominately Eastern Orthodox. An evangelical Greek reviewed the claims of the Greek Orthodox Church for its unbroken continuity; its apostolic succession; its constant fidelity to the traditions of the Fathers, martyrs, and world-synods. He was willing to concede the claims:

> for we know that most of the errors which conflict with evangelical belief crept into the church at an early period . . .

> . . . This it is which makes the Greek so blindly conservative as regards the Church of his fathers. . . . Religious persecution is, to be sure, not so violent as it was a quarter of a century ago; yet it is only fourteen years since the Evangelical Church and Sunday-school at the Piraeus was mobbed and wrecked at the instigation of the priests, and the open avowal of the evangelical faith can be punished in so many ways,—moral and material—that we know of many a Nicodemus, who comes to us by night, but dare not confess Christ in broad daylight.[9]

Bulgaria was also a problem. In that country, church and state were so identified that when a person changed his faith, he was regarded as having altered his nationality: " 'Protestant' has meant to many not only pervert from the faith, but also traitor to the Fatherland. In Macedonia many believe that to become a Protestant is to become an American citizen." [10]

The locus of the problem, no doubt, was the traditional near-identity of church and national loyalties, deeply embedded in the Eastern Orthodox tradition, or at least more deeply embedded than in the West.

At the Zurich convention, a Sunday school missionary in the Balkans reported:

> I have been driven out twice by the Turks and now by the Serbians. I have been spied upon by the police, my house twice searched, my correspondence and papers confiscated. Twice I have been a prisoner. Three purchases of land for the work have been expropriated. In five years I have had to change my place of residence and work four times, and such is the condition of the country for lack of highways and railroads that for more than half of the time I have been deprived of all or a large part of my household goods. I have been privileged to fill up somewhat the "measure of the sufferings of our Lord." [11]

There was a similar account from Russia, where the situation for evangelicals seemed to be worsening. Russian children had been forbidden by governmental decree to attend Sunday schools with the result that:

Several large Sunday-schools in large centers have been practically suspended during the past two years and from all parts of the empire word has come that the free church congregations and Sunday-schools have been either suspended or greatly hampered through interference of the police or priests—in some cases by both. God grant that real religious liberty, based on sane and liberal laws in harmony with the manifests of His Majesty the Tsar (issued in 1905), may speedily come to this great land and people, where out of more than one hundred and sixty-three million souls less than five million know anything about the Bible and a *living* Christ.[12]

Opposition in Roman Catholic countries had not diminished. In Belgium:

The Roman Catholic clergy is hindering our work as much as possible. A little girl attending the nun's primary school was punished because she had been seen at the Protestant school: during playtime she had to kneel in a corner with arms up and stones on the hands; but she came again. A small boy was repeatedly whipped by his father, an unbeliever, but he also came again.[13]

Restrictions were placed upon the work in Austria, governed by the Catholic house of Hapsburg:

. . . even the Sunday-schools of these churches acknowledged by the state dare teach only the children of their own congregations. What the difficulties of the free churches are under these circumstances can be imagined. They are not allowed to hold public services for children.[14]

In Lutheran- or Reformed-dominated European countries, an emerging open situation was observed. Conditions had improved over earlier years, though hindrances were still frequently encountered:

The parish clergyman in Germany, assisted effectually by the village school-teacher, has more than once prevented a school from being started, and such as had been started had to be closed, for want of scholars, they having been forbidden by the teacher to go to a Sunday school of a sect. . . . One other drawback is that generally the children leave the Sunday schools of the Dissenters, when they are not the children of Dissenters, at the age of twelve or thirteen, in order to be prepared for the rite of Confirmation.[15]

In Bohemia (Czechoslovakia), a favorably inclined pastor used an unusual analogy to allay opposition:

"Brethren," he said, "this opposition to anything foreign is very unwise. How about potatoes? A few years ago they were foreign here, but Bohemia adopted them, and you know how we enjoy them. . . . Then, brethren, are you ready to give up your coffee, because it was once foreign? No, no, not one of us could do that. Now then, give the Sunday-school a hearty welcome, and it will soon be as much at home here as in England or America." [16]

Potatoes and coffee had prepared the way for Robert Raikes!

ATTITUDES TOWARD THE ROMAN CATHOLIC CHURCH

Many of the Sunday school missionaries in this period faced formidable opposition from the Catholic church in many lands. It is not surprising that there are reports of anti-Catholic attitudes, some of them extreme and couched in vigorous language. One missionary reported that he had travelled:

> thousands of miles on mission tours, and have met numberless religious devotees, some of the Virgin, others of Joseph, and others of still other patron saints, as yet I have never found outside of evangelical churches, a single devotee of the Lord Jesus Christ! [17]

The morality of people in South America, in 1913, was much to be deplored, according to A. Stuart MacNairn, and he laid the blame upon the Catholic church:

> The curse of South America to-day, and the source of the moral miasma that blights the fresh young life of the rising generation, is that corrupt system which masquerades in the guise of a Christian church and fills the hearts of all thinking men in South America with inexpressible loathing and disgust. There is nothing in human affairs that breeds such corruption and cruelty as a dead religion, however divine that religion may have been when animated by the breath of God. [18]

Relations between Catholics and Protestants in the Philippines were reported as being far from satisfactory. There:

> Athletic games have been organized by the teachers during the Sunday-school hours. Teachers not Roman Catholic have sometimes taken an unfavorable position to please the church.
> It is due to the work of the Sunday-school in an American country that the Sunday-school should be given an equal chance with all religious enterprises and that all barriers to this, direct or implied, by educational authorities should be removed. [19]

In the midst of these shrill denunciations, there was one irenic report recorded which breathes the air of a freer and more open ecumenical day. In 1910 the executive committee reported that:

> . . . indications are not wanting to show that there is in the minds of at least a few of the leading prelates of the Church of Rome a hope that the day will soon dawn when Protestantism and the Church of Rome will find some common ground from which they may conduct a campaign against a common enemy . . .
> . . . despite the recent occurrence in Italy, the Church of Rome is becoming more and more tolerant towards Protestantism. When this shall become as

complete as the toleration with which the Church of Rome is regarded by Protestants, there will dawn a day of exceptional promise for the kingdom of Him whom we love.[20]

THE ANGLO-AMERICAN AXIS

In the "Two Flags over Two Shoulders" of Chapter One we described the strong expressions of solidarity among the three nations of Canada, Great Britain, and the United States, an affinity which today seems to have been over-emphasized, even to the detriment of a Christian agency which declared itself to be an inclusive world body. How did this fraternal bond fare in the period we are now describing?

At Jerusalem (1904), and at Rome (1907), there were recognitions of language differences. A hymnbook, prepared for use at Jerusalem, was expanded and used at Rome. There were fourteen hymns in the Rome edition translated into Italian (including the Italian national hymn), German, and French, including titles in four languages in the index. Most of the hymns, though not all, were of British or American origin.[21]

On the whole, the Anglo-American axis continued strong and vigorous. It was vivid and dramatic when, at the sixth convention in Washington, D.C., after the first and last stanzas of "My Country 'tis of Thee" had been sung, the convention went easily to "God Save the King." [22]

The singing of these two national hymns concluded, E. K. Warren declared that there was only one language which would be spoken at any Sunday school convention held anywhere in the world, and that language was the English tongue. From a practical standpoint and as a simple prediction, Mr. Warren was probably right. The prevalent use of English from that day to the Nairobi assembly of the World Council of Churches proves him to be something of a prophet:

> . . . some speaker said in my hearing that he was quite anxious about the tongue that should be used in heaven. I never thought about that before, but, men and women, it lies with you and me that it shall be the English tongue that shall spread the gospel of the Lord Jesus Christ on earth.[23]

John Wanamaker joined the chorus of 1910 in suggesting that the nations not English wanted an English education, either in American or British schools. Believing in America and England, they have loved President Taft and King Edward VII. As a result of Taft's and Edward's influence and example: "birds may build their nests in cannons' mouths and . . . war shall be no more in any land." [24]

At this 1910 convention, there was reenacted a dramatic episode which had captivated the members of the convention in St. Louis seventeen years before. Mr. Cary Bonner of London ascended the speakers' platform, stood by the side of Marion Lawrance, and clasped his hand. Mr. Warren then ran up to them and threw the Union Jack over the shoulder of Mr. Bonner and Old Glory over the shoulder of Mr. Lawrance. Again, "Two Flags over Two Shoulders."

To make the symbolism perfectly clear so that none would miss it, Marion Lawrance declared: "We have all honor for all the flags of the world, but this means just this, that under these two flags the Anglo-Saxon people have upon themselves the responsibility under God of being the big brother to all other flags." [25]

Only thirteen days before the convening of the Convention of 1910, King Edward VII died. The Convention sent a message of sympathy to Queen Alexandra, and a Memorial Service was held in his honor.

It was not until the seventh convention in 1913 that there is any indication language differences were recognized and provided for in the basic program. There, at least one service had been printed in English, French, and German. As will be noted, three languages were used in the Rome (1907) exhibits. [26]

It was the same story in Tokyo in 1920. At the opening service in charge of the Japanese committee, the Japanese, the British, and the American national anthems were sung. [27] Again the recurring questions come: "If it were natural to sing and hear the Japanese national anthem, why these other two? If these two, why not more?"

General Secretary Frank L. Brown assumed the continuance of American dominance:

> In some way the spiritual condition in America has an immediate effect upon the people of the Orient. When the spiritual thermometer rises in America, it rises in the Orient. Should it fall in America, it will fall in the Orient. It behooves us then to keep the fires burning brightly upon the altars of this country, and in doing so we may feel sure that we are having a mighty influence upon the nations of the East. [28]

W. C. Poole of London and the United States assumed the same dominance, but coupled it with a sense of responsibility:

> The United States and Great Britain can underwrite the world's peace and prosperity if, in addition to perpetuating through secular education the intellectual heritage of the race, they perpetuate the moral and spiritual heritage of the race through religious education. [29]

As before, by far most of the officers of the organization were English-speaking. From 1913 to 1916, for example, there are seventy-seven officers listed. Of them forty-nine came from Canada, Great Britain, and the United States. Australia had three more, and some of those from other countries were English-speaking missionaries. Governance was still firmly grasped in the hands of persons from the three dominant countries. [30]

NATIONALISM AND GOSPEL FIDELITY

The warm Anglo-American alliance merged at times into patriotic expressions and the confusion of loyalties. Critical readers of a more sophisticated age ought not to be too quick to sniff at these expressions. One ameliorating circumstance in this period was the frequent testimony to the virtues of the United States and Great Britain from citizens of other countries. These citizens often displayed a most ardent "American patriotism." This eulogy was spoken in 1910:

> I cannot tell you how much I, an oriental woman, love the Stars and Stripes.
> . . . The world today is looking to Old Glory to send the gospel to it. . . .
> Christian people of America, if you want to exist forever, if you want this Old Glory to float over land and sea for Christ, lift up the banner of the Cross! Lift the Bible high! . . . God bless America! I love this flag. May it ever float side by side with the Union Jack, and may the two Christian countries go forward, lifting high the banner of Christ.[31]

This from a woman from Syria!

An even more impassioned burst of oratory came from a Mexican delegate. After greeting the sixth convention in the name of the National Sunday-school Association of Mexico, and presenting his country's flag to the convention he continued:

> You will notice in the centerpiece we have the Mexican coat of arms. . . . You will note the difference between this eagle and your grand old bird. I am sorry to say that our eagle still struggles with the serpent, the serpents of superstition and idolatry and immorality.[32]

> Help us to flood Mexico with Bibles, help us to multiply the sabbath-schools and one day our noble bird will give the old serpent a final blow and will then soar away [Cheers]. In the clear atmosphere of Mexico, passing over the high volcanoes of Popocatepetl and Iztaccihuatl, high he will soar northward until he shall come to the Rio Grande and meet the American bird, and then as they commune together at the Rio Grande let the people of both nations arise and once more sing the glorious song, "Peace on earth, good-will toward men." [Cheers.] [33]

It may be, of course, that the Syrian woman and the man from Mexico were speaking back, to an Anglo-American dominated Convention, sentiments they believed would be acceptable. There is, however, the other possibility—they may have sincerely believed what they said.

The sixth convention, it will be remembered, was held in Washington, D.C., and in that setting it was only natural that the president of the nation,

William Howard Taft, should attend. He did. He received the Chautauqua salute—the waving of handkerchiefs—gave an address, and then remained for a speech by John Wanamaker.

On May 20, a most unusual action was taken by the United States House of Representatives when, in accordance with House Resolution 700 of May 18, introduced by Representative Courtney Hamilton of Missouri, it adjourned not later than 4 P.M. in order to allow members to march in the Men's Bible Class parade. This parade, even though held in a heavy rain, marched from Tenth Street, Northwest to the east Capitol front and then on to the convention hall. Thousands of men marched, "the highest type of American manhood" bearing eighty or more flags and banners with such devices as "The Saloon MUST Go," "British Columbia For Christ Through The A.B.C. (Adult Bible Class)," "Where Men Go, The Boys Will Follow." State yells stirred the enthusiasm of the dripping marchers:

> *Colorado is big, Colorado is great,*
> *We are the only Centennial State,*
> *We have gold in our mines, we have silver galore,*
> *We have money in banks, and goods in our store.*
> *But the biggest assets in our glorious State*
> *Are the workers for God that our Sunday-schools make.*

Six Missouri congressmen, including Representative Hamilton, marched in the parade.[34]

It would be neither fair nor accurate to say that in these large conventions there was never a critical word spoken, never an admission that state and church may have differing aims, and that history is crowded with instances of each using the other for its own ends. There are such. William T. Ellis reported:

> I sat beside Senator Gore of Oklahoma, at Monday evening's session, and he remarked: "This convention stands for peace on earth and good-will among men; today we passed the naval appropriation bill with one hundred and thirty millions for bloodshed and destruction. The convention sends out one message from Washington; the Senate sends another." [35]

A Sunday school tour party, under the leadership of Henry J. Heinz of Pittsburgh—Sunday school leader, business genius, and philanthropist—bound for the Zurich Convention by way of the Orient, carried with it a letter from William Jennings Bryan, then secretary of state under Woodrow Wilson. In the note Bryan commended the Sunday school because it raised the standards of society:

. . . The Sunday School is a permanent institution and an important factor in the progress of our country. Anything that improves the condition of the youth of our land, as the Sunday School does, vitally concerns the entire community. The religious training of the young raises the standards of society and benefits business as well as other conditions.[36]

A little earlier, the Washington convention had heard from a Y.M.C.A. secretary that some of the profits of the Union Oil Company went to the spreading of the Gospel in the Orient. An oil well producing 43,000 barrels a day was devoted to this cause. And the speaker concluded: "We can trust this God of ours to take care of us, if we stand by him." [37]

Two quotations in the program book for the Tokyo convention of 1920 serve as illustrations of the confusion of faith with worldly concerns. One was from Andrew Stevenson of Chicago: "In the City of Chicago there are forty-eight State and National banks. Forty-five of these are officered by Christian men." The second was from Governor (later President) Calvin Coolidge: "I most heartily endorse a movement for the observance of universal Bible Sunday, and urge upon all a renewal of the study of the Bible that always holds something new for us. If we can but follow its teachings, we shall all be truly good Americans."

This habit of national self-glorification was not easy to shake off. A descriptive background for the Tokyo convention gave expression to the classic sequence: gun-boats came first, the Gospel came next. "The land must be opened for the residence of foreigners and thus a way made for the missionaries of the gospel." [38]

At the same convention Bishop Yoitsu Honda, speaking in the same year (1910) that Japan annexed Korea, and only five years after the winning of the Russo-Japanese War, reported uneasily:

Japan had a reputation once, as you know, for its facility in evangelization, but I say frankly she has lost her fame recently, and now seems likely to have a record of a somewhat different character, which we do not like much ourselves. That is of the army and navy, which are in a sense a heavy burden upon us, and have occasioned many severe criticisms and suspicions from outside nations.[39]

There were also those at the Tokyo convention who were becoming uneasy about the glorification of America. Bishop Herbert Welch of the Methodist Episcopal Church decried the popular slogan, "America for the Americans":

The cry of great Americans is "America for the world." . . . The proudest position any nation can hold is not that of a master of other nations, but of a friend, a helper, and servant of all the nations; that the mission of the strong is to the weak, the mission of the wise is to the ignorant, the mission of the rich to the poor; that God gives that we may give. National service must be put side by side with national loyalty.[40]

Frank Langford struck the same note, relating it to the Sunday school teacher:

> If the leaders could lead the pupils really to pray for those earnest workers who in every sphere of life and in every land are most sincerely serving mankind, the result in elevating the ideals of the pupils would be simply incalculable. Boys and girls would grow up with the realization that the only way to serve one's country is to minister to real human needs; service and cooperation would replace gain and competition as the ruling motives of citizens, and thus, and only thus, are true patriots made.[41]

The "great war" was seen by one speaker at Tokyo as having had a contradictory effect upon the spirit of intense nationalism:

> It is true that the Great War kindled the spirit of intense nationalism. But it is also true that it intensified the eagerness for mutual understanding, respect, and forbearance in order to maintain the common welfare of all nations, which will be a natural outcome of Christian longing for the redemption of the world.[42]

The tide of nationalism did not exactly recede in the years between Tokyo and Glasgow, 1920 and 1924, and at the latter convention the expectations of the nonwhite races of the world were not to be ignored. It was Basil Matthews, missionary prophet and statesman, who asked the Glasgow convention people to:

> Look across the world and everywhere you see how this idea of self-determination—translated into Sinn Fein in Ireland, and Swaraj in India, Egypt for the Egyptians in Egypt, into Thranianism in Turkey, Arab nationalism in Western Asia, and reverberating in the cries, "Asia for the Asiatic" in the Far East, "Africa for the African" in Africa and America—is transforming the political contours of the world.

And in a sadly prophetic passage, Basil Matthews foresaw much of the terrible future of the world, with the outbreak of World War II only fifteen years ahead:

> Five columns on the middle page of yesterday's "The Times" [London] were given up to the vehement and rancorous racial debate between Japan and America over the new action of the American Senate. Responsible men tremble for the peace of the Pacific. There are among the small, new nationalities of Europe today more men in standing armies than there were before the Great War. Western Asia from Smyrna to Persia, is the cauldron of racial hates. White, black, and brown in South Africa are divided by such antagonisms as have led most cautious observers like Lord Selbourne and Lord Gladstone, to warn of the peril of a hideous and bloody race conflict.[43]

A little earlier the American members of the executive committee of the World's Sunday School Association went on record officially opposing the American Japanese Exclusion Act:

It is the unanimous sense of the American members of the Executive Committee of the World's Sunday School Association in session that we herewith
register our total disapproval of the action of Congress on the immigration bills
as affecting immigration from Japan and that we urgently recommend the continuation of the "Gentlemen's Agreement" or some equivalent thereof.[44]

Exuberant nationalism came to the surface often in these conventions. In the
later gatherings, however, warning voices were being raised and at least one
ominous American national policy was opposed.

COLONIALISM

Along with continuing expressions of Anglo-American solidarity, and the
sometimes florid protestations of nationalism, it would be natural to assume
that there was to be found in convention utterances an uncritical acceptance
of colonialism and of the "white man's burden." Such statements are not
difficult to find. An examination of the record reveals, however, that there
were critical voices being raised, and warnings of dangers ahead.

A representative from Algiers was grateful that the proud, intolerant,
fierce, and cruel· Barbary pirate had been conquered. He rejoiced in the
growth of education "along European lines," the development of commerce, and the thousands of miles of highways and railways recently constructed: "Under the grind of these forces Mohammedanism is rapidly disin-
tegrating. . . . Under the shock and wear of these great political, civil, and
commercial forces Mohammedanism is doomed." [45]

As the French had been the cause of material blessings for the Algerians,
so the Americans were seen in the Philippines. Closed doors, rumors of
persecutions, oppressions, and desolations had characterized the islands for
four hundred years, until 1898 when "God called the dreadnaughts of a great
world power to batter down those doors and throw open those islands to the
march of progress . . ."

As a result, so it was claimed, peace had been established, natural resources had been developed, internal and external commerce had been
opened up, postal, telegraph and water communications had been created,
courts and schools had been established. The religious benefits of the conquest were just as gratifying: "Scarcely had the anchors of Dewey's ship
grappled with the glistening sands of Manila Bay before the missionaries and
the Bible colporteurs entered the portals of this pearl city of the Orient to
grapple with this great question . . ." The results? "Fifteen years ago there
was not a single member of an evangelical church in the islands. Today we
have 100,000 as faithful and earnest members as can be found anywhere in
the world." [46]

As in Algeria and in the Philippines, so in Central and South Africa—
colonial imperialism was seen in a humane and beneficent light and as a
friend of Gospel faith. At Rome in 1907, the convention heard an expression

of praise to European imperialism in Africa: "a marvelous event that a whole continent should be divided up between a few European nations." Europe's best statesmen and vast sums of money were to be devoted to "their sublime purposes." Italy, Portugal, and Belgium were now in control of vast areas, and "would to God that the best men of that country (Belgium) could take possession of the Congo and rule it." Germany, France, and Britain had even larger shares of Africa, and Christians should rejoice:

> With the exception of little Liberia on the west and Abyssinia on the east, the whole continent is under the flags of alien peoples, who, in the providence of God, have gone in to take possession of the continent, develop its resources and give the benefits of government to its vast population . . .

The European governors were, on the whole, fair-minded men, reported Methodist Bishop Hartzell, and not a few of them active Christians. Some nations were better than others because of greater experience. One notable exception was the Congo Free State, where the fundamental laws relating to the natives were wrong: "But what a marvelous event it is, that in twenty-five years in this vast continent, governmental authority should be established throughout its entire vast domain, and that all those governments should be Christian!" [47] The conquest of Korea by Japan was justified by the prevailing internal corruption of the country.[48]

Surprisingly enough there came from the lips of an admittedly great missionary leader and statesman, Robert E. Speer, a call for the economic exploitation of South America, coupled with a call to the service of humanity in the countries of that continent:

> In looking out over these 60,000,000 of people in South America, we are looking upon one of the greatest industrial and commercial opportunities in the world, with a continent of immense undeveloped resources, with an unparalleled river system awaiting development, with a people who instead of being effete are only awaiting the touch which is to make of them, as it can make of the individual man, a new creation. For the call of the Latin-American peoples is not only the call of their immense commercial possibilities, but it is the call also of the great opportunity for the development there of noble, serviceable lives.[49]

The uncritical attitude toward the colonialism of the early twentieth century was not shared by all, and a darker, more sombre side was presented about conditions in Africa. Bishop Hartzell, a Methodist bishop and missionary leader, put forth another side of the picture: ". . . Africa is the black man's continent and the black man has been the slave of semi-barbaric and civilized races from time immemorial. In our own day the great Christian nations have had a part in this world-crime against humanity." [50] Bishop Hartzell levied a specific charge against the Congo Free State, ruled, not by the Belgian government, but as the private domain of King Leopold II, who amassed, directly and indirectly, a huge personal fortune from it:

The Congo Free State was established by the treaty of Berlin and our hopes
were high for a speedy development of the country on the best lines. But our
high hopes were dashed to the ground, and we found we were to have a
government of the people, not for the sake of the governed, but for the benefit
of those who were to rule.[51]

It is probable that the Sunday school workers reflected the spirit of the
churches of the day. Examination of records of mission societies, of general
church meetings, and of Bible societies would, no doubt, yield instances of a
similar spirit and attitude. In any case, it is important to point out that it is a
too facile trait of human nature for one generation to caricature and deplore
the ethical imperfections of a preceding era. Sanford J. Ungar believes this
habit is characteristic of our own day and that it can be self-defeating.
"There is an air of examining yesterday's events with today's morality and
an oh-so-much-wiser perspective than that of the last generation." [52]

CHURCH AND SUNDAY SCHOOL RELATIONS

In this period, 1907 to 1924, the old separation between Sunday school and
church begins to disappear. Gradually it is recognized that the teaching
ministry of the church is part of its integral mission, not something to be
added on. The year 1916 seems to have been something like a decision year.

At that time it was decided by the field committee of the American section
that, wherever there is a federation of native churches and missions, the
committee related to that federation should be the committee representing
the World's Sunday School Association.

In that same year it was recognized that, while the Sunday school interests
had been carried on by laymen from the very beginning, the increasing
interest of denominations in the work made a more direct representation of
denominational interests "inevitable" and "valuable." Henceforth, one-half
of the executive committee of the American Section of the W.S.S.A. was to
include twelve from the Foreign Missions Conference of North America and
six from the Sunday School Council of Evangelical Denominations (a
church-constituted body). The other eighteen members were to be nominated, as before, by the world convention.[53] This was the beginning of
denominational control over the affairs of the World's Association. It began
with the American section.

By 1924, the workers in adult Christian education recommended to the
Glasgow convention that:

> . . . a complete "School of the Churches" should be patiently and persistently
> aimed at, whether it be called "Sunday School," "Bible School," "School of
> the Church," "Bible Study and Teaching Service of the Church" or otherwise,
> in which it is sought to enroll "all the Church and as many more." [54]

The church was beginning to be seen by some leaders, at least, as a teaching
body itself, and that by its very nature.

Educational Concerns of the Conventions

CHILDREN'S WORK

The interest of the movement-agency in children continued, but during these two decades a broader, emerging concern for the general rights and welfare of children began to appear. To be sure, this interest was not wholly absent from the earlier conventions, but it was articulated in this period with a new clarity and force.

The Glasgow convention adopted a resolution on child welfare, based upon the "Incarnation and Mission of our Lord" pleading for children everywhere that:

> . . . their essential rights to birth in health, honour, and happiness; supply of adequate food, clothing, housing; education of body, mind, and spirit for the development of all the gifts and powers of life; enjoyment of recreation and companionship, of beauty in nature and in art; protection from neglect and cruelty, abuse and exploitation.[55]

Sunday school and other Christian workers were urged to give leadership in such concerns, "towards the practical application of the Gospel to the betterment of the world's children."

The newcomer to the affairs of the association, Professor Weigle of Yale Divinity School, enumerated the rights of children as five-fold: a good home, wise and loving parents, and a wholesome family life; a good school; a good community; a good church; and a good Sunday school.[56]

CONTINUING ABSENCE OF YOUTH WORK

Work by and with young people hardly comes into focus at all during this period. At the first convention in 1889, consideration was given to work with older teenagers. The problem, at that time, was how to retain them in the Sunday school program. In 1909, a recommendation dealing with the grouping of older adolescents was approved. This step involved taking this age group out of the adult department and putting it with the intermediates, thus grouping together two units dealing with adolescents. The concerns of young people themselves were obliged to wait until a still later period for full discussion.

ADULT RELIGIOUS EDUCATION

Similarly, there was little reference to adult religious education. One item relating to governance does appear. As we have seen, the management of the movement, both before and after its organization in Rome in 1907, was in the hands of men. In 1920, this masculine dominance was modified when "two elect ladies" were appointed to the executive committee of the World's Sunday School Association, one from the Women's Board of Missions, the other representing "woman's interest in the right solution of world problems." The argument justifying this inclusion was as follows:

> The most superficial thought will grant to womanhood the right of way in those realms which lie closest to the problem of rightly shaping a generation—the children under ten and the home—the teacher and the mother, and it is time that we took counsel in the Committee with those who are masters in this field.[57]

For whatever inadequate reasons, women were now to share in the governance of the body, from which they had long been excluded.

THE UNIFORM LESSONS AND OTHER CURRICULA

The educational issues of the period were not particularly related to age groupings. They were chiefly related to curricula, specifically whether the Uniform Lessons, originating from and promoted by American and British Sunday school leaders, were the best means of teaching the Gospel and bringing persons to a saving and effective knowledge of Jesus Christ.

Almost every earlier convention had discussed the issue at length and, during the period, there was a steady (perhaps that is too definite a word) swing away from the Uniform Lessons and toward the use of indigenous curricula. The word is *toward,* for there were not many such materials actually created, but the movement was in that direction. After 1924, a great deal of time and attention would be given to such creations. It cannot be counted as an achievement of this period.

At the first convention, a worldwide International Lessons Committee had been formed with a British and an American section, a body which remained in existence until World War I. In 1917, it was recognized in the American section of the W.S.S.A. that this arrangement would no longer work, partly because of the cumbersome provisions, and chiefly because of war-time problems. The year before the Americans had reported that cooperation between the two groups had ceased, the British were in the midst of the war. For a triennium after the war (1918–1920), lessons were prepared separately in North America and in Britain. Canada was served by the American section, and the area served by the British section of the association was reached by the corresponding section of the lesson committee.

The needs of the mission fields were paramount in the reconsideration of the adequacy of the Uniform Lessons. At the Rome convention, Chairman George W. Bailey pointed out the desirability of securing singing books better adapted to the needs of children in the mission field. Copyright difficulties were pointed out, but it was decided to make the effort of securing a small number of suitable hymns to be translated, operating through mission boards.[58]

While this proposal was not directly associated with the Uniform Lesson

Plan it was a part of the general desire to reexamine the practice of treating all parts of the world as if they were suburbs of London, Chicago, or New York. A step in differentiation came at the fifth convention (1907) as a four-part grading for the Sunday school was proposed:

1. for beginners, uniform
2. for primaries, uniform among ourselves
3. a general lesson for those above primary ages
4. an advanced course [59]

At the sixth convention, the success of the American Sunday schools in using graded lessons for the beginners, primary, and junior departments was reported, along with the smooth transition from the uniform to the graded lessons for this age group.[60]

Dissatisfaction had come about both with the very youngest in the Sunday schools, the beginners, and at the other end of the age span, with adult classes. As a result the lesson committee was beset in two directions:

> . . . we first were set by the International Convention to adjust the work for the beginners, and then, a year later, a session later, we were set to adjust work for the adults; and while we were experimenting on those two ends of the constituency of the Sunday-schools, the movement had grown and developed until there came down upon us the order that we were to undertake not only the beginnings and the closings, but that we were to cover the whole field, and we had that enormous problem thrust upon us, and the constituency that was interested in it demanded that the answer should be given in the shortest possible mode.[61]

A complicating factor brought a complaint from Australia, subject to pulls in two directions. In 1910, lesson outlines from the British section used the King James Version (1611) of the Bible, and explained it by the [English] Revised Version of 1881. On the other hand, American publishers were then leaning toward the use of the American Revised Version (1901), putting it alongside the King James text. The Australian faithful were confused.

The urge for reform persisted into the seventh convention. The India Commission reported to the convention that the Uniform Lessons were not useful in India, even though the series was popular among Indian teachers and people. A growing number of representative missionaries and teachers were expressing a need for a series of graded lessons. "A general claim was that no courses made abroad could meet the peculiar needs of India." [62]

More persuasive than the needs of any single mission field was the growing realization that the Uniform Lessons were not in accord with the psychological needs of children.

The influence of Maria Montessori was widespread and her example in focusing attention upon the child and his possibilities was applauded.[63] In Britain the position of George H. Archibald in declaring that the Sunday school of the future must be decentralized was quoted as being in opposition to the centralized curriculum and the centralized administration which accompanied it:

> The public speaker may seek the crowd, and if that crowd be composed of adults he may secure an atmosphere that will make his message both easy to deliver and easy to receive. If, however, we seek the heart of a little child, he must not be one of a crowd; we must treat him as an individual.[64]

The proposal was clearly made in the Zurich convention (1913) by J. P. McNaughton of Turkey that the world convention prepare a "good system of graded lesson helps that might be used throughout the world." [65] At the same time H. Kozaki argued that a graded curriculum was needed in Japan, as being more in accord with pedagogical principles; as in accord with the new spirit in Japan; as in accord with the Japanese national system of education; and because of the variety of home backgrounds of Japanese Sunday school children.[66]

Nothing came of this proposal, however, perhaps because of two factors. The influence of Bishop John H. Vincent and B. F. Jacobs, the founders and popularizers of the Uniform Lessons, was still strong, and to turn from uniform to graded lessons might have seemed an affront to these revered leaders. In the second place, the growing desire for the creation of indigenous curricula may have cast doubt upon the wisdom of inaugurating a new, centralized world venture, even if it were graded to the needs and capacities of the learners.

At Zurich it was reported that Chicago and London had established operations by which superfluous Sunday school material was being sent to the foreign field: picture rolls, scrap books, papers, books, and teachers' guides; song books and musical instruments; stereopticans; dolls; lesson leaflets; art calendars; and other supplies. The service was named the "Waste Material Department" and it lasted for years, though fortunately, it was renamed in time. It was said to be appreciated by the recipients, even though the suitability of the material for its users seems seldom to have been questioned.[67] The distributed items were running into the millions. It was a logical and practical expression of the American and British paternalism of the times, a function of the Anglo-American Protestant empire.

Four years later, the executive committee of the American section adopted eight resolutions dealing with curriculum aimed at a thorough investigation of the worldwide problem and looking toward the creation of indigenous curricula.

A year was to be spent in studying needs and experiences; indigenous curricula must be created in the field; agencies were to be thanked for the free use of their materials; cooperation from publishers was sought; assistance was to be sought from all bodies, including the YMCA and YWCAs;

gratitude was expressed for the increasing number of indigenous books and pamphlets being produced; satisfaction was voiced for the establishment of standards; and recognition for the attainment of standards was urged.[68]

Two years later the same body decided to confer with the British and American lesson committees, proposing a visitation to foreign fields to ascertain lesson-making needs.[69] In 1920 it was proposed that a lesson committee for the Orient be established, the Sunday School Council for Evangelical Denominations and the Foreign Missions Council to work out details.[70] By 1922 it was reported to the British Committee that uniform lessons were a hindrance to progress in India.[71]

With these and other urgings, action finally began. In 1922 a Joint Commission on Methods and Materials for Religious Education on the Foreign Field was created. An American creation, it included members from the World's Sunday School Association, the International Sunday School Council of Religious Education,[72] the International Lesson Committee, and the Commission on Cooperation in Latin America. The initiative had begun with the Foreign Missions Conference of North America, and thus the cooperation of five American agencies had been enlisted.

It appears that advice was sought from the British section, for Principal A. E. Garvie of the British Lessons Council wrote out his reactions. A uniform lesson course for the whole world is undesirable and impracticable, he said. The two sections of the Uniform Lesson Committee should, however, help wherever they can. A member of the British section should be coopted as a corresponding member. And should a visit to the mission fields be planned, a British representative should be included in the delegation.[73]

By the time the Glasgow convention of 1924 convened the chorus of dissatisfaction with the Uniform Lessons was almost worldwide. The general secretary, W. G. Landes, reported that India found the series a hindrance to progress. Principal Garvie declared that "the day for the Uniform Lessons is over." The children's workers at the convention begged for graded lessons for peace education. Professor Braga insisted that uniform lessons were no longer useful anywhere on the mission field.

Probably the most devastating criticism of the principle of uniformity came from Professor Weigle. The defects were inherent because there was no principle of progression, because younger children cannot find what they need, and because there was no adequate basis for the teaching of the full range of Biblical truth: ". . . many of us in America have come to feel that the continued existence of the Uniform Lessons scheme constitutes on the whole the greatest single obstacle in the way of the more effective progress of religious education in our land and in the world." [74]

As a desirable alternative, General Secretary Landes proposed that the association assist some national committee to devise "a complete scheme of lesson study courses that will more clearly interpret the Christian way of life, and be more definitely identified with the history, climate, ideals, tradition and evils of the people." [75] Secretary Landes saw the proceedings of the joint committee as an initial step in this direction.

With this support from the general secretary, the joint commission made its report. The five agencies constituting it had cooperated and had asked for time on the program. Four consecutive afternoon conferences had been held during the convention with delegates from China, Japan, Korea, the Philippines, India, Ceylon, Burma, and some Moslem lands. As a result a committee of seven was appointed by the World's Sunday School Association to make a comprehensive study and survey and to report back through the executive committee. Weigle was appointed chairman, and the group met at Glasgow to outline its method of work. Weigle set the direction:

> The Glasgow Convention has made it clear that the cause of religious education on the foreign field can no longer be served effectively by the translation of American or British uniform lessons. The problems which are involved in the creation of better curricula for religious education upon the fields of the world appear to be among the most urgent of the problems which the World's Sunday School Association, together with the various missionary societies, faces throughout the next generation.[76]

The newcomer from Yale to the convention was quickly drafted into service. The solution to the problem, now that the inadequacy of the old provisions was commonly recognized, was, however, a long way off. In spite of dissatisfactions, the Uniform Lessons continued to be produced. In many nations and dependencies, whose needs had not been and could not be taken into account, the series continued to be used.

Schools and Seminaries

The years of these conventions, preoccupied as they were with internal educational issues such as the curriculum problem, were not marked by any serious grappling with related concerns—involving other teaching agencies of the church. In 1908 the North American section of the association sent out a questionnaire to 125 Protestant theological seminaries to discover what instruction in Sunday school work they were giving. There were 104 replies, a gratifying number. Ninety-two institutions reported some kind of Sunday school instruction.[77] In spite of this encouraging response, it was reported two years later that many pastors felt themselves ill-equipped by their seminaries for this phase of their work, and the seminaries were urged to make more adequate provisions for such training.[78]

Another questionnaire went to Christian universities in the foreign fields. It went to institutions in the North American area, South America, Moslem lands, the Philippines, China, Japan, and Korea. Of the eighty-three responses, comparatively few offered any work in religious education. Union

Seminary in Manila, the Baptist Seminary in Shanghai, and Kwansei Gakuin in Tokyo had well established departments. It was proposed that world normal school centers be established to train professors in such cities as Tokyo, Seoul, Shanghai, Manila, Cairo, Paris, and Buenos Aires.[79]

The Tokyo convention urged every Christian college to maintain courses on Christian pedagogy and commended "released-time teaching as carried on in the United States, especially as in Toledo, Ohio, and Gary, Indiana"; approving also the North Dakota plan of Bible instruction for credit in high schools.[80]

During the Tokyo convention five programs were arranged in the public schools of the city according to a plan worked out by convention officials and the department of education of the city:

> At one of these the Mayor, Viscount Tajiri, presided, and to four he sent his deputy. These meetings so successfully demonstrated to the authorities that the public schools may be used as community centers that, as a result of these Sunday school convention extension meetings, other similar programs will probably hereafter be given in these and other centers in the city.[81]

Social and Ethical Issues

For the most part, the early conventions in this section were not greatly concerned with social and ethical problems. They were preoccupied with organizational matters. The 1910 convention, however, endorsed the efforts of the Hague conference on universal peace, extolled the virtues of temperance, and urged stricter observance of the Lord's Day.

W. C. Pearce, at this meeting, was optimistic about the success of the Prohibition movement, which banned the manufacture and sale of alcoholic beverages in the United States by 1919:

> The first speech I ever made was a temperance speech, and, God willing, I expect to live to preach the funeral sermon of the last saloon in America and the Bible-class folks are with me in that proposition, and they will be there to shout "Hallelujah." [82]

The Tokyo convention expressed gratification that the United States, Estonia, and Finland had enacted national prohibition, and urged the growth of temperance sentiment in every part of the world.[83]

Bishop John H. Vincent, in the last world convention he was to attend (1913), declared his faith in the social responsibility of the church, asserting that it was a very narrow view of religion to be concerned only, or chiefly, with personal safety after death. The church's aims embrace both culture and service, both God and neighbor, both personal and social health. "The truly organized and regulated church becomes far more than a life preserver at sea or a sanitarium on land." [84]

It is in 1920, at the Tokyo convention, that the first strong emphasis upon the social responsibility of the churches appears. With the exception of Bishop Vincent's address cited above, this is the first convention to hear a sequence of speakers stress the social implications of the Gospel, and the churches' obligation to deal courageously with whatever harms or maims the children of God. William Charles Poole, later to be a president of the association, declared that the Christian program was to be the Christianizing of the social order. J. Williams Butcher addressed himself to the conflicts between labor and capital. "Buy labor in the cheapest market" was condemned, along with the dishonest policy of labor: "The restriction of output." Arthur Black enumerated threats to the welfare of children.

What appear to be the most forthright and vigorous calls to awareness of the social dimensions of the Gospel came from two American Methodist bishops: Walter R. Lambuth of the Methodist Episcopal Church, South, and Herbert Welch of the Methodist Episcopal Church.

Mentioning the convictions of William Adams Brown on social concerns, Bishop Lambuth went on to say:

> The world itself is beginning to realize that the emphasis of Christianity is not upon things but upon men, that its attitude should not be so much to receive as to share, that wealth is a tool, that stewardship of money brings tremendous obligation, and "that property is not a matter of private right but of social responsibility."

Bishop Lambuth continued by reciting and commending the social ideals of the churches as listed by the Federal Council of Churches in 1908.

Bishop Welch called for the same high ideals which manifest themselves in the ministry, missionary callings, and the healing arts to be incorporated in commerce and industry:

> . . . when it comes to business, then we seem to assume that a man is in business primarily to make money rather than to serve God and man—and that is the worst modern form of atheism!

> The stinging indictment brought last spring against the United States Steel Corporation was that its principal object was not to make steel but to make money: and that was a fatal charge.

This in a devotional address! Bishop Welch championed a wide view of the work of the Sunday school, proclaiming, as it were, ample dimensions for a spacious curriculum:

> Anything that will make for human happiness, well-being, goodness, has a relation to the Sunday school. For instance, all questions of relief, the relief of the poor, of the sick, of the sad, are questions for the Sunday school. The question of recreation, which has so much to do not simply with the happiness

but with the moral welfare of the growing child, is a question that relates to the Sunday school. Questions of sanitation, housing, accident, factory conditions, wages,—the question not simply of the living wage but of the comfort wage— all of these are not alien to the purpose of the Sunday school.[85]

The growing dangers associated with urbanization and industrialization were seen, as Margaret Slattery warned Japan and the nations of Asia not to perpetuate the mistakes America had made in the nineteenth century:

A thousand things I see you making and preparing to send out all over the earth. I have stood in the smoke of your cities. Your girls have just begun to go by the thousands into your factories to make things. Our girls have been in our factories for a long time making things. We have made things successfully, but we have not always made girls. God help you, a young nation, making things in your great factories, to make girls. Don't repeat the mistakes of a day whose old ideals must soon perish from the earth.[86]

In Glasgow, four years later, Basil Matthews spoke out of his world background:

Let us forever clear our minds of the illusion that the spread of Western industrialism is in itself a benefit. When we have replaced the minaret of the East with the factory chimney of the West, and drowned the Muezzin's call to prayer in the factory whistle's call to work, we are not an inch nearer to the Kingdom of God. We may, if these are the forerunners of class conflict and interracial war, be nearer to the gates of Hell.[87]

Surprisingly, the British committee, in 1919, uttered an expression of guarded hope for the Bolshevik revolution. The word "surprisingly" is used, for on the whole reports from that body, in those years and thereafter, contain more expressions of anti-Communism than those from the Americans; and more than are to be found in the proceedings of the Association as a whole:

During 1917 the cloud that has long hung over Russia has burst in fury. Amid the turmoil of revolution it is difficult to hear the voices of the children. Yet now and then we get glimpses of the overturning of old educational methods and the dawn of a new day for the neglected children of the peasant population. Corruption in organized religion has been revealed, and the heart of the people is surely turning to seek a purer fountain. After the earthquake and fire must come the day of the still small voice. Then will be the day of our challenge and our call.[88]

In the same year that the British committee expressed this cautiously optimistic hope, Secretary Brown was much more negative and foreboding:

The wave of Bolshevism, which threatens to engulf even intelligent and orderly nations with its reaction of hysteria and class hatred, challenges the organized

Sunday-school forces of the world to train a generation to offset its danger. The leaders in this Bolshevist movement are planning well in the future. In New York City, Bolshevist Sunday-schools are already in operation at fifteen centers with the announced intention of establishing one in each Assembly District. In these schools a catechism is taught including the teachings of Marx, atheistic in doctrine and subversive of government.[89]

The remedy, of course, was more and better Sunday schools. If the British committee's action erred on the side of naive sentimentality, Secretary Brown's excited warning sounds in character with the American "anti-Red" hysteria.

World peace received the attention of several speakers at Tokyo in 1920; naturally enough, since the newly formed (1919) League of Nations was in the news, and winning the confidence of many nations and peoples as a positive good coming out of the dreadful carnage of 1914–1918.

Count Ichida set the tone:

We are now entering upon the new era of reconstruction, and men are crying out for economic and social justice everywhere. . . . The age of Machiavellian diplomacy has passed, and we are living in an age of liberty and progress, equality and justice. . . . No righteous citizens will permit their country to perpetrate wrong. You are indeed missionaries of international good will and ambassadors of peace. If all the nations of the world should adopt the Christian principles of justice and mercy in their national policies, there would be no problems incapable of solution.[90]

Bishop Lambuth saw in the creation of the League a cause for great rejoicing, expressing a hope which was never realized for his own country:

Who is in attendance upon this Convention who fails to congratulate Japan upon her place and share in what will prove to be a brotherhood of nations and ultimately the brotherhood of the world? What American is here present in whose breast there is not the purpose and the prayer that his country shall take her rightful place in any league which has for its motto the Golden Rule, "Do unto others as you would that they should do unto you." [91]

President D. Ebina based his support of the League upon the principle of responsibility for others:

If Christianity becomes the driving force of the League of Nations, it will further accomplish its grand mission for the peace of the world. . . . The nation is not the goal of the Christian programs. Its next step should be the formation of the League, a work of greater, nobler moral effort, a work of genuinely Christian enterprise. . . . The ultimate aim of national progress can be attained only by the organization of free nations in preparation for the coming of the Kingdom of God.[92]

The Committee on Resolutions, evidently, had the matter of world peace much in its mind, because an eight-point resolution was adopted by the convention. It affirmed the solidarity of the human race; expressed appreciation for every movement for mutual obligation; asserted its confidence in the practicability of a world brotherhood; deplored any policy of discrimination; asserted its belief that all international problems are solvable; encouraged brotherhood in relation to the Kingdom of God; warned against provocative national action; and announced its conviction that nothing is settled until it is settled right.[93] As matters turned out, the United States Senate prevented the entrance of the United States into the league. The influence of the Sunday school convention did not prove very effective on Washington's Capitol Hill.

Attention to Area and Continental Needs

Africa received little program attention during this period, even remembering the attacks upon the colonization of the continent by Bishop Lambuth and others. One report from Egypt suggested that the example of Robert Raikes was still being followed: a combination of philanthropic concern and Bible teaching popularized by that Gloucester layman. The street children of Egypt were collected—bootblacks, pickpockets, and other waifs—and brought to the Sunday school:

> Such are collected on Sunday mornings and are taught, in all simplicity, lessons on physical and moral cleanliness. Most of the boys are Mohammedans, and they hear for the first time the story of the life of Christ. A text is usually learned and a song and a simple prayer. Picture cards are welcomed with vehement enthusiasm. . . . In villages the waifs and children of Moslem families are with the regular Sunday-school students, either in special classes or mingled with the church children.[94]

Robert Raikes' faith and works traveled a long road. In the above quotation is a beginning toward an inclusive Sunday school; street-children and "church children" in the same school, sometimes in the same classes.

India had been an object of special concern ever since the first convention made it possible for J. L. Phillips to go to that country. By 1907, the India Sunday School Union was able to formulate and report its seven purposes:

1. To emphasize the spiritual character of Sunday-school teaching;
2. To consolidate and extend Sunday-school work;
3. To educate teachers in the best principles and methods of Bible study and teaching;
4. To produce and foster the growth of English and vernacular literature suitable for teachers and scholars;
5. To encourage special services among the young people;

6. To focus the attention of the Christian Church upon the child as her most valuable asset;
7. To unite for mutual help, all Sunday-schools conducted by Protestant Missions in Southern Asia.[95]

Japan, too, had received the loving and thoughtful attention of the very earliest conventions and in 1893, as we have reported, that concern resulted in the employment of T. C. Ikehara. By 1907 there was a headquarters at Tokyo and thirty-two auxiliary associations, each with its own executive committee.[96] Nine books on Sunday school work were being translated into Japanese.[97] Japanese Christians were so confident of their ability that an invitation was extended at Rome to hold the next World's Sunday School Convention in Tokyo, "the gateway of the East." [98] But Japan lost to Washington, then to Zurich. Finally, Tokyo's turn came in 1920.

The beginning of the work in Japan was made possible by a gift of 1,000 dollars from H. J. Heinz to be used chiefly for a central office and for field work. The Heinz grant was renewed annually, and supplemented by grants from other mission treasuries.[99]

Undiscouraged that the invitation of 1907 had not been accepted, the Japanese delegates of 1913 again made a strong case for Japan and Tokyo. They reported that 10,000 children had recently attended a Tokyo Sunday school rally. An invitation was presented from the Rev. Kajinosuke Ibuka, president of both the Meiji Gakiun and of the Federation of Japanese Churches, and the Rev. Hiromichi Kosaki, president of the National Sunday School Association of Japan. The motion to accept was made by H. J. Heinz, and seconded by Sir Francis Belsey, and so the decision was made.[100]

At Zurich, the delegates were told of the many problems confronting the work in Japan in 1913, problems which were not only political, financial, and industrial but also social. The moral and religious problems were equally complex and perplexing. Western thought and science had shaken the old foundations, and new ones had not yet been constructed. The sociological situation was giving statesmen and educators in Japan the gravest concern.[101]

The Philippines had not been organized until 1911, when already the Sunday school enrollment was 11,000. Now (1913), it was 40,000.[102]

The 1913 convention was informed that the Sunday School Union of China had a full-time secretary and associate Chinese secretaries who were in training, and that graded lessons and teacher training books were then being translated into the vernacular.[103]

The revolution of 1911 and the election of Dr. Sun Yat-sen as president, followed by Yuan Shih-k'ai, was seen as favorable to the development of the Christian faith:

In a wondrous moment the scepter of China's future has been thrust into the hands of the Christian church, and we stand amazed and awed, facing the two hundred millions of the youth and children of China just waking up to a knowledge of their own worth and possibilities.[104]

This encouraging commission report came from one of six delegates who, before the Zurich convention, had toured Europe, South Africa, India, the Orient, Mohammedan lands, and Latin America. The tour party included fourteen business men and Sunday school specialists and their families. At Seoul, Korea, 14,700 Sunday school members and workers were present at a rally, together with four or five thousand visitors. In China an audience was arranged with President Yuan Shih-k'ai, and a service was held in the Temple of Heaven, in Peking.[105]

Mr. Belsey reported that in Britain they were deeply troubled by the drop-outs in the years twelve to nineteen. Some 80 percent of the scholars disappeared in those ages. The situation among the younger children was much more encouraging, though the statistical method of arriving at this conclusion is, to our eyes, rather amusing:

> . . . if you were to sit down and take the statistics, take from our census the children between five and fourteen, and deduct from these the children of the Catholic element, the children in our large public institutions not attending Sunday school—if you were to take some small proportion of the wealthy upper classes, who, I am sorry to say, to a large extent miss the advantages of Sunday-school teaching, and compare these numbers with the reported number of scholars in the various schools of our different denominations, you would find that for a longer or shorter period, every English boy and girl is either in a Sunday or in a ragged school.[106]

Denmark, in 1907, counted about a thousand Sunday schools, five times as many teachers, and about 35,000 children, the numbers having doubled in the last twenty years.[107] France had established an information bureau which assisted 1,200 schools with their 7,000 teachers and 67,000 scholars.[108] French evangelical workers had seized upon Thursday, the weekly school holiday, for the creation of "Thursday Schools," a device that possessed a great potential for evangelization.[109]

In Germany, Sunday school affairs grew more slowly. Four reasons were adduced for the modest gains: the Sunday schools began late in that nation (about 1827), and they were largely confined, at first, to the Baptists and the Methodists. The prevailing attitude of the established churches was: "In the land of Luther we need no Sunday schools." The prevalent skepticism in the university world scorned such efforts, and very probably, Sunday school workers were not as fit as they should have been.[110]

Basic to this slow growth in Germany was a fundamental difference in the philosophy and the means of Christian nurture. A reporter for the evangelical interpretation put the case as follows:

> [Each party] have their own way of looking upon Christian work that is to be done, since according to the one, everyone that is not a pagan or a Jew or a Musselman is a Christian, and according to the others, all that are not converted and hence professing Christians, are not only to be taught the Bible, but are led to accept the Saviour Jesus Christ as their Saviour.[111]

Somewhat the same problem prevailed in Hungary, where the Sunday school was thought by many to be unnecessary because of religious instruction in the day schools. Furthermore, the Sunday school was regarded as being a foreign institution, using new and foreign hymns and taught by those who were not professional theologians. The greatest difficulty was said to be the very few leaders who were equipped to awaken interest in the Sunday schools.[112]

In Norway the established church, as in Germany, was Lutheran. Spreading from the free churches, the Sunday School movement was beginning to win some acceptance from the state church. Progress seemed especially gratifying in the cities.[113]

Russia, dominated by the Orthodox Church, presented difficulties for the growth of the Sunday school movement. But there were significant signs for hope:

> The children are most eager to come; if they are snowed in and see no other way of getting out of the house they would crawl up through the chimney to attend the Sunday-school. The adults are willing to leave the plough to take up the Sunday-school work. Even the want of suitable clothing does not keep the children at home; if a boy has no suitable coat of his own he puts on his father's or he borrows his sister's dress, so it happens that often boys and girls cannot be distinguished.[114]

In Spain the tambourine proved an effective recruiting device, as it had been to the Salvation Army:

> Although the time for the Sunday-school is 10 o'clock on Sunday morning, not a few children appear as early as 8 o'clock. We open the doors and take care of them. Four of the scholars begin to play on tambourines in the inner court connected with the school building. About half an hour before time for the beginning Sunday-school the Director goes out with scholars and with these tambourines, and they march through the principal streets, and by the time they come back to the school they have about a thousand children.[115]

In Sweden the Sunday school movement was organized by a daughter of an English consul in 1833, but hostility thwarted it. Two years later a Wesleyan missionary made a second attempt. He had to flee to England ("the people would have stoned him'') and the little building was destroyed. However, by 1871 a Sunday school union was established in the province of Nerike, and in 1894 the several provincial units were united in the Swedish Sunday School Union.[116]

Swiss Sunday schools were not started by the church but as a result of private initiative. Overcoming initial difficulties and prejudice, by 1907 they were accepted nearly everywhere and enjoyed grateful acknowledgement and sympathy.[117]

By 1906 the West Indies had been added to the field over which the North American committee had supervision. There were Sunday school associations in British Guiana, Trinidad and Tobago, Barbados, Antigua, and St. Kitts. There were also working committees or district associations in Montserrat, Nevis, Dominica, St. Lucia, St. Vincent, Granada, and Cuba.[118]

Statistics showed, in 1907, that fifteen percent of the population of the United States was enrolled in Sunday schools. Headquarters for the International Sunday School Association was in the Hartford Building, 140 Dearborn Street, Chicago; the affairs of the association were in the hands of an executive committee of ninety-six business and professional men, each of whom served for three years. There were 14,000 Sunday school conventions held in the single year of 1906.[119]

By 1913 every state in the United States had a Sunday school organization, all but three of them with employed secretaries. Many states employed from one to five additional workers. More than 15,000,000 were in the Sunday schools of the land, and one out of ten officers and teachers was taking a teacher-training course. New members were being added to the Sunday school forces at the rate of more than 1,200 per day, and 1,000 scholars, for every day in the year, were making decisions for Christ.[120]

Structures and Programs for Conventions

References, containing new terminology, have appeared from time to time in the development of this chapter. It is time now for the several conventions in this period to be described as entities in themselves, and as creators and supporters of program. There are important organizational developments.

ROME, 1907
The Fifth World Convention (Rome, 1907), proved to be a turning point in the life of worldwide Sunday school work. Until this time, the affairs of the movement were in the paternal hands of the two Sunday school associations: one British, the other American and Canadian. The arranging and administering of the consecutive conventions seemed to be in the hands of one or the other of these associations, depending upon the locale of the meeting, and perhaps upon other circumstances. Such interim business and program as

was carried on was the responsibility of interim committees. Very few original documents of the work of these interim groups remain; what is available comes from secondary sources: convention reports, addresses, references, and the like.

At Rome, it became clear that, as the Sunday school organizations increased in numbers and strength, and as they became related to the several foreign mission movements and societies of Europe, Britain, and the United States, a more adequate structure would be needed.

Marion Lawrance delineated the essentials of Sunday school work. He said that the Sunday school is a church service,[121] and that it stands for the teaching of God's Word. Our Lord has commanded us to carry the Gospel to every corner of the earth and to every creature, a commandment which carries with it the responsibility of sending persons and providing for them.[122]

With these basic essentials in mind, the Rome delegates set about framing a statement of "Its Purpose-Policy-Field," a document dated May 22, 1907. The World's Sunday School Association was organized for four purposes: to extend the work of the conventions; to increase the efficiency of Sunday schools, "especially in those regions of the world most in need of help"; to improve methods of organization and instruction; and to promote the formation of Sunday school unions and associations.

There was to be an executive committee composed of the elected officers of the convention (president, four vice-presidents, two secretaries, treasurer, past presidents), six members each from the United States and Great Britain, two from Canada, and not fewer than ten from other parts of the world. The treasurer was to be elected by the executive committee. The governance of the association, when the convention was not in session, was to be vested in this executive committee. It was to have power to frame a Constitution and, if advisable, to secure an act of incorporation.[123]

Immediately following the adjournment of the Rome convention, a meeting was held in London at which it was decided that a North American section should administer work in North Africa, Korea, the Philippines, Turkey, and Japan. A British section would assume responsibility for work in South Africa, India, and China.[124] There is no record that people in these areas were consulted on this arbitrary division. Here again is evidence of the paternalistic assumptions of the executive committee.

Organizational matters were not the only concern of the convention at Rome. A Sunday school missionary was employed for the northern Levant. A commissioner was chosen for Korea. A world visitation was considered for the president of the organization, and plans were made for beginning work in China.[125]

National reports were given by the Continental Mission (Europe) and also by thirty-one other regions or nations, and in between the sessions the delegates took time to inspect and enjoy the exhibits which involved 7,000 separate pieces, all of them prepared by noncommercial firms and houses. Later, these displays were distributed to all parts of the world by a special commission appointed for that purpose. In the exhibits three languages were used: English, French, and Italian. The sixteen convention departments included maps, curriculum materials, music, periodicals, and other items.[126] English was no longer the single language.

The delegates supported laws and treaties to prohibit the sale of intoxicants and opium "to uncivilized races"; asked for the observance of World Sunday School Day (the third Sunday in October); reaffirmed the convention's faith in the Bible as the inspired Word of God; supported observance of the Lord's Day; deplored the actions of Greece in forbidding circulation of the Bible in the vernacular; commended the services of the home department, cradle roll, and adult Bible schools; expressed hope for the success of the International Peace Conference at The Hague; condemned the atrocities in the Congo Free State, and urged Belgium to improve its colonial administration, requesting other nations in Europe and America to influence the Belgians to that end.[127]

"Sunday School Tours" were characteristic of this period. They were outgrowths of the tours arranged in connection with earlier trips to the conventions in London and Jerusalem. So successful had these expeditions been that the third convention, in 1898, had been requested to appoint a committee with one member each from five countries to "consider and plan for a tour of the world by several representative men, in the interest of the Sunday school cause." [128]

I have found no evidence that this instruction was carried out, but the convention of 1907 returned to the subject, declaring: "an around-the-world 'Sunday-school visitation' is one of the great plans in the minds of the [members of the] Executive Committee." It was a plan that envisaged a chartered ship and a world tour of several hundred Sunday school leaders, to be engaged in study and counsel.[129]

Henry J. Heinz proposed an ambitious plan which was adopted and referred to a committee. It was to be called "World Sunday School Visitation." Its purpose was to confer and cooperate with Sunday school workers, especially in Japan, India, and China. The delegation was to be composed of practical Sunday school workers willing to bear their own expenses; no financial responsibility was to rest upon the W.S.S.A. A ship was to be chartered and to sail about December, 1908.[130] This ambitious venture actually came to pass, though not in the year originally contemplated. It sailed in 1913, just preceding the Zurich convention.

Other tours by smaller groups or by individuals took place from time to time. Dr. Frank Brown of Brooklyn made trips to the Orient in 1907 and 1912; and in 1909 a visit was made to South Africa by Arthur Black. A visit

to the same country was made in 1920 by Charles Francis.[131] The visitations
and tours, made either by individuals or by groups, were becoming a part of
the unofficial programs of the conventions. No doubt because of them, delegates were arriving at convention cities better informed and more aware of
Sunday school needs in the visited areas.

WASHINGTON, 1910

The Washington convention gave American Sunday school workers an
opportunity to attend a world convention in their own country for the first
time in seventeen years, and they turned out in enormous numbers. The
presence of President Taft, and the adjournment of the House of Representatives for the parade, gave the convention a patina of governmental endorsement.

More important than the location of the meeting, Carey Bonner and Marion Lawrance were elected joint secretaries. Thus began official leadership
for the conventions. No longer were the proceedings and interim affairs of
the conventions to be dependent upon volunteer efforts. Seventy-five thousand dollars was raised for three years' work (60,000 had been the goal), and
it was decided to send Mr. Brown to the Orient, Arthur Black to Africa, and
H. S. Harris to South America for Sunday school investigations.[132]

At the time of the Washington convention some modifications were made
to the agreements about the areas of the world for which the British and the
American sections held responsibilities. The Middle East, South America,
and the West Indies were added to the North American responsibilities, and
Europe was explicitly assigned to the British committee.

The British Committee seemed in difficult financial circumstances from its
very beginning. It was agreed to grant $2,000 a year from American funds to
the British committee, and to incorporate the organization in the United
States, an action which was accomplished in 1917 under the laws of the
District of Columbia.[133]

The Washington convention was not all work. Some of the earlier exuber-
ance carried over, as is evidenced by the high spirits of the Iowa delegation,
which presumably did not stand alone in its enthusiasm for its home state
and for things of the Sunday school. Before the call to order the contingent
of seventy-two persons arose in a body and gave its yell:

> *Who are-who are-who are we?*
> *We are-we are-we are the*
> *P-E-O-P-L-E*
> *Iowa, Iowa I-O-W-A.*

Then to the tune of *Maryland, My Maryland* they sang:

We are bound for Washington, D.C.,
   Iowa, O Iowa!
To at the World's Convention be;
   Iowa, O Iowa!
We are passing through the comet's tail,
We'll make the trip and never fail,
And from the shadows onward sail;
   Iowa, O Iowa.[134]

ZURICH, 1913

This convention was the first and, as events turned out, the only convention ever held in central Europe. Zurich had not been the first choice for the gathering. Geneva had earlier been selected. In 1911 it was discovered that Calvin's city was not a possible site, and other possibilities were considered by the central (American) committee: Constantinople, Edinburgh, Berlin, London, Paris, the Orient, and Frankfurt. The committee decided on Frankfurt. Meanwhile the British section had been meeting in London, and it recommended Zurich, a choice which was then made unanimous.[135]

A decision was made to use both German and English for the convention and its reports. The hymns were to be printed in at least these two tongues. The addresses were to be printed also in Italian and French.[136] This procedure was the first significant concession in the conventions to the realities of the difficulties caused by the Tower of Babel.

Preceding the Zurich convention, Marion Lawrance spent ninety days in thirty-five cities in Britain promoting the meeting. Why he had to make this effort, why the promotion could not have been done by Carey Bonner and members of the British Committee is not clear.

In 1913, H. J. Heinz with his party made a tour of the Orient, and then went by rail across Siberia and Russia to Zurich. This remarkable expedition deserves more than a passing notice.[137] The twenty-nine persons in the party had visited many cities on the journey, spending three weeks in Japan, two in Korea, three in China, passing through Siberia and European Russia on their way to Zurich—a total of six months' travel. Mr. Heinz had agreed to pay the expenses of those members of the party who could not meet them. *En route*, two members of the expedition had also visited the Philippines.

On the Pacific steamer Mr. Heinz had suggested the desirability of holding the next convention in Tokyo. Upon arriving in Japan, he discussed that possibility with the National Sunday School Association of Japan, the Federation of Japanese Churches, and the missionary bodies.[138] The party brought to Zurich with them two distinguished Japanese clergymen bearing an invitation for the next convention, an invitation supported by some influential laymen in Japan. By the time the Tokyo convention was called to order in 1920, however, Mr. Heinz was dead. He did not live to see the consummation of his proposal. He had, though, at Osaka earlier participated in a special conference with missionary and Japanese leaders, looking forward to a thorough organization of Japanese Sunday school work, and the engagement of a specialist for training leadership.[139]

Of more than 2,600 delegates at Zurich, twenty-two were missionaries, 447 were pastors, 601 were Sunday school superintendents and other officers, 983 were Sunday school teachers, and 356 were scholars. Seventy-five denominations were represented among the delegates, and fifty-one countries. Every province in Canada was represented and all but two of the United States.[140]

Sir Robert Laidlaw was elected president; Henry J. Heinz, chairman of the executive committee; and $125,000 was contributed by delegates for the work of the next three years. The executive committee was reorganized to be made up of the president, the past-presidents, the five vice-presidents, the two joint treasurers, the two joint statistical secretaries, and the two joint general secretaries (with no vote), plus twelve persons nominated by the North American section, an equal number named by the British section, two from Canada, and twenty corresponding members named from the rest of the world.[141]

At Zurich a problem arose about the real unity of the new association, and an ambiguous answer was given that proved to be "no answer" for four decades and more to come:

> As a general principle hereafter, the World's Sunday School Association carry on its work as a solid unit so that without materially interfering with the prerogatives of either Section of the Committee, the various fields shall realize that it is the Association as a whole and not a section of it (as at present) that is endeavoring to help them solve their Sunday School problems . . . that bearing in mind this principle, each Section known respectively as American and British, raises its own money and controls its own expenditures.[142]

The World's Sunday School Association attempted to solve the organizational problem in a manner which was to become characteristic up to 1964 and beyond: to affirm the unity of the organization and then to make such allowances for practical necessities as to make that unity almost impossible.

These organizational ambiguities were not the ordinary delegates' concern, however, and the reports from the convention indicate there had been a warm, evangelical tone to the sessions:

> One night, in particular, it seemed that a "Billy" Sunday revival had broken loose. This was when Mr. Heinz was introduced and the Pennsylvania delegation gave him an ovation. On this occasion the report of the "Sunday-school Tour Around the World" was delivered. Mr. Heinz was a member of this tour, and had much to do with the thrilling report that was brought to the convention.[143]

One reporter saw the convention as a testimony to the unity of the church, to the central place of the Bible school in the life of the church, and to the importance of the missionary movement. He predicted that sooner or later every Sunday school would adopt the principle of grading in its lesson materials.[144]

TOKYO, 1920

The enthusiasm generated by the report of the Heinz party was responsible for the unanimous acceptance of the invitation from Tokyo. There was to be, however, a seven-year interval occasioned by World War I, and all its disruptions of international travel. Meanwhile, there was dissatisfaction with the time schedule. Marion Lawrance felt that the Zurich convention had hurt the attendance at the Fourteenth International Convention, held at Chicago in 1914. It was agreed, then, that the W.S.S.A. would hold conventions at quadrennial intervals, the International Association to do the same, but in other years.[145]

With the outbreak of the war, recognizing that Americans could not travel to Europe, General Secretary Frank L. Brown organized a Sunday school tour of South America in 1915. It lasted eighty-three days, covered 17,000 miles, eleven countries, twenty-one cities, and was marked by forty-five meetings in the interest of Sunday school work, attended by about 15,000 people, meetings in which the World's Sunday School Association salute was given—"a handclasp over the head." [146]

There was a problem of financing delegates for the long trip to the postponed Tokyo convention. The secretaries of the association were allowed commissions for securing delegates; these sums were to be used for their own travel expenses.[147]

In 1919 there arose an unexpected complaint about the decision to go to Japan. Protests had come from Korean Christians, from the China Sunday School Union, from individuals, missionaries, and from one missionary body.[148] Korea's and China's grievances against Japan grew out of the international tensions of the times. The facts were presented to the executive committee, together with a report that the United States State Department desired the convention to be held. In October of 1919 the decision to go to Tokyo was reaffirmed.[149] Presumably the State Department was pleased.

The China Sunday School Union was not happy that the decision held, and presented a statement from its executive committee explaining its objections. It was agreed to distribute this Chinese protest to the executive committee of the association, but not to the members of the convention.[150]

The cause of the protests from Korea and China was the existence of the notorious "Twenty-One Demands upon China" of 1915, followed by fresh demands the following year relating to Manchuria and Inner Mongolia. In 1919 rioting and rebellion in Korea had been put down without mercy, by the Japanese, subduing a Korean independence movement. The first protest made by national Christian bodies to the World's Sunday School Association failed and planning for the Tokyo Convention went steadily forward.

Meanwhile, three steamers were engaged and reserved exclusively for the convention; sailing from Pacific ports were the *Empress of Japan* of the Canadian Pacific line, the *Siberia Maru* of the Tokyo Kisen Kaisha line, and one other of the same company. Later the *Monteagle* and the *Suiva Maru* were added.[151]

As the delegates in Tokyo were actually preparing to make their way to the convention hall (completed especially for this convention), one of the most disastrous, unnerving, and spectacular disasters in the history of these conventions occurred. As a convention choir, under the direction of Professor H. Augustine Smith of Boston University, was practicing for the opening service, a defective piece of wiring ignited a section of the stage decoration and, in a few moments, the welcoming arch was in flames. The choir was dismissed and no lives were lost; nor were there any serious injuries. At that same moment, the executive committee of the association was in session in a nearby meeting room:

> At this point, at 3:48 P.M., Mrs. Frank Brown came into the room and quietly announced that the beautiful Convention Hall, just outside the hotel and across the Station Plaza, was in flames. All rushed to the windows and gazed at the burning building which in about twenty minutes became a mass of ruins.

The committee reassembled, gave thanks that no lives had been lost and no injuries had occurred, voted appreciation to its Japanese friends and to the architect, R. Furukasi, to Baron Sakatani, and Viscount Shibusawa. Before adjourning the committee voted "to open the Convention tonight at the scheduled time, at 7 o'clock at the YMCA and to hold an overflow meeting in the Salvation Army Hall." [152] And it was so. To be sure, the opening of the convention was twenty minutes late, but under the circumstances we may assume none of the delegates complained. No doubt many were thinking, "What would have happened if the late afternoon fire had broken out this evening?"

The crowded YMCA and Salvation Army meeting places were replaced the next day, as the prime minister of Japan offered the Japanese House of Parliament for sessions on October 7. It seems that this offer was declined in favor of meeting in the Imperial Theatre, perhaps more conveniently located, where the sessions were held through the end of the convention.[153]

The convention had its moments of dramatic pageantry. H. Augustine Smith's pageant, "The Sunday School from Bethlehem to Tokyo," so excited the admiration of Baron Shibusawa, one of the patrons of the convention, that he asked that it be repeated at the patrons' reception for the delegates, at which there would be a great many prominent Japanese, celebrities not otherwise identified with the convention. The baron's request was granted, and again the Imperial Theatre was:

. . . crowded from top to bottom with this splendid group of men and women who had been invited by the Patron's Association to be their guests for the afternoon. From the singing of the Wise Men in the beginning to the closing chorus, "From the Eastern Mountains, Pressing on They Come," one could not help feeling that the message of individual responsibility must reach their hearts. And one hears after the Convention of individual Japanese who feel that business men in Japan must take responsibility as they have never before.[154]

During the proceedings of the convention, J. W. Kinnear of the United States was elected chairman, John Wanamaker, president, Frank L. Brown, general secretary for three years, Paul Sturtevant, treasurer, and W. C. Pierce, associate general secretary, a totally American slate! Mr. Wanamaker died before assuming office, and J. H. McLaren of Canada was chosen as acting president. The election of Paul Sturtevant marked the beginning of a long period of service (until his death in 1957) for this New York layman, and after his death a scholarship, raised in his honor, memorialized his name.[155]

During the convention $145,000 was subscribed for the work of the association. After its conclusion four tour parties passed through China and were deeply touched by the human suffering occasioned by the famine in the country. Members of one of these tours, meeting in Peking, subscribed $2,000 for famine relief that night. On board the *Tenyo Maru* on the return voyage to America, additional pledges were received to bring the total sum to $5,000.[156]

It appears that the convention gave a significant impetus to Sunday school work in Japan. A group of Japanese leaders, at a reception given for them in New York two years later, said, "it is necessary merely to open a room and place over the door the sign 'Christian Sunday School' and the place will be filled to capacity by those who are eager to study the Bible." [157] These reports may have been overly enthusiastic and tailored to the desires of the New York hosts, but they are part of the record.

The decisive role played by H. J. Heinz in bringing the convention to Tokyo, stemming from his appointment at Washington and his efforts on the tour during the months immediately preceding Zurich, was remembered in the eighth convention book:

It is a profound regret that the great leader of that Commission, Mr. H. J. Heinz, did not live to see in the Convention the fulfillment of his plans and dreams. His spirit seemed to pervade the Convention arrangements, and it was felt by all the members of the committee that he would have rejoiced in the way the East and the West came together to build a new world by claiming for Christ and his service this generation of the world's childhood and youth.[158]

Not all the judgments upon the Tokyo convention were favorable. *The Christian Standard*, a conservative Disciples of Christ periodical, charged the convention with compromise: "Delegates gathered from all over the world attending the Tokyo World's Sunday School Convention, sit by while their Lord is sold for the price of a nice, hearty, fraternizing handshake with paganism." [159]

GLASGOW, 1924

At the ninth convention there were 2,810 delegates registered from forty-four countries. An executive committee met during the convention and accepted Syria as a member unit. The British members, reversing an earlier decision, reported that their committee had agreed to accept again the administration of all work on the continent of Europe, with the assistance of the New York office.

After the Tokyo convention adjourned, the general secretary, Frank L. Brown, died (1922). He had been the first full-time general secretary, with worldwide responsibility, and had been succeeded by W. G. Landes of the United States. At Glasgow the services of James Kelly, a Scottish Sunday school leader and a layman, were secured for four years, as part-time secretary. Thus began, as was the case with treasurer Paul Sturtevant, a long and distinguished service with the association. Kelly's secretaryship lasted until 1948, when he resigned. He continued, however, as a member of the board of managers until 1962, thus contributing a total of thirty-eight years of service through some of the most difficult and troublesome decades of the life of the organization. His coming was with the understanding that the Scottish Sunday School Union would continue to provide his salary, and that the W.S.S.A. would provide expense money not to exceed £350.[160]

A proposal to change the name of the organization to World Council of Christian Education was made at Glasgow but no action was taken. It was to come up again twenty-three years later with more success.

A new feature of the Glasgow meetings was a Conference of Association Officials held immediately preceding the ninth convention. This was a significant step in the professionalization of the organization. A new profession, that of religious education, was emerging. New leaders from seminaries, and those with accumulated practical leadership in the field, would gradually eclipse the services of lay persons, so conspicuous in the earlier years of the association.

There were findings on general information, on curriculum, on leadership training, on religious education extension, on finance, and on statistics. A similar meeting was held in Los Angeles in 1928. This was the prototype of similar gatherings of the World Council of Churches, bringing together the general secretaries of the various national councils of churches around the world.[161]

A "tightening" of its membership occurred, as the by-laws were reviewed and an article 2 adopted, stipulating that: "Only persons holding what is commonly known as the 'Evangelical Faith' shall be eligible for membership." No definition, no specifying of the content of "Evangelical Faith" was then or later attempted.

Officers of the Conventions and Association

At Rome in 1907 fifty-six officers were elected, of which thirty-six came from the familiar nations of Britain, Canada, and the United States. At Tokyo in 1920 there were 129 officers elected, of whom ninety-two were from the three nations.[162] The Anglo-Saxon dominance continued. Similar proportions could be cited from the other three conventions of the period.

During this period three leaders of the association died. Sir Francis Belsey, its first convention president, died in 1914. As has been noted, H. J. Heinz died on May 14, 1919. On that day the executive committee of the W.S.S.A. was meeting in New York. Mr. Heinz had planned to attend the sessions. "When the news came Mr. Wanamaker bowed his head, the tears streamed down his face, and he said, 'A great man is gone.' "

Mr. Heinz's world Sunday school interest began at the Toronto International Convention in 1905 when he pleaded that organized Sunday school work be extended to Japan, and offered $1,000 for it. In Rome the creation of a World Sunday School Visitation came about as a result of a suggestion made by him. The world tour has already been reported, and at the Zurich convention, partly because of his urging, the decision to hold the next convention in Tokyo was made. This intention, though delayed, was realized in 1920. At his death, Mr. Heinz left the association $100,000 for its further work.[163]

John Wanamaker, elected president of the convention in 1920, had had a distinguished career as a Philadelphia merchant, a committed Sunday school superintendent, and as postmaster general of the United States. "When Mr. Wanamaker was Postmaster-General he continued his activities in the Bethany Sunday School in Philadelphia and made it the rule to return each Saturday from Washington that he might be in his place in the home school on Sunday." [164] Before the next convention met in Glasgow, however, Mr. Wanamaker died (1922).

Staff

The conventions, which grew into an association, had only unpaid leadership until 1910. The period 1907–1924 marks a turning point from unpaid, part-time, and volunteer leadership to a salaried executive and administrative staff. Up until 1910, as Marion Lawrance declared, "never has any officer or worker connected with it received a dollar in salary or remuneration." [165] The term *movement* is not inaccurate. An unsalaried staff, a minimum of structure, a dependence upon mass conventions, and infrequent meetings of an interim body were characteristic of the association, which was to move, however, in the direction of a more formal organization led by a professionally trained staff.

B. F. Jacobs and Marion Lawrance on the American side, and Edward Towers and Carey Bonner on the British side, served as unsalaried secretaries.

In 1910 Marion Lawrance was placed on a half-time salaried basis with a full-time secretary, but he found that carrying two responsibilities—the international and the world associations—was too heavy a load, and he resigned in 1914. Frank L. Brown was then elected as joint general secretary.[166] He had served for two years as a full-time field secretary. Mr. Brown died on March 23, 1922, and W. G. Landes was elected general secretary in his place. Landes first declined, but later reconsidered; he was elected and took office on November 6, 1922.[167]

With this change in American leadership, Arthur Black, honorary secretary of the British committee, asked the executive committee to delay appointing a European secretary for the present, and not to initiate work in any land touched by the Continental Missions Committee of England and Wales.[168] This was a rather extraordinary request, since the British committee was not able to function; a request that nothing be done by the only body which could act, the American section, now empowered by common consent to act for the entire association.

Field Services

One of the principal activities of the association through this period, in the earlier years, and in the decades to come was the service which secretaries gave to "the field." Personal contacts with Sunday school leaders in many lands were frequent and, judging from the record, appreciated. Particularly useful were visits to countries torn by the recent war or to lands where the Christian community suffered severe political or social sanctions.

Not only were such visits made by the volunteer and later the paid staff, but officers and supporters of the movement and association took upon themselves this opportunity of giving fraternal assistance to Christian workers in other lands.

We have mentioned above the H. J. Heinz world tour of 1913. This expedition took place at a time when, in the history of the United States, Oriental prejudice was strong and reports of the United States exclusion acts had already reached Japan. The American Sunday School leaders were aware of this serious affront, not only to relations between Christian communities, but also to two powerful nations and peoples. That they sought to alleviate some of the tension, as they appeared on behalf of the Sunday school work, is attested by a report from Frank L. Brown. After describing visits to several centers in Japan and Korea, and again in Japan, he reported that members of the American party were guests at cordial receptions and large rallies:

And, mind you, all of this occurred while the California land bill matter was in the air, and the press in the next city was calling upon the people to go to war at once, for the Japanese people have been and are greatly disturbed by the discrimination against their nation in the California bill. We were beseiged by newspaper men at every point for an expression of our views, and in the public meetings we spoke on the subject by request, and sought to let the real situation be known and to inform concerning the friendly sentiment of the mass of our American people. Touching the strategic centres as we did, nearly thirty-five of them, our presence and spirit and message did, we hope, help toward a better understanding between the two nations. The Japanese people are exceedingly friendly, our trade relations are important. But they are a proud and sensitive people, and our politicians in America are apt to go further than is wise and just in classing the Japanese with other nations, some of them from the Occident, who are vastly inferior, and who are admitted to rights of citizenship denied a nation which has 98% of its children in public schools.[169]

Secretary Brown collated reports from places visited. Japan needed help for its 65,000 members. Shintoism and Buddhism had lost their hold upon people, and agnosticism was strong. A larger percentage of Christians were in leadership positions in the nation than the small membership would suggest.

Hawaii had benefitted from American annexation, and missionaries of the American board had done effective work, though teacher-training was needed. Korea had seen a rapid growth of Christians, and the Sunday school was popular. Teacher-training was also needed here. In China the influence of American colleges and universities was noted.[170]

A committee on Moslem lands was formed in 1914, with Bishop J. C. Hartzell as chairman and S. M. Zwemer as secretary. Headquarters were in Cairo, and visitations to Moslem lands were included in its program.[171]

In 1916 the New York office of the association began to provide some Sunday School training to missionaries on furlough with the expectation that, returning to their stations, they would be better equipped for educational leadership in their own areas. On December 4, 1916, Frank L. Brown proposed that state and provincial council secretaries be alerted to the presence of furloughed missionaries in their area. Eighteen books were suggested for study, with authors such as Athearn, Slattery, Barclay, Weigle, Alexander, Hartshorne, and others. Campus YMCA secretaries, Bible schools, and colleges were also urged to make similar efforts in their schools and areas.

In 1921 requests came for help from Greek and Russian Orthodox churches and from the Egyptian Coptic Church for Sunday school assistance. These appeals created a problem for the association, for it had not forgotten the opposition of some of the Orthodox churches to Sunday school extension before and after the turn of the century. Even then it was aware of the minority status of the evangelical people in the very lands where these churches were so strong. It was aware of its own evangelical membership requirement. What to do?

The question that we face is whether, without compromise of principle, we shall give all help possible to the leaders in these three movements, trusting to the truth to win out and to the superiority of our product, both as to material and in the results in character-making to justify our cause.

It is to the ecumenical credit of the association that in 1921 it found a way to answer these requests affirmatively. It was voted:

that we approve of the policy of giving Sunday-school assistance where requested to the reformed movements within the existing non-Roman Catholic Church systems in the Near East, which teach the Saviourhood of Christ and which are seeking our help in the work of the general religious education of their young, as well as to those new evangelical movements which have been broken away from the old church bodies.[172]

Perhaps the most sustained, personal efforts in field visitation were put forth by James Kelly who, after the close of World War I, was indefatigable in visiting the associations and the churches in Europe, ravaged and impoverished by the war.

Activities of the Regional Committees

From its very beginnings, the world Sunday school movement took shape and form around two nations—Britain and the United States. As the conventions required more and more interim work, and since a united secretariate was not yet created, the two sections came to be more and more twin centers of authority and program initiation, indeed administration.

We look in turn, therefore, at the work of these two sections, remembering that while there was clearance by mail and that, at the conventions themselves, there was face-to-face contact, most of the work of the World's Sunday School Association centered in London and Chicago (later New York). There was an outward facade of a united organization; but this was merely ceremonial.[173]

North American Section

The first meeting of the American section in this period seems to have been in October of 1907, when it voted funds for a secretary. In 1908 it began calling itself "the central committee," a change for which no authorization has been discovered. It was a vigorous and enterprising body. It opened work in Italy and in the Belgian Congo. It affirmed that it should take responsibility for all of South America. It began to enlist the help of foreign mission boards. It undertook to translate the uniform lessons into one of the Philippine languages.[174]

Cooperation, in 1908, between the American section and one of the

Methodist Sunday school boards had resulted in the setting aside of one of their missionaries in Korea for Sunday school work. In December of that year the section heard a report from President F. B. Meyer, detailing his trip to South Africa, and entertained his offer to visit China, Japan, Korea, and India the following year in the interests of the association.

At a meeting in the Pittsburgh home of H. J. Heinz, plans were made to finance work in Italy and Japan. A worker was appointed to organize Sunday schools in the Congo free state, and a report was heard from Dr. Bailey, the committee's chairman, of provisions for religious education in 125 Protestant theological seminaries.

An office worker for the Chicago office was hired in 1910, and Marion Lawrance began on a part-time salary. In 1911 the "central committee" assigned $1,000 to the British section to purchase Sunday school materials in China and $330 for materials in Turkey. In 1913 the American section received £400 as the first of an annual gift for work in Egypt. There was, thus, some crossing of section lines in carrying on the work.

In January 1913 the American section proposed an annual budget of $100,000 for the coming three years. Both general secretaries had visited Zurich in preparation for the coming convention, and reported that conferences had been held with Swiss Sunday school leaders who feared that an undesirable emphasis upon American patterns would characterize the convention.

In the autumn of that year Marion Lawrance was employed as a full-time general secretary, an appointment of short duration. Then an extraordinary episode took place. Mr. Lawrance named his own successor by rising from his place, walking over to the chair of Frank L. Brown, and pinning his own convention badge on him. Members of the committee approved the irregular procedure, the pinning, and the virtual appointment in January 1914. With the election of Mr. Brown, the headquarters were moved from Chicago to New York.

By the time of that meeting almost $45,000 had been raised for work in the Moslem lands in the Middle East, and in February 1915, the American section sent $1,500 to the British committee for work in China.

Still another request came from the British committee for the Americans to take over a part of its assigned responsibility, that is, a share of the work in China. The American section declined responsibility, but promised financial assistance.

The British committee restated its plea for relief and this time the American group said yes:

> Whereas, the British Section of the Executive, owing to the stress of war conditions, finds itself unable to continue the work of the World's Sunday School Association in China, and
> Whereas, after long and careful consideration, they have unanimously re-

quested their American brethren to undertake the responsibility of that work in the future,

Resolved, that realizing fully what this responsibility means, and regretting the conditions of the world which necessitate the request and remembering the admonition of Christ to "bear one another's burdens," we hereby comply with their request to take up the work subsequent to July 1, 1917, appreciating the voluntary offer of the British executive to forward any contributions raised for China to the Executive Committee of the American Section.

Resolved, that we request the General Secretary to convey to the brethren of the British Section by letter the spirit of the meeting at which this resolution was passed.[175]

In 1916 the American section reported that British-American cooperation in the Uniform Lesson Committee had ceased, and that separate and independent lessons were now being prepared on either side of the Atlantic. It was also reported that, in cooperation with the American Bible Society, more than a million testaments for soldiers (at five cents each) had been provided.

In 1918 the American section mapped out a two-year program for itself which included six points: to train a native and missionary Sunday school leadership; to develop literature; to extend organization to new areas and fields; to emphasize the social outreach of the Sunday school; to increase evangelistic emphasis; and to broaden the publicity effort for Sunday school in all fields.[176]

In 1918 and 1919 there was a merger of the Foreign Sunday School Association and the American section of the W.S.S.A. The former body had been founded in 1856 by Albert Woodruff, a layman, who was convinced that lay, voluntary cooperation in world evangelism was necessary but neglected. After he retired from business, he set about working at the problem, spending a winter in Italy organizing Sunday schools. At Heidelberg, in 1863, he met William Broekelman, a retired merchant from Bremen, and the two joined forces. They chose Berlin as their center, and quickly organized nine Sunday schools there. When Mr. Woodruff traveled through the Netherlands and England on his way home to the United States, he left unions or committees behind him to carry on the work. In Germany some of these creations became a part of the "Inner Mission."

Back in America, Mr. Woodruff attempted to merge his projects with an existing agency, but later decided to remain independent. A group of women organized themselves into a committee of correspondence, Spanish, French, German, and Portuguese with subdivisions. Illustrated Sunday school papers for children were produced in six languages. Translations were made for Sunday school libraries: twenty-eight books in twenty-one languages, 125,000 volumes in all.

> . . . We were among the earliest pioneers and for a long time the field was pretty lonely. To touch a country is very different from occupying it, especially if the country is Russia or China.

With the rise and growth of the World's Sunday School Association, the almost confusing similarity of the names, the likeness of the work and the removal of the headquarters to New York, the question presented itself and was asked whether some closer affiliation could not be reached . . .[177]

After consideration and negotiation, a union of the two bodies was effected in November 1918, and $8,672 was transferred from the Foreign Sunday School Association to the W.S.S.A., followed later by another $6,000.[178]

In 1918 and the early 1920s there were several proposals for joint funding of the International Sunday School Association and the W.S.S.A., the first proposal being a continent-wide campaign to raise $20,000,000 for the budgets of world, international, state, and county associations for four fiscal years.[179]

A later proposal, or perhaps a refinement of the earlier one, was heard at a meeting of the American section in Toronto in February, 1919. The I.S.S.A. was to assume all of the financial obligations of the campaign, and was to receive the first $63,000. Thereafter, the W.S.S.A. was to receive one-third of the receipts, and the I.S.S.A. two-thirds. The joint venture was a failure and the I.S.S.A. asked the W.S.S.A. to accept twenty percent of receipts from the Ohio association as full settlement. The W.S.S.A. accepted the proposal and terminated the joint endeavor.[180]

In May 1920 another attempt was made at joint fund raising. This time the W.S.S.A. was to receive fifty percent of the first $50,000 raised.[181] Nothing seems to have come of this proposal, but the idea would not rest, for in 1922 the business committee drew up six governing principles for such a campaign. Two years later it was decided that the plan "be held in abeyance until the debts of both Associations have been covered." [182]

By 1920 the British section was unable to discharge even the residual responsibility left to it after the American section had taken on much of the work five years earlier. The Americans, in assuming much of the British work, asked the British section not to disband but to make every effort to hold together. Carey Bonner brought the request from London to Tokyo, and in response to his request, the American executive committee was reorganized and expanded and the British were asked to set up a consultative committee. The British, upon the return of their delegates, felt they had gone a little too far in abdicating all program responsibilities. Therefore, they requested the return of administrative responsibility for India. This request was granted by the American section.[183] Even so, the 1920 decision made the agency more than ever an American association in staff, location, ethos, and support.

BRITISH SECTION

In 1908 the British section undertook a five-year program for a Sunday school worker in China. Arthur Black was sent (at his own expense) to South Africa, and it hoped to send F. B. Meyer to Australia and New Zealand.

Both men were to promote Sunday school work in the Antipodes. The next year, the British section appointed a second Sunday school secretary for India, A.E. Arnoff; and it was able to announce that £500 was available for five years' work in China.

By October 1909, Arthur Black had returned and reported on a four-month tour involving 226 meetings in seventy centers in South Africa. He reported that it would be inadvisable to have a national organization in South Africa at that time. The reason for the negative conclusion is not recorded.

In preparing for the Zurich convention (1913), Carey Bonner was given secretarial assistance and Marion Lawrance was asked for comments on the draft program. A difference of judgment manifested itself when Lawrance suggested that all credentials come from him. The British committee preferred to send credentials to all those from countries assigned to its domain.[184]

In 1913 there is a record of the encouragement given the work by John R. Mott, acclaimed as a missionary statesman and world leader:

> With reference to dealing with these innumerable masses of youth in the rising nations all over the non-Christian world, you are operating at the very basis of our problems. More and more is this becoming apparent that the agencies which mould youth in plastic years make for the best results of our high and holy aims. The battle is going to be fought and won down at this great basis. Yet at times it is fairly overpowering when we think of the surging life to be brought into subjection with the life that is life indeed. It is nothing less than marvellous in point of claim and possibility. To my mind the time has come when your agency should greatly enlarge its energy. The problem to be faced is so intricate, so complex, so doubtful, that we must multiply the number of experts.[185]

In June 1914 the section applied for affiliation with the Interdenominational Missionary Board, but by October the British section felt itself so enfeebled that it appealed to the American section for help in its areas of responsibility, including China. This weakness appears to have been caused by declining contributions.[186] In February 1915 (Britain was then at war), $1,500 was sent from the American section to alleviate, in part, the distress of their British colleagues.[187] At the same time, the American section, after repeated requests, took over the British section's responsibility for China.[188]

During the same year, it was agreed that the chairman of the W.S.S.A. should be an American, and that the presidency should alternate between Britain and America. The possibility that either of these two chief officers might be from some other nation was not considered, or if it was considered, no record has endured.

Responding to the requests for the transfer of all the work to the American office, the section responded by trying to encourage its British coworkers:

We feel that now as never before, we should *retain* and *maintain* our Anglo-Saxon impact upon the world need at this juncture of reconstruction of the world, which can be done only as we undergird it all by a wider application of the Gospel of Jesus Christ through Sunday-school effort.[189]

When the Tokyo action, concentrating the work in the American office, was taken in 1920, the British established a consultative committee to assist in future conventions, to collect funds, and to give limited help where and when it could assist.[190]

An appeal, in 1922, to have the work in India restored to British supervision was granted, but with the condition that the return transfer should be "under some arrangement that would secure general secretarial supervision from the World Office." [191]

In 1923, even though the foreign work of the National Sunday School Union (the British counterpart to the International Sunday School Association) had been merged with that of the British Committee,[192] the unhappy limitations of work in Europe and elsewhere elicited a discouraged comment:

This [British] section of the World's Executive Committee labors at present under severe handicaps. The disturbed conditions in Europe and throughout the world resulting from the aftermath of the war and seriously affecting British interests at home and abroad has prevented the British committee from accepting the full measure of responsibility for promoting the work the committee desires to take.[193]

If the low point in the British activity was reached about this time, 1924 marks the turning point, for in that year it was announced that the British committee was prepared to accept entire responsibility for administering and supervising the work on the continent of Europe, and in India as well.[194]

The intention of the British committee was supported by the executive committee, and it was asked to secure the part-time services of James Kelly (secretary of the Scottish Sunday School Union) for work on the continent.

The two actions were tied closely together. Indeed, it is almost an inescapable conclusion that the evidence of new life in the British committee was a transfusion of morale from James Kelly himself, and his coming proved to be the beginning of a revitalization of a body which was almost on the verge of organizational death.

Shortly after James Kelly's arrival, the "Ladies' Auxiliary for Scotland," a supporting and fund raising body for the work of the association was formed. It continued for many years, and while the individual sums it brought to the association were small, it did provide a way for many Sunday schools and lay people to contribute to and to feel themselves a part of the worldwide teaching ministry of the churches.

Financing the Association

During these seventeen years, the association was financed in various
ways: by appeals from the convention platform; by three-year pledges; by
contributions from the state, provincial, and county Sunday school councils;
and by generous bequests. We have already seen how quickly convention-
goers responded to Sunday school missionary appeals. B. F. Jacobs was of
this mood and of this time:

> In a brief but pathetic address he [Jacobs] reminded the committee not only of
> its agreement [to send a Sunday School worker to Japan] but of the open door
> of opportunity which awaited its action. So profound was the impression made
> by Mr. Jacobs' remarks that after some moments of perfect silence it was
> suggested that prayer be offered for guidance. It seemed as though the Holy
> Spirit filled the room where the committee was gathered. Arising from their
> knees, the members of the committee pledged nearly $3,000. for Japan, and a
> vigorous campaign was entered upon to find someone to introduce the work.[195]

Other financial developments not included in the narrative above are:

1912   To employ Frank L. Brown, John Wanamaker offered to raise his annual
       gift from $1,000 to $5,000.
1917   Persons giving $1,000 per year for four successive years became honor-
       ary life members.
1922   James Kinnear died and left $50,000.[196]

With the coming of James Kelly to the executive staff of the British committee, and with the introduction to the work of Luther A. Weigle from New
Haven and Sir Harold Mackintosh of Halifax, three strong leaders were
joined to the association. Their official association continued until 1961
when, at the meeting of the Board of Managers in New York, the three were
together for the last time.

All in all, the seventeen years from 1907 to 1924 comprised an eventful
period in the life of the World's Sunday School Association. The evangelistic
and missionary impulse continued and, in the later years, new alignments
were made with established and official boards of foreign missions. A formal
organization was established in 1907. Salaried executive leadership was inaugurated, and new professional leadership emerged from university circles.
All of this led to an increasing institutional and professional complexion for
the agency. Lay leadership, while still prominent (Wanamaker, Heinz, Belsey, and others), was diminishing. Male dominance seemed taken for
granted.

Similarly, the dominance of Anglo-Saxon leadership continued. Though
diversities of language increased in convention sessions, the governance
remained firmly with English-speaking persons. Confusion persisted be-

tween national goals and aspirations (chiefly American) and Gospel imperatives.

Sharp dissatisfaction with the Uniform Lessons increased and the popularity of graded curricula grew. Toward the end of the period, the social awareness of the conventions increased; militarism, world revolution, war and peace, and industrialization being of special concern.

A tradition of long terms for the chief office-holders took root. Harold Mackintosh, Luther Weigle, Paul Sturtevant, and James Kelly each served thirty or forty years, in time becoming the "elder statesmen" or "the old guard."

While the W.S.S.A. during this period was a single organization in theory, the fact was that much of its program was administered by one or the other of the two regional committees, and increasingly by the North American body. This trend was caused by the fiscal and organizational weakness of its British counterpart. Inevitably, an organizational problem arose, one which persisted in various forms and in greater or lesser degree throughout the next two periods, almost to the end of the life of the association-council.

3

A Federation of Autonomous Units
1924-1939

Characteristics of the Conventions

BY THE TIME this third period in the life of the world Sunday school movement began, the fervent expressions of evangelistic concern had diminished. The intense, personal evangelism which accompanied the revival efforts of Dwight L. Moody, the preaching of Charles H. Spurgeon, and which was an expression of the general Protestant climate of the latter half of the nineteenth century, was gone.

Gone also was the optimism of the earlier period which so often seemed to assume that the coming of the Kingdom was just ahead, certainly within the lifetime of the next, if not the present, generation. The coming of World War I, followed by the social disasters in so many European countries and the Bolshevik revolution in Russia, all contributed to the chastened social and spiritual outlook of the twenties and thirties.

Luther Weigle summarized this outlook more vividly than any other person in the twelfth convention in Oslo in 1936:

> The present is not an age of faith, we must confess. It is for many an age of disillusion, of bewilderment, of distrust, of fear and even hate. The happy sense of progress, the triumphant belief in the natural and inevitable perfectibility of the human race, which was so characteristic of the nineteenth century, is gone. Its easy optimism has disappeared. Its paeons of praise to the laws of evolution are hushed.[1]

There were also improvements for the Sunday school movement to be discerned. The Catholic opposition to the expansion of the movement seemed (from the convention records) to have greatly diminished. Italy appeared to be the only reported offender, and at that, sporadically:

The Sunday-schools have enjoyed peace and liberty, except here and there throughout the wide field where they have been exposed to the old and sometimes fierce insidiousness of the old enemy of the pure Gospel, the regular and the secular clergy. The nuns especially have been in the front ranks of this battle and to wrench the souls of our little ones from the Sunday-schools, they have done all they could, but, if hard fought, the battle has borne them little fruit. It is true that at present, on account of the protection afforded to it, the enemy has become very powerful and has found a new way to injure the work seriously by pointing out some of our superintendents and teachers as disloyal citizens and so exposing them, according to their own pious designs, to the blows of the authorities.[2]

Nine years later the metaphors were still those of conflict, not to say of military engagement:

Italy, Pastor Guido Comba reported, had only seven thousand five hundred Sunday School children in a nation of forty-one million people. The Evangelical Churches are fighting the Catholic Church on all fronts, and he asked, "Can 579 teachers in Sunday Schools hold such a line?" He concluded an impressive statement with an appeal—"Pray for Italy." [3]

Earlier conventions had heard professions of Anglo-American solidarity in terms which often sound effusive to modern ears. Such fraternal excesses are absent in this period, though it is still true that the reality was there in the governance of the association. Later in this chapter we shall report the formation of a "Board of Managers" to direct the affairs of the association. At its first meeting in 1934 in New York, seven members were present: five from the United States, two from Great Britain, and no others. The second meeting, held the next year in London, had nine members present: four Americans, five British. The association was still in the hands of the "Anglo-Saxon cousins." The body had become "a federation of autonomous units," but governance was something else again. Lack of funds prevented attendance, of course, of persons from the younger churches as well as those from European countries.

Nationalism, too, had faded, and where it came to the surface critics pointed out its dangers and aberrations. It was frequently stressed that missionary endeavor must not contravene the legitimate national aspirations of people in developing nations:

One of the chief objections to mission work in all foreign countries has been that it tended to denationalize the converts and create in the nation a body of men who were largely controlled by foreign ideals, not only in their religious practices, but in their entire mode of life and thought. We are beginning to understand in mission work that it is not necessary to denationalize in order to christianize.[4]

Old attitudes of established countries toward the newer nations on the global map died slowly. As a foreward to a 1925 report on visits to Europe, the British secretary used a quotation from John Ruskin as a keynote for the narrative:

> Everything that you could hold in the stability of the Continent . . . every kind deed that you could do in relieving distress and preventing despair on the Continent, would have a tenfold reaction on the prosperity of England, and open and urge, in a thousand unforeseen directions, the sluices of commerce and the spring of industry.[5]

The content of James Kelly's report is much more discriminating than the Ruskin foreword.

The aspirations of the indigenous churches were described by a Filipino at the Los Angeles convention:

> To the Christians of America who are supporting the different mission boards in the Philippine Islands, may I give a word of warning? Nationalism is growing more intense every year. There are already many strained relations between missionaries and native workers in different denominations, and unless you give the native workers ample freedom and participation in the shaping of policies and greater autonomy in their exercise of initiative and resourcefulness, something serious will happen.[6]

Another need was expressed on behalf of Mexico, that of atonement, in words which must have startled many at Los Angeles:

> Dr. Schweitzer, the great missionary to Africa, has said, "Anything that we can give to Africa is not benevolence but atonement." The same might be said with regard to our obligations to Mexico. More than half of Mexico's territory has been taken by the United States. American citizens own more than half of Mexico's present wealth. Americans have shared in the merciless exploitation that has been the cause of so many of Mexico's present problems. We Americans have much to atone for.[7]

The attitudes toward non-Christian religions were changing as well by 1928. The seminar on world friendship and cooperation, which commented earlier on the U.S. Japanese Exclusion Act, commended also an open and understanding attitude toward indigenous religions:

> The Christian approach to this problem must be that of the Great Teacher himself who "came not to destroy but to fulfil." It is the business of the Christian teacher to cooperate rather than compete, to plant a seed rather than to uproot, to discover what is good in other cultures and contribute something which will make them still better. This demands, on the part of the Christian teacher, an attitude of humility and respect, a willingness to learn, a sympathetic appreciation of what is regarded as sacred by his fellowmen, while at the same time he is unshaken in his confidence that Jesus Christ has shown us the way to God and to attainment of the best for all men. With utter candor and sincerity he will seek to contribute the Christian dynamic to the thought and life of other cultural groups, quite content that each shall integrate this into its own cultural inheritance.[8]

The seminar found the Japanese Exclusion Act an "international catastrophe" and recommended the admission of Asiatics into the United States on a quota basis.

"Childhood" . . . "Daybreak"

The paramount interest for children in the earlier years does not appear explicitly in the period between 1924 and 1939. It does not leap out of the pages of the convention books in just the same way as heretofore. It is to be found by reading between the lines of minutes, implicit in much of the work of the association. One interesting revelation comes to light which both symbolizes the continuing interest of the association, and at the same time by contrast reveals the differences in emphases, which grew larger with almost every year, between the London and the New York offices. The cable address for the British office in 1936 was CHILDHOOD, GLASGOW. That for the New York office was DAYBREAK, NEW YORK. The two differing selections tell their own story.

The association's emerging interest in youth work began in this period. It will be discussed at greater length in the later chapters. It was at the tenth convention in Los Angeles (1928) that a seminar on youth work was held. Four years later, in 1932, a "youth council" met in connection with the eleventh convention at Rio de Janeiro. This youth council was the first of its kind, a meeting predominately directed to the interests of youth, and managed and controlled, to a large.extent, by them.

At Oslo in 1936 the Rio pattern was followed. A separate youth council met and recorded its convictions on the economic bases of modern wars, on the futility of nationalism, and on the separation of the church from economic and political systems. The Christian church can, the young people declared, educate on vital social issues, seek to reconcile differences, engage in social pioneering, and inspire motivation by relating people to the resources that are in Christ.[9]

In the spring of 1938 the W.S.S.A. became involved in a broader venture: the Amsterdam World Conference of Christian Youth. Correspondence was carried on between R. H. Edwin Espy, the executive for the conference, and James Kelly of the W.S.S.A.'s Glasgow office.[10]

The conference was sponsored by the Provisional Committee of the World Council of Churches, the World Alliance of YMCAs, the World's YWCA, the World's Student Christian Federation, the World Alliance for International Friendship through the Churches, and the International Missionary Council, in addition to the sponsorship of the W.S.S.A. James Kelly was a member of the conference executive committee. The conference was announced on page 39 of the 1938 report of the British committee, but, curiously enough, no summary or report of the conference is included in the 1939 report.

The Amsterdam conference helped to make possible proposals for youth work in the yet-to-be-formed World Council of Churches, and made necessary the involvement of the W.S.S.A. in these plans and in the resulting structural provisions.

As was the case with work for children, there are only a few specific references to Sunday school work with adults in this fifteen-year period. Oslo, again, produced an age group reference in the nature of "suggestions" and "guidance" from the adult education section of that convention:

1. We declare that religious education must continue after childhood into the whole term of life, both for the sake of those whose own childhood and youth missed the heavenly vision, and for the sake of those children for whom every adult, in one way or another, is partly responsible.
2. We maintain that Christ is the Power of Life, not alone for the liberation of the individual from selfishness and fear and sin, but for the whole Social Life of Mankind in all its relationships.
3. Adult Education, we therefore say, must lead individuals to a personal share in the redemption of society—especially in these directions:
    (a) Home Life . . .
    (b) The Industrial Life . . .
    (c) International Relations . . .
    (d) Co-operation . . .
4. We welcome the wider educational opportunities whereby Christian Life can be enriched and made effective.[11]

Continuous growth; the relevance of Christ for the social order; individual responsibility for its redemption—here were challenging perspectives from the Oslo meeting.

Curricula for Indigenous Religious Education

The continuing interest in the perplexities of providing adequate curricula for worldwide Christian nurture extended through this period and into the next. In December of 1923 courses for beginners, primary, and juniors were reported to be in print in Spanish, and others were in preparation, along with teachers' reference materials in Spanish. In the next spring it was recorded that other countries were writing courses based on the group-graded outlines produced by the International Council of Religious Education. At Glasgow, Professor Weigle reported that it had been agreed that the British and the North American Committees should outline group- or department-graded series of forty lessons which could be used in North America, in Britain, and in mission fields.[12]

Both China and India expressed a need for indigenous curricula in the early years of this period:

It is gratifying to find that more and more it is possible to prepare the lesson material *first* in Chinese. All Sunday-school work must increasingly become "indigenous" if it is to root and grow in the Orient. It is as it should be that the illustrative and teaching material used by missionaries and Chinese alike should be translated from Chinese into English, rather than from English into Chinese . . . the Lesson Notes for the International Uniform Lessons as far as they contain *new* indigenous material will have that material largely prepared in Chinese first and then translated into English.[13]

From India came a similar expression of need: "We need a system of lessons, graded of course, that fit the conditions of the country. The Old Uniform System, or even the newer Graded Lessons that were assembled to fit American and English conditions, do not fit our conditions." [14]

Needs such as these expressed from China and India gave rise to a statement of curricular generalizations in Los Angeles. A. Lowell Ryan, in speaking on "The Needs of the Field for Indigenous Lesson Courses," enunciated six basic principles:

1. A curriculum should be indigenous, scientific, unified, and comprehensive.
2. A clear understanding of what is meant by indigenous.
3. Some kind of world unity.
4. A scientific approach and procedure.
5. Curriculum must be unified and comprehensive.
6. In most mission fields (the curriculum) must be "subvention" (subsidized).[15]

This ferment resulted in a 1930 curriculum conference in Japan. It was a gathering limited to twenty-five persons: directors and those with experience in curriculum-making.[16]

Taking these protestations and new developments into account, and remembering the earlier dissatisfaction with the uniform lessons, we would expect that there would be recorded instances of turning away from the Uniform Series in the direction of indigenous productions on the one hand and toward grading on the other. This is exactly what happened. The British section had been disillusioned about the usefulness of the Uniform Lessons in its own country. Ernest H. Hayes, secretary of the British Sunday School Lessons Council, stated at Oslo that the council he served had been committed to the graded principle from its earliest beginnings, and had discouraged the international uniform plan.[17]

At Oslo in 1936 there was a sharp break with the international uniform principle. It was agreed there that the British and American lessons committees should unite on using a group-graded basis for their series, that the courses should be arranged topically for annual periods, without assigning lessons to particular dates or days, and that publishers be asked to prepare accompanying source material.[18]

Social and Ethical Issues

The Los Angeles convention took place soon after the historic Jerusalem meeting (1928) of the International Missionary Council. Luther Weigle had been at this Jerusalem assembly and, together with J. H. Oldham, secretary of the International Missionary Council, had produced a significant report on world religious education. In his mind the social implications of the Gospel could not be forgotten or ignored:

> The definite assumption of the meeting [see above] was that Jesus Christ seeks to redeem the whole of life, and that even the staggering problems and wrongs of today do not lie beyond the power of the Spirit of God, as he moves the minds and hearts of men. It was seen that the social gospel and the gospel of individual redemption are indissolubly associated; and that no issue which bears vitally upon the moral well-being of mankind lies outside the concern of the Christian churches cooperating in the missionary enterprise.[19]

At the Los Angeles convention Nannie H. Burroughs was passionate and explicit in denouncing human exploitation:

> . . . The human family has degenerated until races organize to take from each other their inalienable rights instead of enjoying and sharing with each other their common heritage. They organize to work each other instead of working together.
> They set up industrial boycotts. Millions of men are denied the God-enjoined privilege of earning their bread. All denominations are pleading for funds for the missionary enterprise at home and abroad. If Christian people would only lift the industrial boycott and let men and women into shops, factories, and all other employments, on their merit, instead of on their race or color, they could work for themselves, and givers to charity would not be strained to support them or their families.[20]

It will be remembered that 1936 was one of the years of the worldwide depression which had so disastrously affected the Western industrial nations, and because of their adversities, all the rest of the world. The deep concern of the speaker for full employment must be understood in the light of that dark economic situation.

The year of the Rio convention, 1932, will not be remembered as one of the happiest of years in the Western world, both north and south. As the delegates began their work, Luther Weigle spoke frankly and objectively to them about the kind of world and culture in which they lived:

> We live in a confused and bewildering time. In a world of plenty, multitudes are threatened with starvation. In a world that hungers for peace, we are yet arming for war, and the passions of mankind threaten to destroy the race. A modern paganism has emerged, which knows no reticence, abhors restraint, and acknowledges no standards except the impulses of desire and the fluctuations of fashion. Secularism masquerades as freedom; and atheism denounces the scruples of piety.[21]

One of the problems seen by the missionary forces in Brazil at that time was the nationalization of schools. The missionary schools, therefore, which had been able freely to impart religious education, were no longer able to do so, and it was clearly seen that the responsibility for Christian nurture was thrown back upon the churches themselves.[22]

Gonzalo Baez-Camargo, who was to become a long-time member of the Board of Managers and who had already become an effective Christian education leader in Mexico, declared that Latin America needed a religion which had social justice at its heart:

> . . . We must struggle to project our spirituality toward social justice and well-being. It must be remembered that the gospel was first preached to the poor, to the captives, and to the oppressed. And it must be courageously recognized that the basis on which our present social order is erected, could not stand before the judgment, inflamed with love and justice, of the spiritual revolutionary of Nazareth.
>
> From Peru, the young communist leader, Mariategui wrote that the new spirituality could conquer the heart of America only if it decides to pronounce bravely and openly against the injustices of our present social order. And that brother of race and idealisms of the illustrious Brazilian, General Rondon, who was called Benito Juarez, the great Indian President of Mexico, doubtless was thinking along the same line when he said, "The Indian needs a religion which will oblige him to read, and not to spend his savings in candles for the saints." [23]

George Stewart (Presbyterian, U.S.A.) spoke to the convention on the theme, "The Challenge of Christ to Modern Youth," an address which had a strong social content. He declared that we must deal conclusively with an economic order which had become intolerable, that the challenge is to reconstruct politics in the interest of the total population, that along with that obligation went the need to reconstruct the ideals of citizenship, to deepen the spiritual life of our own churches, and to link our own lives with the living Christ.[24]

One of the seminars dealt with cooperation in Christian education, a topic which included some very pressing social concerns:

> War being the first peril of the peoples of today, this group declares its explicit adherence to the movement on behalf of peace. . . . Observing the functioning of society at the present time, we consider that great modern problems spring from the low evaluation of human personality. . . . We believe that the Christian church cannot escape its responsibility for the present chaotic situation because it has not understood the ample character of its redemptive mission.[25]

The youth council, which met for five days at Rio, was attended by a hundred persons, with an average attendance of sixty-four. It considered four themes: Christ and nationalism, Christ and the social order, Christ and war, Christ and personal conduct.[26]

A throwback to an earlier kind of national imperialism came as one speaker, after reviewing the potential of an awakened and Christianized Africa, declared "that the civilizing and Christianizing thrust must come from South Africa." [27]

While many of the addresses and findings at Rio dealt with the broad and pressing social issues of the world of the early thirties, the formal resolutions of the convention dealt with familiar and traditional concerns. They deplored the use of alcoholic beverages, recommended temperance education, endorsed the Hague agreement on drugs, opposed gambling in all its forms, deplored the inferior and immoral character of many films, and appreciated the services of international radio. [28]

As might be expected, international relations were a concern to the participants in the conventions of this period. Few happy developments from World War I had been seen. A worldwide depression had begun; the rising popularity of fascism, especially in Germany, Spain, and Italy, had dismayed those who had counted on the inevitable acceptance of the democratic way of life.

The president of the convention, Sir Harold Mackintosh, set the tone at Oslo:

> At this time of crisis in the world's history we are more than a gathering of Sunday School workers, we are a spiritual League of Nations, working for the healing of the nations through the children of all lands. There is in this Convention enough spiritual power to change the next generation. The world is sick economically, politically, spiritually, but most of all spiritually. At any rate, the quickest way to ease all these ills is to repair the spiritual side of mankind, to rouse afresh the faith of mankind in the power of the spiritual life. What better way, what surer way, than in bringing the millions of boys and girls, youths and maidens of every land to the Master's feet? The Sunday schools are indeed the hope of the future. [29]

Another speaker saw in the disorder of the day a need for effective teaching of the young:

> It is a dreadful thing to conscript youth for war for want of consecration to the needs of their earlier childhood. How easy it would be to teach them that Armaments are not a Divine manufacture because all the nations are members of God's family. Teach children to spell out the implications of the Fatherhood of God, and they will spurn the implements of destruction. The Sunday School process of moving into World Peace on the feet of children "taught of the Lord" would first result in "spears being turned into pruning hooks," and then, that no spears were forged to await industrial transformation. [30]

Before the Oslo convention adjourned, it brought forth resolutions on the issues of world peace. These resolutions were not able to accomplish much in averting the threatened cataclysms ahead but, nonetheless, they called the constituencies of the W.S.S.A. to new specific endeavors:

The World's Sunday School Association . . . is conscious of its opportunity and responsibility in these days of world crisis when the Christian religion is being seriously challenged.

Education and statesmanship cannot dispel the fears or quell the passions that menace the future of mankind. It is our conviction that the world's greatest need is for deeper, truer and more complete faith in Jesus Christ, and a more resolute acceptance of His way of life.

Acknowledging with penitence our failures and our sins and expressing anew our faith in Him, who is able to transform all human relationships, we affirm our purpose to inaugurate and maintain in our educational work such definite programmes of teaching and worship, based upon the Word of God and interpreting the life and teaching of Jesus Christ, as shall lead to inter-racial understanding, international concord and the abolition of war. We labour and pray for the coming of the Kingdom of God, that His Will may be done on earth as in heaven.

We call upon all our constituent units to give effect to this resolution in such ways as may be deemed wisest and best, so that men and nations everywhere may accept the sovereignty over all life of Him who is the Prince of Peace and the Hope of the World.[31]

At the Oslo convention, Toyohiko Kagawa was the speaker at the third morning session. He had already become world famous for his sacrificial labors in the metropolitan slums of Japan, for his identification with the poor and outcasts, for his passionate evangelistic zeal, and for his following of young people and college students. Kagawa set forth the essential unity of evangelism and religious education, documenting his thesis with stories from his own experience:

When Paul discovered that ordinary evangelism in the city of Ephesus was a failure he changed his technique. He went to a study room and started a lecture course, and with that method he upset the whole atmosphere of Ephesus. When the ice is thick we must dig down through the ice, cutting deeply in order to draw water. Religious education is the only method to dig the holes in the ice. Thus, educational evangelism becomes the most effective method of evangelism.[32]

When the Oslo convention adjourned in 1936, another would not be convened for fourteen years because of World War II—a sharp contrast to the regular three- or four-year intervals. It was the longest span between conventions in the history of the association.

In the spring of 1937, the American section, apparently following the counsel of the Oslo resolution, formed a committee on peace education. It was headed by Philip C. Jones, later to become a staff member of the W.C.C.E.[33] In establishing this committee, the cooperation of the British committee was sought, but there is no record that a similar committee was formed there.

Area and Continental Needs

Each of the three conventions of this period met on a different continent: North America, South America, and Europe. As was always the case, the delegates tended to come from the churches and Sunday schools nearest at hand. So it was that, in a very real sense, the conventions met some of the needs on each of the three continents. Perhaps that was most true of the convention in Rio de Janeiro, for in the other two cities and countries strong cooperative Sunday school units were already at work, equipped to do much for their own constituencies.

EUROPE

The organizational picture in Britain became somewhat more clear when, in 1925, the National Sunday School Union transferred responsibility for overseas extension to the W.S.S.A.[34]

In 1931 the first European Sunday School Convention was held in Budapest with many more to follow in the postwar years. There were 335 delegates from twenty-seven nations and twelve denominations. Morning conferences, practical demonstrations carried on in German, Hungarian, and English, and public meetings were held. A proposal for a Continental committee of Sunday school workers was rejected in favor of continuing leadership and assistance from the British section of the W.S.S.A., an action which must be interpreted as a testimony to the effective help given by the British section.

James Kelly reported that out of this convention there emerged a strong sense of the unity of the teaching mission of the church:

> Among the many indications forthcoming during the convention days two were especially outstanding. First, that the Sunday School is not an adjunct to the Church, but an integral part of the Church's life and work, and second, that Sunday Schools are not regarded as an end in themselves. Nothing short of full and active membership in the Church of Christ is the desire of those leaders in the modern Sunday School movement for every boy and girl whose loyalty to Jesus Christ has been deepened and developed as childhood has given place to adolescence.[35]

Surveying the European political horizon in 1933, an influential member of the British committee saw some signs of hope where no hope really was to be found, and recorded his optimism in words which before long he himself was to see as unfounded and misleading:

> Much interest and comment has been aroused in the new Italian postage stamp which has recently been issued by Signor Mussolini. In the centre of the stamp there is a large open Bible standing on a pedestal, the word "Evangelium," meaning Gospel, being printed across its pages. Behind the Bible stands a Cross—not a crucifix—and near the Cross are the Fascist emblems. In the left

top corner is the Star of the Royal House of Savoy. The flags of Italy are shown bowing down and saluting the Bible, while underneath is the word "Credere" (Believe). Surely the issue of such a stamp is very encouraging as being another indication of the desire of Signor Mussolini that the Bible—the Word of God—would spread throughout Italy.[36]

Of course, the full measure of the evil of Italian fascism was not known in 1933. The directions were obvious, however, even though the signing of the four power pact (England, France, Germany, and Italy) in that year may have obscured the political realities, a situation which was revealed by the invasion of Ethiopia two years later, and the overt support of the Franco rebellion against the legitimate government of Spain about a year after Italy's Ethiopian invasion.

ASIA

In 1932 at Rio de Janeiro, Chester Miao, secretary of the new Council of Christian Religious Education of China, pointed to the growing strength of Communism in China:

> One of my friends in China made a study of 400 new books published between 1928 and 1930 by a few small book stores on one of the busy streets in Shanghai. Seventy percent of them deal with the social sciences, and 20 percent with literature such as novels, poems, and essays. Of the 70 percent social science books, five-sevenths are about Marxism and materialism. Of the 20 percent so-called "literature books," three-fourths are about the proletarian movement. My friend has also found out that the majority of the readers of these new books are of the student class.[37]

China was remembered in the generosity of the convention, 1500 dollars (gold) being received in cash and pledges.[38]

A reference to the religious situation in Japan was made in 1928 recommending cooperation among leaders of the world religions:

> Jesus said that he came into the world not to destroy the law and the prophets, but to fulfill them. In Japan the time has passed for Christians and Buddhists to fight one another. They are coming more and more into close contact. Just a month ago, in the city of Tokyo, Shintoists, Buddhists, and Christians sat together with a common purpose in their minds, namely, the spiritual and moral welfare of our people. They are trying to cooperate in the common cause, that is, a fight against Radicalism and Materialism now prevailing among young people. These are a menace to the younger generation.[39]

In 1929 a Korean National Sunday School Convention had been held and the spirit and the dramatic effectiveness of the meeting are so remarkable that a full excerpt from the record is justified:

> On Monday in the midst of the convention, a great consecration meeting was held in the Central Church (in Pyengyang), 2,200 people inside the building,

and half as many more looking in at the doors and windows. About 1200 yen in cash and pledges were taken in. Women stripped off their wedding rings and bride ornaments; men gave their watches; five different people, who did not have money, gave their spectacles. The money poured in in an endless stream, pennies, dimes, and an occasional dollar. Doctor and Mrs. Hopkins, General Secretary of the World's Association, were present and saw it all. Their laps were piled high with these sacrificial gifts.

The enthusiasm did not diminish overnight:

The next day the Association members met for a business meeting and it was noted that some members present had not been at the church the night before. Someone said that it surely was not nice to let the ordinary members of the convention do all the giving and that those present should also help. In a few moments two hundred yen more were pledged or paid.

The fervor continued to the closing session:

On the last night of the convention, Secretary Chung spoke on the Four Year Forward Program that is to be carried out from now till the next National Convention. The second year of that is to be "Sacrifice Year," and he pled that the members start a campaign to raise an endowment fund that would finance the whole Sunday School Movement in Korea without foreign help. Just before the meeting a telegram came from the country from a man who had not had a chance to give on the offering night. It contained a gift of one hundred yen. Doctor McCune sprang up as Mr. Chung finished speaking, showed the telegram, and asked if there were not others present who had not had the privilege of giving before. A wave of enthusiasm swept the audience, and again the pledges and cash poured in, a total of 600 yen more for the evening, making about 1,800 yen for the week, over 800 of which had been received in cash. When one considers that the day's wage for an unskilled laborer is about 30 cents here against five dollars in America, it is seen that 1,800 yen means 3,000 days or what a $15,000 offering would mean in America, and every penny of it was "widow's mite" money.[40]

The old, spontaneous generosity of Sunday school conventioneers was not dead. Some of it had been transplanted to Korea!

LATIN AMERICA

Latin America, during this period, did not receive very much attention, save for the holding of the Rio convention in 1932. At the Los Angeles convention four years before, one speaker declared that our responsibilities for the "Mexicans in our midst" were at least fourfold in nature: spiritual, moral, educational, and economic.[41]

Structures and Programs for the Conventions

LOS ANGELES, 1928

At Los Angeles there was a two-day conference preceding the convention. It was composed of representatives of national Sunday school associations around the world and was in the pattern of the meeting four years before in connection with the Glasgow convention. There was also a conference in children's work attended by 1,200 persons. In addition to these meetings, popular conferences were held in four centers of the metropolitan area. National and area group meetings were included, seven seminar group conferences were held, as well as nineteen denominational gatherings.[42]

The convention proper was largely attended: there were 7,636 delegates from sixty-one countries. The membership was noted for more than its size if a reporter's words are to be taken at face value:

> In all my convention experience, and these are getting to be many, I have never seen a group brought together who took their task more seriously. They were there for the program's first session and they stayed for the last session. . . . Notebooks were in evidence everywhere and they were used, too . . .[43]

An item of special interest was the proposed election of two joint secretaries by the executive committee of the association upon the nominations of the respective sections. Robert Hopkins, from the American section, was a new nominee. James Kelly, from the British section, had already served for four years, though on a part-time schedule.

There was sentiment for a name change. As early as 1919, H. J. Heinz reported to the executive committee American section that the word "international" applied to one organization and the word "world" to an entirely different agency, creating confusion.[44] In 1922 Dr. Hugh Magill had become the general secretary of the International Council of Religious Education (its later name). He found the name, World's Sunday School Association, unfortunately narrow and restrictive. At the convention he moved to change the name of the body to "World Council of Christian Education." His motion was deferred to a later meeting and, when the issue came up for question, it was voted that the name should be changed to "World Sunday School Council of Christian Education." [45]

The decision was one of the association's many compromises. There came in time another, both decisions leaving the organization with a long and awkward name—a title which, however, did reflect the program and administrative ambiguities which continued to characterize the body.

The convention attempted to set forth the integral role of religious education in the missionary enterprise by declaring that it should be central, that a clear statement was needed about the nature of religious education, that a constant and ever larger use was needed of modern educational science, and that the sphere of religious education was not only to be located in church and school, but also in home, community, nation, and in human society as a whole.[46]

A Committee on Reference and Counsel was established to be the interim body of the executive committee of the association. It was composed of Weigle as chairman and L. W. Sims (Canada), H. G. Chesser (England), Sir

Harold Mackintosh (England), W. C. Poole (England and U.S.A.), Hugh R. Munro (U.S.A.), and Hugh S. Magill (U.S.A.).[47] The first meeting was held in Los Angeles on July 17, 1928, with Chairman Weigle and four other members present, plus Secretaries Kelly and Hopkins.[48]

Perhaps the most enduring action of the Los Angeles Convention was the election of Sir Harold Mackintosh as President and Luther A. Weigle as Chairman of this Committee of Reference and Counsel, a body which later became the Board of Managers of the Association. Brief statements about these two men will appear in the section on the officers of this period.

RIO DE JANEIRO, 1932

In the early 1930s the executive committee of the association met at yearly intervals. In 1930 in Toronto thirty-one representatives from thirteen nations were present. At that session, the National Sunday School Association of Germany was received as a member unit.

London was the site of the 1931 meeting. Nineteen members from seven national units were present. Organizational questions were disturbing the Americans and the meeting was largely given over to discussion of them.

When the executive committee met in Rio in 1932, at the time of the convention, forty members from twenty-four member units were present, a greater representation than in earlier meetings. Of the forty, only sixteen were from the United States, Canada, and Great Britain. At this meeting new by-law amendments were endorsed, effecting changes which clarified the role of the North American and the British sections, now to be known as the North American Administrative Committee and the British Administrative Committee. Approval was given for the making of grants, when justified, from undesignated capital funds. Clarification of constituent membership rolls was made, the number being determined as forty-six in forty-eight countries.

In an attempt to establish priorities for the association, there was a recommendation to all units that consideration be given, during the next quadrennium, to the relative importance of aspects of the work of the general secretaries—preparing for conventions; raising and administering funds for appropriations to fields; field visitation and deputations; and clearing house, research, and educational assistance.[49]

The 1932 convention was unusual for four reasons: it was the first to be held in the southern hemisphere; it was the first to be held in the midst of a turbulent political situation; it was characterized by a smaller percentage of leadership from the predominantly Anglo-Saxon nations; and it included a parallel "youth council." [50]

Of the 1,849 participants, 889 were from Brazil itself, distributed among sixteen Brazilian states and the federal district. These Brazilians came from seven denominations with fifty-two not so specified.[51]

The newly elected president, Sir Harold Mackintosh, did not attend, but the chairman, Dr. Luther A. Weigle, was there, this time accompanied by his wife, Clara. For the first time, a youth council met in parallel sessions with the convention, with its own agenda and procedures.

Delegates to the Rio convention may have looked forward to the session with mingled feelings. In contrast to the anticipation of traveling to a beautiful city in South America, there may have been some feelings of apprehension, for civil and political strife lay ahead in the nation to which they were traveling.

Two years earlier there had been a widespread revolt in the southern provinces led by Getulio Vargas, who later became president of the republic. In the middle of the convention year a revolt broke out in Sao Paulo which was broken by the central government, but not without turmoil and disorder. The convention book reported that:

> Civil war was raging in Brazil while armed conflict and political upheaval were rampant in several other South American nations. So serious were conditions in some sections that important railroad trunk lines suspended operations entirely while others were running on reduced schedules.[52]

There was one delegate, however, who looked forward to the convention with zest and verve, utilizing as he was going to do, a new method of convention-ward travel—H. L. Gelwick of Mechanicsburg, Pennsylvania.

> "I am expecting to fly to Rio de Janeiro, Brazil, next year to the Convention. We will take off from Harrisburg airport about May 15, 1932, and fly by short hops by way of Texas, Mexico, Central and South America." Mrs. Gelwick makes up the "we" and two passengers will be taken with them.
> This is the first flying itinerary that has come to the office of the World's Sunday School Association. It is a decided innovation in proceeding from home in one continent to a World's Sunday School Convention in another continent.[53]

The atmosphere at Rio was cordial and friendly. Samuel Guy Inman, an established authority on Latin American affairs, reported:

> The possibilities for attacks by super-nationalists and religious fanatics were many. . . . The convention was a great international gathering which the Brazilian government, Protestant churches, and the general public entertained with characteristic Latin warmth and enthusiasm . . .
> Memorable among the hundreds of interviews I have had with heads of governments was the one [Robert] Hopkins and I and a few others had with President Getulio Vargas, who told us of his great regard for Protestantism as necessary for the development of democracy in South America, and reminded us that he had named one of his sons for Luther.[54]

There was also pageantry at Rio. H. Augustine Smith, of Boston University, produced a pageant which was given twice, once for the delegates and once for Rio citizens. Professor Smith had been the music and pageant director at the Tokyo convention in 1920. The interests of the convention included discussions of vacation church school work, weekday religious education, and religion in schools and colleges—fairly new concerns, these, for Sunday school convention-goers.

It had been voted at the Los Angeles convention to change the name of the association. Legal advice had been sought in the interim, and at Rio it was decided that any change in the name would be undesirable. It would be interesting to discover the nature of this legal opinion, for later a name change was made without any legal problems, save for the complexities which competent lawyers proved perfectly capable of solving. The Committee of Reference and Counsel, established at Los Angeles, became at Rio the "Board of Managers," a name which the body continued until the dissolution in 1971.[55] It was the executive *ad interim* body functioning between conventions.

At this convention there was a change in the terminology for the two regional governing bodies. They became known as the North American Administrative Committee and the British Administrative Committee, and were the functioning bodies of the association.[56] A meeting of the executive committee was held with forty members present from twenty-four constituent units of the association.[57]

At Rio there was essayed that most difficult of program understandings: the establishment of priorities. Discussions were held, inconclusively, on: preparation for the conventions, raising and administering funds for the fields, field visitation, and service as a clearing house and resource center for member units.[58]

After the Rio convention closed, for the first time a report volume was published in a language other than English. The English volume was entitled *The Living Christ;* the companion volume in Portuguese was called *O Cristo Vivo*.

As had been the case with other conventions, there were postconvention meetings in 1932. They were held in Montevideo, Buenos Aires, La Paz, Asuncíon, Santiago, Valparaiso, Lima, Buenaventura, and Port of Spain (Trinidad). [59]

The influence of the Rio convention was felt to have been widespread and deep, especially in Latin America:

The Convention has made a profound impression upon the public. It has contributed as no single event of the past to raise the Protestant Evangelical Church and Sunday School movement in Brazil and elsewhere in the estimation and respect of the people generally. The effect and influence of the Convention on the mind and heart of workers, foreign and national, and the community of believers in Brazil and throughout South America has been, and will be, increasingly to dispel the sense of isolation heretofore keenly felt. From time to time, tourists seeking pleasure, scientists in search of knowledge, educators and others on missions of good will, capitalists, engineers and business men looking for investments and for commercial and industrial expansion, in increasing numbers have been coming to South America, but never before has so large and representative a group from thirty-three nations of the world visited this continent on business for the King.[60]

OSLO, 1936

In 1936, after twenty-three years, the association returned to Europe for its convention, this time to Oslo, the capital city of the Kingdom of Norway. The planning for the convention revealed that hotel space was limited and that many delegates were expected to be housed in private homes.[61]

In spite of the shortage of hotel space, there were over 3,000 delegates at the convention, coming from about sixty countries. Of them, 877 were registered from North America, and between two and three hundred others attended. Robert Hopkins reported that it was the largest number from North America ever attending a Sunday school convention outside the United States. About 1,200 came from the four Scandinavian countries. Two hundred and seven came across the North Sea from Great Britain and Ireland.[62]

A new problem arose in preparing for Oslo: how to minimize nationalism in decorating the meeting place? It concerned flags which had been so conspicuous in earlier conventions. James Kelly wrote to Robert Hopkins, asking what the Americans thought about the matter, and the North American Administrative Committee, in replying, said it would be best if no flags at all were used in the convention hall. If, however, the local committee urgently requested the use of flags, then, the Americans said, either a single Norwegian flag or the four flags of the Scandinavian countries might be used, but under no circumstances any others.[63] It is not difficult to understand the problem: the National Socialist flag, the swastika, and the flag of fascist Italy would have appeared along with the others. But Dr. Kelly, by his alertness, forestalled the whole problem and only the Norwegian flag appeared.[64]

A racial problem also arose in connection with the Oslo convention, or to be more precise, in connection with tours associated with it. Thomas Cook and Son, the travel agency, found that a few "Negro delegates" had enrolled for some of the tours and repeatedly raised questions with the North American committee about the matter. Robert Hopkins conferred with Hugh R. Munro and Luther Weigle, and then responded to the agents that no discrimination could be tolerated. The N.A.A.C. also issued a statement to all delegates and prospective delegates:

A question has been raised as to whether there are any limitations as to race or color in the invitation issued for the World's Sunday School Convention. Those who have attended these Conventions in the past are of course well aware that the most cordial invitation has been extended to people of all lands and races who are properly certified by their respective evengelical bodies. There will be no departure from established practice in this respect in connection with the Convention at Oslo.[65]

That response seems to have settled the matter. The issue was to come up again in planning for the next convention, and that time not by a travel agency, but by the entertaining body.

Before the convention adjourned, it voted to hold the next meeting in South Africa. Other invitations had come from Toronto, Tokyo, New York City, Oakland (California), and Jerusalem. The decision was for South Africa, and the arrangements were left to the North American committee.[66]

DURBAN

Herbert G. Chessher of Herne Bay, England, raised the first recorded misgiving about the choice. In a letter to Dr. Weigle dated July 29, 1936, he warned about the racist nature and unrepresentative character of the South African Sunday School Association.[67]

Apparently, Durban was not altogether to the liking of Secretary Hopkins, and back in the United States he sought the advice of several unnamed mission leaders. These persons felt it would be wise for Dr. Hopkins to go to South Africa, "as soon as possible to make sure that the conditions imposed by the World Council in accepting this invitation were fully complied with in the interest of a successful convention." [68] Hopkins brought the results of his inquiry to the business committee, and it agreed he should go to South Africa to sound out the situation.

The planning for "the-convention-that-wasn't" was important, even though the meeting itself, prevented by the outbreak of World War II, was never held. The planning chiefly revolved around the problems created by the segregated society and culture in South Africa, and the involvement of the churches in that pattern.

Soon after the close of the Oslo convention, the North American administrative committee met and agreed that "one of the most difficult of these problems will be the interracial character of the gathering." [69] Seeking the opinion of North Americans knowledgeable about the South African situation, the business committee invited nine counselors, most of them mission executives, to discuss the wisdom of holding a convention in South Africa. An entire afternoon was given over to the issue. The minutes record:

> No votes were taken but it was the unanimous judgment of those who participated in the discussion that adequate representation of all the church forces in South Africa should be secured in forming the Convention organization and equitable representation should be accorded all races.[70]

Durban was seen as the preferred city. Robert Hopkins went again to South

Africa to survey the scene and cabled home, "Durban meets all conditions." [71] On July 23 the mayor of Durban had indicated that he did "not anticipate much difficulty."

A mid-October meeting proved to be important. Invitations had been received from Durban, Johannesburg, and Cape Town. Durban was officially chosen, and the dates were set for July 22–28, 1940. John L. Dube, a Bantu, had assured the business committee that "non-Europeans" ("non-whites," that is) need anticipate no hostile treatment in Durban. Maurice Webb of Durban and J. Rheinallt Jones of Johannesburg, both attached to the South African Institute of Race Relations, agreed that Durban was the best city in South Africa for the "color bar." George E. Haynes of the Federal Council of Churches of the U.S.A. was not reassured, however, and urged that clear understandings be secured about hotels, trams, buses, and the like.

It was evident at the meeting that there was a redoubtable South African opposition to the holding of the convention as an official communication from the Synodical Council of the Dutch Reformed Church in the Orange Free State was read:

> . . . such a Convention tending as it will to propagate the policy of doing away with differences of race and colour and bringing to us speakers who are not adequately conversed with the views and circumstances in our country will without doubt endanger the sound development of the extensive missionary endeavour of the Dutch Reformed Church, the propagation of the Sunday School activities and will also unjustifiably disturb the relation of the races in South Africa to one another;
>
> This council therefore resolves that we cannot participate in the proposed World Sunday School Convention and—for the above mentioned reasons and also because nobody in South Africa can guarantee the desired friendly treatment of all the delegates at all places and at all times in our country—request the leaders and all parties concerned to abandon the proposed plan for the sake of the delegates as well as for the cause itself . . .
>
> (signed) P. H. van Huyssteen,
SCRIBA SINODI

Robert Hopkins had been to South Africa twice, and had met with both black and white church leaders in twelve cities. Cape Town, Durban, and Johannesburg had given assurances that a convention could be held in each place with no racial discrimination and that both English-speaking and Afrikaans-speaking churches could be served. It was admitted that in the cities themselves, the color bar would be encountered. Secretary Hopkins had learned, ahead of the formal notification, of the action of the Synod of the Orange free state. [72]

Obviously, serious difficulties lay ahead. After a time the question was raised in South Africa if its National Sunday School Association might take over organizing the convention, substituting for the W.S.S.A. Hopkins was agreeable, provided the association could make full use of the Dutch Reformed Church, whose Sunday school enrollment was half of the total in the country, and "also the large non-European Christian element in South Africa." [73]

By mid-1938, it was reported that the Synod of the Cape Province, the largest of the four synods of the Dutch Reformed Church, was deeply divided on the matter of supporting the proposed convention, and it had therefore taken no action upon it. [74]

Toward the end of the year, Hopkins having gone for the third time to South Africa to try to straighten matters out, the Transvaal Dutch officially requested that their delegates to the convention be seated apart and that in all social gatherings their delegates be sequestered, a kind of self-segregation. Such provisions, Hopkins cabled home, were necessary for the participation of the Transvaal people. Professor Charles Loram of Yale University thought this provision was acceptable, provided full racial equality be preserved in meetings and discussions. Weigle agreed. Hugh Munro was afraid of making this much of a concession. Meanwhile the convention council in South Africa accepted these stipulations and welcomed the Dutch Reformed Church to the coming convention. By June of 1939, however, the Dutch Reformed Church had second thoughts and voted not to give official recognition to the convention.

In September of that year World War II began. All the planning and all the attempts to achieve a consensus became irrelevant with the invasion of Poland and the involvement of the British empire in the conflagration. For a time there was a difference of judgment in W.S.S.A. circles as to whether the convention had been postponed or cancelled, and it was decided to leave that decision to the council of the association scheduled to meet in 1940. Before that time, however, it became more or less tacitly assumed that the convention was cancelled and that, when and if another became possible, plans should be made for a new place, a new convention, and a new approach.

This was the first time in the history of the conventions and the association that a racial problem proved serious in planning and arrangements. Events beyond the control either of the South Africans or the association interfered with a clear settlement of the issue. The first serious instance of racial discrimination in the conventions themselves was also, fortunately, the last. [75]

Association Officers

During this period, as had been the case in the earlier days, the management of the association and the formulation of its policies was in the hands of leaders almost exclusively from Great Britain and the United States. If there was sentiment for a greater variety of elected leadership, there are no records to attest to it. As the Los Angeles convention reported, there were seventy-nine elected officers chosen from Great Britain, Canada, and the United States, together with forty-six from other countries. At the close of the Oslo convention, the proportions were evenly divided: Great Britain, Canada, and the United States had fifty-five; forty-two other nations had precisely the same number, almost all of them one or two each. The Board of Managers, which came to be the effective governing body, was composed in 1936 exclusively of persons from the United Kingdom and the United States, half from each country.[76]

In 1938 Miss Dorothy Cadbury of Great Britain and Mrs. Clifford J. Heinz of the United States were chosen as vice presidents of the association and began a long service as officers and as members of the Board of Managers.[77] In February of 1930 J. Arthur (later Lord) Rank was chosen as chairman of the British committee, a position which he held and to which he gave active service until 1958, when he resigned the post.[78]

The two officers who were elected during this period and who furnished a large share of the leadership of the association for many years were Sir Harold Mackintosh and Dr. Luther A. Weigle. They were named at the Los Angeles convention in 1928, having previously attended the Glasgow convention four years before.[79] Sir Harold, in time to be elevated by several stages to the title of Viscount Mackintosh of Halifax, had already served, in a conspicuous way, the National Sunday School Union of England and Wales. In 1924 and 1925 he visited many parts of the country in the interests of the Sunday school.

He had grown up in Halifax, where his home introduced him to the joys of reading: "My early home turned me loose among the Victorian classics, and Church and Sunday School soaked me in great stories and drama, narrated in the matchless prose of the Authorized Version. If there is a better way of learning English, I should like to know of it." [80]

This early interest in the Sunday school was a matter of pride to him as attested by his reporting of a citation in his home Sunday school on Queen's Road, Halifax, a wall plaque which read: "There was once a boy who was a scholar in this School and later a teacher and became President of the World's Sunday School Association." Lord Mackintosh declared that: "among all the honours that I have been fortunate enough to receive this I hold very high." [81]

Mackintosh, a British Methodist, was active in the circles of his church, influential in its policies, and committed to the Wesleyan heritage. He declared that there was more of Methodism than Marx about the Labour Party and, as he saw matters, the Sunday school had given to Britain a variety of gifts, many of them usually unrecognized by the general public:

What has the Sunday School done for the nation and in its quiet way for the world, since Robert Raikes lived and laboured? The blessings direct and indirect are beyond all calculation. Not only has our land been richly blessed by the training of the children in that "righteousness which exalteth a nation" but at the same time they have been fitted for all kinds of service, involving both faith and works. In many and varied responsibilities are to be seen men and women who received their first training in the Sunday Schools. They taught themselves in teaching others and large numbers learnt the art of public speaking at their Sunday school desks.[82]

Even though Sir Harold was not present at the Rio convention, he was reelected, and, at Oslo in 1936, he was chosen for a third term. He accepted the unprecedented honor, but said that this third term should be his last and that at the next convention another should be chosen.[83] The next convention after Oslo was a long time in coming (Toronto, 1950), and again he was chosen to hold the presidential office. At Tokyo in 1958 Dr. Weigle having retired as chairman, Lord Mackintosh became chairman in his place, an office which he held until his death during the Christmas season of 1964.

In 1936 there was a minority sentiment for a change in the presidency. Arthur Black thought that a choice of a North American, or a person from another area, a person to travel, speak, write, and preach for the association would be a wiser choice, and in that event Sir Harold might be made chairman for the next four years.[84]

After Lord Mackintosh's death, Nelson Chappel, who had worked so closely with him for ten years, gave this testimony:

> He was a man of many parts, who always seemed to be able to give more time to public affairs in the nation and the world than to his own personal business where he also was eminently successful. He was never too busy to turn aside from other tasks to give consideration to the work of the WCCESSA. We respected him as a great leader and loved him as a great friend.[85]

Luther A. Weigle, elected at Los Angeles as the chairman of the Committee on Reference and Counsel (later to be called the Board of Managers), was called in the same year to be dean of the Yale University Divinity School where he had been professor of religious education since 1916. His father was a Lutheran minister in Pennsylvania. He did his undergraduate and seminary work in that state and completed his graduate studies at Yale University.

Dr. Weigle had done graduate research in philosophy, rather than in education, and was greatly influenced by Professor William James of Harvard and George T. Ladd of Yale. The writings of Immanuel Kant had influenced him deeply, especially *The Critique of Practical Reason,* and his dissertation was entitled *An Historical and Critical Study of Kant's Antinomy of Pure Reason.*

Weigle had been a professor and later dean of Carleton College in Northfield, Minnesota, where he transferred his ministerial standing from the General Synod, Lutheran Church, to the Congregational Churches.

His book, *The Pupil and the Teacher,* published in 1911 on assignment from the Lutherans, was widely read, used by many denominations, translated into several languages, and sold over a million copies. The book caught the eye of a Yale professor and, as a result, the Carleton dean was called to become Horace Bushnell Professor of Christian Nurture at Yale University.

Weigle had been a leader in the International Sunday School Association (Canada and the United States), taking an early interest in matters of curriculum, especially the inadequacies of the International Uniform Lessons, then the most popular of any single lesson system. His service as chairman for the association (council) was to continue for exactly thirty years. He was replaced as chairman by his long-time friend and associate, Lord Mackintosh.

Weigle had been, since 1917, a director of the Congregational Education Society and the Congregational Publishing Society. In 1924, the year he attended the Glasgow convention, he became chairman of the Commission on Christian Education of the Federal Council of the Churches of Christ in America and, four years later (the year of the Los Angeles Convention and his election as Chairman of the W.S.S.A.), he was made chairman of the Administrative Committee of the Federal Council. He later became the president of that body. In 1929 Weigle was elected chairman of the Standard Bible Committee of the International Council of Religious Education, a committee which published the Revised Standard Version of the Bible (1946 and 1952). He held this chairmanship until he turned it over, in 1970, to Professor Herbert G. May of Oberlin College, an undertaking which engaged the concentrated attention of his later life, indeed, to and beyond his ninetieth year.

Dean Weigle had a high regard for the human mind. The intellectual life served as a kind of foundation stone for his career in education and in the W.S.S.A. He made such a testimony in his writings and in public address on a number of occasions:

> Protestantism trusts the human mind. It believes in the competence of man to apprehend God, to respond to Him with faith, and to gain new insights and increase of power by the experimental method of basing activity upon such knowledge as we have and such faith as we dare venture. Grant, as we must, that the being of God lies beyond the power of our finite minds fully to grasp, comprehend, and formulate; grant, too, that these minds of ours are too commonly blinded by sin, biased by complexes, prejudiced by the traditions of yesterday, and cramped by the social pressures of today—yet these minds are the only minds we have. If we cannot trust them, we can trust nothing. Protestantism . . . insists that such minds can cope with the problems of value as well as with matters of fact; that they can seek and find God as well as probe the laws of nature.[86]

Echoes here of Immanuel Kant! The professor of Konigsberg and the professor in New Haven had much in common.

From the convention of Los Angeles onward, Mackintosh and Weigle—the one a practical man of affairs, nurtured in the pietistic tradition of Methodism, the other a Lutheran student-of-philosophy-turned-educator—were to join their differing talents to the task of worldwide Christian education. In the course of that conjoining, a deep personal friendship was created.

Staff

Mr. W. G. Landes had succeeded Frank L. Brown as general secretary with reluctance. He served in this position until 1927. A decision was made in Heyst, Belgium, concerning the organizational nature of the association with which Mr. Landes disagreed. How much this difference in judgment affected his commitment to the organization is impossible to say. What we do know is that he received a call from the New York State Sunday School Association and decided to accept it. His resignation took effect October 31, 1927.[87]

In his place as North American general secretary, Robert M. Hopkins was elected and installed at the Los Angeles convention. Dr. Hopkins was a minister of the Disciples of Christ, and had attended the conventions of the W.S.S.A. at Zurich in 1913 and in Glasgow in 1924. He served during the time of the Rio convention and the Oslo convention as well. He was the executive in charge of the planning for the Durban convention, with its difficult problems of racial discrimination and its eventual postponement. In 1938, having received a call from the principal missionary agency of his brotherhood, the United Christian Missionary Society, Dr. Hopkins decided to reenter the service of his own fellowship. The W.S.S.A. was reluctant to let him go:

> Dr. Munro read a letter from Dr. Hopkins regarding his election as President of the United Christian Missionary Society and the action that should be taken looking toward the appointment of a successor as general secretary of the World's Sunday School Association. It was VOTED that the committee approve proposal #4 in Dr. Hopkins' letter whereby he would continue as part-time general secretary until the Durban Convention and in the meantime an associate general secretary be secured to help with the work in the office and the routine of the general secretary.[88]

Hopkins continued part-time service for a period, and Forrest L. Knapp was elected associate general secretary with a view that he would be proposed as the American executive at the Durban convention.[89] With the Durban convention postponed or cancelled, Dr. Knapp was presented at a Lake Mohonk, N.Y., meeting of the Board of Managers in 1940 as the general secretary-elect.

At this same Lake Mohonk meeting, a testimony to the effective work of Robert Hopkins was adopted by the W.S.S.A. Council:

> . . . He has led in adapting the structure and program of the Association to the needs and conditions of the present day; he has deepened the good-will towards the Association, and widened its circle of friends; and he has carried large responsibility for developing and strengthening cooperation in Christian religious education in China, in Mexico, in Puerto Rico, in Brazil, in Egypt, in the Bible Lands, and in other parts of the world. Much of the cooperative program in Christian religious education in various sections of the world is a living monument to his skill and devotion. . . . His record of achievement is indelible and our affection for him will abide through the years.[90]

Dr. Samuel D. Price served the American section as business secretary for several years. He died on May 17, 1932, and Archie Lowell Ryan succeeded him in that position.[91]

On the British side, the association also suffered the loss of a friend and, in this case, the former general secretary. Carey Bonner died on June 16, 1938, having served from 1907, the year of the organization's founding in Rome, to 1920 as joint general secretary of the association.[92]

James Kelly continued through this period in the life of the association and well into the next, the British counterpart of both Robert M. Hopkins and Forrest L. Knapp. He served during a difficult time in Britain and in Europe, much of the earlier period being devoted to works of reconstruction and reconciliation.

There is much in the record which attests to the affectionate regard in which he was held by European Sunday school secretaries. His continuing service as chairman of the British committee in the next period, after the resignation of J. Arthur Rank, is evidence of the esteem in which he was held by his British contemporaries.

In the midst of this distinguished service a curious compliment was paid him by the association's president, a tribute which seems decidedly ambiguous to many Americans brought up in a tradition of church-state separation, and aware of the 1975 and 1976 revelations of the misuse of American missionaries and church leaders by the Central Intelligence Agency. Sir Harold said:

> It is understood that upon his [Kelly's] return to England after journeying through the countries of Europe he should call upon the Foreign Secretary of his country, giving his opinion of the conditions in the countries visited as seen through the eyes of the Christian people in those countries.[93]

It should be remembered, of course, that this reporting was done more than forty years ago, that the British Foreign Office served two countries,

England and Scotland, in each of which there was an established church, and that James Kelly was a faithful member of one of those denominations. Perhaps the reporting served, in some instances, to make easier the lot of Christian workers in some difficult European places.

Field Services

Field services during this period offered four chief types of assistance: visits by the employed staff; visits by officers of the association; service by resident Sunday school missionaries, often subsidized by one or the other of the two headquarters offices; and grants made to expedite the work in a specific country.

In 1924 there were three full-time Sunday school missionaries: in Italy, France, and Hungary. There were also grants made to Norway, Poland, Latvia, and Spain. By 1928 there were eleven full-time Sunday school missionaries at work in Europe.[94] The 1925 yearbook listed nineteen names as being part of the field staff, working in Argentina, Austria, Brazil, Ceylon, China, Czechoslovakia, Europe (*sic*), Hungary, India (5), Japan, Korea (2), Moslem Lands (2), and the Philippines.[95]

Staff and constituency visitations were frequent. South Africa, the Congo, India, the Near East, China, Europe, Brazil, the United States, Canada, and other nations, areas, and continents were visited.[96] The Rio de Janeiro convention made possible side trips to other South and Central American countries.

Perhaps the most significant field service of this period was that rendered by Luther Weigle in 1935.[97] He journeyed from New Haven and arrived in China in February 1935, accompanied by his wife, a daughter Ruth, and a son. Richard Weigle, then a young man of twenty-three, had served for three years at Yale-in-China, Changsha. Dean Weigle was scheduled to be present at the biennial meeting of the National Christian Council in April, and to meet with a selected group of people at Kuling during July. Before he arrived, a survey team had worked for six months collecting information for him on the educational and religious situation in China.

On the way, Dr. Weigle had spent a few days in Japan, but the bulk of his time was spent in China. Departing on August 3, his stay had lasted 164 days. He reported that, in this period, he used 133 days for work and thirty-one for travel, and he visited sixteen centers.

His invitation to the country came from three bodies: the National Committee for Christian Religious Education, the National Christian Council, and the China Christian Educational Association. During the time he was there, he visited all of the "higher grade" theological seminaries, all but two of the seminaries of "lower grade," and all but two of the colleges and universities.

The conference at Kuling came off as planned, composed of 111 educators and church administrators. Discussions were held on eleven major topics in church education, theological education, education of women, and inter-church cooperation.

Upon the completion of the visit, Dr. Weigle listed the outstanding results as they appeared to him at the time:

1. Assumption by the National Committee for Christian Religious Education of responsibility for a program of education for lay service;
2. Adoption by the Nanking Theological Seminary of a program for expansion and cooperation;
3. Outlining of a national policy providing for three grades of theological seminaries: theological colleges, theological training schools, and post-graduate schools of theology.
4. The organization of the China Association of Theological Seminaries.[98]

Two testimonies to the worth of this visit may be quoted in support of the subjective comment above, one made at the time by those directly involved and one by an American missionary statesman.

The Kuling meeting minutes note the following:

> The members of this enlarged meeting of the NCCRE assembled in Kuling desire to place on record their deep sense of gratitude to God for the visit of Dr. Luther A. Weigle during these past months since February, culminating in this present conference. We have appreciated the rare gifts that he has brought to this study of education for service in the church in China; his broad experience of church life, of the work of theological seminaries and of Christian education; his ready grip of the essential problems and quick insight into the needs of China; his open minded hospitality to suggestions from any quarter; his power of lucid exposition as a preacher and speaker; his single-minded devotion to the work entrusted to him; and not least his persuasive friendliness and infectious humor. We believe that the labors of these six months in collaboration with the Survey Team will mark the beginning of a new period in the history of the church and that the Report soon to be published will prove a classic that will guide our policies for many years to come.[99]

The observations of John R. Mott, distinguished missionary leader, inspirer of many ecumenical movements and bodies, were equally warm:

> The timeliness of the visit of Dean Weigle, a man that has such a profound grasp of the whole range of religious education, who is so responsive to the voice of the need of the youth of the world, who combines with that long experience in the practical work of the church, and on top of that a leader of one of the most important schools of religion, is beyond doubt. I am much pleased with his thoroughness. He is taking time to expose himself all over the place, out of the usual beat, into the interior touching every point you could mention today. My last individual interview save one in China was with Dr. Weigle. He is going to bring in leading minds all over China and have judgment

on his findings before bringing them back. This year was the most pertinent time to have him over there. Last year, I believe would have been too soon, next year, too late. He challenges attention and goes on to guide us, and presents this matter in a way to arrest attention not only over there, but here.[100]

The board was as appreciative of this impressive field service as the Kuling colleagues and Dr. Mott had been earlier:

The Board of Managers of the World's Sunday School Association met in London in the month of August under the Chairmanship of the Rev. Dean Luther A. Weigle, D.D. of Yale University, who had just returned from a visit to China where he had spent six months giving help and guidance to the Chinese Churches in the work of Christian education. Dr. Weigle spent most of his time travelling. He gave one month each to North, South, East, Central and West China. In co-operation with Chinese Ministers and European missionaries he studied the needs of Christian Theological colleges and Bible Training Schools, the indigenous churches, the Training Centres for the teaching and training of leaders and teachers for lay service in the church, and the whole policy and programme of Christian education. Dr. Weigle's service to the Chinese Christian Church and the ongoing of the Kingdom of God in that great and needy land has been of inestimable value as is very evident from the report prepared and issued by the Committee in China responsible for his visit.[101]

Activities of the Regional Committees

As was the case in the preceding chapter, the association operated largely between conventions as a dual organization, with most of the program planned by the British and the American committees, with clearances made and some common planning projected at the annual meetings of the Committee on Reference and Counsel, later the Board of Managers.

THE NORTH AMERICAN ADMINISTRATIVE COMMITTEE

Each of the two committees was, in principle, subordinate to the executive committee (later to the Board of Managers), and an action was taken that the executive committee should be authorized to grant to either of the administrative committees amounts in emergencies not to exceed $25,000.[102]

In 1925 the executive committee, meeting in New York, decided to recommend that the association should become a federation of autonomous units, each of which would be represented on the executive committee. The British committee was to be responsible for India and Europe, the American committee for South America, Burma, Ceylon, China, Egypt, North Africa, Syria, Palestine, Turkey, Japan, Korea, and the Philippines. It was a division heavily weighted on the American side.[103]

In 1926 there is recorded one of those actions (not uncommon in church agencies) which never seems to have been carried out, and seems to have died with the recording of the motion. It was recommended by the executive committee that, as soon as possible, the world office of the W.S.S.A. should be in Geneva, Switzerland, but that the legal headquarters should continue as before in Washington, D.C.[104] It was not until 1963, thirty-seven years later, that a functioning program office was actually located in Geneva, and not until 1965 that the chief administrative and executive office was established there.

In June, 1930, the executive committee was to meet to consider a name change to "World Sunday School Council of Christian Education," a proposal which had been approved once before and then reversed. Here again there was no record of follow-up on the matter, and the proposed change seems to have been dropped.

About this time there appears to have been some tension and friction between the International Council of Religious Education and the W.S.S.A. in matters of program and support. A special committee headed by Dr. Weigle brought in recommendations which were accepted. These proposals provided that the I.C.R.E. would make adequate provision in its meetings for world Christian educational concerns; that the constituent denominations of the I.C.R.E. would nominate members to the Board of Managers and to the North American section of the W.S.S.A.; that the I.C.R.E. would contribute annually to the budget of the W.S.S.A. and support the association in its financial efforts; and that the I.C.R.E. would accept a quota of 500 delegates for the 1932 Rio convention. Other recommendations were not accepted, viz., a proposal from Dr. Hugh Magill for the I.C.R.E. to take over full responsibility for the budget of the North American section; the education commission of the I.C.R.E. to determine the W.S.S.A. program, thus eliminating the North American section of the association; and a proposal to have the I.C.R.E. ratify the 1931 budget of $70,000.[105]

A new step in the services of the North American committee came about when Robert Hopkins called a conference to consider the needs of the West Indies. Eleven committees of the conference were convened, each considering two questions: "What is Being Done?" and "What Needs to be Done?" In 1938 a National Convention on Christian Education was held in Camaguey, Cuba, and out of this convention came a decision to form the Cuba Council of Christian Education. It was later organized and annual conventions were held thereafter. In May 1941, this council became the Department of Christian Education of the Cuba Council of Evangelical Churches.[106]

THE BRITISH ADMINISTRATIVE COMMITTEE

During the quadrennium between Los Angeles and the Rio de Janeiro conventions (1928 and 1932 respectively), the British section (later the

British Administrative Committee) maintained contact with nearly every country in Europe except Russia, relations sustained chiefly through the travel and labor of James Kelly. Sunday school committees were reorganized and councils of Christian education set up in many lands. During the period the British section gave financial support to Sunday school missionaries in eight countries, and in addition grants for teacher-training and production of literature in large numbers.[107]

In the spring of 1930 it was decided to terminate the "pass-it-on department," an operation which had been known as the surplus materials project; by 1918, to cite a typical year, it had distributed more than 28,000 picture rolls alone to various countries.[108]

An important item in the work of 1931 was the first All-European Sunday School Convention in Budapest, in August of that year. Even though a financial crisis in Europe made travel and enrollment difficult, 235 delegates from twenty-seven nations and twelve denominations attended. The entire cost of the convention was met by a few friends in Scotland and England. We may conjecture that J. Arthur Rank, Sir Harold Mackintosh, and Miss Dorothy Cadbury were among those few.[109]

The 1930s were, of course, the years of the rise of National Socialism in Germany. James Kelly found that the increasing oppression of the churches by the Nazis reached the state churches first, the free churches only later. In late January 1933, Adolf Hitler had become chancellor, the Reichstag was dissolved, and a month later its building was destroyed by fire. There were channels for the Nazis to reach the state churches and the pressure became so intense that the breakaway of many pastors and lay people to form the Confessing Church was the only way out for many a conscience's sake.

In the beginning, however, Kelly found that the actions against the free churches were not so severe:

> The Free Churches have scarcely been touched by the Ecclesiastical conflict which has affected the Lutheran Church, and whereas all the Youth work in the Lutheran Church has been adversely affected as a result of the situation which has arisen between Church and State, the Free Churches have not suffered quite the same, and have been able to carry on to a considerable extent their Sunday School work. The situation changes rapidly, but the Leaders of the Churches are convinced that there never was a time when Christian Education was more needed in Germany than now, and granted a satisfactory readjustment of relationships between Church and State, and between the Nazi Youth organization and the German Evangelical Youth Movement, a great opportunity will present itself for Evangelical Christian teaching.[110]

The "satisfactory readjustment of relationships" never came about, of course, and two years later Kelly saw the church situation in grimmer detail:

> Reports from Germany indicate that although the work maintained by the National Sunday School Association (Lutheran Church) has been sadly cur-

tailed, the Association is still maintaining its hold and exercising a great influence upon the youth of the church. We rejoice in the growing number of Christians in Germany associated with the Confessional group of Protestants who decline to bow to Caesar where the crown-rights of Jesus Christ are concerned, even although it means restriction of their activities and much personal hardship. As we write the School of Theology at Elberfeld has been closed by the Secret Police. The School was founded nine years ago with the cordial support of the Reformed communities, and was recognized by State and Church alike. No explanation was given for the closing of the School.[111]

In 1938 Kelly saw the issue for what it really was, a deadly confrontation over ultimate values and the nature of ultimate reality. Speaking of Europe, he wrote:

There are few lands in which the rising tides of nationalism and secularism, and the shadow of a totalitarian State, claiming the primary or exclusive loyalty of all its citizens, do not fall like a dark shadow across the future. We are all too sadly familiar with the aim and object of many of the youth movements existing today in an increasing number of European countries which are subversive of the highest and best interests in life, and which seek to instill in the minds and hearts of their followers the grim doctrine that there is no higher loyalty than the State.[112]

With the rising nationalism, the temper of the times and the increasing difficulties of travel, the work of the British committee, so largely focused on Europe, was becoming increasingly difficult. Matters would get a great deal worse in the years immediately ahead, as the shadow of which James Kelly spoke deepened into almost continental darkness.

Financing the Association

The period began, fortunately, with no deficits from the Glasgow Convention. Expenditures were less than income, a substantial balance was turned over to the British committee, increased by generous donations after the convention had closed.[113]

In the United States united financial campaigns continued to interest the American committee. Representatives of the American section of the world association met with officials of the International Council in 1926, a conference which may have led to a three-party proposal in 1929 involving these two bodies and the Southern California Council of Religious Education as well. The sum of $15,000 was approved to be raised during the life of W. C. Pearce, and $3,000 was to be raised in southern California during the month of March for Christian religious education in China. Nothing more is recorded about the tripartite effort, save for the laconic comment that about $915 came in for China work. It does not seem to be one of the more successful financial efforts.[114]

In 1928 there was a $20,000 bequest from David C. Cook, an independent Sunday school publisher of Elgin, Illinois, one who had been long interested in the work of the association. Because of the financial needs of the British committee in that year the Americans voted to pay annually for that Committee's work the sum of $4,250.

The same year it was agreed to consolidate the American and the British budgets ($65,000 and $30,000 respectively), with the understanding that the two sections raise and administer their own funds. "Consolidation" would seem to have small meaning in the light of the proviso.

The Rio meeting of the World Executive Committee learned, in 1932, that Sir Robert Laidlaw, who had died in 1930, had left to the association £47,700 (about $235,000). The Robert Laidlaw grant proved to be the largest bequest ever left to the W.S.S.A.[115] The income from this bequest was to be divided equally between the two administrative committees. The British committee, however, voted to surrender its claim to $9,500 to permit the North American committee to pay off a deficit.

The American need stemmed from the effects of the depression, severely felt by the North American committee. Robert Hopkins was having a hard time making ends meet. The American section reported to the Rio meeting of the executive committee that:

> The budget of the North American section for 1932 totals $61,000, but unless the financial conditions improve the actual expenditures for 1932 must be held to a figure below the expenditures for any of the four years of the past quadrennium. We do not feel that this failing income is due to slackening of interest in the work, or that it has been caused in any sense by bad administration or lack of promotion. On the contrary these friends and supporters who are finding it difficult to maintain former standards of giving are emphasizing in their letters which they send in response to our appeals that they greatly regret that present financial conditions make necessary for a time the withdrawal or the reduction of their support for the world work.[116]

In 1934 at the meeting of the board of managers, a finance committee, consisting of Paul Sturtevant, Hugh Munro, Sir Harold Mackintosh, and S. B. Chapin was appointed.[117]

The financial stringency of 1932 would continue for several years. The British committee was especially handicapped because of the war. By 1935 there were capital funds equivalent to $355,000, two-thirds in dollars, one-third in pounds sterling.[118] The income from these funds was used for current programs.

During this third period in the life of the association, the early optimism diminished and merged into a more realistic appraisal of the social and religious outlook. Disillusionment with the results of World War I, the postwar economic catastrophes in Europe, the swift emergence of Russian Communism, the changed theological outlook—all these factors contributed to a more sober point of view.

The problems and opportunities of a ministry to young people, almost ignored before the twenties, began to engage the attention of the world conventions. The engagement was erratic, at best, for there is scant evidence that work with and for youth was a continuing concern between convention sessions.

This period saw the continuing trend toward graded Sunday school lessons. The demand for indigenous curricula increased, though little was devised to meet the need.

Social and ethical issues received considerably more attention than at the earliest conventions. Racism, unemployment, economic collapse, exploitation, war, and fascism were condemned and national associations were urged to combat these evils.

During the period, the first (and last) convention south of the equator was held, and although another had been planned for the southern hemisphere, it was cancelled because of the outbreak of World War II. In the planning for this convention, the association met the problem of racism head-on. The outcome was inconclusive, and it will never be known whether the association would have insisted upon a completely unsegregated convention or if some compromise with local leaders and national churches would have opened the way for a partially or optional segregated pattern.

Two long-time leaders began their service in 1928. Sir (later Viscount) Harold Mackintosh of England and Dr. Luther A. Weigle of the United States. James Kelly gave many years to the British committee in this period and the next, first as its executive, later as its chairman.

The field service of Dean Weigle to the theological seminaries of China in 1935 was characteristic of the growing professional service and competence of the association, a type of field offering beyond the skill of well-meaning laymen, however consecrated.

The vigor and zest of the early days was not forgotten, however, and at a 1935 meeting of the board of managers in London it was agreed to celebrate the jubilee of the beginnings of the W.S.S.A. (July 1889) during 1939. A forty-page booklet was produced, but there was no general celebration. Adolf Hitler had other plans for Europe that summer and early autumn.

4

Difficulties, Achievements, and Strains
1939-1953

IT IS NOT USEFUL to continue the description of the characteristics of the conventions as in the three earlier sections. From now on the association will be seen as a body which held conventions from time to time as one among many types of program activities. The association will no longer be perceived as an organization created by conventions, operating in a convention tradition, and responsible to successive conventions for initiations and authorizations of program. The two regional committees and the Board of Managers will take over these functions.

A few general observations, however, before we look at the age-group interests of the period. The Anglo-American dominance of the association continued without interruption. In 1941, for example, there were fifteen officers and members of the Board of Managers. Six were from Great Britain, eight from the United States, and Switzerland had the remaining single place. What is different about the period, however, is the sound of the first voice raised to call for a wider and more representative leadership. Forrest Knapp, the North American secretary, observed in 1947:

> We need to strengthen ourselves by means of developing a more active partnership among the constituent organizations of the World's Association. Too largely in the past many of the constituent units have tended to think and to act as if the World's Association is chiefly a British-American enterprise. Each of them should take upon itself the responsibility of helping to determine the policies and practices of the World's Association.[1]

The reader who has noticed the characteristic governance of the association through the years will conclude that "the constituent units" tending "to think and to act as if the World's Association is chiefly a British-American enterprise" were seeing organizational matters as they really were. And he will be right.

Children's Work

Throughout this period the British committee saw the worldwide task of the Christian education of children as being the primary, if not the only, responsibility of the association. In this position, the British were consistent with the Association's history.

The North American committee, however, with the passing of the years and with a wider concept of Christian education, saw children's work as one of many areas of concern for religious education forces.

Toward the latter part of the period there came an attempt to give specialized attention and professional competence to children's work as carried on by the association, or council, as it was then called.

The North American administrative committee held a conference on children's work, at Buck Hill Falls, Pennsylvania, in March 1947. It was attended by persons from different lands who described the children's work in their countries. From this session, twenty practical suggestions were given to the W.S.S.A. to facilitate its services as a professional resource agency.[2]

In connection with the Toronto convention of 1950, the council called a conference on children's work, attended by specialists from a number of countries. A number of questions, programmatic in nature, had been raised by that conference, and to deal with them in an adequate fashion, the North American program committee appointed a Children's Work Advisory Committee. Florence Stansbury of the American Baptist convention staff was appointed chairman, and Erich F. Voehringer of the New York staff was to provide executive services.[3]

By the end of 1951 this new body had accepted four main tasks:

1. To compile a list of Children's Work correspondents.
2. To send out circular letters and packets of materials.
3. To call a conference to study the matter of providing specialized training in the Christian Education of children.
4. To prepare curriculum guidance material for "Pictures for Children Everywhere."[4]

The chief activities of this committee lay ahead and will be discussed in the next chapter. The reference to the picture project will also be developed later.

Youth Work

As one looks back over the record, it is apparent that the association was very slow in giving any sustained and specialized attention to the religious education of young people. At the first convention, in 1889, there had been some consideration given to work with older teenagers, particularly to the problem of retaining them in Sunday school and church. A seminar on youth work had been held in Los Angeles in connection with the 1928 convention and the pattern had been repeated in Rio four years later. The W.S.S.A. was one of the sponsors of the 1939 World Christian Youth Conference in Amsterdam.

The first conference of evangelical youth from the Western hemisphere was held in Cuba in 1946, following the Latin American Congress of Evangelical Youth. It was sponsored by the Latin American Union of Evangelical Youth and the United Christian Youth Movement (United States and Canada), with the cooperation of the W.S.S.A. and the Committee on Cooperation in Latin America (a cooperative body of mission boards).[5]

It was not until the Birmingham assembly met in 1947 that authorization for the creation of a youth department was secured, and the department and committee were authorized to explore the field of youth work with the World Council of Churches, then in process of formation.

The year before, the Board of Managers had voted to participate in the 1947 World Christian Youth Conference (the successor to the earlier Amsterdam gathering) scheduled for Oslo.[6] This youth conference met in July of 1947, with about 1,000 delegates present from seventy-one countries, representing 181 churches and organizations. Two hundred sixty-three young people and thirty-seven adult leaders were present as representatives of the (North American) United Christian Youth Movement.[7]

A clear desire for closer cooperation among the agencies involved in Christian world youth work grew apace, resulting from the sponsorship of the Oslo conference, and of the associations in the meeting itself. A large amount of correspondence ensued, and frequent rewordings of agreements and understandings with other world bodies were made by W.C.C.E. secretaries, chiefly by Forrest Knapp.

It was agreed that there should be a World Christian Youth Commission for purposes of program information and fellowship among youth workers. Its first meeting was held in July of 1948. A second meeting was held the next year in Lausanne. This body was composed of representatives of the World Council of Christian Education, the World Council of Churches, the World Alliance of YMCAs, the World's YWCA, and the World's Student Christian Federation. It was to act as a kind of clearing house for world programs.

The Birmingham assembly approved, with stipulations, cooperation with the World Council of Churches in youth work and authorized participation in a joint committee. It empowered the board to establish a youth department and committee.[8]

The stipulations were not drawn carefully enough, however, to avoid tension in the procedures of appointment of a youth secretary. Forrest Knapp reported to the British committee that the North American committee had indicated its understanding that a youth executive would be appointed by *one* of the general secretaries. The British committee took exception to this understanding, one-sided as it appeared to them, and recorded its judgment that if it was to be expected to contribute to the expenses of the youth department, it should be a full partner in the venture: "While the direction of his work would be in charge of one Secretary, he should work in close cooperation with BOTH secretaries, and should be responsible to the Board of Managers." [9]

Meanwhile, the World Council of Churches, still in the process of formation, determined to make some kind of provision for youth work and a youth secretary. As this intention became clearer, during the years of 1945, 1946, and 1947, a real dilemma was created for the World Council of Christian Education. It could demit its concerns for youth work and establish some kind of cooperative relationship with whatever the World Council of Churches created; it could establish a separate youth entity of its own; or there might be a joint venture of a kind and scope as yet unknown.

The administrative difficulties of the second and third options were those of knowing that some influential members of the British committee were either indifferent or opposed to the creation of a youth department, and yet the establishment of youth work representing only the North American interests was seen to be anomalous. Once again, the real nub of the difficulty was the dual structure which had grown up across the years, and the differences in basic program assumptions resulting from the divided council.

In 1948 the first assembly of the World Council of Churches was held in Amsterdam. Immediately afterwards, at Laage Vursche in the Netherlands, the organizing meeting of the youth department was held. By this time it had been agreed that there would be a Joint Youth Department Committee of the two bodies with most of the members appointed in common, and with some members appointed independently by the two councils.

These arrangements were administratively cumbersome. The Youth Department Committee proposed to the Toronto assembly (1950) that the World Council of Christian Education recognize the Youth Department Committee of the World Council of Churches "as the representative forum of church youth." The W.C.C.E. declined to accept this act of abnegation and it voted to continue the existing arrangement, standing ready with the fullest possible cooperation with the W.C.C.E., and looking to the Board of Managers for guidance in a long-term policy.[10] Following the Toronto meetings, the Youth Department Committee met at nearby Whitby with forty-one members present from twenty-four countries. Preparations for the youth meetings in Canada had been carefully made by Wilmina Rowland, youth secretary in the New York office.

In mid-1951 one British observer felt that the committee members were chiefly attached to the World Council of Churches and that the involvement of the World Council of Christian Education was of doubtful worth, and further: "There is little doubt that the brains and the drive at this Joint Committee are both found on the Geneva rather than on the New York side of the Atlantic." [11]

In the same year, Secretary Knapp reported the completion of a study of worldwide youth work.[12] In 1953, operational difficulties having arisen, working agreements were hammered out at a meeting of the two youth committees in Alwaye, India, as the two groups met in connection with the World Christian Youth Conference in Kottayam, Travancore, India, in December 1952. This conference was sponsored by five world bodies, including the W.C.C.E. More than 350 persons were present.

Adult Work

Specialized concerns for adult Christian education in this period generally took the form of planning for enlarged services in family life education. The North American committee had authorized a survey of needed services, an inquiry which went from the New York office to thirty-five countries. Fourteen replied, and to these responses there were added thirteen more which were routed to the London office. Three main questions were asked of the religious education forces in these nations:

   i   What is being done in your country to encourage Christian Education in the Home and to provide practical assistance?

   ii What would you say are the dominant needs in your country with respect to the furtherance of Christian Family Life and Christian Education in the Home?

  iii What help would you like to have from outside your country in meeting these needs? [13]

Curriculum

The matter of curriculum seriously engaged the interest of the association-council during this period. The more so because by now it was accepted by all that no single curriculum—the Uniform Lessons or any other system, graded or ungraded, prepared in New York, London, or any other center—could possibly meet the needs of a Christian education world, so wondrously and so bafflingly complex in its needs.

Addressing this problem, Forrest Knapp reviewed the history of the curricular services of the council, effective and otherwise, for the North American committee. The review recapitulated the developments reported in these pages.[14] Dr. Knapp's proposed line of advance was to make possible assistance to workers in the national councils desiring to prepare their own curricula. This auxiliary or enabling role was a radical departure from precedent. Knapp proposed the establishment of a supporting operation at the

New York office and also the London office, to the extent that it (London) felt itself able to extend such assistance. In any case, the help was to be extended in the name of the body as a whole.

Dr. Knapp was not alone in sensing this need and in proposing the kind of steps he saw possible to meet it. At the 1947 Birmingham assembly meeting, Chester S. Miao, the China secretary, articulated the same need:

> In the old days when many of us were pupils in Sunday schools, we studied the International Uniform Lessons. However, as different national units have become more and more conscious of their respective cultural and social heritages, there has been a growing dissatisfaction with the old scheme. The new demand is for each national unit to prepare its own material in accordance with its own spiritual and moral needs . . . no literature in Christian education can be called truly indigenous when it fails to take into consideration the cultural heritage of the people and the present-day moral and social conditions of the country.[15]

Turning from a description of a transition and a statement of need, Chester Miao indicated the type of services which might helpfully be given to its member units by the association (council). Chester Miao's address and Forrest Knapp's earlier suggestions met with favor as the Birmingham assembly heard a report of its Committee on Curriculum, urging more attention to this problem as a principal service.[16]

With the support of the Birmingham assembly, the North American committee and staff proceeded to prepare such guidance material. The first production was called *Preparation of Curriculum Materials* and was a twenty-eight-page booklet; it was the second in a four-part series called *Christian Education Guides*. The text was divided into nine chapters, following an introduction:

1. Suggestions for Using this Guide
2. Examining Your Present Situation
3. Characteristics of Good Curriculum Materials
4. The Foundations of Christian Education
5. The General Plan
6. Preparing the Outlines
7. Writing and Editing the Materials
8. Adapting Existing Materials
9. Preparing the People; Distribution; Revision.

This guide was widely used, and, as Dr. Knapp's successor took over the general work of the council and began assisting national and regional curriculum makers with his own personal professional service, the usefulness of this guide was extended, even though other written materials were later used to supplement it.

In late April and early May fifteen leaders from eight Latin American countries, together with consultants from the United States, met in Cuba as a Latin American curriculum commission. Good progress was made in preparing outlines for curriculum materials for Sunday schools of different sizes beginning with the very small.[17]

Schools and Colleges

In 1950 the council held a one-of-its-kind conference—a Joint Seminar on Church-Related Colleges, sponsored jointly by it and the World's Student Christian Federation. It was held in connection with the 1950 Toronto meetings, clustered around the Thirteenth World Convention. Moulton College of the University of Toronto was the site. Twenty-eight persons from thirteen countries attended.[18]

The conference was modest in size, but distinguished in the quality of its participants. Sarah Chakko of India was chairman (she was at that time one of the presidents of the World Council of Churches), Professor A. J. Coleman of McMaster University was the secretary. Most of the participants, limited in number to thirty persons, were college presidents, deans, or distinguished professors. E. Fay Campbell of the Board of Christian Education, Presbyterian Church in the U.S.A. was the executive and the inspirer of the gathering.

The conference dealt with the crisis of the Church college, including its economic existence, accommodation to the spirit of the age, and conflict with national cultures. A three-fold task was seen as imperative for the Christian college in whatever nation, culture, or set of circumstances it might find itself located: to win, train and develop for Christ and the church those students brought up in the Christian tradition; to provide for its students a community which, like the Christian home, will foster a sense of Christian vocation; to teach all courses of instruction so as to challenge the secularization of thought so common in the university world.[19]

The conference came down hard on cultural religion:

> Especially in the United States, but not only there, the place of democracy in social faith and practice bears a curious relationship to Christianity. On the one hand, the democratic ideals of liberty, equality, and fraternity have some kinship with Christian ideals, and contribute to a climate of opinion favorable to the Christian message. On the other hand, there is a tendency to corrupt the Christian message by identifying it with various creeds of political democracy or by deifying the "common man". . . . An industrial, capitalistic, metropolitan culture, with unprecedented media of mass communication, including radio and motion pictures, has blanketed culture, imposing its set of values which are often un-Christian. The people confuse bourgeois values with Christian ideals and make of Christianity a successful cult.[20]

As we have said, this was the only conference of its kind. Later in the year the National Protestant Council on Higher Education (U.S.A.) merged with other interchurch agencies into the National Council of Churches, finding its place in the Division of Christian Education. New interests and responsibilities engaged its time and energy. The concerns of the Christian college were not conspicuous in the W.C.C.E. The World's Student Christian Federation was generally entrusted with responsibility for issues in higher education, not only for student affairs. Accordingly, a combination of factors was probably responsible for the fact that no other conference on this subject was convened.

Conventions

The outbreak of World War II prevented further planning for the proposed Durban convention, and the continuing hostilities led first to the postponement and then to the cancellation of what would have been the thirteenth convention, the second to be scheduled in the southern hemisphere, the first on the continent of Africa.

MEXICO CITY, 1941

As it began to be clear that no world convention would be convened in the immediate future, the North American committee began to plan for some substitute. Taking care not to call it a world convention, the committee began arrangements for an international gathering in Mexico for 1941, designed for those who could attend. Obviously few, if any, from Britain and Europe were expected in that year with the German submarine blockade at its most effective stage.

A planning group met in Cuernavaca in the summer of 1940, with 137 persons involved.[21] As the larger meeting convened in Mexico City, there were 925 delegates present, 508 of them from Mexico, the host country. At least twenty-six countries were represented by one or more participants.[22]

While the "International Congress on Christian Education," as it was called, was not exclusively concerned with Latin American Protestantism, as was the case with most world gatherings, it did take on much of the texture of its surrounding culture. It seemed to have a considerable influence for the cause of cooperative Protestantism in Mexico, according to one experienced and informed commentator, Gonzalo Baez-Camargo:

> The Congress brought to the Mexican churches a word of encouragement . . . helped to win the recognition of the Mexican evangelical forces by the Government and people of Mexico . . . gave a tremendous impulse to evangelical cooperation in this country . . . the common study and plans and methods and the sharing of experiences have left the Mexican churches with a much wider horizon and a deepened consciousness of responsibility.[23]

A year later, influenced in part by the Mexico City congress and by his own trips in Latin America, Forrest Knapp presented a paper, "Some

Suggested Next Steps in Latin America," to his administrative committee. The "next steps" were five: the development of better plans for various agencies of Christian education; support to interdenominational literature committees; education for Christian service; fellowship; and personal counseling.[24] Full authorization of this ambitious program could not be given, until the Board of Managers or the Assembly was able to meet again. Reception by the North American body was, in the meantime, warm and cordial.

TORONTO, 1950

The thirteenth convention in Toronto in 1950 was a far larger meeting than the congress in Mexico City. In addition, there was an unprecedented cluster of meetings, most of them in Toronto, some of them in nearby cities, scheduled about the convention, some before it, some after.

These associated meetings included a Christian Education Study Institute, a Seminar on the Christian College, a Children's Workers' Conference, a session of the (North American) International Convention, a meeting of the Assembly, a meeting of the Board of Managers, and a meeting of the Joint Youth Department Committee.

It had been recommended in 1947 that the convention, the first since Oslo, should be in North America and Toronto was later chosen as the city. It was then decided that there should be an institute, a new type of meeting. The sequence should be: institute, convention, assembly.

These decisions were made, however, subject to some pulling and hauling on the part of the British committee, unconvinced after the decisions had been made that the plan was a wise one. The executive committee of the British administrative committee resolved, in 1949, that in view of the economic situation in Europe, the Near East and Britain, the Toronto convention, then far along in preparation, should be considered an "international convention," similar in status to the Mexico City congress of nine years before.

In a cable, Drs. Weigle and Knapp protested, and the North American business committee wrote the executive committee in Britain, explaining the reasons why the world convention could not be abandoned and why plans should continue on the basis of agreements already reached.[25] No records have been found indicating that the British executive committee reconsidered or retracted its resolution. The supposition is that it simply let the matter drop.

The convention was preceded by a careful preparation of study materials, an endeavor which extended well over a year before the convening in Toronto. Two principal documents were prepared: *Christian Education Today and Tomorrow, A Pre-Toronto Study Guide,* and *Christian Education Around the World Today.* The careful study of these documents by institute and convention delegates created an informed body of delegates, the first volume being a sourcebook in contemporary Christian education practices, and the second constituting a substantial encyclopedia on the church educational situations in more than forty nations.

The study guide, after explaining the purposes of the Toronto meetings, the nature of the guide, and how to use it, turned to a section on basic theory under the heading "Jesus Christ—Teacher and Lord," the theme of the convention. This section was treated in eight parts.

The second main section dealt with "Your Situation Today and Your Goals for Tomorrow." Five subsections on theory and principles of Christian education were followed by discussions of age group, societal groupings, leadership education, curriculum, help provided by national and world bodies, and other matters. It was a useful sixteen-page booklet.

The second piece was a more pretentious volume (over 300 pages in length). It set forth a survey of the actual situations in forty-two countries.

Each correspondent was asked to reply to a list of nine topics, responding in as full and comprehensive a manner as this person chose. The headings were: biblical, theological, and psychological foundations for Christian education; the scope and nature of Christian education; purposes of Christian education; principles of Christian education; the life of the people and the world in which they live; the Christian education of children, of youth, of adults; and Christian education in the home. The worth of such an almanac diminishes, of course, with the passing of each year; but when current, it was a handy compendium of information, conveniently arranged, and not available anywhere else in Christendom.

The work of the Toronto institute will be reported in a separate place in this chapter. It became the first in a series, which was repeated in 1958, in 1962, and in a modified form in 1967 and 1971. We continue here with the reporting of the convention proper.

So far as attendance was concerned, the Toronto convention was gratifyingly successful. The official report listed 5,044 registered delegates from sixty-two countries. The United States sent 2,957 delegates, and Canada sent 1,735. The fears of the British executive committee seemed to have had some foundation, for only 126 came from all of Europe, while Asia accounted for ninety-five.[26] Leadership was largely Anglo-Saxon and European—fifty-three out of eighty-seven.[27]

There were plenary sessions held in the evening at the Coliseum of Canada's National Exhibition Grounds, on Sunday evening in Toronto's Maple Leaf Gardens. In the mornings and afternoons there were divisional meetings; a general division and three age-group divisions, each meeting in nearby colleges, churches, and seminaries. The International Quadrennial Convention, which would have been held in 1951, was advanced one year, and consisted of one session on Tuesday, August 15.

An impressive feature of the opening night was the presentation to Lord

Mackintosh of the *Canadian Welcome Book,* bearing the names of more than 27,000 Sunday school persons from all over Canada. Representatives of the various provinces presented their provincial books, one by one, to the president of the convention. The books contained names and, associated with each name, was a contribution of a dollar or more, an expression of affection and unity on the part of the Sunday schools of Canada.

The executive in charge of local arrangements for all the Canadian gatherings was the Rev. Nelson Chappel, then secretary of the Department of Christian Education of the Canadian Council of Churches. His efficient and understanding services to delegates was one important factor in his later election as general secretary of the World Council of Christian Education.

It had been fourteen years since a world convention had met, a devastating world war had intervened, and the Toronto convention and related gatherings did much to restore to the council an awareness of its worldwide nature and mission.

Toronto Institute

An innovation in the planning of the Toronto meetings was the projection of a "World Institute on Christian Education," designed to be a smaller gathering of professional leaders holding responsible national positions. It was to meet for a sustained period of study and discussion immediately before the convening ·of the convention which, as was the case with its predecessors, had been planned as a popular meeting, appealing to lay teachers, officers, and superintendents of local Sunday schools as well as to trained professionals.

The institute measured up to most of what its planners hoped. There were 230 members and the regional spread was most impressive: Europe, fifty-six; the same number for Asia; West Indies and Central America, twenty; Canada, thirteen; South America, eighteen; South Pacific, four; Africa, fifteen; U.S.A., thirty-four; staff and part-timers, fourteen. Fifty-two countries were represented. The geographical distribution was more impressive than that of the convention itself, much more representative than the meeting of the Board of Managers, at which there were only two representatives of the younger churches. The institute met in three sessions daily for two weeks and three days, and was characterized by serious study, discussion, and writing. It was presided over by Principal A. Victor Murray, of Cheshunt College, Cambridge University, England.

In the closing sessions of the institute, reports were brought in by the twelve discussion groups which had been meeting during the past fortnight: Christian education of children, of youth, of adults, in the home, in the church, in the school; preparation of curriculum materials; preparation for service in Christian education; audio-visual aids in Christian education; the

Bible in Christian education; purposes and principles of Christian education; and denominational and interdenominational service. The twelve reporters came from ten nations and five continents—a wide span of backgrounds.[28] A subsequent evaluation included these statements: "a memorable experience for its members and had meanings which cannot easily be put into words"; ". . . a deep sense of responsibility for producing conclusions which would be useful to others"; ". . . a mind-stretching endeavor to consider subjects as broad as The Everyday Life of the People, The Wider World in Which the People Live, The Christian Conception of Man and His Salvation, The Gospel Message and the Christian Community, The Christian Conception of History." [29]

Assemblies

There were three meetings of the Assembly (Executive Committee or World Council, as it was formerly called) during this period of fifteen years, a remarkable sequence in the time of a world war:

LAKE MOHONK, 1940

The coming of a new general secretary to the New York office on September 1, 1939, naturally sparked many new interests on the part of the North American administrative committee, in spite of the outbreak of war in Europe on that same date.

One prompt result, with the freedom from preparing for the Durban convention, was a decision to hold an enlarged meeting of the administrative committee at Lake Mohonk, New York, in the spring of 1940. It was to be in the nature of a conference, with some official business included. The persons to be invited included not only members of the committee, but also representatives from denominational mission boards and competent Christian nationals and missionaries from abroad who were nearby at the time or could come especially for the occasion. For example: Dr. Chester S. Miao, general secretary of the National Committee for Christian Religious Education in China and Dr. Hachiro Yuasa, president of Doshisha University (and after the war, of the new International Christian University) in Japan.

Rather intensive preparatory work was done. A workbook was compiled containing information about Christian education in countries which the New York office was responsible for serving. Much of the meeting time was spent in small working groups.

BIRMINGHAM, 1947

The first postwar meeting of the governing body of the association convened at Westhill Training School, Selly Oaks, Birmingham, England. The Lake Mohonk meeting had been called during the war and there was not a representative attendance. For the first time since Oslo (1936), there was an opportunity for the assembling and the deliberating of a truly representative world body.

There had been suggestions from time to time in earlier years for a change in name. The matter had again been before the Committee of Reference and Counsel in 1929. It decided to postpone action until the executive committee met in June 1930. But no change was made.

In 1946 the matter came before the Board of Managers once again. A recommendation was made for the name "World Council of Christian Education." Some feared that this change in name meant altering the aims of the organization. But Dr. Weigle, at Birmingham, reassured them that the aims of the association would not be changed, because they had already been broadened.[30] The change of name, he said, was merely keeping up with the already evolving organizational situation.

Thus reassured, the Assembly voted to change the name, but with the subtitle, "Incorporating the World Sunday School Association." The matter seemed settled. But not for long, as we shall see in the following account,of the Toronto meetings.

Other actions of the Birmingham assembly included the reception of the Trinidad and Tobago Sunday School Union and an agreement that the next convention, the first after the war, should be in North America in 1950.

TORONTO, 1950

When the "Assembly," as it was then called, met in Toronto in 1950, it was understood that the "Assembly" took the place of the former "Executive Committee" and that the Birmingham meeting in 1947 was its immediate predecessor. It was composed of representatives of the member units of the council, with the number from each based upon the Sunday school enrollment in each individual nation.

The change of name voted at Birmingham had caused difficulty with some constituent units, and the British committee was especially disturbed at the change, feeling that a distinct loss had been incurred by dropping the words "Sunday School" from the name of the organization. This regret developed even though Sir Harold Mackintosh had made the motion for the change. Most of the members of the American committee had been pleased with the Birmingham action, but in order to achieve the greatest good for the organization, they were willing to consider a modification of the three-year-old action. A compromise was worked out, and the name became, for operating purposes: "World Council of Christian Education and Sunday School Association," with the legal name remaining: "World Council of Christian Education." The operating name was to be used until near the end of the life of the organization and, while cumbersome, did represent the full scope of the agency. It was also a symbol of its lack of organizational unity.

The Toronto assembly was also preoccupied with a growing realization of the bifurcated nature of the organization, and took steps to overcome it. (These endeavors will be described in the next section in the interests of a continuous narrative, though at the expense of chronology.)

An action was taken at this assembly which represented a break with past practice. Membership in the future was to be extended to church religious education agencies. From now on, the council was not to be composed exclusively of national councils or associations, though they would continue in numerical preponderance. It was to be a council of councils (associations) *and* church bodies.[31] A statement defining the scope of services to be offered was also adopted.

Both the proceedings of the institute and the convention received attention at the Assembly, its positioning at the end of the series of meetings making this review possible and natural. The reports of the institute commissions were to be edited and made available to the member units, the New York office assuming this responsibility. There was to be a short, popular report to be written by Dr. Baez-Camargo. A statement of needs was referred to the Board of Managers and the two administrative committees, and authorization was given for a special committee on the Bible.[32]

A European statement presented at the Assembly declared that both the institute and the convention had tried to do too much. Represented by J. W. van Kooten of the Netherlands' Sunday School Association, the Europeans said that too much time had been spent on details of program and not enough on basic principles. They also felt there had been too much emphasis upon geography and not enough on confessions, thus establishing a false basis for consensus when a more adequate one might have been chosen.[33]

A Canadian correspondent for the *Christian Century* (a nondenominational weekly magazine published in the United States) had another reaction. He wrote: "The cause and program of Christian education have been lifted to a new level." Then he outlined what the convention had brought to the 5,000 delegates under the theme, "Jesus Christ—Teacher and Lord." It was, he said, "a *world gathering* which brought, among other values, a full and varied program, the extensive use of visual aids, and the conviction that the task of Christian teaching in our world is a common task." [34]

At this Assembly Japan and India each invited the next convention to meet in their country. The time and place were referred to the Board of Managers with the recommendation that the next convention be held not sooner than 1955 and not later than 1960, and if 1960 is selected, consideration be given to holding regional conventions in the ten-year interim.[35]

Officers

There were not many changes in the principal officers of the council during this period. James Kelly was appointed by J. Arthur Rank as vice-chairman of the British committee, and Lord Mackintosh as its honorary treasurer.[36]

In 1950, the convention year, V. M. Koshy of India was elected to membership on the British committee, probably its first non-British member, and by the end of the year representatives from France, the Netherlands, and Denmark were also chosen.[37] The membership base of the British committee was broadening.

For the North American Administrative Committee, the chairmanship passed successively from Hugh R. Munro to William A. Shimer to Judge Lewis L. Fawcett and then to attorney Coleman Burke in 1953. That year, Gerald Knoff was elected chairman of the North American Program Committee.

Staff

NORTH AMERICAN OFFICE

The coming of Forrest L. Knapp to the New York general secretaryship of the council was a significant event, so important that the years of his tenure form the beginning and the ending dates of this fourth section of the history. For a year he was to work with Dr. Hopkins and then succeed him as the principal New York executive.

Dr. Knapp had been director of leadership education in the International Council, and had carried with this portfolio, responsibilities in research. Later, he was the part-time director of field work in that agency.

Before coming to the International Council, Dr. Knapp had been superintendent of religious education in the Cleveland Church Federation.[38] Dr. Knapp had received a Ph.D. in religious education from Yale University, and so became the first professionally trained general secretary in the history of the council. The earliest predecessors in the New York office had been laymen and, while Dr. Robert Hopkins was a minister in the Disciples of Christ Brotherhood, he was more of a skilled administrator and vigorous promoter than a professional educator. Soon, the quality of the material issuing from the New York office attested to the competence and statesmanlike qualities brought by the new incumbent.

Before long, Dr. Knapp surrounded himself with a number of staff members in the New York office. Jennie M. Doidge came as associate secretary in September 1942 to carry a variety of functions, including fund raising. She left at the end of 1944 to continue graduate study. E. Harold Bredesen joined the staff to direct public relations, but decided to leave to enter a more personal type of ministry.

While these two individuals gave short-term service, 1946 and 1947 saw the accession of two men who remained for much longer periods. On September 1, 1946, Erich F. Voehringer, with missionary experience on the Gold Coast of Africa, came as associate secretary. He held, in addition to a divinity degree, a Ph.D. in African languages and anthropology from the

University of Berlin. Everett M. Stowe was added to the staff on November 1, 1947, as associate secretary with particular responsibility for serving the Joint Commission on Christian Education, referred to elsewhere in these pages. A graduate of Boston University School of Theology, he had a doctor of education degree from Columbia University. He had done some general missionary work in China, was director of religious education for a section of the Methodist Church there, and was a professor in the School of Education and acting dean of Foochow University.

Dr. Knapp apparently found it difficult to fill the post of associate for public relations and finance, lacking adequate funds for such work. After Mr. Bredesen's departure, North Callahan came, made one report, and left in about a year to work for Cornell University. Then E. Earl Breon began this work in June 1948, only to leave after the Toronto convention.

In 1947 Dr. Knapp and James Kelly were reelected as general secretaries during the course of the Birmingham assembly. Phillip C. Jones joined the staff in 1949 as associate secretary for the Toronto convention, coming to this position from long service as director of Christian education for the Madison Avenue Presbyterian Church in New York City.

Miss Wilmina Rowland joined the staff on March 16, 1949, at first for part-time service, but soon for full-time, as associate secretary for youth work. Her major immediate task was to prepare for the youth work aspects of the Toronto convention. She had earned degrees from Union Seminary in New York and from Yale; had taught missionary children in China; had acted as traveling secretary for the Student Volunteer Movement (United States); and had been professor of religion in the Woman's College of the University of North Carolina.

By the time the Toronto assembly met, Dr. Knapp was able to enumerate his New York staff as follows: Marie E. Wissel, secretary; Erich F. Voehringer, audio-visual aids; Everett M. Stowe, World Fellowship in Christian Education and Study and Research; Chester S. Miao, field service in east Asia; W. Earl Breon, public relations and finance; Phillip C. Jones, 1950 convention; and Wilmina Rowland, youth work.[39]

In early 1947, Dr. Chester S. Miao accepted an invitation from Dr. Knapp to become a part-time associate secretary to provide field service for the association to the countries of east Asia other than India. Dr. Miao held a Ph.D. in religious education from the University of Chicago, and had participated in several world gatherings of the W.S.S.A. and other world meetings. He was to serve the association with a third of his time.

Chester Miao was not able to be present at the Toronto meetings because of political restrictions, but the assembly received a greeting from him as he sent his prayer for the Assembly: "'Paul's words sound good today; namely 'But take heed, lest by any means this liberty of yours becomes a stumbling block to them that are weak.' "[40] The years ahead were to bring great deprivation to Mr. Miao, with little abatement until his death.

In December 1953 Erich Voehringer resigned to become professor of Christian education at the Lutheran Theological Seminary (Mt. Airy, Pennsylvania), and in April of the next year Marie E. Wissel received a well-deserved advancement when she was made administrative assistant.[41]

As an outcome of Toronto discussions, Nelson Chappel was secured to become the general secretary of a yet-to-be unified organization, to take up duties on September 1, 1953. Philip Jones was to serve as the acting Executive of the New York office from March 1, 1954, until a successor to Dr. Knapp could be chosen.[42]

BRITISH OFFICE

In the office of the British Committee during this period there were also a number of staff changes. F. R. Morrish had served the committee in deputation work and in fundraising, but not with the success anticipated, and there was a separation in 1949. Percy N. Corry became the staffperson for audio-visuals in 1948, but his services were terminated in 1949. Then Edgar G. Youdell came as associate general secretary with a major responsibility for audio-visual aids. He was a graduate (M.A.) of Mansfield College, Oxford, had served as a pastor for five years and as a lecturer at Gaddesden Training College.

Generous grants from J. Árthur Rank made his services possible.[43] With similar generosity, Mrs. Clifford S. Heinz, a daughter-in-law of Henry J. Heinz, carrying on a family tradition of support and involvement in the cooperative teaching task of the churches, made possible services in New York from Erich Voehringer.[44]

By far the most important change in the staffing of the British office came when James Kelly relinquished the general secretaryship, after twenty-five years in that position. His departure from the salaried position brought up long thoughts in the British committee as it reflected upon the quality and variety of his service:

> The Protestant Churches of Europe were guided by his counsel into a united effort to further Sunday school work. What was begun in war-stricken regions of an earlier day was continued through the years of an uneasy peace and has outlived a second holocaust. What was begun as an adventure of faith has become an experience in fellowship in the Continents of Africa, Asia and Europe . . .

> . . . We recall his selfless devotion to the cause of the Gospel, his balanced judgment, and his quiet faith. His body may have paid the price of such devotion, but his spirit is reaping the reward.[45]

A report from Europe testified to his solicitude and tirelessness:

. . . Dr. James Kelly even after Munich, hurried to the dismembered Czecho-slovakia to encourage the bleeding hearts of the Sunday School workers. We shall never forget his fatherly interest in those dreadful days. Through Mr. Loertscher in Switzerland he tried to remain in touch with us, but the Gestapo soon discovered the connection and persecuted for it the leader of the International Bible Reading Association, Rev. Lanstjak.[46]

At the assembly meeting in 1950, it was voted to accept the resignation which indeed had already taken effect, and it was declared that:

No minute can express the affection and regard in which Dr. Kelly is held personally by all members of the Board [of Managers], nor can it ever put on record its full appreciation for the great services he has rendered to the Council in building up the work of the British Administrative Committee from very small beginnings over twenty years ago.[47]

Kelly was quickly made the vice-chairman of the British committee and, accordingly, his accumulated experience and background continued to be at the disposal of the council.

At this time a selection was made of a successor: the Rev. James Turnbull was elected general secretary for the British administrative committee. Turnbull, like James Kelly, was a Scot, and held an M.A. from Glasgow University. Unlike Kelly, he was a Baptist. He had previously been a missionary and headmaster of a school in Peru. His (1948) election was confirmed by the Toronto assembly.

Field Services

Field Services during this period were no longer conspicuous activities of the officers of the council. That role was performed by the staff; and, since the number of the New York staff was growing, those persons carried on the greater amount of field visitations.

A large amount of field service was undertaken by Forrest Knapp during this period, and some was also shared by the associate secretaries in the New York office. Dr. Knapp sought to do careful planning by correspondence with leaders in the countries to which he was going so that the energy, expended by all involved, would be multiplying in its effects. He was less interested in making speeches than in sharing in planning by the responsible leaders of the national, interdenominational agencies. Decisions for constructive next steps to meet local needs, and information as to how the World Council of Christian Education could help, were among his tests of success. He thought of a field visitor as a channel for exchange of information between countries and as a catalytic agent to stimulate new endeavor. Dr. Knapp was especially mobile in South America (four trips), in Africa (two trips), and in Asia (one trip). At least thirty-seven countries were visited during his administration, some several times.

James Kelly found that his great task was to assist in the rebuilding of the Sunday school associations and the churches devastated by the war. It was a responsibility for which he was fortunately equipped by his experience following the close of World War I. One imagines that many memories must have come to him as he made his way, in the 1940s, to nation after nation, recalling similar journeys made twenty years before.

In 1943, while the war was still going on, the British committee felt a postwar fund of at least £25,000 should be raised for reconstruction. Kelly, in proposing this goal to his colleagues, reported that he had himself already raised over £5,000 and had "intimations of promises" of £3,400 in addition.[48]

This desire, and the need for discussion of common concerns, led to a proposal that James Kelly be brought to the United States for consultation and fund raising:

> It was reported that Dean Weigle and the general secretary [Knapp] had presented a request to the British Ministry of Information to bring Dr. James Kelly to the United States for a period of about six weeks early in 1943 for conferences with American members of the Association, and to present to American audiences some information regarding the present Christian education situation in Great Britain and Europe. It was
> VOTED, that if the British Ministry of Information accedes to the request, the North American Administrative Committee will care for Dr. Kelly's expenses while in the United States, it being assumed that there will be some income toward his expenses as a result of the speaking engagements arranged for him.[49]

By the autumn of 1943, Kelly was in the United States. It should be remembered that, in December 1942, submarine warfare against Allied shipping in the North Atlantic was deadly, more than 7,000,000 tons of shipping having been lost by the end of July 1941. While much of the German *Luftwaffe* was busily engaged in combatting the recent invasion of North Africa by the American and British expeditionary forces, the skies over the English Channel and over Great Britain were neither quiet nor friendly. For Kelly to be willing to make such a trip in such a wartime period was a testimony to his commitment to the cause he loved and served.

Kelly desired also to visit the Near East "as soon as circumstances permitted," hoping to call a few small regional conferences there and in Europe.[50]

This concern of the British for the post-war reconstruction of Christian education work was shared by those on the other side of the Atlantic. *A Memorandum of Understandings* between the General Secretaries was recorded in 1943 which included the following points: The Association was "to help in the reconstruction of institutions which are directly concerned with children and adolescents." Toward this end, a World Fellowship in Christian

Education was to be established in New York City. It was to serve an interpretive and promotional role. There was to be a proposal for a worldwide study of Christian religious education sponsored by the W.S.S.A., the International Missionary Council, and the Provisional Committee for the World Council of Churches—Dr. Knapp to take the major responsibility.[51]

Out of the proposal for a world fellowship came occasional bulletins and, after a time, the quarterly, *World Christian Education*. To assume responsibility for the worldwide study, Everett Stowe joined the North American staff.

One approach in the interests of this postwar reconstruction fell on its face. Forrest Knapp had expressed a desire to ask King George VI and Queen Elizabeth of Britain, King Haakon of Norway, Queen Wilhelmina of the Netherlands, and other royal persons to become members of a World Christian Education Fellowship. The British leaders took an exceedingly dim view of this proposed venture:

> The Secretary [Kelly] stated that Sir Harold Mackintosh and he had given very careful consideration to this matter some time ago. They knew, of course, that no such approach could be made to King George and Queen Elizabeth, and they questioned the wisdom of approaching the other Royalties suggested. After full consideration the Committee decided to intimate to Dr. Knapp that they did not think it wise to approach such Royalties and to seek statements commending the work of the W.S.S.A. It was one thing to solicit the patronage of a Crowned Head for a National gathering in a particular country, it was an altogether different thing—and a by no means easy thing in these days—to solicit the patronage or support of a Crowned Head for an International and Inter-racial movement.[52]

And that was the end of that proposal!

Dr. Kelly went, in late 1946, to Norway, France, Holland, and Czechoslovakia, discovering great need everywhere for Sunday school and youth literature. Returning, he was able to enlist help in meeting such needs.[53] James Turnbull spent a part of May 1949 and the greater part of June in Sweden and Finland. Earlier he had been in France.

By the time of the Toronto convention, Forrest Knapp, in writing a chapter in a compendium, delineated his concept of the current program of the council. Field visitation by secretaries headed the list of eleven activities. The holding of world conventions was number eleven.[54] In his mind, at least, there was a marked change of priorities, even admitting that there was considerable overlapping in some of his items.

It is interesting to read of a report by Wilmina Rowland as she reported on the work of the youth department in 1953. She recounted:

> . . . that Philip Potter, a pastor in Haiti and active in the Youth Department Committees of both the W.C.C. and W.C.C.E. had been asked by them to make

a trip to West Africa, visiting Nigeria, Gold Coast, Angola, Liberia, Sierra Leone. She said he had done a remarkable job in these countries, getting at the root of the problems and bringing back some interesting challenges.[55]

This may have been Philip Potter's first trip to Africa, but it was not his last. A quarter of a century later, he was still "getting at the root of problems and bringing back some interesting challenges," as general secretary of the World Council of Churches.

Activities of the Regional Committees

As has been the case in earlier periods, much of the actual program services of the association-council was carried on under the supervision of one of the two regional committees. Since this present period included the years of World War II, when travel was severely curtailed—impossible across the Atlantic and Pacific—the functioning of the two separate administrative committees tended more and more toward virtual independence. We look at each in turn.

NORTH AMERICAN ADMINISTRATIVE COMMITTEE

In 1940, the New York office moved from 51 Madison Avenue (the Metropolitan Life Insurance Tower) to 156 Fifth Avenue. The move was made, primarily, to be near the offices of the Foreign Missions Conference of North America, with which a close consultative relationship was needed. It was not long before something closer than a consultative relationship was being advocated. A few persons in the F.M.C. said the North American Administrative Committee should become a committee of the F.M.C. The view of Forrest Knapp, and some others in the W.S.S.A., was that the F.M.C. should become a member unit of the W.S.S.A., paralleling the International Council of Religious Education. Finally the latter view prevailed, and constituent membership was applied for and enthusiastically granted.

A conference on Christian education for world order was held in 1943 in Pennsylvania, with seventy-three persons from twenty countries attending. Another conference, in Ohio, was held the next year, its concern being Christian youth work. Forty-three persons from nineteen nations took part in this meeting. A Western hemisphere Christian youth conference was held in Havana, in 1946, sponsored in part by the W.S.S.A.[56]

A conference was held in Schwenksville, Pennsylvania, in 1952, concerned for the training of missionaries and foreign students for Christian education. The resulting document, after setting forth a general view, indicating the training needed, and suggesting the means of available training, set forth specific suggestions for the work, the needed training, and the means of training for general evangelistic workers and pastors, for specialists in Christian education, and for agricultural, industrial, urban, and medical workers, along with teachers and administrators in educational institutions and hostels. The conference was sponsored jointly by the North American Administrative Committee and the Committee on Missionary Personnel of the Division of Foreign Missions of the National Council of Churches, U.S.A.[57]

Remembering that the complex series of Toronto meetings in 1950 was also under the administration of the New York office, it is clear that the administration of conferences during this period was a heavy responsibility for the American staff.

The administration of conferences and other meetings was not at all the only activity of the N.A.A.C. In 1950, for example, grants-in-aid were given. Field Service, scholarship assistance, and study and research were carried on. The world fellowship, *World Christian Education,* audio-visual aids, *Pictures for Children Everywhere,* curriculum preparation assistance, and youth work were administered by the New York office.[58]

In 1951 there was a proposal made for a special conference on religious education in the Belgian Congo and, that same year, the Christian Council of Nigeria voted to set up a youth board which was to be an information gathering body and a potential convener of youth conferences.[59] Both of these ventures were encouraged by Dr. Knapp during the course of a long trip in Africa.

In the same year, Dr. Knapp posed four basic program questions for his committee to consider:

1. What are the major local needs?
2. What provisions should be made for denominational and interdenominational service?
3. What help, if any, is needed from outside each country?
4. Who is to provide the help? [60]

In the months preceding 1953, a substantial amount of time in the New York office was given to the preparation of a series of booklets, the Christian education guides. Forrest Knapp was the chief writer. Nothing like these documents had ever before been prepared, with national and regional groups within the Third World particularly in mind.

The first was called *Planning the Local Program of Christian Education.* There were sections on the Christian education of the familiar three age groups, and on Christian education in the local church, in the home, in the school, and through press, cinema, radio, and television. A summary, a synthesis, and suggestions for next steps brought the booklet to a conclusion. The guide was, however, more than a "how-to" booklet. Earlier sections dealt with basic foundations and theory.

The second guide has already been reviewed in connection with the discussion of curriculum. The third was titled *Preparation for Service in Chris-*

tian Education. Ten sections dealt with the following topics among others: motivation for service and training in Christian education; characteristics of a good training program; aims of the training program; and methods, agencies, and materials.

Planning Denominational and Interdenominational Service was the title of the fourth guide. Some of the topics treated were: examining your present situation; the program of service in the future; stimulating concern and spreading information; and finance in denominational and interdenominational service.

The Division of Foreign Missions of the National Council of Churches became a member unit of the W.C.C.E. in 1953, taking its place alongside the Division of Christian Education of that Council, successor to the International Council of Religious Education.[61] Its entrance vastly strengthened the work of the W.C.C.E. as it provided informed people for its work, persons much more knowledgeable about the work of the church in the developing nations than were most associated with the Division of Christian Education. The new alignment symbolized the significance of the Christian education movement in the foreign mission program of the churches.

In 1953 Dr. Knapp recorded many activities of the New York office. Participation in the World Conference of Christian Youth at Kottayam, Travancore, India, was noted; in the work of the World Christian Youth Commission; and in meetings of the youth department committees. Two South American institutes had been held, one in Santiago, the other in Sao Paulo. The quarterly magazine, *World Christian Education,* had been established and published. Letters and packets had been sent out on vacation church schools; audio-visual aids; youth work; Christian education in schools; adult work; home; and Christian education in theological seminaries. Evaluations of audio-visual aids had been distributed; an exchange of children's workers had been carried on; the ''Pictures for Children'' project had been administered; and the Christian education guides were in preparation.[62]

BRITISH ADMINISTRATIVE COMMITTEE

Judging from the available records, the British Administrative Committee, during this period, was chiefly involved in two endeavors: the reconstruction of the Sunday school forces in continental Europe and the personal visitations and travels of James Kelly. Perhaps it could be said that there was mainly a single involvement, the second being auxiliary to the first.

In 1941 Kelly reported:

> In these days of War it is difficult for us to remember that in Germany there are still Christian men and women who have refused to allow their love of country to take the place of the worship and service of God. These German Christians need our prayer in these days for their lot is indeed difficult. The Confessional Church has carried on against extreme opposition though the extent of this

varies in different parts of the Reich. . . . The number of Confessional Pastors known to be in prison is twenty-six, but very many more have to suffer the even greater hardship of being nominally at liberty, but not allowed to preach or teach.[63]

The next year, the Netherlands having been invaded, Kelly wrote:

Special prayer meetings take place and prayer for "all the needs of Christendom" is made with a reality hitherto unknown. One hundred Pastors of the Dutch Reformed Church have been arrested since the invasion of Holland, of whom seven have died in concentration camps.[64]

After the war was over the task continued, and financial assistance in the undertaking was secured.

The task of reconstruction is the outstanding need in all Christian work today. This is more vital in those countries which have been ravaged by the War. The World's Sunday School Association's British Committee is cooperating in this great task particularly as it affects youth on the continent of Europe. . . . For this purpose the World's Sunday School Association's British Committee inaugurated a special fund for relief and reconstruction, aiming at a total of at least £25,000. It is encouraging to report that that target has now been passed.[65]

During much of this period, a serious difference in viewpoint arose between the British committee and its American counterpart; and also between the British committee and the organization of the council as a whole, as it took actions in its assembly and Board of Managers. Illustrations of this divergence follow.

As Forrest Knapp matured plans for the World Christian Fellowship, he told of the plan and invited British participation in it. This venture of public relations, interpretation, and educational re-enforcement was received coolly by the British. Its recorded action was that, after careful consideration, the proposal should lie on the table so far as it was concerned.[66] This action was not, after all, of major importance. Different countries have had different opportunities, different limitations, different ways of working, and the declination may have been well justified.

The next incident was more serious in its revelation of disunity. After the Toronto convention had been authorized by the council, after the plans were well advanced, the British executive committee requested that the meeting be reduced to the status of an international convention, representing only the United States and Canada. There was an exchange of views in 1949, and the British proposal was not approved. So far as I have been able to ascertain, there is no record that this appeal was authorized by the British administrative committee nor that it was reported back to it in 1949 or 1950. The loss, or the absence of the minutes of the British executive committee, makes it impossible to say why this extraordinary request was made or who originated it.

The Birmingham assembly, after careful thought and discussion, voted, in 1947, to establish a youth department. Less than three years later, the British committee decided to seek a reversal of this action. The recommendation reached the Board of Managers.[67] It was not approved, and the permanency of the youth department was assured.

The name of the organization proved to be divisive. The British were unhappy with the decision of the Birmingham assembly, changing the name of the organization from World's Sunday School Association to World Council of Christian Education. At the meeting of the Board of Managers in London in 1946, Sir Harold had asked if the time had not come to enlarge the name of the W.S.S.A. Next, Robert Denholm, general secretary of the National Sunday School Union for England and Wales, suggested as a new name, "World Council of Christian Education" with letterheads, documents, and literature carrying prominently the words "incorporating the World's Sunday School Association." This suggestion by Mr. Denholm was accepted by the board upon the motion of Sir Harold, and recommended to the Birmingham assembly, including both the main change and the subline, and the assembly so decided.

This change, however, came to be unacceptable to many of those within the influence of the British committee. At its February 1950 meeting, the matter of the 1947 name change was brought up for discussion, covering some of the ground Hugh S. Magill had worked over many years before. Lord Mackintosh had recently been to South Africa, and reported that South Africans thought the change a mistake. Arnold Clark characterized the change as a "deplorable mistake." Lord Mackintosh reported that he had voted rather reluctantly for the change at Birmingham, and that he entirely agreed with Mr. Clark. In this agreement, Lord Mackintosh probably forgot that four years before the Birmingham assembly meeting he had, himself, proposed that the organization change its name to "World's Sunday School Association for Christian Education." (Perhaps the double wording, a variant of which was finally accepted, made the difference.) Accordingly, the double name, "World Council of Christian Education and Sunday School Association," was adopted at Toronto because most European member units were Sunday school associations, more or less independent of the churches.[68]

At the Toronto assembly, a far-reaching organizational decision had been reached—which will serve as much of the content of the next main chapter—a resolution to work toward a unified organization, with *one* general secretary at its head, and with each administrative committee clearly answerable to clearly defined bodies, the Board of Managers, and the Assembly.

Though again this was a considered action of the whole representative body, the British committee could not accept it as wise, and recorded its desire to return to the pattern of two equal general secretaries. In early 1950, J. Arthur Rank had been in the United States and had tried to reach the chairman of the board, Dr. Weigle in New Haven, but had been unable to do so. He was able to interview Forrest Knapp to ask him the implications of the action of the N.A.A.C. Knapp replied that the N.A.A.C. had a conviction:

> that under the present policy the W.C.C.E. is weaker than it should be and weaker than it would be with greater unity, and that it is handicapped in cooperating with other world bodies. The view was expressed that a plan which may have been satisfactory in the past is not necessarily adequate to the present.

Upon request, Knapp wrote down his understandings of the implications of the Toronto decision: the British and the North American committees would continue though perhaps with changed functions; fuller participation in W.C.C.E. policy and program by leaders in other parts of the world would be encouraged (pointing out that the Board of Managers' membership is almost wholly British and American, Knapp put forth his conviction that "the W.C.C.E. is not now truly a world organization in the way it functions"); there would be one chief executive with a principal associate in New York and one in London (this person, Dr. Knapp thought, should not be an American). Knapp declared that the chief need was for the W.C.C.E. to study the issues involved.

When Lord Rank reported back to the British committee the exchange of views, Lord Mackintosh questioned whether Knapp's ideas could be put into practice. Norman Goodall stressed the importance of a wide range of nationals on any policy committee, and Rank agreed that the Board of Managers could be made more representative. Alexander McLeish made the sage comment that the underlying question had to do with two concepts of function. All comments, the record says, were critical of the American position.[69]

The outcome of the meeting was a recommendation that a new name should be either the "World Council of Christian Education and World's Sunday School Association" or "World's Sunday School Association for Christian Education." As a result of the discussion in Toronto, a double name was agreed upon, though not quite in the wording the British committee had recommended.

An unintended revelation of the differences between the two committees comes in examining the covers of the booklets setting forth the work of the British committee. The books of 1947, and from 1949 to 1953 inclusive, have covers bearing photographs of children, always little children. There are no pictures of junior-high age children, none of young people, none of adults, none of families. These representations occurred at the time the American committee, and indeed the organization as a whole, was vigorously broadening its concerns for the Christian education of persons of every age group, and in every kind of social grouping.

A geographical change took place in 1948 as James Turnbull succeeded James Kelly in the British office and the headquarters were moved from Glasgow to "Annandale," Golder's Green, London, a building owned by the British Student Christian Movement. The Glasgow office continued but only for the purposes of financial solicitation, chiefly among Scottish givers.

The Quarterly, World Christian Education

Forrest Knapp, in seeking to broaden the constituency base and the financial base for the North American Administrative Committee, conceived the idea of amassing a list of persons who would receive frequent news about the program of the association and, in time, be induced to contribute to its work. These persons would constitute the World Fellowship in Christian Education. Such an effort was started in 1942, and occasional bulletins were sent out from the New York office. Members, meanwhile, had agreed to write a letter at least once a year, sending information about their work and paying $1.00 a year ($2.00 in the United States) to defray costs. By October of 1945, nine occasional bulletins had been mailed.[70]

That idea did not prove very fruitful for the purpose of developing a giving constituency, and a metamorphosis took place by which the World Fellowship in Christian Education came to be intended for key persons in Christian education throughout the world who were interested in international fellowship in the common task.

Growing out of these developments, by the beginning of 1947 occasional bulletins appeared bearing the name *World Christian Education,* and its inauguration was reported to the Birmingham assembly. Dr. Knapp was the editor at the outset, but before long responsibility for editing the quarterly was assigned to Everett Stowe, and he was responsible for its publication until the end of his service with the council in 1964.

By the time the Toronto assembly met, the magazine had commended itself sufficiently that it was made the official magazine of the whole council, not merely that of the world fellowship, or of the North American Administrative Committee. It was to be edited and published in New York, as heretofore, but with editorial consultants from other lands.[71] It contained articles on the theory and practice of Christian education; news items from various countries; preparation for and reports from world conventions and institutes; and reports and items of interest from other world bodies, such as the International Missionary Council and the World Council of Churches.

Through 1951, the emphasis of the magazine was on national, regional, and continental reporting. Thereafter, there were more general articles and, from the last quarter of 1951, there was a unifying theme for each quarter. There were book reviews in every issue, mostly of books in English, though there were occasional reviews (in English) of books written in French, German, or Spanish.

Most of the years of *World Christian Education* were to be in the next period, but here it may be helpful to see a classification of the special topics treated. In their entirety, they comprise an impressive worldwide compendium of reporting, the like of which exists nowhere else for these years:

Age Groups and Family Education

Learning for Life—Adult Christian Education	Fourth Quarter, 1951
The Home as Christian Educator	Fourth Quarter, 1952
Third World Conference of Christian Youth	Second Quarter, 1953

Bible, Theology

The Word in Our World	First Quarter, 1953
Teaching and Faith	Third Quarter, 1953

Nature of Christian Education

Evangelism through Christian Education	First Quarter, 1952
The Teaching Church in a Revolutionary Age	Third Quarter, 1952

Leadership Education

Leadership Education	Second Quarter, 1952
For Better Leaders	Fourth Quarter, 1953

The magazine was often criticized for the subsidy it required, criticisms coming frequently from members of the British committee. It continued through the period and on into the two next periods, though frequently under review about its value, its audience, and its general content. Many testimonies are on record, however, praising its worth, particularly in creating and nurturing a lively sense of a worldwide fellowship of Christian educators.

Audio-Visual Services

The postwar years were characterized by an immense amount of interest in audio-visual resources for Christian education purposes. Part of the interest had grown because of the employment of such devices in the military, some of it because of the success secular education had experienced with such aids to learning.

In British Sunday school circles, much of the impetus came from J. Arthur Rank, who had been vigorous in promoting the use of audio-visual materials in his own Methodist denomination and among the churches served by the National Sunday School Union in Britain.

At the meeting in Birmingham, presentations were made by him and by Dr. Erich Voehringer who had, the September before, been brought to the New York office for leadership in this work. In the course of the ensuing discussion, it was voted to establish a department of audio-visual aids, with a staff of at least one secretary each in New York, London, and Geneva. The department was to serve as an information center, to provide counsel, and to promote wider interest.

It was announced that Lord Rank would provide a secretary for the London office, and Mrs. Clifford S. Heinz then arose and said that she would provide funds for a secretary in the New York office.[72] No "angel" appeared for a Geneva installation, therefore nothing came about in that city.

Dr. Voehringer was already at work in New York, and the British committee began its work in this field, first with Percy Corry, then with Edgar Youdell. Some research had been done at Westhill Training College in the use of audio-visuals in the curriculum. (Youdell was an Oxonian M.A. [Mansfield College].) Things seemed to be off to a good start in London.[73]

In Britain and in the countries associated with that office, Youdell was a useful person for consultations on the field relating to the practical uses of audio-visual aids in the teaching program of the church. He was also interested in basic research. In 1953 he studied the use and effectiveness of visual aids in Christian education. The conclusions may seem obvious to us today. They were not so commonly accepted twenty-five years ago.

1. The good teacher is the most important factor in learning.
2. Increased effectiveness comes with use of both films and filmstrips.
3. Films must be integrated into the session.
4. The effectiveness of a film seems to rise with the age of the group, the effectiveness of a filmstrip seems to remain static from about age 8 upwards.
5. Color is important only if it is of first class quality.
6. Assistance in installment buying would be welcomed by many churches and schools.
7. A central film and filmstrip library should be set up.
8. There is an urgent need for training in utilization.
9. The W.C.C.E.S.S.A. Evaluation Service needs expansion.
10. Joint viewings of both films and filmstrips should be set up.
11. Inquiry should be made of the provision of film-slides.[74]

Another study, made at about the same time, dealt with the use of films in evangelism.

An evaluation service was begun in New York and, by early 1948, a group of missionaries and nationals from abroad had reviewed well over one hundred motion pictures, film strips, and slide sets.[75] Subsequently, several articles appeared in *World Christian Education* giving information on the latest developments in equipment and procedures for use of visual aids.

The Board of Managers

Even through the war years, the services of the association to its member units continued, though on a reduced scale. There were some readjustments of responsibility made or considered during the period. In 1943 it was reported that the South African association had requested it be related to the British administrative committee, and it was suggested that Ceylon be placed there as well. No action was taken, probably because a full meeting of the Board and the Assembly was impossible.[76] In the case of South Africa, a second reason for delay was seen—a visitation by Forrest Knapp already being planned. The restoration of the Greek Evangelical Church to the British committee was also sought, and an informal meeting of the board of managers, held in New York, agreed to recommend this change to the N.A.A.C.[77] Later, the shift was made.

Luther Weigle reported to the Birmingham Assembly that, at the Board of Managers' meetings in 1940 and 1946, three national units had been elected to membership: one a church body, Synod of the Evangelical Church in Guatemala; the other two interchurch agencies, the Confederation of Evangelical Churches of the River Plate and the Evangelical Alliance of Angola.[78]

The above dates should be explained by saying that there had been no full meeting of the Board from 1940 until 1946, when it assembled in London, the first step toward a resumption of the association's worldwide services. The 1940 meeting had been held at Lake Mohonk, New York, and welcomed Forrest Knapp as North American general secretary. After 1946 yearly meetings were held in Birmingham, 1947; New York, 1948; London, 1949; Toronto, 1950; and New York, 1952. Unofficial meetings took place in London and New York in 1949, 1951, and 1953.

In 1950, at the Toronto assembly, the Japan Council of Christian Education and the Korea Council of Christian Education were received into the membership of the council.[79] The Board heard a report from its previously appointed special Committee on Policy and Program.

During this period the Board approved two ventures involving relationships with other world Christian bodies. It decided to join with other ecumenical bodies in sponsoring the World Conference of Christian Youth scheduled for Oslo in July 1947; it also approved a proposal for the formation of a joint World Commission on Christian Education, to be composed of representatives of the World Council of Churches, the International Missionary Council, and itself.[80]

So far as composition is concerned, the Board of Managers remained almost completely Anglo-Saxon, continuing the pattern of the previous years, and that of the Committee of Reference and Counsel before it. At the Birmingham council meeting, for example, there were thirteen members;

seven of them were from the United States, four from Britain, and one from Canada. The remaining single person was from Czechoslovakia. A representative composition of the Board of Managers lay in the future.

Finance

Throughout this period, each administrative committee was largely responsible for raising and managing its own funds. One exception was a capital fund established by two bequests. Income from that endowment was divided equally between the two committees.

The needs which ought to be met by the North American Administrative Committee, as seen by Forrest Knapp in 1940, required at least $41,000. An analysis of the projected income indicated forty-three percent in individual gifts coming from about 650 persons, and eight percent coming from fifteen boards of Christian education and missions. No effort had been made to increase income from agencies. All of this persuaded Dr. Knapp that a new and vigorous fund raising effort was needed. The staff was creative. The program was expanding. New needs were felt. It was unthinkable that inadequate financing should limit the promising future.

Accordingly, Knapp proposed that new contributors be sought, that Sunday schools and churches be asked to increase their present giving, and that present and former donors be asked for increases.

In 1942 Dr. Knapp announced four new sources of income which he hoped would bring the financial resources of the North American branch of the association closer to its felt needs. To that end, there was to be inaugurated a plan for "World Religious Education Associates." He announced that twenty persons had already been secured. A company of "World Friends of Christian Education" was to be formed, and thirty-five persons had already joined. Contributions from denominational boards of Christian education were to be solicited and the assistance of foundations and endowments was to be sought.[81]

The next year Dr. Kelly arrived in New York on his wartime journey to the United States, pleading the need for the postwar reconstruction effort already referred to. He asked for a grant from the capital funds of the organization for this purpose. In response to his appeal, a grant of $10,000 was given to each administrative committee to be used for postwar reconstruction.

More productive than other efforts was an imaginative project on behalf of the North American Administrative Committee which enlisted the cooperation of Captain Edward V. Rickenbacker. He had been cast adrift on a raft during the war in the Pacific, and he testified later about the courage and steadfastness which came to him as a result of earnest prayer. His experience and later testimony had made a deep impression upon the American public and he had become something of a war-time folk hero.

Knapp succeeded in interesting Rickenbacker in the work of the W.S.S.A.; and he agreed to sign letters to 7,000 individuals and 2,000 corporations on its behalf. A promotional dinner at the Waldorf-Astoria Hotel in New York, with Princess Martha of Norway as the guest of honor, inaugurated the campaign. By the next April Dr. Knapp was able to report that the number of contributors had grown from 700 to about 6,500, and that the net gain on the mail campaign had already totalled over $30,000.[82] The North American Administrative Committee continued to harvest good fruit from this "Rickenbacker appeal" for many months afterwards, as contributors at annual intervals were asked to continue or increase their gifts. Much of the staff and program expansion of the North American committee was made possible by this campaign.

Statistics of Sunday Schools

I come now to a subject which gives me trouble—the statistics of the Sunday school movement. The difficulty is not with lack of material; figures are available in great numbers. The early friends of the Sunday school movement in America and in other countries were fond of figures. They loved to count, but whether they knew *how* to count is a debatable question.

Gathering statistical information is a twentieth-century skill, and even today the technique of gathering church statistics is something less than a scientific process.

The Yearbook of American Churches is perhaps as sophisticated a compilation as any, and great care is taken by its editor to ensure accuracy and reliability. Even so, the annual volumes of this publication bear words of caution. Those in the 1972 yearbook are typical: "A Guide for the User of Church Statistics" is prominently displayed at the beginning of the book. The editor reports that of the 236 denominations reporting, some have computerized data and accurate banks of information. Most assemble statistics by conventional hand methods. Many operate upon the basis of "educated guesses." Four major qualifications are advanced: church statistics are always incomplete and pass through many hands, some skilled and some unskilled; they are not always comparable; they are not always current; much important data (church attendance, socio-economic data, and participation records, for example) simply does not exist.[83]

If these caveats had to be sounded in 1972 for a body of data from two countries only (United States and Canada), how much more difficult is the task of reporting Sunday school figures from 1889 onward for scores of countries and denominations from every continent!

The development here will be simply to try to convey some of the fascination the Sunday school leaders, during these periods, had with figures. In the early years, generous blocks of convention time were given to the reporting of these figures, and deep satisfaction with them is recorded in the pages of the reports as audiences must have glowed at the numerical advances put before them.

The classifications of statistics were not always uniform, making comparable tabulations difficult. An illustration of the discrepancies in available figures is from the reported enrollment in the Sunday schools of the world in 1936, as reported at the Oslo convention. The convention book reported 34,139,624. Arthur Black, writing in *The Golden Jubilee of the World's Sunday School Association,* gave 37,285,000—a nice round number.

And in 1950, at the Toronto meetings, I was surprised at the figure reported for North America: 23,610,946. I had been responsible for gathering statistics for the International Council of Religious Education, figures reported by the denominations of the United States and Canada. The two totals did not agree at all, and no reasonable tabulation from Mexico would have made them come out any closer.

When I questioned where the figures assembled by the World Dominion Movement came from, Alexander McLeish, the compiler, did not attempt to justify his figures, but merely replied to me rather testily, "We have our own sources of information."

With these cautions, therefore, some statistics as reported to the convention or assembly from time to time are set down in comparable categories.

	Sunday schools	Total teachers and scholars
1889	183,390	19,715,781 [84]
1907	255,544	25,148,664
1910	286,000	28,011,194
1913	310,057	29,848,041 [85]
1920	287,426	30,296,531 [86]
1924	347,001	32,677,611
1928	356,146	33,014,952 [87]
1932	361,145	36,546,829
1936	369,510	34,139,624 [88]
1950	437,338	37,387,384

The enumeration of convention delegates was a much easier task and, allowing for some variations in defining just who is or is not a "registered delegate," the statistics for the several conventions probably are more reliable than the Sunday school enrollment tabulations.

In 1950 the Board of Managers agreed that statistics gathered by the World Dominion Movement "be published by the World Council of Christian Education." [90] From this year on, there was little attention paid to the compiling of statistics. The council had more rewarding work to do.

The account of this period represents a paradoxical impression that in perhaps the most difficult period of the association-council's history, some of

First Convention	1889	London	904
Second Convention	1893	St. Louis	882
Third Convention	1898	London	1,154
Fourth Convention	1904	Jerusalem	1,526
Fifth Convention	1907	Rome	1,118
Sixth Convention	1910	Washington	2,500
Seventh Convention	1913	Zurich	2,609
Eighth Convention	1920	Tokyo	1,814
Ninth Convention	1924	Glasgow	2,810
Tenth Convention	1928	Los Angeles	7,636
Eleventh Convention	1932	Rio de Janeiro	1,626
Twelfth Convention	1936	Oslo	2,700
Thirteenth Convention	1950	Toronto	5,044
Fourteenth Convention	1958	Tokyo	4,700 [89]

its most creative and restorative outcomes came about.

The war, of course, was the "great destroyer." The Durban convention was made impossible and, if the segregation problem had been successfully overcome and if an adequate program had been devised, it might have achieved significant results in divided South Africa. But this was not to be.

To say that the war destroyed the unity of the association is to say too much. By preventing trans-Atlantic and other contacts, however, such unity of aim and purpose as did exist was diminished. Inadequate clearances and infrequent consultations led to mistrust, frustrations, and the hampering of forward movement.

Still, with all the problems, the early fifties found the World Council of Christian Education a stronger and more vigorous body than before. The Toronto convention had brought a new vision. A youth department had been established. Youth relations with the World Council of Churches, though strained at times, remained effective. Programs in audio-visual Christian education were beginning. All over western Europe, Sunday school associations were responding to the organizational and pastoral ministry of James Kelly, who brought healing and reconciliation folded within his well-used passport.

Basic decisions had been hammered out at Toronto about the unity of the council, and in the next chapter we shall see what happened because these determinations had been made.

5

A Partially Unified Council
1953-1965

IN THE LAST CHAPTER, a brief reference was made to the growing uneasiness about the divided nature of the council, with its separation into two program and administrative units, which often operated independently of each other. The account was not developed, however, and was reserved for this chapter in the interests of telling the whole story in one place.

The efforts to achieve a greater unity in the organization were inseparably bound up with the administration of a new figure, Nelson Chappel. Formerly of Toronto, Chappel was called to a new position as general secretary, and was responsible for unflagging, though only partially successful efforts to bring New York and London to accept a common yoke, the better to till the world Christian educational field. The concentrated effort began in 1950, but there had been earlier, though sporadic, efforts.

Early Attempts at Unifying the Council

At the Zurich Convention of 1913 there was a resolution stressing the importance of a unified program but, at the same time, so emphasizing the autonomy of the two committees that it made program unity virtually impossible.[1] Forty years later, Nelson Chappel accurately described the gradual, but steady development:

> Each Administrative Committee had its own staff and budget and became more and more involved in initiating and interpreting the work and program of the world organization. The three thousand miles of distance which separated the two offices together with different emphases in Sunday school and youth work in Europe and America made it inevitable that the work of the WCCESSA was more and more divided into two programs, each largely created and administered by an Administrative Committee whose individual programs were usually effective only in that part of the world served by that particular Committee.[2]

A quarter of a century before the Toronto meetings, it was sensed that the dual structure of the association might be inadequate for its present needs.

The executive committee voted in 1926 that, "as soon as practicable," the headquarters should be located in Geneva, Switzerland; and that regional committees in such areas as North America, South America, Britain, Australia, and other places should be established. The legal headquarters should remain in New York City; there was to be a unified staff; and the convention of 1928 in Los Angeles was to ratify these radical proposals.[3]

At the next meeting of the executive committee, however, the headquarters were established in New York City, and no mention was made of a unified staff. Sometime during the winter and spring the proposals got the organizational axe. The convention approved the conservative substitute.[4]

Robert Hopkins brought the matter up again seven years later, in 1933. "The suggestion which has been made should be carefully considered that the World's Sunday School Association as 'the greatest movement in the world working for the spiritual education of the rising generation' should be ably represented in Geneva." [5] This time something happened, though the action could scarcely be called precipitate. A proposal was discussed at the end of 1936 to establish a Geneva office with Dr. Adolf Keller occupying it at minimum cost to the W.S.S.A. The space was to be in the old League of Nations building—the Palais Wilson—on the third floor, a little to the left of center, facing Lac Leman. Further discussion was held in early 1937, and in August of that year the British committee was asked to pay half the sum needed, an amount of $75 or $100 for each of the two committees.[6]

During the 1940s Forrest Knapp stressed the desirability of a truly unified organization and pointed out the inadequacies of the existing structure. In 1942, only three years after his election as North American secretary, he raised a basic question about relationships between the two administrative committees, parallel and equal in authority and responsibility. He expressed the hope that after the war they could be brought into much closer functioning relationships.[7]

Nothing happened, and a year and a half later Knapp tried again. He declared forthrightly that the dual structure "ought to be modified as soon as possible." He was not content with temporizing answers:

> To say that other ecumenical bodies confront and have only partly solved the same problem does not change the facts for the Association nor eliminate the need for something more satisfactory . . . the Association could be the means of world fellowship in Christian education in the fullest sense of that term, rather than being too largely a "foreign" missionary society.[8]

Again, in his 1945 report to the North American Administrative Committee, Dr. Knapp repeated his concern for a broad council "with appropriate organization and relationships." [9]

The next year the Board of Managers heard Knapp's convictions that there was needed:

> A conscious effort to modify the conception that the World's Association is chiefly a missionary outreach by Britain, the United States, and Canada, and

the further development of the Association into a full partnership of national and international bodies in which each gives and each receives.[10]

At the Birmingham assembly of 1947, with representatives of many national councils present to hear him, Forrest Knapp declared that "We should inquire of ourselves, now, and from time to time in the future, whether or not we have within our organization that measure of unity in organization, in policy, and in administration which makes for the greatest effectiveness and efficiency." [11] It was clear to those who were acquainted with his earlier utterances, that Knapp's answer to his own question was "No."

Whether from the needs sensed from the representatives of the member units at Birmingham, or in response to the prodding from Forrest Knapp, the Board of Managers decided to make a study of allocating to the two general secretaries those responsibilities which "need to be carried out for the Council as a whole." [12]

A committee reported a year later and assigned youth work to the N.A.A.C., audio-visuals to both committees, and authorized a General Policy and Program Committee to serve the W.C.C.E. as a whole.[13]

A New Structure in the Making

The structural innovation, the General Policy and Program Committee, was appointed early in 1950. Weigle served as its chairman, and a meeting was held in Toronto on August 7 and 8.

Meanwhile, the North American committee had given serious thought to the proposal and to the general future, and had advanced three possible plans, with a preference expressed for its Plan Three, providing for a unified staff and a more unified administrative structure.

On May 15, the British committee moved in a contrary direction. It recorded its desire to return to a position before the Birmingham assembly, to reconsider the decision taken there to establish a youth department, and to reconsider the new name, "World Council of Christian Education." [14]

Dr. Weigle seems to have been the initiator of the American proposal for a unified structure and program:

> He stated his willingness to have a person from Great Britain as general secretary to be located in the London office, and proposed that he be nominated by a Committee representing both areas of administrative responsibility. He proposed the continuance of two associates as "executive secretaries" to be located in the two offices.
> This proposal assumed that the general secretary would serve as the secretary of the Board of Managers and that the executive secretaries would serve as secretaries of the respective administrative committees.

In approving the proposal of Chairman Weigle, the Board of Managers voted to appoint a committee of six to explore this proposed unification—the members to be the president, the chairman, and two from each of the administrative committees.[15]

The proposal of the Board of Managers was approved by the assembly, work was to begin promptly, and a special meeting of the board was authorized to be called when necessary.[16] The assembly action did not settle matters, however, and critical discussion followed for many weeks.

In an attempt to defend the plan and to win British approval of it, Weigle outlined, for the British Committee, his reasons for support. He saw as advantages the enabling of the world association to increase the amount and effectiveness of its services throughout the world, and the possibility of a more effective deployment of personnel and resources. Dr. Weigle declared that a Britisher should be sought as chief executive, and that he should operate from a British base. In the ensuing discussion, Norman Goodall and Herbert A. Hamilton supported Weigle and the proposal. Negative reactions were recorded from members McLeish, Cowlan, Hayes, Kelly, and Miss Brown.

In spite of this, the British committee gave general support to the plan—one wonders, in view of the record, how it could have done so—and Weigle won the day for the ''Toronto reforms.'' [17] By the end of the year, it was possible to articulate three agreements: there should be one chief executive for the W.C.C.E.S.S.A., a staff under his leadership should be responsible for program, and the chief executive was to maintain relationships with other worldwide bodies.[18] Some earlier terminology had not survived. The title ''executive vice-chairman'' for the chief executive was discarded for the traditional wording, ''general secretary.'' The two executives in charge of the London and the New York offices were to be ''associate general secretaries.'' [19] The idea had originated with James Turnbull.

The title was of less importance than finding a qualified person, and a search was soon begun for such an individual, who was to have been a resident of Great Britain. Such a person had not been found by the time the Board of Managers met in 1952, and the search turned to other parts of the world.

In New York the searchers found their man—a Canadian by birth, training, and experience, and a well-known colleague. Nelson Chappel, elected in 1953 as general secretary of the W.C.C.E.S.S.A., had been a chaplain in the Royal Canadian Air Force during World War II. Born in Ontario, educated in Canada's midwest, he had become the secretary of the Department of Christian Education of the Canadian Council of Churches. In this capacity, he served as the host for the series of Toronto meetings of 1950, and won widespread appreciation for his efficient and understanding services to the 5,000 delegates from the sixty-two nations represented there. Soon after, he became general secretary for the John Milton Society for the Blind, and moved to its headquarters in New York City.

Chappel was well known to American leaders, but it was important that he have the confidence of British leaders of the council as well. Dr. Kelly interviewed him, giving him

> . . . a full statement of the background of the work and told him what the position was with regard to the General Secretaries so that there would be no misunderstanding if he felt disposed to accept the appointment. He had found him a most likeable and humble man.[20]

With support evident from both sides of the Atlantic, the Committee on Integration formally invited Chappel to the new position on July 23, 1952. Chairman Weigle followed this invitation by polling members of the Board of Managers on October 7.

It was specified in the call that Nelson Chappel was:

> . . . to provide executive leadership to the Assembly and the Board of Managers in the determination of policy, plans and budget for the Council and its Administrative Committees. He will . . . have ultimate responsibility as head of the Staff for administration of the policy and plans of the Council.[21]

Chappel accepted the position, agreed to begin on September 1, 1953, and at a meeting of the Board of Managers in New York on September 9 and 10, 1953, he was chosen.[22]

It wasn't long before Chappel had a confrontation in Britain which nearly occasioned a rupture. He tells the story in a letter to me:

> Jim Turnbull, who was opposed to the integration of the WCCESSA, had prepared a plan which he presented at my first meeting with the Executive of the British Committee (Lord Mackintosh, J. Arthur Rank and Dr. Kelly) apparently with their consent. His plan left the administration as it had been and I was to be largely a figurehead. I was taken aback and said to them, "If this is what you want, now is the time to make it plain; but this is definitely *not* integration. You are not stuck with me, as there are other things I can do." I told them that I had thought they wanted integration. Jim Kelly saved the day when he said, "You are quite right. This plan is not integration, and we are committed to integration." [23]

In New York, there was great satisfaction with these decisions and this election. The business committee reaffirmed its view that the North American share of the new expense should be a first claim upon income, and that other cuts would be made, if necessary, to provide it.[24] The North American committee voted to express appreciation for the step and to indicate its readiness to relinquish to the new world office responsibility for *World Christian Education,* the youth department, or any other present service.[25] The offer was repeated before the meeting of the assembly, held the next year in Frankfort.

The legislation at the special New York assembly in September, 1953, provided specific details for the new administrative establishment. There was to be an assembly, as heretofore, the governing and legislative body. While the program was to be unified, national member units were to be free to request, accept, or reject programs. The general secretary and the two associate general secretaries were to administer the program and the organization. Two administrative committees (British and American) were to recommend program to the Assembly, to administer specific projects, and to seek to strengthen national units. Christian education work, in new areas, was to be referred to the world office. Administrative committees were to nominate the associate general secretaries and other staff members in their respective offices, in consultation with the general secretary. Each administrative committee was to be responsible for the maintenance of its respective office and staff. When possible, administrative committees were to provide funds for the world office for overseas grants. The world office was to be the executive office for the assembly, and the Board of Managers. The world office was to prepare a unified budget in three sections: British, North American, and general. Present area responsibilities were to be retained for the present for reasons of expediency, but additional regional committees were to be created, if needed, in the future.[26]

With these provisions made, with the new title authorized, the two current general secretaries, Knapp and Turnbull, resigned and were reappointed as associate general secretaries with the New York and London offices as before. Chappel was elected at the special meeting of the assembly, in September 1953, and established his office in the same building, though on another floor, as the office of the New York committee, 156 Fifth Avenue.[27]

The organizational decisions of 1950 and the selection of Nelson Chappel in 1953 marked a distinct change in the self-understanding of the W.C.C.E.S.S.A. Notwithstanding the misgivings of the British committee, the direction was now set to achieve a unified program under a unified organizational structure, with a single administrative head. The general direction was rather more easily set than the necessary practical steps, but the decision was a most important one for the council's future. Chairman Weigle's hopes expressed the expectations of many: "The Council can be more truly a world-wide fellowship, and all its services will be more readily accessible to every part of the world." [28]

The World Educational Services Committee

It was seen, before long, that if there was to be a really unified program for the agency, there had to be a single program-creating and reviewing body. The Board of Managers, by this time, had too much on its hands to perform this role well and thoughtfully, and a new committee, responsible to the board, able to give time and thought to emerging and needed program, was essential.

Fortunately, the North American Administrative Committee had had such a body, and it had been working well for several years. A program committee had held its first meeting on September 12, 1945, with Eric M. North as its first chairman. Its program recommendations went to the North American Administrative Committee, and in turn and in time to the Board of Managers, and sometimes to the Assembly. Gerald E. Knoff had become the chairman by February 1951, and continued in this responsibility when he asked to be relieved in 1957. He was succeeded by David R. Hunter, in April 1958.[29]

The successful functioning of this New York program committee was seen as a possible model for the world body and, accordingly, a World Educational Services Committee was established in 1954.[30] The N.A.A.C. named to this body Gonzalo Baez-Camargo of Mexico, Alvin J. Cooper of Canada, Luther A. Gotwald and Gerald E. Knoff of the United States. The British committee recommended postponement of nominations until after consultation with the general secretary, but the board, at its 1955 meeting, approved the North American names, and urged the British to make their nominations as quickly as possible.[31] They complied, and named A. W. Andrews, Borge Forsberg, H. A. Hamilton, and J. K. Meir as their representatives. Forsberg was a Swede, the others were English. Luther A. Weigle presided at the beginning of the first meeting of the World Educational Services Committee, 1956, in London, turning over the chair to Gonzalo Baez-Camargo who was elected by it as its presiding officer.[32] The committee, thereafter, met each year immediately preceding the Board of Managers, and reporting to it.

With the new Educational Services Committee working well, with a general secretary in charge (in principle, at least) of the program of a unified organization, there was guarded hope that the W.C.C.E.S.S.A. had made significant steps in becoming one agency. The British committee felt that the three-way relationships had considerably improved by 1957, and one of the members of the Board of Managers reflected, at the close of the 1956 meeting, that "all the tensions within the W.C.C.E.S.S.A. have now gone." [33]

Nelson Chappel was not quite so sanguine and commented:

> I am glad to say that there is a great deal of truth in that remark, but the tensions will always be with us—tensions created by our past history—tensions created by the fact that the World Office is situated in New York and thus appears to be more clearly related to the North American Committee than to the British Committee—tensions created by the world situation itself.[34]

Chappel saw that the remaining problem was the not yet unified budget. It proved to be a difficult issue because of differing financial standards around the world, and he advanced this concern as a principal agenda item for the quadrennium, beginning with the 1958 Tokyo assembly.[35]

However, these achievements were not great enough to satisfy the North American committee which desired something more radical and impressive to show for the nine elapsed years following the decisions of the Toronto assembly, and the election of a single general secretary. It passed a motion which, after complimentary words about the achieved progress, called for more. The N.A.A.C.

calls upon the Board of Managers to study ways in which the work of the W.C.C.E.S.S.A. can be further integrated. In further integrating the work the suggestion of having more area committees than two might be considered. This matter should be brought to the attention of the Board of Managers.[36]

The Future Planning Committee

The timing was right, for the Board of Managers was scheduled to meet in Glasgow later that summer. The position of the North American committee was heard, supported, and an enabling action taken. A Future Planning Committee was created to

study the work of the W.C.C.E.S.S.A. in the light of its purposes, principles and policies; and taking into account its present relationships with other inter-denominational and ecumenical bodies, to prepare a program for developing and intensifying the work of the W.C.C.E.S.S.A. in Christian education in the life of the churches throughout the world and plan the financial support for this future program.[37]

The committee was to report through the World Educational Services Committee to the board, and Lord Mackintosh was named as chairman. Serving with him were to be Coleman Burke as vice-chairman, Luther Gotwald, H. A. Hamilton, James Kelly, Gerald Knoff, and the three principal staff persons.[38]

It was not possible for the new committee to meet soon as a whole and, as a consequence, separate meetings of the North American and of the British members were held, a pattern of work almost inevitably leading to the perpetuation and deepening of the very differences it was established to overcome.

In February of 1960, the British members raised further questions about the scope of the agency's work, and six weeks later the American members agreed that a statement of purpose for the organization should be broad and general and that it should not be limited to work with children, an often repeated conviction. Leadership education and assistance were seen as primary needs by both sections of the committee.[39]

The budget of the council proved, as expected, to be a stubborn problem. A staff report came in which indicated that it was not possible at that time to unify the budget and the council's financial operations. Some partial steps were proposed and approved.[40]

A more basic difference which made a consensus in this committee difficult was "Who is to be served by the organization?"—the same old and persistent cleavage. In February 1960, the British members

emphasized that we should always remember that the W.C.C.E.S.S.A. came into being primarily to care for the Church's work among children, and indeed is the only ecumenical body which is doing this. This should be in the forefront of our thinking and of our program. There were too many national church councils which did not appreciate the importance of this work nor were aware of the services of the W.C.C.E.S.S.A.[41]

Established in the summer of 1959, the committee met as a group for the first time in Berlin in 1960. The British committee had recommended a statement of scope stressing children and young people; the North Americans formulated a wording which did not refer to age groups. The Berlin meeting adopted a wording similar to the North American recommendations and the next year in New York a similar formula was approved.[42]

As the committee presented a resumé of its findings to the 1961 meeting of the board, it was cast in the form of a three-point program for the coming quadrennium—1962–1966—and was most modest in scope, compared with the spacious terms of reference given to it at its creation. The council was seen as "assisting churches in West Africa, West Indies, Chinese in southeast Asia, Burma and the Philippines with Sunday school and week-day schools curricula." It was to provide "further emphasis upon leadership training; and it was to encourage and assist the formation of organizational and promotional centres in Asia, Africa and Latin America." [43]

At this meeting of the board, Dr. Chappel reviewed the unsatisfactory and halting steps toward the unification of the program of the council, the responsibility to which he had been called:

.Originally we thought of the World Office as a central planning office where policy and program and staff work would be considered in consultation with the secretaries of the two Administrative Committees to make an integrated program for the W.C.C.E.S.S.A.; meetings of the Board of Managers, of the Assembly, and World meetings such as the World Institute would be the major administrative problems, and fund-raising would be left to the two Administrative Committees. However, as our program built up in recent years, the World Office, for various reasons, has undertaken more and more responsibilities for program administration.[44]

Dr. Chappel identified the several curriculum projects being carried forward with his assistance as the chief programs involved.

The Future Planning Committee really did not live up to its authorization. For the most part, the unsatisfactory situation continued, though now there were really three educational programs being carried on, each receiving official review only at yearly intervals.

New Proposals for an Integrated Council

Two years later, Chappel made a second try. This time he decided to bring recommendations to the board by way of the senior staff: the two associate general secretaries and himself. As these three staff officers analyzed the problems of the council, they saw a basic conflict between an area concept of its work, held largely in London, and a functional interpretation, dominant in New York:

> Our British Committee has tended to emphasize area responsibility and to question the right of staff members with functional responsibilities to make their services available "anywhere in the world" especially where they feel that these assignments have been given without full consultation with the whole organization and do not seem to be "under the direction of the World Office."
> The North American Committee has tended to emphasize functional responsibilities and to question the necessity of waiting until new program and staff appointments to serve the whole world have been acted upon by the whole organization, or of taking area responsibilities into account in giving service to the whole world.[45]

The most significant of the recommendations from the three staff members, going to the two administrative committees for review and comments were: all proposals for new programs are to be approved by the World Educational Services Committee and the Board of Managers before implementation; all executive staff appointments are to be made by the Board of Managers upon the recommendation of a small personnel committee; all program services are to be under the supervision of the world office, the general secretary being able to delegate administrative responsibility for a particular item; where existing or approved work is transferred to the world office, present financial support should be continued as long as possible; an equitable division of support for the world office should be arranged; and meetings of the finance committee of the council should be held during the period of the meeting of the Board of Managers with the two associate general secretaries present.[46]

From Dorking, England, where the secretaries' meeting had been held in 1963, the proposals went to the two administrative committees. As would be expected, there were agreements and divergences in their substantive responses, and the two committees differed also in the manner of their reviewing processes.

The British committee took up faithfully, one by one, the proposals from the staff. It stressed the role of the area committees as over against the World Educational Services Committee, it agreed in principle with the proposals for executive staff appointments, for program supervision by the world office, for continuing support for transferred work, and asked that the finance committee itself discuss financial support for the world office and the scheduling of its own meetings. The British committee also made some suggestions of its own: that the Board of Managers' meeting should be extended to cover four days; that an executive committee should be established to meet at half-yearly intervals between the sessions of the Board; and that both administrative committees should be consulted about new proposals.

The North American committee went about its task in a wholly different manner, feeling that the real solution of the problems of the W.C.C.E.S.S.A. went far beyond the recommendations of the secretarial staff. It made three main and eleven secondary recommendations. The three of prime importance were: transfer the world office with a unified program and staff to Geneva; call a special world assembly to consider reorganization of the council; and at this assembly carefully consider suggestions from both administrative committees and from all member units.

The accompanying eleven suggestions were: transfer both the North American and the British offices to Geneva; retain only a mailing address and desk space in the two cities; dissolve both present administrative committees, and in their stead create a North American and a British Interpretation and Program Advisory Committee; ensure that these two new committees have no administrative power and no program authority; treat the Churches' Television Training Centre in London as a special case; increase the membership of the Board of Managers to about fifty, and on a representative basis; increase the membership of the World Educational Services Committee to about thirty, of which sixteen should be members of the Board; the Board and the W.E.S.C. should meet once a year at the same place and near the same time, with the W.E.S.C. sessions preceding those of the Board; subcommittees of the Board were needed; so were subcommittees of the W.E.S.C.; and an executive committee of the Board and of the W.E.S.C. should meet midway between the annual meetings.[47]

As the Board of Managers met in Ottawa in 1963, it was clear that major and far-reaching decisions would confront it. The recommendations of the secretaries and the actions of the North American committee dealt with matters which might have been included under the terms of reference of the earlier Future Planning Committee, but which were not adequately faced and dealt with by it. The task remained.

Again, the Board voted to record its determination to unify the council by recognizing the final responsibility of the Assembly and the Board in the determination of policy, assignment of subunits, determination and supervision of program, budgets, and the appointment of all staff above office assistants. A planning committee was established with ten members, these persons to meet from July 13 to 18, 1964, in or near London.

It is true that most of these determinations had been expressed before, and all of them were either explicit or implicit in the actions of the 1950 assembly in Toronto, thirteen years earlier. Now, however, there was a new determination to carry through to completion the reforms and reorganization. This resolve was strengthened by the forthright statement of the situation by the general secretary: "In 1963 I reluctantly reported to the Board meeting in Ottawa that administrative difficulties had become so great as to make a more complete integration of the organization inevitable if it was to survive." [48]

Soon after the close of the Ottawa meetings, the membership of the newly constituted planning committee was named, and staff papers by H. A. Hamilton, Andrew Wright, and Nelson Chappel were begun. In early April of 1964, the chairman of the council, now Lord Mackintosh, and the chairmen of the two administrative committees met with the three senior staff members for purposes of discussion and common understanding.[49]

The planning committee met in Wimbledon, Surrey, England, for intensive work sessions in the spring of 1964, and as the report was completed it was clear that most of the general positions and specific points taken by the North American Administrative Committee had been supported, and that a radical change in the operation of the council was needed.

The British committee was disturbed by the schedule. It felt that the sessions of the planning committee were much too close to the time of the Paris meeting of the board, leaving little or no opportunity to involve member units in basic decisions, goodwill and support being so vital to the future. Realizing that consideration by member units might not be possible in the midsummer of 1964, the British committee urged such reference after the board meeting, with an executive committee created to take final action after responses from national units had been formulated and reported.[50]

At the deliberations of the Paris meeting, Nelson Chappel put the necessity for a fundamental reorganization in the strongest possible manner:

> It is now essential that ways be found to make the authority of the Board of Managers and the Assembly effective in the determination of new program and the appointment of new staff. While the accomplishments of the W.C.C.E.S.S.A. in recent years have given cause for much gratification, they would have been much greater had it not been for the tensions which have arisen between our two area committees and our three offices because of our divided administration.[51]

The radical actions of the board included an order to begin spending on a unified budget on January 1, 1965; to move the headquarters to Geneva at the earliest possible date; to take from the two administrative committees all responsibilities for program initiation and supervision, lodging these duties with central committees of the council; and referring the actions and the appropriate by-law changes to the two administrative committees and to all member units of the council for comment and action, with final confirmation scheduled for the next assembly in 1966. The Paris sessions marked a real revolution.

The British committee, receiving the actions of the Paris board meeting, called a special meeting to consider the substance and the implications of the Board of Managers' actions. On December 2, it found itself in agreement with the efforts to strengthen the final authority of the assembly, board, and general secretary.

The British believed, however, that inadequate attention had been given to helpful services the regional councils or committees and member units could render to the common cause. It urged that these bodies be consulted on projects particularly concerned with their areas; that they be consulted on appointments, locations, and duties of staff there involved; that they have a responsibility for raising funds within their areas, with a proportion retained, if agreed upon, for local use; that the traditional relationships of member units with London or New York be retained until other regional committees were established; and that staff members should be related to one or other of the regional bodies, acting where desirable as secretaries for such bodies.[52] At a subsequent secretaries' conference, most of the findings of the British committee were seen as useful and supported. The action relating to fund sharing, however, was not endorsed.

By the time the board met in Mexico City for its next session (1965), Nelson Chappel was able to report the reactions of the member units to the proposals for the centralization and integration of the council. They were supportive but not quite unanimous. Canada, the British Lessons Council, Finland Evangelical Lutheran Church, Finland Swedish Association, Australia, (Evangelical) West Germany, India, Jamaica, Japan, Korea, New Zealand (Youth Committee, N.C.C.), the Philippines, Spain, Swedish Lutheran, Swedish Mission Covenant, Tanganyika, and the Division of Overseas Missions, N.C.C.C. in the U.S.A. approved. The Division of Christian Education in that council approved with reservations, as did Ireland and Switzerland. Only Scotland disapproved.[53]

With these board actions of a year past taken, and with this support from the member units, a new kind of World Council of Christian Education and Sunday School Association was brought into being. Actions actually preceded the 1965 meeting of the board, as Dr. Chappel reported:

The British and North American Committees as administrative bodies have, in effect, gone out of existence. They have been replaced by a European Regional Committee which will meet for the first time next month in Sweden and by a North American Regional Committee which held its first meeting in Pittsburgh, Pa., U.S.A. on May 24 and 25.[54]

At last, a unified organizational structure was provided for, but it took more than fifty years after the question was first raised at the 1913 Zurich convention. No one could complain that the council had taken hasty action.

Tokyo Convention and Associated Meetings, 1968

The council, through this era, had concerns other than its internal reorganization. To be sure, that attempt occupied a large share of the time of staff, the officers, and the governing committees, and had achievements come more easily and promptly, effort and energy would not have been so diverted. The servicing of educational needs had not been neglected, however, and the providing of program services was constant and under annual review.

One of the most conspicuous program developments of this "Nelson Chappel period" was the holding of the Tokyo convention and associated meetings in the summer of 1958. The meetings were an impressive display of the program unity and strength of the council, but in the early discussions cleavages of judgment were also displayed.

The Toronto convention was five years in the past when, in 1955, the council began discussing plans for the next. The old, quadrennial schedule had not been observed since 1936, when Oslo followed Rio.

At the meeting of the Board of Managers in Cleveland in 1955, a meeting held just following the Twenty-Third International Convention, both invitations and demurrers were received. Invitations from Berlin, Switzerland, and Japan were received. W. Zimmerman of Berlin pointed out that Christian teachers from behind the Iron Curtain could attend meetings in Berlin (this was before the construction of "The Wall") and, coming there, teachers from other countries could see what it is to live and teach under an atheistic government.

Emanuel Jung, stating the case for Switzerland, mentioned Zurich and Lausanne as possible cities, and some of the "old timers" on the board recalled that Zurich had been the host of the convention of 1913.

The successful invitation, however, came from the energetic Jonathan Fujita of the National Christian Council of Japan, urging that, for the first time since 1920, the convention should be in a country with a non-Christian culture; specifically in Asia, more specifically in Japan, most specifically in Tokyo. Furthermore, Japan's Christian Council had already agreed to raise between $30,000 and $60,000 for the meetings.[55]

In making such a decision, the board felt it was important to ascertain the judgments of the two administrative committees. Each body had considered the matters earlier, and each came out with different answers.

The British committee opposed the holding of any convention at all in 1958. Rather, regional meetings of smaller working conferences should be held in various places. A world assembly should be held in Japan in 1958 for legislative purposes, and before or after it, inspirational meetings should be scheduled for various places in the Far East.[56]

In May the North American committee reached another conclusion. There should be a convention—and in Japan; there should be a ten-day institute preceding it, patterned somewhat after the Toronto institute; and there should be visitations in various countries before and after the convention.[57]

The Board of Managers adopted the recommendations and pattern proposed by the North American committee, including the acceptance of the Japanese invitation and, as the sessions adjourned, the staff was charged with the complicated and arduous tasks of planning for a world convention on the other side of the world. The British committee loyally accepted the decision and in time sent some of its most able and distinguished members to participate in the several meetings.

One of the most immediate tasks was to prepare a resource book, setting forth in fairly comprehensive fashion the situations in which the teaching work of the churches was being carried on in the late 1950s. Ten general headings organized the findings, with several continents or regions surveyed in each: "Rapid Social Change"; "The Christian in His Community"; "The New Interest in the Bible"; "New Insights in Theology"; "The Christian Education of Children"; ". . . of Youth"; ". . . in the Home"; "Leadership Training"; "Theological Education"; and "Evangelism." The accumulated findings made an impressive compendium.

When the eventful summer was over, no less than eleven separate series of meetings had been held, the largest of which, of course, was the Tokyo convention.[58]

At the Seminar on Training Ministers, sixty persons from nineteen countries were present. More than two-thirds of these individuals were principals, deans, or professors from thirty-six seminaries. C. E. Abraham of India and Elmer G. Homrighausen of the United States served as co-chairmen.

To the above list of meetings, directly relating to the meetings in Japan, should be added a series of twelve deputation meetings in Japanese cities led by four or five visitors from abroad immediately after the convention, and by six international teams in Asia, Australia, and Africa as they made their way home from Japan.

The convention, of course, was the largest and most spectacular of these meetings. There were about 1,200 overseas delegates from sixty-four countries. A Japanese delegation of 3,000 was enrolled. At each of the three plenary meetings in the sports arena, there were 12,000 persons present, 11,000 of them Japanese. Other sessions drew as many as 10,000.

The Japanese goal of raising 5,000,000 yen for the expenses of the convention was exceeded by sixty percent. At the opening night, a friendship book in forty volumes (an idea taken from the Toronto convention) was presented to Japan's National Christian Council bearing 75,000 names from sixty countries, and representing gifts totalling about $18,000. Half of the sum was reserved for the travel of convention delegates from Latin America, Asia, Africa, and the minority churches of Europe. The other half went to the National Christian Council of Japan.

As the convention began its daily schedule, many of the facilities of the Christian colleges of Tokyo were taken over for seminars and discussion groups. Five divisions met each morning in the Aoyama Gakuin, a Methodist college.[59]

As with the earlier Toronto institute, the Second World Institute, held at Seiwa and Kobe Colleges, afforded its participants a study period far exceeding in length and intensity the convention sessions. Michio Kozaki, son of the Kozaki who was so prominent in the 1920 convention, served as the director, and Professor Paul H. Vieth of Yale Divinity School as the dean. Six groupings made possible intensive study in as many subjects: the Christian education of children, of youth, in the home; leadership training; Christian education in theological education; and evangelism through Christian education.[60]

Participants in the institute were enriched by a most helpful study guide, prepared in the earlier months by H. A. Hamilton of Brighton, Sussex, England. A section dealing with Jesus' use of the educational method was followed by discussion topics and questions on background issues and institute study topics.

Christian C. Baeta of Africa made what was generally regarded as one of the outstanding addresses of the convention:

> . . . Christian education has made astounding progress in the matter of provision of teaching materials and aids of all kinds. But there still remains a load of which these helps cannot relieve us. They cannot relieve us of the necessity of personal engagement with the substance of our subject, namely the basic issues of life: the question of God, the question of who and what man is, of where we come from, what we are supposed to be doing here, and where we go from here.[61]

Jonathan Fujita and other Japanese leaders later gave very high appraisals of the convention and its related meetings and of the effects upon the Christian churches of Japan and their educational programs. Mission leaders and other western church officials were, in like manner, appreciative.

Belfast Institute of 1962 and Other Conferences

When planning began for the next institute, to be held in Belfast in 1962, the Toronto and the Tokyo experiences proved invaluable. By 1960, only two years after the Japan meetings, the schedule for Belfast shaped up as follows: a theological education seminar; a children's work consultation; an institute of Christian education; a meeting of the World Educational Services Committee; centenary celebrations of the Sabbath School Society for Ireland; and meetings of the Board of Managers and the quadrennial assembly.[62]

As Herbert A. Hamilton had been asked earlier to prepare a study guide for the meetings in Japan, so Randolph Crump Miller of the Yale University Divinity School was requested to write a volume of similar nature for the 1962 Belfast gatherings, all of which were held in or near Queen's University. The contents of the study guide included sections on: the church in the Bible; Christian education in the church; the parish-wide program of Christian education; the relation of the Sunday school to the parish; family and church; and youth in the church.[63] The study guide appeared in January 1961.

The Lilly Endowment of Indianapolis had generously agreed to contribute $30,000 to defray delegates' travel expenses in order to assure a representative attendance, provided the council raised an equal amount. It did, and thus more than $75,000 became available for this purpose. Many of these delegates attended several of the meetings, the institute, and other gatherings.

The institute delegates came from eighty-one countries, and worked under the theme, "The Educational Mission of the Church in Today's World." Dr. J. Kenneth Meir of England served as institute chairman, and Bishop Sante Uberto Barbieri of Argentina as dean.

Work was done in three sequences: addresses and small group discussions formed the first; three commissions on "The Impact of Today's World" the second; and programs on future planning and programs the third. Unconventional worship services led some to thought, others to provocation, and several opportunities were given for institute members to become somewhat acquainted with Ulster's religious life. Since the dates included the anniversary of the Battle of the Boyne, delegates observed the political-religious sentiments of Ulster's Orangemen.

A World Theological Education Seminar was held from June 30 to July 7 at Assembly's College, Belfast. Kathleen Bliss of England served as the presiding officer of the seminar, and thus began the first of three valued services which this gifted British leader—long active in the affairs of the World Council of Churches—gave to the concerns of the World Council of Christian Education. The second and third of these involvements took place in the last period of this study.

Competence in education was seen by the participants as a requirement for those who teach in any seminary curricular offering: "The qualifications for membership in a seminary faculty should include not only competence in a field of study, but equal competence in the art of teaching." [64] A mutual benefit might occur if the W.C.C.E.S.S.A. and the theological seminaries stayed in close touch with each other, and in this relationship the council might help the seminaries turn outward to the world:

> The seminary traditionally is oriented towards the church. It must move to a larger perspective; it must be directed towards the world. . . . Since it is of the nature of academic activity to be more or less isolated from the world, consistent and conscious attention should be given to seminary life and teaching to ensure their relevance to the revolutionary, collapsing, expanding, and rapidly changing world. [65]

The seminary must be conscious of its identification with the church, for,

> . . . while not a church, [it] ought to partake of the nature of a Christian community, where problems common to students and faculty will be discussed, where the sacramental and devotional life will be deepened, where pastoral care will be provided for students, and where the "priesthood of all believers" will become a reality. Within such a community, we may ultimately hope for the integration of the learning process with Christian nurture in the life of the student. [66]

Practical suggestions for seminary curriculum revision and construction were made. The seminar was appraised by those who participated as most valuable. For nearly all participants it was the first experience of its kind.

Curriculum Services

Next to the planning for and the administration of the 1958 series of meetings in Japan and the 1962 series in Ireland, perhaps the curriculum services of the council occupied most of its attention. In making that judgment, however, one has to remember, as always, that there were important programs directed under the auspices of the London and the New York offices, sometimes with clearance with the other, sometimes without, and sometimes with less than complete awareness of them in the office of the general secretary.

During Forrest Knapp's administration in the New York office, curriculum assistance had been given both by personal visits in the field and by a helpful guide: *Preparation of Curriculum Materials*.

By 1959, something more contemporary was needed, and Mary Burnie of the Westhill Training School, Birmingham, England, and Bernard J. Mulder of the Board of Christian Education of the Reformed Church in America began work on manuals on leadership training and on curriculum, respectively.

The impulse for indigenous curriculum development grew during 1954 and 1955, and ventures in Latin America, the Philippines, India, Africa (west, east, central, and southern), and the Near East began to emerge. In most of them, the personal services of Nelson Chappel were involved.

Chappel had many gifts for this type of service. He quickly won the confidence of curriculum constructors by his friendliness, his competence, and perhaps above all, by his self-effacing manner and his disposition to be an enabler and neither a manager nor a North American expert. The growing demand for service of this kind, prompted the convening of a Consultation on Curriculum, which was held in Cleveland in connection with the Twenty-third International Convention in 1955. Paul H. Vieth was the chairman of the sessions.[67]

The British committee saw this type of activity as a helpful service for the council to render. It properly stipulated that such ventures should be authorized by the whole body, and that they not expand into direct publication, distribution, and promotion.[68]

From the Atami assembly on, there were reports every year from Dr. Chappel of Christian education curriculum ventures in different parts of the world. In most of these he was involved in the initial stages, only to withdraw at an early period, in the interests of genuine local responsibility. At Atami in 1958 he reported that W.C.C.E.S.S.A. responsibility for the India curriculum had ended, but that continuing support was being extended to efforts in Africa, the Near East, and the Philippines. Requests were then in hand for assistance in curriculum construction in West and East Pakistan, for the Chinese in southeast Asia, and for the English-speaking Caribbean.[69]

At the Glasgow board meeting a year later, books of the India Sunday school curriculum were displayed, volumes which were to be published in from twelve to fourteen of the major languages of that country. Two full-time editors and a hundred writers were at work in Africa. In the Near East a full-time Egyptian editor was employed, assisted by a part-time missionary; and in addition to works in Arabic, an Armenian version was planned. A curriculum conference had been held in West Pakistan, while East Pakistan planned to use a revision of Indian materials or some other. Work had begun that year in the English-speaking Caribbean, which included British Honduras and British Guiana. The Chinese in southeast Asia were at work on their project, as initially discussed in Tokyo.[70]

In 1960 Chappel reported that ninety percent of the African three-year cycle was written and that translations into nine African languages had begun. A curriculum conference for East Pakistan was planned, a director, David Mitchell, had been employed for the Caribbean English-speaking area, and a curriculum conference was being planned for Hong Kong. Seven of the ten levels planned in Latin America were fully written, the Japanese curriculum had been completely revised, the Philippine course greatly revised after experimental use. Daw Win Mya from Burma enrolled at the Pacific School of Religion and later returned to help with a Burmese curriculum for day schools.[71]

At the New York meeting of the Board of Managers in 1961 Chappel made clear that the W.C.C.E.S.S.A. had not initiated a single one of the curriculum projects (there were eight new ones that year). Requests came only from the churches or agencies in the areas concerned. Upon receiving such a request the council helped organize a formal curriculum conference and provided technical and financial assistance. "No W.C.C.E.S.S.A. staff person has ever written a single word," he declared.[72]

By the time of the Belfast assembly in 1962, it could be recounted that such curriculum activity had been carried on in sixty-nine countries, 101 languages, 1,706 volumes had been produced, with total publications of more than 1,811,000, involving 231 church bodies.[73]

It was felt that a general guide might be helpful, and a manual was produced in 1963, *A Guide on Writing Curriculum Materials for Christian Education*. Its contents included: "Teaching as Jesus Taught"; "Communicating with Your Particular Audience"; "Pointers on Style and Manuscript Preparation"; "Keeping Faith with the Outline"; "The Editor's Role in the Production of Curriculum Materials"; "Bibliography." [74]

With such activity going on in so many places, it was most natural that there should be a demand for a conference on indigenous curriculum construction in order that experiences might be shared, and some general, guiding principles formulated. Accordingly, a World Consultation on Curriculum was convened in the delightful resort town of Füringen, Switzerland, in late June 1964. Leaders in curriculum preparation from forty-one countries were present, coming from forty-six church bodies. William A. Morrison, general secretary of the Board of Christian Education, United Presbyterian Church in the U.S.A., served as chairman. A comprehensive report of its findings was issued later that year.

When Nelson Chappel turned over the general secretaryship to his successor in 1965, he was able to look back upon an impressive amount of curricular activity. And in one way or another Nelson Chappel was involved in all of it. Later critics of such curriculum ventures might (and did) see many faults in such undertakings.

First steps are first steps, however, and at the very least these ventures gave self-confidence and self-understanding to Christian educators in many lands. Upon their efforts others would build.

In later years, Dr. Chappel was to look back upon these curriculum ventures with satisfaction, but also in critical retrospect. He wrote:

> One general frustration came from my attempt to try to let the younger church people develop their own indigenous teaching materials and leadership. At curriculum conferences they showed great aptitude in trying to understand or develop the real purpose of Christian education, and to understand the people for whom the materials were being prepared and their spiritual needs today, and therefore what the gospel had to say to them in this situation. But only a few of the writers ever got to the curriculum conferences, and most of the writers went at their work with their own ideas of what was needed without the thinking that had gone on at the conference. . . . Thus in the writing of the curriculum materials one saw most of the educational ideas and methods that had been discovered "go out the window." We did not have funds for conferences for the writers. Thus when each curriculum came out in finished form, the indigenous quality had been largely diluted by good people who were foreign to the environment and just did not realize what we were trying to do. I came to the sad realization that a first curriculum could not be really indigenous, but only a first step on the road to truly indigenous teaching materials. But progress toward that goal was made.[75]

Children's Work

Alongside this intensive curriculum activity in many parts of the world, age-group programs were also being carried on, though usually under the supervision of one or the other of the administrative committees. The British committee continued to encourage the Christian education of children in the countries for which it had responsibility, and in North America a Children's Work Advisory Committee had been at work since 1950. That it did not seriously influence the work of the British committee is in itself another instance of the divided nature of the Council.

This advisory committee had strongly recommended that a full-time staff person be employed by the council for children's work and suggested that the person be neither an American nor a European.[76] Its hopes were realized in mid-1962 with the appointment of Epiphania Castro, of the Philippines.[77]

A concern which was strong in the minds of the professional workers with children was the lack of books and other materials for leaders of children in the younger churches. A beginning was made in meeting this need in the Caribbean in 1957 when libraries, each with a nucleus of sixty-six books, were established in Trinidad, Jamaica, British Guiana, and Barbados. A year later, the youth department of the council added books on youth work to this initial collection.[78] The idea grew, and in 1965 Dr. Chappel reported to the board that sets of books were to be assembled and made available to Christian centers in Asia, Africa, and Latin America.[79]

Interest in work with children grew, and a Consultation on Children's Work was authorized and held in Belfast on July 4–6, 1962. Dr. Ruel Howe of the United States served as chairman. About sixty persons participated in the three-day meeting.[80]

The main interest of the North American Children's Work Advisory Committee, at this time, centered in art—art for the religious education of children, and art produced by children themselves. The earliest discovered reference to this interest was at the Cuernavaca conference in 1941. There it was agreed to outline a simple plan for producing and distributing a limited number of Bible pictures. A leaflet dealing with pictures and their uses was also to be prepared.[81] It is not clear from the record what resulted from this decision, but by 1949 an action was recorded that a project, "Pictures for Children Everywhere," was to be begun.[82]

Bible pictures were selected by representatives of the Children's Advisory Committee. The cooperation of the Providence Lithograph Company (a firm which had long and various connections with denominational publishing houses) was secured. Printing on the cards, or on the reverse, was either eliminated entirely or held to an absolute minimum in order to obviate language difficulties. Packets were made available at minimum cost and their acceptance was swift and numerically almost overwhelming. It was reported to the assembly in Frankfurt in 1964 that nearly a million large pictures, and 8,750,000 small pictures, had been shipped to ninety-one countries.[83]

Two hundred eleven persons had been enrolled as correspondents and a new series was being planned to be called *Stories of Jesus for Children Everywhere,* to be published in English, French, Spanish, and Portuguese. In the first year of its life, this series reached 300,000.

By 1958 more than 1,800,000 booklets had gone to 113 countries in twenty-one languages and dialects. Contributions of $131,880 for the venture had been received.[84] By the time the next quadrennial assembly met in Belfast, the total number of pictures in the picture project had increased to more than 13,000,000, and the booklet, *Jesus, Friend of Children Everywhere* (a new title), had reached more than 3,000,000. Instead of the original four languages, it was available in sixty-two, and had gone to 115 countries.[85]

At board and assembly meetings, criticisms of the pictures were frequently raised as being of an old-fashioned style, not in a contemporary art form. Attempts were made, from time to time, to provide more varied and representative pictures. With the modifications, the series continued to grow. Approximately 50,000,000 pictures had been distributed by 1963.[86] Encouraged by these successes, the North American committee made ready a third offering in 1962, *Stories Jesus Heard*, an Old Testament series.[87]

In 1965 Dr. Chappel reported that efforts were being made to revise both the pictures and the story booklets. Two years later, at the Nairobi Assembly, it was voted that the series be officially terminated at the end of 1968, and gradually phased out. Steps were to be taken to replace it with contemporary resources as needed and requested.[88] Not much was done, however, to provide such resources in the remaining years of the council's life, though informal encouragement was given to local and regional efforts.

The second aspect of this interest in art came in 1961, initially from A. Wilson Cheek, New York associate general secretary, and Mrs. Vivian Russell, a member of his staff. The idea was to deal directly with artistic creations done by children themselves, and the purposes were described as three-fold:

A. To discover whether children can communicate basic Christian teaching through art.
B. To discover whether children are interested in each other's art work, keeping in mind that this is a world-wide effort in which language and cultural barriers must be crossed.
C. To discover what the participation accomplished with the child and the extent to which this process motivates the child in his own understanding.[89]

Responses came in large numbers, and the New York office received hundreds of pictures done by children in nearly every part of the world. So numerous were they, and of such high quality, that the interest of the Metropolitan Museum of Art in New York City was aroused, and in December 1962 an exhibition of children's art was held in its halls, attended by an estimated 40,000 persons. The exhibition and the collection were featured in *Newsweek* magazine and on television stations of the ABC television network during the Christmas season of that year.[90] The publishing firm of Thomas Nelson and Sons published a volume, *Away in a Manger,* containing selected paintings from this collection in full color and with accompanying texts from the Revised Standard Version of the Bible. By June 1965, 145 exhibitions had been held in various cities and centers, composed of these pictures by children, and in addition they had been seen on many national and local television programs.[91]

With interest generated both by the picture and stories series, and by the

Children's Art Project, a recommendation was approved by the North American committee for an *ad hoc* committee on "The Use of the Arts in Christian Education." [92] In November 1963, an exploratory conference was held on the subject, but soon after it became apparent that the council could not financially sustain any significant and continuing effort in the use of the arts, and it was decided that the project would have to be terminated in mid-1965.[93] An overture was made to the National Council of Churches in the United States to assume responsibility for the project,[94] but this body also proved unable to do so.

The North American committee could not have been faulted during this period for not displaying an interest in the Christian education of children.

Youth Work

During the earlier period (roughly, the administration of Forrest Knapp), the general outlines of youth work had been established, involving close cooperation with the Youth Department of the World Council of Churches and the creation of a supervising committee, with most of its members jointly appointed by both councils.

American youth secretaries involved in the work of the World Council of Christian Education felt, however, that there was need for a second committee dealing with youth work and differentiated in its role. Accordingly, a Youth Services Committee was authorized by the W.C.C.E., this group to be composed of adults active in the leadership of denominational young peoples' bodies, fifteen in number.[95]

About this time, an invitation came to the World Christian Youth Commission (the W.C.C.E. a member), which caused Nelson Chappel considerable concern. The overture came from the World Federation of Democratic Youth, a secular agency of youth groups involved in the political left in several nations. The proposal was for a meeting with the agencies of the World Christian Youth Commission. The W.C.C. Youth Department supported the holding of informal staff conversations. Some "adult group within the W.C.C.E." had said no. Thereupon, the W.C.C.E.'s Youth Department asked for a reversal, protesting that others seemed to have made a decision about a concern of the Youth Department without that group being involved.

Nelson Chappel had written Lord Mackintosh on February 17, 1955, relating his previous unsatisfactory experience with a unit of the W.F.D.Y. It had seemed to him to be a communist-dominated agency, and one with small regard for truly democratic procedures.

Staff members of the W.F.D.Y. met in Geneva on April 15, 1955, with representatives of the World Alliance of YMCAs, the World's YWCA, the World's Student Christian Federation, and the Youth Department of the W.C.C. The report of the meeting was not very revealing:

In the course of a friendly conversation, questions were freely asked and answered and information was exchanged about the respective programmes, publications and concerns of each organization. The participants expressed their satisfaction with the meeting and with the fruitful exchange of views and information which resulted.[96]

Youth Department people from the W.C.C.E. were not present at this meeting. They felt a need for some contacts of their own with the W.F.D.Y. In an effort to work out some understanding, a committee of three from the board was appointed to confer with representatives of the Youth Department.[97] However, other matters rose to greater prominence, and nothing more is recorded about the relationships of the council with the World Federation of Democratic Youth.

The next organizational problem came about as an almost inevitable consequence of having two world church councils—each with a youth department—housed on either side of the Atlantic Ocean. Both departments were interested in a common venture, World Youth Projects (by which means, assistance was given to programs and projects involving church young people all over the world), but a staff member was related to only one of the departments. Youth movements in Europe, Africa, and Latin America were inadequately represented. Geographic separation had caused problems. Committee meetings were poorly attended. The two staffs had somewhat different training. The W.C.C.E.S.S.A. staff was particularly interested in strengthening "teen age work," which, it felt, was a neglected emphasis.[98]

In this unsatisfactory situation, it was thought wise by authorities of both councils to hold a consultation on these problems, and accordingly, at Yale Divinity School in 1957, on the occasion of the meeting of the central committee of the World Council of Churches, a consultation was called to order by Roy G. Ross, general secretary of the National Council of Churches, U.S.A.

After discussion, it was decided that in the future a single committee should be responsible for youth services in both councils. This committee was to be composed both of young people and experienced adult leaders of youth. It was to be known as the W.C.C./W.C.C.E.S.S.A. Youth Committee. Through this common committee, all youth ventures—world youth projects, educational youth services, and others—would report to the parent bodies. If staff assignments were to be made, such proposals were to go to the general secretary of the agency concerned before they were implemented.

The two youth departments adopted revised statements of aims and functions in 1960. In the preparation for the above, it was discovered that there was considerable duplication between the two bodies.[99] The Division of Ecumenical Action of the World Council of Churches (in which its youth department was administratively lodged) urged more evidence of identity of concerns in place of the former agreed-upon division of labor.[100]

In 1961 identity of purpose and function had gone so far that it was proposed that there should be a single committee, and that three subcommittees should be accountable to it: an ecumenical youth services committee, an educational youth services committee, and a world youth projects committee.[101]

This formulation did not entirely correct the tension and differences between the two youth emphases. Therefore, at the meeting of the committee, following the New Delhi (third) assembly of the World Council of Churches in 1961, differences in understanding were reported:

> The Youth Department staff [of the W.C.C.], interpreted by Dr. Knoff, saw the Christian Education forces at New Delhi as a stumbling-block to fostering Ecumenical Education—for reasons of affluence, self-sufficiency, complacency, etc. The W.C.C. sees its task as continually facing us with our brokenness in the Church.
>   Dr. Irene Jones concurred in Dr. Knoff's observations, and also called attention to the new Division of World Mission and Evangelism with its implications for Christian education.[102]

The continuing separateness of the two councils was seen as one cause of the difficulties of the two youth departments, but in the meantime, the Belfast assembly was urged that no youth projects be put into operation until complete clearance with the Joint Youth Committee was assured.[103]

One contention between the two youth departments was the role of the Ecumenical Youth Services Committee of the W.C.C.E.S.S.A. The World Council of Churches people usually contended that there was no need for it; the World Council of Christian Education representatives usually supported it. Evidently, in time, the committee became less and less useful, and in 1963 there was a recommendation to the board that it be abolished, and that its functions be taken over by the Joint Youth Committee.[104]

The termination was made and, at the close of his administration, Nelson Chappel could report to the board that the work of the two departments, merged under one committee, was a unity. By then Donald O. Newby was housed in Geneva, as W.C.C.E.S.S.A. youth secretary, and Albert van den Heuvel, his counterpart in the W.C.C., and he were sharing in the support of youth secretaries in the East Asia Christian Conference, in the All-Africa Conference of Churches, and in the Latin American Evangelical Youth Organization.[105] In a real sense, what the two councils finally achieved in 1971 by an organizational merger, their youth departments had brought to pass more than six years before.

Adult Work and Family Life

In contrast with children's work and with youth work, there was not a great deal of activity in this period in the specialized field of the Christian education of adults. What activity there was centered in leadership for Christian education, and in education for Christian family life.

In 1960 a week-long conference was held in Nyon, Switzerland, to discuss leadership in the churches' programs. Representatives of the World Council of Churches, the World Council of Christian Education, and the world organizations of the Y.M. and Y.W.C.A. attended. Dr. Paul Limbert of the World's Y.M.C.A. served as chairman.

In 1961 the N.A.C. recommended to the board that a world committee on "Adult Work and Christian Education in the Home" be established, and the board was asked to suggest to other world bodies the joint calling of a consultation as soon after the Belfast meetings as possible, looking forward to a possible World Conference on the Christian Family in 1967.[106] Later, interest and approval were expressed by the World Y.M. and Y.W.C.A.s, from the World's Student Christian Federation, and from the World Council of Churches—each body making suggestions and raising questions.[107]

At about this same time, the council carried on a worldwide survey on theological schools and family life and a bulletin, incorporating its findings, was published. A study of young parents and Christian home life was also being pursued—an inquiry involving ninety persons in different parts of the world. Packets on family life had been sent to fifty-five seminaries.

Lack of staff time handicapped this aspect of the council's work. Everett Stowe, with this responsibility in the New York office, found his time preempted with the contents and the affairs of the quarterly, *World Christian Education.* When that assignment was turned over to H. A. Hamilton in Geneva in 1963–64, he found his duties with the Joint Study Commission were paramount.

Audio-Visual Services

We have seen in the previous chapter, that two programs of audio-visual education were established, one in New York and one in London. These ventures were the result of the generosity of Mrs. Clifford S. Heinz and J. Arthur Rank, respectively. While there was communication between the two staff people, Erich Voehringer and Edgar Youdell, the arrangement intensified the dual nature of the council, already evident in other ways. In New York a helpful relationship had been established with a radio and audio-visual operation in the Division of Overseas Ministries of the National Council of Churches, and 2,500 copies of a useful brochure, *Sight-Sound,* were being distributed five times a year. With the departure of Dr. Voehringer for a seminary teaching position, the services were consolidated under Mr. Youdell in London.[108]

In 1959 a second and even more generous gift from J. Arthur (now Lord) Rank was announced, as he made possible a facility in London known as the Churches' Television Centre. Alert to the educational and religious potential of television, Lord Rank made possible and helped to organize a central training facility for television ministries which, while primarily designed to serve British trainees, was to be of service, in so far as was possible, to the wider Christian educational constituency of the World Council of Christian Education and Sunday School Association. The total expense was to be covered by Lord Rank. Its program and affairs were to be in charge of a management committee which was to be appointed by the British Committee of the W.C.C.E.S.S.A.[109] The offer and arrangement were approved and accepted by the board. Elaborate equipment was made available; intensive training courses were offered; and in time the installation was removed to more spacious and quiet quarters in Bushey, Hertfordshire, a London sub-urb. By 1965, 3,000 ministers and a few hundred laity had passed through the Centre and had completed the courses.[110]

A detailed report of the workings of the centre was made to the 1966 meeting of the Board of Managers by members of its staff. Some members of the Board were not convinced that the Centre was offering a worldwide program, but there was general appreciation for the unique service it was giving to English-speaking leaders.

For those not close to the operation, there was a continuing uncertainty about what significant relationship the British committee had to the Centre, about the strength of the British committee's influence upon the manage-ment committee, and the day-to-day operations of the Centre. "Outsiders" came to the conclusion that the relationship was slender and tenuous, and that the Centre was largely an independent installation doing a large amount of significant and specialized work. This conclusion seemed to be upheld when, in the negotiations for merger with the World Council of Churches, it was agreed in time that the Churches' Television Centre was not involved and that it would continue in Great Britain as an independent venture.

"World Christian Education"

This quarterly, begun in the period covered by the last chapter, continued its double work—that of serving as a substantive, educational journal and as a medium of information to Christian workers in many lands.

There were problems, and rising costs was one of them. Investigations revealed that the magazine could be printed more cheaply in England than in the United States, and the function was accordingly transferred to a firm in Nelson, Lancashire.[111] Determination of useful content, always a problem for an editor, came under frequent discussion. In 1960 a readers' survey was taken, asking for expressions of desired priority in the contents of the magazine.[112] As a result of the survey, these priorities appeared and were accepted: leadership training; theory or principles of Christian education; reports on teaching techniques or methods; practical experiences; the use of the Bible; Christian education in the family; news items; Sunday schools; and children's work.[113]

After the findings of the survey were codified and reported, the Board of Managers approved a statement on the nature of the magazine:

. . . this magazine is primarily intended for key persons in Christian education around the world, particularly in the younger church areas. Since these persons represent a wide range of training and experience, there should be some elements in the magazine which will be of interest to executives and professors . . .[114]

With the retirement of the editor, Dr. Everett Stowe, scheduled for 1964, new decisions had to be made about editorial direction. In 1960 it was decided that responsibility for the quarterly was to be shifted from the North American to the world office, and that a widely representative editorial committee was to be established.[115] The transfer was made at the end of 1964, at which time the magazine had 2,001 subscribers in 117 countries.[116] Editorial responsibility was to be parceled out among the members of the staff, each in turn taking responsibility for an issue. Business responsibility was transferred to the London office, where easy communications would be possible with the Lancashire printers.[117]

English, being the first or second language of most of the readership, continued to be the language used, though some articles in Spanish, German, and French were printed in the fourth quarters of 1966 and 1967.

The following analysis of contents will give an idea of what the magazine covered during the period, 1954–1965, and continues the analysis in the previous chapter.[118]

Age Groups and Family Education

Church and Home, Partners in Christian Education	First Quarter, 1956
A Redemptive Fellowship and the Christian Nurture of Children	Second Quarter, 1959
Relationships in Christian Youth Work	Third Quarter, 1959
Christian Adult Education	Fourth Quarter, 1959
Young Parents and Christian Home Life	Second Quarter, 1963
Faith Coming of Age: The "People of God" of Adult Years	First Quarter, 1964
For the Religious Growth of Children	Second Quarter, 1964
Youth Work in the Life of Church and World	Third Quarter, 1964

Bible, Theology

Christ, the Hope of the World	Third Quarter, 1954
The Gospel and Secularism	Fourth Quarter, 1954
Biblical Theology and Christian Education	Fourth Quarter, 1955
Christian Faith and Contemporary Culture	Second Quarter, 1956
Using the Bible in Christian Teaching	Fourth Quarter, 1956
The Renewal of the Church	Fourth Quarter, 1957
Teaching the Bible Today	Fourth Quarter, 1960
Theological Foundations of Christian Education	Third Quarter, 1961
Interpreters of Christ	First Quarter, 1965

Nature of Christian Education

Fellowship	First Quarter, 1954
Local Programs of Christian Education	Second Quarter, 1954
Worship and Christian Growth	First Quarter, 1955
Church, State and Christian Education	Second Quarter, 1955
The Christian Vocation of the Laity	Third Quarter, 1956
Relation Between Evangelism and Christian Education	First Quarter, 1957
Group Relations and Christian Growth	Second Quarter, 1957
The Church Must Teach	First Quarter, 1958
Christian Education, 1958	Second Quarter, 1958
Four Background Topics (Nishinomiya Institute)	Third Quarter, 1958
World Meetings in Christian Education	Fourth Quarter, 1958
Some Next Steps in Christian Education	First Quarter, 1959
The Local Church—The Whole Congregation Teaches	Second Quarter, 1960
Educational Evangelism in an Industrialized Society	Third Quarter, 1960
Our Teaching Mission	First Quarter, 1961
Image and Symbol	First Quarter, 1962
The Educational Mission of the Church: Summary of a World Survey	Second Quarter, 1962
Previews of the 1962 World Institute on Christian Education	Third Quarter, 1962
World Meetings on Christian Education	Fourth Quarter, 1962
Some Next Steps in Christian Education	First Quarter, 1963
The Church as a Redemptive Community	Third Quarter, 1963
The Curriculum of Christian Education	Fourth Quarter, 1964
Religion in Day Schools	Second Quarter, 1965
Africa	Third Quarter, 1965
Sunday Schools in Transition	Fourth Quarter, 1965

Leadership Education

Christian Teaching Through Mass Media	Third Quarter, 1955
Preparing Leadership for Tasks in Christian Education	Third Quarter, 1957
The Christian Teacher: Interpreter of Jesus Christ	First Quarter, 1960
Leadership Development	Second Quarter, 1961

Sabbatical Services Project

The Lilly Endowment made possible a new service during this period—
"The Sabbatical Services Project." Nelson Chappel was convinced that
there was a large, unmet need in the theological colleges of the world for
assistance in the training of students for an educational ministry. Accordingly, a sabbatical services committee was established, headed first by
Luther A. Weigle and later by Dean Elmer G. Homrighausen of Princeton
Theological Seminary. The project was an attempt to enlist theological

seminary professors on sabbatical leave, and put them in the service of other seminaries, particularly those of the younger churches.

The objectives of the project were stated in order of priority:

a. To serve as consultant to the Boards and staffs of theological colleges and seminaries concerning the training of ministers for their teaching ministry, especially in the field of Christian education;
b. To counsel with a teacher (if someone has been set aside to teach Christian education subjects) in planning the entire Christian education syllabus in general and to outline in detail the particular courses within that syllabus;
c. To serve as leaders at conferences on Christian education for pastors and others which the Seminary may organize;
d. To teach one course in Christian education as a demonstration.[119]

The following schedule describes in outline the scope of this venture in enriching the pattern of theological education.

Year	Professor	From	To	Country
1957–58	Donald M. Maynard	Boston University School of Theology	Tainan Theological Seminary	Taiwan
1961–62	Elmer G. Homrighausen	Princeton Theological Seminary	Campinas Seminary	Brazil
1961	Helen Garber	Biblical Seminary	Tainan Theological Seminary	Taiwan
1963–64	Robert Boehlke	Princeton Theological Seminary	Djakarta United Theological Seminary	Indonesia
	Elmer G. Homrighausen	Princeton Theological Seminary	Djakarta United Theological Seminary	Indonesia (also Korea, Japan, the Philippines and other countries)
	Clayton Kitchen	McMaster University	Baptist Theological Sem., Kakinada, Eastern Theological Coll., Assam, Serampore College	India
	William Overhold	Boston University School of Theology	Central Philippine Univ., Iloilo	Philippines
1964–65	Robert Boehlke	Princeton Theological Seminary	Djakarta United Theological Sem.	Indonesia
	Gordon Jackson	Pittsburgh Theological Seminary	Campinas Seminary	Brazil

Year	Professor	From	To	Country
	Margaret Lobb	Pacific School of Religion	Seiwa College and Cibu Methodist Seminary	Japan & Sarawak
	Norma Thompson	New York University	Chiengmai Theol. Seminary	Thailand
	George Tuttle	Union Seminary, Vancouver	St. Paul's Sem., Limuru	Kenya
1965–66	Ralph Chalmers	Pine Hill Divinity Hall	United Theological Coll., Bangalore	India
	Benjamin Guansing [120]	Union Theol. Sem., Philippines	Pacific School of Religion	U.S.A.
	Donald M. Maynard	Boston University School of Theology	Trinity College, Accra	Ghana
	Lois Tupper	McMaster University	Emanuel Theol. Coll., Ibadan	Nigeria
1966–67	J. Gordon Chamberlain	Pittsburgh Theological Seminary	Evang. Fac. of Theol., Buenos Aires	Argentina
	Randolph Crump Miller	Yale Divinity School		Far East, Near East, South Pacific, and Australia
	Grant S. Shockley	Board of World Missions Methodist Church	United Evangel. Center, Mexico City	Mexico
	Erich Voehringer	Mt. Airy Theol. Semin.	Federated Theol. Seminary, Alice	South Africa
1968	Irene S. Caldwell	School of Theology, Anderson College	United Theol. Coll. and Jamaica School of Theology	Jamaica
1970	William C. Moore	Boston Univ. School of Theology	National Christian Council	Ceylon
	Paul Irwin [121]	Southern Calif. School of Theology	Trinity College	Singapore

In all of these arrangements, the institution in which the visitor held his permanent appointment paid his continuing salary; the host institution provided local entertainment (meals and housing), and the council paid the roundtrip travel expenses and made initial and subsequent arrangements. When the foundation money ran out, the program had to be terminated because the council itself could not support the expenditures.

Field Services

In all of this period, the staff was on the move, both from London and from New York. Records are not complete for all their travels, and even were they in existence it would be wearisome to recount them. A sampling will suffice for an understanding of the travels of these men and women in the interests of the council they served. James Turnbull was in Spain and Portugal in 1954 for seventeen days. His successor, Andrew Wright, was in Poland, Portugal, Finland, and Sweden in 1960. Wilson Cheek spent six weeks in seven countries of Africa in 1962. In May of that year, he was in Jamaica. Epiphania Castro, in 1958, visited eastern Asia, in connection with the Tokyo meetings.

Nelson Chappel's travels have been recorded most completely. Five years after his appointment (1959), he reported that he had been in forty-three countries. In 1960 Chappel had been to several countries in Europe and Africa, and to Hong Kong, Australia, and New Zealand. He reported that, in the single year of 1963, he had traveled 75,000 miles and had been on all six continents.[122]

In addition to these contacts by individual staff members, many leadership training conferences were held in various parts of the world. In the quadrennium, 1954–1958, two conferences for leaders in northern Europe were held, and two for leaders in the European Latin countries. In 1956 there was an all-European leaders' conference, and another for those in the Caribbean area. In 1955 a conference was held in the Djakarta, Indonesia area, and in 1957 a conference on religious films was held.[123]

The Tokyo convention provided an opportunity for extensive field visitations, both as delegates went to and returned from the meetings in Japan. These efforts have already been detailed. A visit to Yugoslavia in 1960 provided the first contact with Protestant and Orthodox educational forces in that country since the beginning of World War II in 1938.[124]

A large and significant program never came to fruition, though Nelson Chappel and other staff members worked energetically on it for many months. Called "The Leadership Team Project," it was designed to send a number of persons, at scheduled intervals, into different countries for sustained leadership education efforts. Persons from the educational work of the churches and from their organized mission boards were to be used, and age group and other specialists were to be included. Some ventures were completed, but as a whole the program did not flourish. Perhaps it proved too complicated to organize and administer, perhaps it was too expensive. It was a dream that exceeded the grasp.

Officers of the Council

There were not many changes in the officers of the North American committee during the period. Robert Diefendorf had served as chairman of the executive committee, and upon his resignation in 1956 he was succeeded by John N. Irwin, II. Irwin resigned in 1957, to become deputy assistant secretary of defense in the Eisenhower administration. The North American committee did not accept his resignation but asked Diefendorf, then vice-chairman, to assume his duties. In 1958 Irwin made his resignation final and complete.[125]

Coleman Burke served as chairman of the North American committee for four years, but resigned in 1957. Dale Fiers, president of the United Christian Missionary Society of the Disciples of Christ, was chosen to succeed him.[126]

The British committee also had changes of leadership. Lord Rank resigned in 1958 as chairman, and he was succeeded by James Kelly, the former long-time British secretary.[127] Dr. Kelly continued as chairman until 1964, when he retired and was succeeded by Dr. C. Ernst Sommer, president of the Methodist Theological Seminary in Frankfurt-am-Main. Dr. Sommer's accession symbolized the enlarged self-understanding which the British committee had gained, and indicated that it was seeking to be a regional rather than a national committee.[128]

Changes also were made in the general leadership of the council. Ernest H. Hayes and Gerald E. Knoff were elected to membership on the Board of Managers in 1956. Paul Sturtevant, the council's long-time treasurer, died in 1957, and Coleman Burke of New York City was chosen to succeed him.[129]

At the Tokyo convention in 1958, Bishop Shot K. Mondol of India was elected president; Viscount Mackintosh, chairman; Luther A. Weigle, chairman emeritus; and Coleman Burke, treasurer.

In this period a new practice was begun, that of having the president serve for a single four-year term. In 1962, at the Assembly in Belfast, Sir Francis Ibiam, the governor of eastern Nigeria, was elected president, himself a ruling elder in the Presbyterian Church of Nigeria.

Coleman Burke resigned as treasurer in 1963, and Constable MacCracken succeeded him.[130] That same year, Dorothy Cadbury resigned as a member of the board, ending a long period of faithful service.

A severe shock came to the members of the council when they learned that Viscount Mackintosh had died suddenly on the 27th of December, 1964. He had been active since 1924—exactly forty years. He had been president of the association-council from 1928 to 1958, and chairman from 1958 to 1964. A memorial service was held at the meeting of the board in Mexico City in 1965.[131]

The *London Times* wrote of him:

Lord Mackintosh's attachment to non-conformity was part of his life, and largely patterned it. Through his parentage he belonged to one of the minor and less orthodox sections of Methodism, the Methodist New Connection Church, which was firmly established in Yorkshire in the early part of the nineteenth century; but when, in the nineteen twenties and thirties efforts toward full Methodist unity began, he warmly supported them and he was one of the first and most prominent laymen to take high office.[132]

Nelson Chappel, a colleague and a friend of Viscount Mackintosh for many years, and wrote in the magazine of Mackintosh's many interests, which included:

. . . a Methodist Ladies' College, the Home Mission Board of the Methodist Church of Britain, committees on cancer, the restoration of Westminster Abbey following the war, the founding of the University of East Anglia, of which he had been only recently elected Chancellor and was to have been installed in that post next May.[133]

Bishop Reuben H. Mueller (Evangelical United Brethren Church) of the United States was elected chairman of the council to succeed Viscount Mackintosh, and he held this position until the end of the life of the organization. Bishop Mueller had been a vice-chairman since the assembly of 1954, and before he was made a bishop in his own denomination, he had been the general secretary of its board of Christian education. He was serving at the time as president of the National Council of Churches in the U.S.A. and earlier he had been the chairman of its Division of Christian Education.[134]

At the meeting of the Board of Managers in 1965, in session in his own city, Gonzalo Baez-Camargo resigned as a vice-chairman and as a member of the board. It was remembered that, in 1930, the association had assisted the National Evangelical Council of Mexico to employ Baez-Camargo as its general secretary of Christian education.[135]

In 1963 C. H. Hwang, principal of Tainan Theological Seminary, Taiwan, was chosen as chairman of the World Educational Services Committee, a position which he occupied until 1965, when other duties connected with his new work with the Theological Education Fund prevented his continuance.[136]

Staff

In the spring of 1953, with the transition to the new structure made and a new general secretary chosen, Forrest Knapp resigned as associate general secretary in New York. He had pressed vigorously for a unified structure and in the end he was successful. In so doing, however, he knew that he was making it impossible for himself to be that new chief executive, since there were those who doubted the wisdom of the new plan and who were not pleased with his championship of it.

The Board of Managers adopted a minute of appreciation:

> As the Council proceeds under the guidance of a unified Staff, we believe that it will become increasingly apparent that the faith and vision of Dr. Knapp have been a large factor in the development of the plan for administration which holds out, we believe, such great hope of a strengthened service to the whole world. Dr. Knapp came to a large position, but because of his rare qualities, he left the position larger than he found it.[137]

Dr. Knapp went to the Massachusetts Council of Churches, and was succeeded by Philip C. Jones of the New York staff, as acting associate general secretary. In 1955 Russell F. Harrison came from the Disciples of Christ headquarters to succeed Dr. Knapp.

At about this time James Turnbull resigned as associate general secretary in the London office, the action to take effect on August 31, 1955. Andrew Wright, son of China missionaries and coming from the British Christian Endeavor Society, succeeded him. Thus, there was a whole new trio in charge of the affairs of the general secretariate of the council: Chappel, Harrison, and Wright.[138]

When James Turnbull left his work, he was remembered in a citation given by V. M. Koshy of the India Sunday School Union: "In India we shall remember for a long time the vigour and alertness with which he fulfilled the exacting obligations of a strenuous three-month itinerary which he carried out in this sub-continent." [139]

Within a few weeks of Russell Harrison's assumption of the work of the New York office, one of his predecessors died: Robert M. Hopkins, general secretary from 1928 to 1940. Harrison had just come from the United Christian Missionary Society, Disciples of Christ, in which he was secretary of youth work, and it had been to this same agency that Dr. Hopkins had gone, as president, in 1940.

The business committee of the North American Administrative Committee happened to meet three days after Dr. Hopkins' death, and it adopted the following minute:

> . . . Notable achievements which are remembered gratefully are his arduous labors in connection with the Council's World Conventions on Christian Education which were held in Los Angeles, Rio de Janeiro, and Oslo, and his careful planning of the projected Convention scheduled to be held in Durban which was cancelled because of World War II. . . . During the depression years, he husbanded the resources of the Council with particular care, astutely maintaining its organizational structure unimpaired.[140]

Russell Harrison carried responsibilities for the New York office until he was called by his own brotherhood, the Disciples of Christ, to become head of its Missionary Education Department. He assumed his new work at the end of August 1959.[141]

Replacing him was A. Wilson Cheek, who had been director of the Department of Youth Work and executive secretary of the United Christian Youth Movement and later director of the Department of Adult Work in the National Council of the Churches of Christ in the U.S.A. He continued as the associate general secretary of the W.C.C.E.S.S.A. in the New York office until 1965, when he left to become the associate general secretary of the Religious Education Association of the United States and Canada.[142]

Umeko Kagawa came to the New York office on July 1, 1959, as director of World Youth Projects for the W.C.C.E.S.S.A. and the W.C.C., spending part of her time there, and part in Geneva.[143] She continued until 1961.

By 1960 the Board of Managers felt that an official plan for the granting of sabbatical leaves should be established, patterned somewhat after the arrangements made for staff members of the National Council of Churches, U.S.A. Seven stipulations were formulated to make the plan both productive of future usefulness, and a clear change from the regular work of the staff member. Nelson Chappel was urged by the board to bring in such a proposal for himself.

He did so in 1961 at the New York board meeting, but his proposal was not approved, as being too much of a "bus-man's holiday," doing work which he was doing anyway in the course of his regular duties.[144] He was urged to bring in another plan, one which would give him a significant change from his continuing tasks.

In 1963, because appointments had been made to staffs of the regional offices without the full involvement of the general secretary, restrictive legislation was passed. "It was agreed as a general principle that in all future cases the General Secretary should be informed in advance of any proposed appointment with full details; if he thought it desirable, such details would be submitted to both committees for consideration." [145]

Carrying out an action of the Belfast assembly in 1962 which authorized the opening of a Geneva office of the W.C.C.E.S.S.A., Dr. Chappel persuaded a member of the board, H. A. Hamilton, then pastor of the Union Congregational Church in Brighton, Sussex, England, to accept this appointment. He had been a leader at the world institutes at Nishinomiya, Japan, in 1958, and at Belfast in 1962. From 1945 to 1954 he had been principal of the Westhill Training School, Selly Oaks, Birmingham, England. His Geneva appointment was for three years, beginning September 1, 1963.[146] At about the same time, Donald O. Newby, who had been serving in Africa since 1961, was to go from there to Geneva to make, with Mr. Hamilton, a two-person office in the Ecumenical Centre of the World Council of Churches.

During his stay in Geneva, Mr. Hamilton shared executive responsibility with Father Paul Verghese of the W.C.C. for the Joint Study on Education, a venture of the World Council of Churches and the World Council of Christian Education. Mr. Hamilton also fulfilled many roles and served as a general liaison person with the manifold activities and the large staff of the World Council of Churches.

So effective was this liaison role, that the general secretary of the World Council of Churches, Dr. W. A. Visser 't Hooft, asked him to come to the staff of the W.C.C. as assistant general secretary for one year after September 1, 1965, with the understanding that he would give half-time to the W.C.C.E.S.S.A., until the end of 1965, and some portion of his time in the following year.[147] The general secretary and the board agreed, with reluctance, to this proposal and to the partial separation of Mr. Hamilton, though realizing that by that time a new general secretary who was to reside in Geneva had been chosen. This prospect made the loss of an experienced, full-time person in the ecumenical centre somewhat less forbidding.

In 1965 it became clear to Nelson Chappel that his severely diminishing eyesight handicapped his work. Accordingly, he offered his resignation to take effect at a mutually agreed-upon date. July 31, 1966 was fixed, he to continue as a special consultant for a time before that with a new general secretary to be brought in as soon as a person could be found.

With this change in executive leadership in mind, and knowing also that there was to be a change in the New York office, Chairman Mackintosh had appointed a Special Personnel Committee in 1964, "to review the whole situation of the Secretariat in view of impending retirements and the financial situation, and to recommend action" and to "examine the salary scales of the Secretariat." [148]

Area meetings of this committee had been held in Enugu, Nigeria, in London, and in New York. A meeting of the committee as a whole was held in London in the spring of 1965 with the chairman of the council, Bishop Mueller, presiding, Viscount Mackintosh having died meanwhile.

The committee nominated Ralph Norman Mould of the United States as general secretary, and the nomination was supported at the next meeting of the Board of Managers. According to an agreement, the appointment was to begin on October 1, 1965, with two months' orientation in New York, and a departure to Geneva thereafter.[149]

Mr. Mould had attended the Toronto meetings in 1950, the Tokyo meetings in 1958, and the Belfast assembly and other sessions in 1962. In the Belfast assembly he was one of the prime movers and authors of the motion calling for closer relationships with the World Council of Churches. Therefore, by his election, he was given responsibility for carrying out that which he had urged as an assembly member. Meanwhile, he had served as a Presbyterian member of the North American Program Committee. His service in the recent years had been with the Board of Christian Education of the Presbyterian (later the United Presbyterian) Church in the U.S.A., as director of children's work, and as coordinator of leadership development over a twenty-year period. He had also been active in the Division of Christian Education and in the Broadcasting and Film Commission of the (U.S.A.)

National Council of Churches. Mr. Mould had served as program chairman for the 1955 international convention held in Cleveland.[150]

In addition to the responsibility of nominating a new general secretary, the special personnel committee also stipulated the need for staff in the three offices. There was to be, it said, a general secretary in Geneva, together with a deputy general secretary and a secretary for studies. There was to be an executive secretary (notice the change in terminology) in each of the London and New York offices. In the London office, in addition, there was to be a secretary for audio-visual education and three executive staff members for the Churches' Television Centre, these four to be supported by the J. Arthur Rank Trust and to remain in London.[151]

As a consequence of these actions, Ralph Mould as general secretary, Rafael Garcia-Mely of Puerto Rico as his deputy, Donald O. Newby for youth work and Katharina van Drimmelen as secretary for study and development were located in Geneva by mid-1966—thus providing a substantial presence in the Geneva Ecumenical Centre, representing the interests and work of the W.C.C.E.S.S.A.

A third responsibility laid upon the committee was to arrive at some formulation about salary scales in the three cities, and to make other staff recommendations as it saw fit. The committee recommended that salaries in Geneva were to be in line with those of the World Council of Churches; in London, with those of the British Council of Churches; and in New York, with those of the National Council of Churches in the U.S.A. Normal retirement was to be at the attainment of age sixty-five with exceptions allowed for an additional year at a time. The North American members of the committee, in consultation with the general secretary-elect and the New York Advisory Committee, were to place a nomination for that office before the board. H. A. Hamilton was to serve part-time after his retirement on August 31, 1966, until the close of the 1967 institute and assembly, but his serious illness prevented this continuance. While October 1967 was the normal date for Andrew Wright's retirement, it was extended until December 31, 1968. Coleman Burke was to replace Dorothy Cadbury on the board, and its membership was to be increased from twenty-three to twenty-six, with at least two of the new places to go to persons from the younger churches.[152] This action was in the direction of a more representative board membership, extending efforts toward that end made in earlier years.

NORTH AMERICAN OFFICE

In the North American office, Wilmina M. Rowland, the youth secretary, left in 1954, to join the staff of United Church Women, N.C.C.C.U.S.A., after serving for five years in the W.C.C.E.S.S.A. The duties of the portfolio were rethought, and in the next year Epiphania Castro (from the Philippines) became field secretary for youth work, with responsibilities centering in Asia. Her term was extended to the end of 1959, and a second extension was made. She resigned this work in 1961, and was elected to a new position—secretary for children's work—from mid-1962 to mid-1965, at which date she left the employ of the council to be married and to pursue further study.

Phillip C. Jones, who had managed the Toronto convention and who had given interim leadership to the work of the New York office, reached retirement age in 1956. It was said of him at the time:

> Dr. Jones has promoted well the work of the Council through his outgoing friendliness and enthusiasm for the W.C.C.E. and its service around the world. He has many friends who recall the warmth of his personality and his pleasant manner. No one can really replace Dr. Jones because he has truly made a place for himself in the lives of many good and loyal friends across the years.[153]

In an effort to increase financial support for the New York office, Homer B. Ogle was brought to the staff in the autumn of 1956 as finance and public relations secretary. The work proved difficult and not productive and, in a little more than a year, he resigned and the North American committee decided to terminate the position.

Laurence Kirkpatrick was brought to the New York office for youth work in February 1961, and Andrew Kim began as associate youth secretary in Asia the next year as regional secretary. Kirkpatrick left at the first of the year, 1963, to assume duties for the World Convention of the Disciples of Christ, his own denomination.

In 1961 Mrs. John H. Amen and Miss Edith Groner were brought on the New York staff for part-time financial efforts. Dr. Everett Stowe, editor of *World Christian Education* for seventeen years, retired in 1964 and, noting this occasion, the Board of Managers recorded its appreciation of his services: "Nothing but the best could for him be either 'Christian' or 'Education.' He has given to this Council a shining image by the consistently high quality of his grooming of its quarterly appearance before its member units and friends in many lands." [154] Mrs. Vivian Russell, who had directed the Children's Art Project, left on June 30, 1965.

By the middle of 1963, the W.C.C.E.S.S.A. was supporting, in whole or in part, an impressive youth staff in Geneva and elsewhere. Dr. Soritua Nababan had become youth secretary for the East Asia Christian Conference, and the North American committee was supporting the work with $3000 annually. Gabriel Setiloane was the full-time African Youth Secretary, with support of $1000 from the NAC. In Latin America, Oscar Bolioli was giving full-time to the Union of Latin American Evangelical Youth, with an annual support of $4000 coming from the NAC.[155]

BRITISH OFFICE

The changes in the British office during this period were fewer in number. Edgar Youdell left the audio-visual work in May 1957, having accepted a position as lecturer in the department of education at Leeds University.[156] He was replaced by Arthur Lomas, who came in the summer of 1957, and who continued in that position until 1970.[157]

British Committee

During these eventful thirteen years, much of the actual program of the council was under the direct supervision of one or the other of the two regional committees. Often, there were adequate program clearances between a regional committee and the office of the general secretary, sometimes there were not, and it was these lacks which led to the clear conviction of Dr. Chappel, during the latter years of his administration, that a tighter structure and tighter administrative practices must be established.

Liaison between the London office and the general secretary's office usually seemed good, though distance, of course, was a factor always to be reckoned with. Distance, however, was not great between the two New York offices and even there communication was not always the best.

Soon after Dr. Chappel came to the work, a European Sunday school convention was held in Wuppertal, Germany, under the sponsorship of the London office. Coming at the close of the Board and Assembly meetings in Frankfort, it enabled some members of the Assembly from non-European countries to participate. Leaders of the Latin countries of Europe met in Italy in 1955, and in Cret Berard, Switzerland in 1957. A German-speaking leaders' conference was held in 1956, and a second European conference was held in the Netherlands that same year. A conference on European youth work was sponsored in 1961, with major responsibility carried by the Youth Department of the World Council of Churches.[158] By 1958 another conference for the Latin countries in Europe had been planned for 1959, this one to be held in Belgium; and a conference for German-speaking leaders was scheduled for Berlin or Austria for that same year.[159]

An observant reader is able to detect differences in emphases as the British committee reported its program from about 1955 onward. Before that time, the reports were largely given over to resumés of what was happening in various Sunday school councils, mostly European, from Austria to Yugoslavia. Now, the reports of the British committee became more and more program-centered, more space being given to the corporate planning and program of the committee itself. One gains the impression that the British committee became less of a London clearing house and more of a program-planning body than it had been before that time, a development, it seems, of the Andrew Wright administration. The popular reports were discontinued in 1961.[160]

In 1962 there came two disjunctions with the past, relating to headquarters. The failing health of Miss G. L. Griffiths led to the closing of the

Glasgow office, which had been, during the service of James Kelly, a center for the association's work. Concern was caused in London by the possibility of having to vacate space in Annandale, Golder's Green, a building owned by the Student Christian Movement which needed more space.[161] New facilities were later found in Bushey, Hertfordshire.

The caution of the British committee about the organizational changes proposed for the Belfast assembly may well have been prompted by a new sense of its own identity. As the years went on, it slowly became less and less of a *British* committee, and more and more representative of European constituent units. Membership on the committee had been extended to all European member units, and each unit was invited to appoint its own representative or representatives.[162] This broadening of membership was accompanied by actual extension of involvement. By 1958 there were members from twenty-four countries.[163] In October of 1958, present at its meeting, in addition to persons from the United Kingdom, were representatives from Austria, Denmark, Finland, France, and Germany. In 1960 as the committee met in Boldern, Germany, thirty-four persons were present from eighteen national member units.

The British Committee thus achieved an international character which the North American Committee never reached, it remaining to the end, virtually a United States organization, with participation now and then from a few Canadians, and almost none from Mexico or the islands of the Caribbean.

North American Committee

There were changes in the nomenclature of this committee during this period. The North American section of the World's Sunday School Association had become the North American Administrative Committee as a result of actions taken at the Rio convention in 1932.[164] The name proved generally satisfactory until the mid-1950s, when it was felt that it was really not an administrative committee, and that it had acquired, necessarily and naturally, other functions as well. Accordingly, it was proposed that the word "administrative" be dropped, and that the body become known as the North American Committee. At the same time it was proposed that the business committee, in existence since 1917, acquire a new name: the "Executive Committee." All members of the present business committee were to be made members of the North American committee. It was hoped that the British would follow the recommendations and adopt similar terminology for themselves.[165]

Programs under the North American committee continued and new ones were added. Over 400 correspondents were chosen in sixty countries, and by 1954 packets were issued on five themes: children, youth, adults, church, and school.[166]

Two curriculum conferences for Latin American countries had been held by 1954; the first in Buenos Aires in 1949, the second in Cienfuegos, Cuba.[167] A curriculum conference was held in April 1963, in Burma. Money for this project had been contributed by children in weekday religious education classes in the United States.[168]

Two regional bodies in South America and in the Caribbean were initially sponsored by the W.C.C.E.S.S.A. and in time achieved their own independent existence: the Caribbean Committee for Joint Christian Action (C.J.C.A.) and the Latin American Evangelical Commission on Christian Education (C.E.L.A.D.E.C.).[169]

The Belfast actions, urging closer relationships with the World Council of Churches, were greeted with approval by the North American committee. Indeed, the Belfast actions were made possible by the actions of the North American committee the year before. In 1961 it recommended

> to the Board of Managers that it explore with the World Council of Churches all possible aspects of relationships and cooperation between the two bodies, and that appropriate representatives of the World Council of Churches and the World Council of Christian Education and Sunday School Association have a consultation on the subject of youth work relationships prior to the New Delhi meetings in November 1961.[170]

In 1965, as this period closed, it was reported that a Latin American Leadership Training Conference had been held, with forty-five persons present from twenty-five countries. The meeting was held in Costa Rica, under the auspices of C.E.L.A.D.E.C., of which Gerson Meyer was general secretary. Four Christian education institutes were to be held in Asia, in 1966 and in 1967, in India, Malaysia, Japan, and Indonesia. Several hundred persons had received training in educational radio and television at the Churches' Television Centre in London, and a large number of youth leadership conferences were being held in Africa, Asia, and Latin America.[171]

A change in the leadership of the committee had come in 1960, as Robert Diefendorf resigned as chairman of the executive committee and became vice-chairman. E. Townsend Look was elected Chairman.[172]

Board of Managers

Through this period, the Board of Managers was responsible, in theory, for the program and administration of the council and, in spite of the tendency of the regional committees to operate at times as if they were virtually independent bodies, the annual meetings of the board and of its World Educational Services Committee were guarantees of considerable program unity. The schedule of meetings of the board was as follows:

1954	Frankfurt, Germany	1960	Berlin, Germany
1955	Cleveland, U.S.A.	1961	New York, U.S.A.
1956	London, England	1962	Belfast, Ireland
1957	Toronto, Canada	1963	Ottawa, Canada
1958	Atami, Japan	1964	Paris, France
1959	Glasgow, Scotland	1965	Mexico City, Mexico

Early in this period, an action was taken to admit denominational bodies or boards to membership in the council. An action stipulated what was required: a denomination, holding "the evangelical faith," autonomous and self-governing; a generally recognized church having a communicant membership of significant size, with an organized Sunday school work or Christian education program.[173] The requirements were admittedly imprecise, but through the years they seemed to serve the body without dissent or controversy.

Through the period the following units were admitted into constituent membership in the council:

National Councils	*Church Bodies*
1954 West Pakistan Christian Council	Sunday School Council of the German Free Church Federation
Youth Department of the National Christian Council of New Zealand	General Assembly, Greek Evangelical Church
Protestant Federation of Sunday Schools of Portugal	Sunday School Board of the Church of Sweden
Sunday School Board of the Federation of Protestant Churches of Belgium	Spanish Evangelical Church
Jamaica Christian Council	Children's Service Board, Evangelical Churches of Germany
Division of Foreign Missions, National Council of Churches, U.S.A.	
1955 British Lessons Council	Congregational Union of England and Wales
Malayan Christian Council	Methodist Church of Great Britain
1956 National Christian Council of Ceylon	Educational Board, Evangelical Church of East Germany
1958 Christian Council of South Africa	Mission Covenant Church, Sweden
1960	Ondo-Benin Diocese (Anglican), Nigeria
1961 Christian Council of Ghana	Church of the Province of Uganda and Ruanda-Urundi (Anglican) [174]
1962 Council of Churches in Indonesia	Board of Church Education and Sunday Schools, Coptic Orthodox Church
Hong Kong Christian Council	Children's Council, Board of Education, Church of England
	Diocesan Synod of Ibadan, Nigeria

In Cleveland in 1955 the closing session of the Twenty-third International Sunday School Convention was turned over by the Division of Christian Education of the National Council of Churches (U.S.A.) to the North American Administrative Committee, and the only offering of the entire convention was taken at that afternoon meeting—the proceeds ($1400) went to the work of the W.C.C.E.S.S.A.[175]

A Cleveland session of the Board also approved the holding of a world convention, institute, and assembly, all to be in Japan. It also authorized a youth services committee in response to a need felt by the council's youth executives and denominational workers.[176]

The meetings of 1956 and 1957 confirmed many of the arrangements then being made for the Tokyo meetings, transferred most of the work in audio-visual aids from the North American to the British office, and approved a Joint Consultation on Youth Work with the World Council of Churches. At Atami (1958) it was announced that the world office would be in the newly constructed Interchurch Center at 475 Riverside Drive, New York.[177]

When the board met at the Johannesstift in West Berlin in 1960, there was a weekend provided for the members to meet with Christian education leaders and pastors in East Germany (German Democratic Republic) for purposes of understanding and mutual sharing of interests and concerns:

> They told in simple language of their problems, thinking of these rather than the privation and very real hardship they personally experienced. So much so, that all who shared this experience were humbled by the devotion and dedication of these our fellow-labourers. They expressed their encouragement at this interchange; it probably meant even more for us.[178]

In 1962, at the Belfast meeting of the Assembly, the size of the Board was increased to twenty-three voting members in the interests of wider representation.[179]

Assemblies

During this period, there were four assemblies: 1953 in New York; 1954 in Frankfurt; 1958 in Atami; and 1962 in Belfast.

The New York assembly was specially called for the chief purpose of officially electing and installing Nelson Chappel as general secretary. The Frankfurt assembly was reported, in *World Christian Education,* as "An Undivided Organization," a designation which proved not wholly true.[180] The 1958 assembly increased the membership of the Board of Managers from eighteen to twenty-one and received an invitation from Belfast for the next assembly and associated meetings.[181] This 1958 assembly also elected six members from the younger churches to the Board of Managers, and reported that five out of the twelve members of the World Educational

Services Committee were from younger churches. At this assembly, the purpose of the council contained in the by-laws was changed to read:

> Since the work of the Council is an integral part of the mission of the Church, its special objectives are to develop Christian education through all available agencies, including organized Sunday schools, to encourage the study of the Bible, and to participate in the church's ministry in the world.[182]

Beyond a doubt, the most important and far-reaching action of the Belfast assembly was a request addressed to the World Council of Churches, asking it to join with the W.C.C.E.S.S.A. in setting up a Joint Study Commission on Education, an invitation which was later accepted by the central committee of that body.[183]

The action authorizing this collaboration in a specific venture was accompanied by language which clearly set forth the organizational openness of the W.C.C.E.S.S.A. to the future and which made possible conversations with the World Council of Churches. These conversations led, in turn, to the "merger" of the two organizations in 1971. The account of those developments, and the spirit and actions which led up to them is the theme of the sixth and last chapter of this account, and is reserved for that next section.

Finances

It was feared, initially, by some that the creation of a world office would put strains upon the finances of the council which, up to that time, had supported only its two regional headquarters. The members of the North American committee, supporting this new centralization, agreed in 1954 to transfer its grants-in-aid to the world office. It also agreed that consolidated financial reports, including those from the two administrative committees, should be prepared annually.[184] The initial fears proved to be unnecessary. Large grants from individuals were received and Nelson Chappel was able to secure generous appropriations from mission and other church agencies.

The British committee now operated on a balanced budget, at times even putting aside some monies in reserve for future conference and scholarship expenses.[185]

The financial situation of the North American committee was not so favorable, even though it contributed more funds to the central budget than the British were able to do. By 1961 it was clear that the New York office was overspending every year.[186] The executive of the North American committee excused this excess by an ingenious rationalization:

> Fortunately our deficits of the past two or three years have been more than offset by increases in the value of our investments. Even so, it has been necessary to authorize the use of reserve funds up to the extent of $15,000 a year to assure full underwriting of the 1961–62 budget which totals $152,700.[187]

The efforts of Miss Edith Groner and Mrs. John H. Amen had helped, but not enough. By 1963 the North American deficits were so large that the Board of Managers was asked for a grant or grants not to exceed $25,000 if such a request became necessary during the quadrennium. By the next year, it proved necessary to make such a request. By this time, the planning committee had met and had approved a grant to the North American committee of $25,000, and a like amount to the British committee for its program. By the time the 1964 closings were made, however, the New York office was able to meet its operating deficit by utilizing balances and special gifts. Thus, it did not need the $25,000 it had requested from the capital funds of the council. This result came to pass even with the turning over from the North American Committee to the general funds of more than $40,000.[188]

The world office budget was gradually assuming some central expenses as it was able. In 1957 it took over the travel expenses to Board of Managers and Assembly meetings for members from the younger churches. Its resources were increased for this and other purposes. Before that date, ten percent of the general funds had gone to the world office, and forty-five percent to each of the administrative committees. After that date, twenty percent went to the world office and forty percent to each of the two committees.[189]

A welcome source of support came from the Swiss Sunday School Association in 1962, when $10,000 was presented to the council, and gifts followed from that association at frequent intervals.[190] By 1962 a scholarship fund, honoring the long service of Paul Sturtevant, the association's treasurer, had reached a total of $10,000.[191]

By 1965 it was clear that commitments from a number of educational and mission boards would be necessary to support the growing program of the council. Accordingly there were a number of consultations held in the United States and in Canada with educational and mission executives of the denominations, pleading the cause of the council as an integral part of the worldwide educational and mission outreach of the churches. "Fair-share" support amounts were suggested. A "quadrennial appeal," adopted by the 1962 assembly, had met with little response, except for the gift from the Swiss Sunday School Association noted above, and a pledge of support from a "Week of Compassion," planned by the Christian Church, Disciples of Christ (U.S.A.). A general mail appeal to local churches in the United States and Canada in the early 1960s produced less than $1500.[192]

The financial stringencies did not abate with the retirement of Nelson Chappel and the election of a new general secretary. They persisted into the administration of Ralph N. Mould, a period of greater centralization of administration and program.

The twelve-year period of Nelson Chappel's administration was characterized by attempts to make one council out of what came very close to being two agencies. Brought to a newly created office of a single general secretary, and even with supporting legislation behind him, he nevertheless found it difficult to bring reality into correspondence with the avowed intent.

With funds—either actual or optimistically projected—at its disposal, the North American office sometimes acted without assured clearances, sometimes with the British office, sometimes with the general secretary, located in the same building. The British committee sometimes revealed its desire to return to a simpler day with a program chiefly for little children, and to revert to the original name and dual structure.

Even with such difficulties, the council widely expanded its program. Dr. Chappel's curricular services were a conspicuous feature of the period. In a way these efforts created a third, virtually independent, council program, for the New York and London offices were not involved in them to any great extent. The establishment of a Geneva office, in the later years, aided immeasurably in relations with the World Council of Churches and other world bodies, but it did not increase the unity of the Council itself. There were now four offices to be coordinated and administered: Geneva, London, and two in New York.

Just as dissatisfaction, prior to 1950, led to the restructuring of the council and the calling of Nelson Chappel, so at the close of this period a second sense of inadequacy led to the calling of Ralph Mould, as Dr. Chappel, because of his failing eyesight, took early retirement.

The supporting legislation of 1964 and 1965, and the personal charge laid upon Mr. Mould were unambiguous: "Set yourself up in Geneva, improve relationships with the World Council of Churches, make of the World Council of Christian Education and Sunday School Association a single body, and see to it that New York and London support you in that grand design."

6

Common Ecumenical Study and
Progress Toward Merger
1965-1971

THE COUNCIL NOW HAD its general headquarters established in the Ecumenical Centre in Geneva with a single general secretary in charge. Belfast had directed that overtures for common effort with the World Council of Churches be made. During the six last years of the life of the W.C.C.E.S.S.A., the possibility, and later the likelihood, of such closer relations or complete merger with the World Council of Churches dominated its interest and energies. This was not the only interest of the council, however, and its educational program went on apace during these final six years.

Institutes

Even before Ralph Mould was chosen as the new executive head of the council, preliminary plans had been made for a 1967 institute, carrying on the sequence of Toronto, 1950; Nishinomiya, 1958; and Belfast, 1962. Graham Hudson, a Canadian layman, had been chosen institute chairman in 1964, and plans were made for the committee to meet in March of the next year.[1]

NAIROBI, 1967
The committee settled upon the theme, "The People of God in God's World—Living, Learning, Teaching." The purpose was to engage participants in conditions for openness "both those whose ministries were in their 'secular callings' and those whose ministries were in the direct service of the Church." [2] The influence of lay chairman Hudson was pervasive. It was hoped and planned that a large percentage of those attending would be lay men and women, not professionally engaged in the work of the church. That

expectation was not realized, for when the final tabulations were made only 12.3 percent of the participants were lay folk. North American denominational executives from the start were dubious that large numbers of lay people would attend the institute.

In other respects, however, the Nairobi institute was a widely representative gathering. For the first time, Roman Catholic observers attended a W.C.C.E. institute. Africa supplied forty-two percent of the 370 delegates, North America fifteen percent and Australia five percent. The participants represented seventy-five countries: sixteen of Asia, Australia, and the Pacific Islands; thirteen of Europe, twenty-two countries of Africa, five of the Middle East, sixteen of Latin America and the Caribbean, and the United States and Canada.[3]

Roy Neehall, senator from Trinidad and member of the board of managers, gave the keynote address, based on I Peter 2:9, 10. The present ecumenical climate, he declared, is an invitation to the churches to reinterpret their denominational emphases in the light of the ecumenicity of the world. We need to become more relevant to the realities of the world in which we live, he continued, and the church needs to recognize its involvement in the world. The world in which we are living is a world of change, one in which people never have time to settle down to anything.[4]

The substantive work of the institute was done in seven commissions supplementing the institute's general theme: in daily work; in the structures of church and society; in the tensions between the generations; in the midst of racial and cultural differences; in state-controlled or state-supported education; in the search for a just and peaceful international order; and in public and private worship.[5] These commissions devoted great attention to the problems of relating the educational work of the churches to the specific social, economic, and political settings in which they were carried on. Detailed requests were made of the W.C.C.E. for specific services.

As the commissions brought in their reports after their several sessions, they were reported to a plenary session and later reproduced in the pages of *World Christian Education.*

At the close of the institute, the participants were asked to evaluate the program in terms of its impact upon them. Twenty-eight percent described it as extremely helpful; sixty-six percent as helpful; five as having no particular effect; and one percent as not helpful. About the same reactions came from a question about the methods and procedures in the small groups. Twenty-seven percent regarded them as extremely helpful, sixty-three percent as helpful, and nine percent as not helpful.[6]

Professor C. Ellis Nelson of Union Seminary, New York, provided a summary and interpretation of the institute in an eighteen-chapter report. General Secretary Mould asked what was the big, critical issue at stake in the institute. He answered his own question:

It was whether Christian education through its many forms was just to keep on the traditional limited tracks of transmitting the faith in often ingrown, narrow, churchly pietistic terms, or whether it was to take a sharp turn and become truly oriented to real persons amid real life situations—the total milieu—and actually prepare them at all ages for Christian understanding of the world, themselves, others, the acute human problems of society and the Christian life in terms of active worship, witness and service in community and world as committed members of God's One Whole World people. Nairobi chose the second orientation.[7]

It was only regrettable that the findings went for the most part to the clergy and to those in church-related vocations. Not many lay people were there to get the message.

During the preliminary discussion of the plans there was some thought given to holding this institute and the 1967 assembly in Rome, to celebrate the founding of the agency there sixty years before. On the other hand, there was strong support for having these meetings in the land of one of the younger churches, and it was this concern which prevailed. The founding of the association was to be remembered later that year in a special commemoration held in Rome, and it was celebrated in the same Methodist church where the association was founded in 1907. The anniversary was tied in with a meeting of the European regional committee. Three language groups—French, German, and English—met to discuss the Nairobi institute recently concluded and its follow-up.[8]

LATIN AMERICA AND HUAMPANI, 1971

As the time approached for the next assembly, the question arose as to whether there should be another institute, or whether the pattern, begun in 1950, had pretty well run itself out in the subsequent twenty years. The answer, in time, was supportive of another institute, but according to an entirely new pattern. Smaller groups were to meet, previously, in various cities and countries and to make, subsequently, their individual contributions to an "institute-assembly."

A word from the Spanish language was selected for these scattered meetings, *encuentro*. No doubt it was thought that a Spanish word was simply most appropriate for meetings held in the Caribbean-Latin American world, though those who knew both English and Spanish asserted that there was a richer connotation in the Spanish term than was true of the nearest English equivalent, "encounter." The "over-meanings" of the Spanish word were said to connote "dialogue," "openness," "an honest searching for truth."

In any event, the experiences of those who met more or less simultaneously in seventeen cities in the Caribbean, Central America, and South America were rich indeed. The *encuentros* were widely spaced, ranging from Haiti and Jamaica in the north to Argentina and Chile in the south.

Each of the 380 official participants in the assembly was assigned to one of these smaller gatherings. Resources about each country were available in written form, but the most frequent and effective resources came from the people who were invited to meet with the members of the groups in conversation and informal addresses—over six hundred of them. Carman Hunter, who directed the program, had formulated the purpose of the week-long sessions: "to develop as complete a picture as possible of education, both Church and general, its purposes, scope, resources, methods and problems in each country." [9]

An amazingly wide variety of persons responded to the invitations for appearances: university, seminary, general education people; Roman Catholic dignitaries and fundamentalist preachers; labor leaders and union members; "main line" Protestant missionaries; poor people; government officials; literacy workers; Sunday school workers; and others.

At the end of the venture, Mrs. Hunter saw both discouraging and encouraging observations. She listed as discouraging an emphasis upon individual understanding of salvation; a tendency toward teacher-directed Bible-centered transmission; a dependence upon content and methodology from other nations and cultures, chiefly the United States; a lack of programs in adult education; a lack of trained persons and resources; and a limited use of audio-visual aids.

Alongside these items she perceived some encouraging developments: the emergence of the Latin American curriculum, *New Life in Christ,* which sought to combine evangelical concerns with a passion for social justice; an increased creation of indigenous material; more emphasis put upon creative participation in learning; some pioneering in producing life-centered curricula; and some rethinking on the teaching tasks of the church by groups such as the Latin American Evangelical Commission on Christian Education.[10]

Coming from these intense and broadening experiences in the seventeen regional sessions, the delegates met at the Huampani assembly grounds, a government conference center located in the foothills of the Andes, a few miles east of Lima. The opening sermon of Methodist Bishop Federico J. Pagura continued themes struck again and again in the Encuentros:

> If there is some hope that brings us together here; if there is some good news that we must examine and proclaim together to the world, they are born in the fact that God lives, God hears and God acts. On his ears, so different from the deaf ears of bad rulers and the fossilized and insensitive religious leaders of our time, has fallen the cry of the oppressed; at the same time he understands the misery and tragedy of the oppressor. In other words, as the great Quaker, Rufus Jones, expressed it: God is not the great "I was" but rather the great "I am." [11]

Though unexpressed, the single word *liberation* might have served as the theme and keynote of the Huampani institute-assembly. The note was struck in its closing message to the churches:

> Liberation is much more than an idea or an ideal. It is God's work in the world for the elimination of the causes of slavery and for the full realization of a new life which becomes actualized in community, solidarity, respect, and equality, according to the truth revealed in the Gospel.
>
> As Christian educators we ask what it means to educate. In this Assembly we have heard a disturbing challenge; to educate is not so much to teach as it is to become committed to a reality in and with the people; it is to learn to live, to encourage creativity in ourselves and in others; and, under God and His power, to liberate mankind from the bonds that prevent the development of God's image.[12]

Bishop Pagura had earlier been a member of the Costa Rica group, and his challenge to missionaries was a provocative and challenging litany:

Missionary Go Home . . . Or Stay

If you cannot understand what is happening on this continent at this time which is awakening the dawn of a new liberation
   MISSIONARY GO HOME
If you aren't capable of separating the eternal word of the Gospel from the cultural molds in which you brought it to these lands
   MISSIONARY GO HOME
If you are not able to identify with the sufferings, agonies and aspirations of these people made prematurely old by the unequal struggle which seems not to have end or hope
   MISSIONARY GO HOME
If your allegiance and faithfulness to your homeland is stronger than your loyalty and obedience to Jesus Christ who came to "put down the mighty from their thrones and exalt them of low degree" (Luke:1.52)
   MISSIONARY GO HOME
If your dogmatism is such that it doesn't permit you to revise your theology and your ideology in the light of all the biblical witness and the events of these times
   MISSIONARY GO HOME
If you are not capable to love and respect as equals those for whom one day you came to evangelize as "lost"
   MISSIONARY GO HOME
If you are not able to rejoice with the entrance of new people and churches into the newness of maturity, independence and responsibility, although at a price of committing errors such as those which you and your countrymen also made in the past
   THEN, NOW IS THE TIME TO RETURN TO YOUR HOME
BUT, if you are disposed to undergo the risks and pains of this hour of birth in which our American people live, while at the same time denying yourself, if you begin to rejoice with them for the feeling of happiness that the Gospel is not just an announcement and affirmation of a remote hope but rather of a hope and liberation which is even now transforming history, if you are disposed to put more of your time, your wealth, your life to the service of these people who are

awakening, then STAY, for there is much to do and there is a lack of hands and blood for a task so large, in which Christ is the pioneer and protagonist.

Assemblies

When the 1967 assembly was called to order at the University of East Africa, Nairobi, there were ninety-four persons plus members of the staff present, fifty-nine of them representing forty-one member units. Fifteen were board members not otherwise counted, sixteen were representatives of countries without member units, and four were fraternal delegates.[13]

In addition, there were others present who had attended the institute and who became observers at the assembly.

The general secretary made a report of his observations about the state of Christian education in various countries. It was not optimistic:

> . . . we have participated in seventeen Christian Nurture Consultations held in selected countries to discover the conditions and most pressing needs in their Christian education. I wish it were possible to tell you that all is well with their programs but this would be contrary to fact by their own accounts. True, there is some promising self-evaluation, though nothing like enough; there are some innovations and reforms in education which are fruitful in beginning ways. There is some worthy work being done and without it people would be much the poorer. But over-all the picture is not too reassuring; in fact it is formidable if not frightening.[14]

As President Charles Malik assumed office, recognizing the critical nature of the years immediately ahead involving possible merger, he asked for the creation of an *ad hoc* committee designed to study the basic future educational program of the council. There was considerable feeling, below the surface, on the part of the World Educational Services Committee that this proposal failed to take into account that it had been doing just that for many years past, and that the stage was being set by Dr. Malik's request for conflict, duplication, and misunderstanding.

The assembly, and later the board, supported the proposal of the new president, and the *ad hoc* committee was established under the chairmanship of Dr. Clifford Wright of Australia, with Phillip Jefferson of Canada as secretary. Eight others were named to the committee, including the president. Later, two more were added.[15]

The *ad hoc* committee held sessions in Nairobi and in the following year in Frankfort, in the latter city assisting in the early negotiations with the World Council of Churches, and carrying on preliminary studies in order for the W.C.C.E. delegation to be well-prepared for their roles. At the 1969 meeting of the board, the *ad hoc* committee was terminated.[16]

At the Nairobi assembly there was an action taken regarding the name of the organization. It had been World's Sunday School Association, World Council of Christian Education, then World Council of Christian Education and Sunday School Association. Now it was to be again the "World Council of Christian Education," and under this name it carried on its negotiations with the World Council of Churches.

Board of Managers

During this time (1965–1971), as a new general secretary began his work, as negotiations with the World Council of Churches became more numerous and significant, and as the two program committees relinquished much of their former functions to the World Educational Services Committee, the Board of Managers continued its oversight of the council's affairs. Indeed, it intensified this supervision, as symbolized by the authorization of an executive committee which met in mid-winter in 1968 and 1971.

The regional committees had been appointed in place of the administrative committees of New York and London in 1965. At the same time, action was taken to enlarge the membership of the Board of Managers from a maximum of twenty-three to a maximum of thirty, to be done "in a manner which will guarantee a more equitable representation of geographical and confessional interests. Representation of younger churchmen is also assured." [17]

When this recommendation came to the assembly in Nairobi in 1967 a rider was approved, to the effect that membership on the Board of Managers be limited to two quadrennia, after which term of service a person should not be eligible again for four years. The provision was to become effective after the next assembly.[18]

There was a strong feeling on the part of some members of the 1967 assembly that the board had allowed too many members to serve too long and that an infusion of new blood was needed. There was a broad geographical range of membership. Of the thirty, three were from Africa, six from Asia, one from Australia, one from the Caribbean, nine from Europe, eight from North America, and two from South America. The president was a Lebanese, the chairman was an American, and of the three vice-chairmen, one was from Switzerland, one from the United States, and one from India. The Anglo-American axis was no longer the real or potential power block it had been in earlier decades.

In that assembly year, the World Educational Services Committee reviewed a paper on ecumenical commitment, originating in the joint youth department; reviewed progress reports on nine indigenous curricular projects; reviewed already existing educational ventures and referred new ones to the Board of Managers; expressed a need for some basic educational research; referred to the staff concern for and research on weekday kindergarten and nursery schools under church auspices; discussed the scholarship program and new developments at Westhill Training School; and heard reports from the youth secretary and the magazine, *World Christian Education.*[19]

At the 1967 assembly five new member units were received: the National Council of the Lutheran Churches in Germany; the Anglican Diocese of Gambia and Rio Pongas; the Reformed Church of Yugoslavia; the Methodist Church of Samoa; and the Syrian Orthodox Church of India. All of these new member bodies were denominational units, bringing the total number to over seventy in more than sixty countries.[20]

North American Regional Committee

The North American committee had, by this time, been transformed into the North American regional committee, a body composed of 160 persons from seven categories; viz., North American members of the W.C.C.E. assembly; advisory committee to the New York office; persons from North American denominations; state, regional, and provincial councils; related agencies; members-at-large and consultants. The first meeting was scheduled for Pittsburgh on May 24 and 25, 1965.[21]

The purposes of the N.A.R.C. were set forth as follows:

1. To review the program of the W.C.C.E. and assist in implementing it.
2. To make recommendations concerning the program of the W.C.C.E. either in terms of modifications or suggestions for new program.
3. To interpret the program of the W.C.C.E. to North American churches.
4. To solicit funds for the support of the program of the W.C.C.E.
5. To perform such other functions as may be requested by the Assembly or Board of Managers and accepted by the North American Regional Committee, as appropriate for this committee.[22]

By 1968 it was generally agreed by those closest to its work that this ambitious program and this comprehensive committee structure had failed, and that the hopes for the usefulness of the N.A.R.C. had not been realized. At the 1968 meeting of the Board of Managers, it received a request from the N.A.R.C. that it be dissolved and a transfer be made of some of its functions to the National Council of Churches. This request was supported by the Board of Managers, giving to the N.C.C. most of the program functions of the N.A.R.C., but retaining the interpretation and fundraising role for North American members of the Board of Managers as a nucleus of an advisory committee.[23] A final meeting of persons involved in the North American concerns met in Toronto on May 21 and 22, 1969.

Program formulation was now no longer being undertaken in New York. It was concentrated in the World Educational Services Committee. The supervision of practical matters relating to the New York office remained in the hands of a small committee, easily accessible to the executive in charge. The program unification of the council, so long sought and with so many frustrations, was seen by the North Americans as having been accomplished. Most persons involved seemed pleased with the changes, and on both sides of the

Atlantic and elsewhere the feeling seemed to be that the council now had a unified educational program, centrally administered.

Officers

The most important change in the elected leadership of the council came at the Nairobi assembly as the Honorable Charles Malik of Beirut was elected president, succeeding Sir Francis Ibiam of Nigeria. Charles Habib Malik, at that time, was distinguished professor of philosophy at the American University of Beirut. He had formerly been the Lebanese ambassador to the United States. He had been a signer of the charter of the United Nations, and had been the chairman of the delegation of Lebanon to the United Nations and president of the thirteenth session of its General Assembly, 1958–1959.[24]

The nominating committee and the delegates to the Nairobi Assembly were fully aware that the next quadrennium would be a critical one in the history of the council. Relationships and possible merger with the World Council of Churches would clearly require strong elected leadership. Dr. Malik provided these qualities. A loyal son of the Eastern Orthodox communion, he had a profound understanding of Western religious and philosophical thought, and understood well the Protestantism of western Europe and of the Western hemisphere.

Bishop Mueller continued as chairman, along with many of the members of the Board of Managers. At Nairobi, Emanuel Jung of Switzerland, Gerald E. Knoff of the United States, and V. M. Koshy of India were elected vice-chairmen. Bishop Mueller's long administrative experience and his knowledge of the program of the World Council of Churches were tremendous assets to the W.C.C.E. in these negotiating months. His level-headed and judicious habit of working helped greatly at many critical points.

Staff

Just as Ralph Mould began his administrative service with the council in November of 1965, an unusually large number of staff members in the three offices terminated their services for reasons of their own. Everett Stowe had retired a year earlier as editor of *World Christian Education* and as a program secretary in Adult Work and Family Life. Epiphania Castro, Vivian Russell, Wilson Cheek, Herbert Hamilton, and Donald Newby had resigned, either to take up other positions or because of budgetary limitations. About the time Mould arrived in Geneva, J. Martin Preston found that service with the joint study commission was not to his liking and left. Marie Wissel, a veteran of forty-one years of service with the council, retired, having served under W. G. Landes, Robert M. Hopkins, Forrest L. Knapp, Phillip C. Jones, Russell Harrison, and Nelson Chappel. Andrew Kim was to have terminated his work at the end of 1965, but the Childrens' Work Advisory Committee asked that he be continued on funds of the Story Picture Project, and so he stayed in service until the end of 1966.

Separations called for replacements, though there were not adequate funds for a one-to-one replenishing of the staff ranks. The first to be appointed was Loren Walters, replacing Wilson Cheek as the executive in the New York office. He began his work in November of 1965. Mr. Walters had been director of the educational program of the United Church of Christ in the U.S.A. He had been coopted as a member of the staff of the Division of Christian Education of the N.C.C. for a period of two years, organizing and promoting the Twenty-third International Convention of that body in Cleveland in 1955.

In January 1966, Rafael Garcia-Mely of Puerto Rico joined the Geneva staff as deputy general secretary. Dr. Garcia-Mely had received a B.D. at Yale and a Ph.D. at New York University. When invited, he was on the staff of the Inter-American University in San Juan, Puerto Rico.[25]

To expedite the work of the study commission occasioned by the loss of Martin Preston, Theodore Gill was called to be a joint director by Mould and Father Paul Verghese of the World Council of Churches. Dr. Gill had occupied a number of responsible positions in religious circles in the United States, including the presidency of the San Francisco Theological Seminary (Presbyterian) and the editorship of *The Christian Century,* an influential and ecumenical weekly published in Chicago.

In 1966 two staff actions were taken by the Board of Managers: Nelson Chappel was made general secretary emeritus, and Katharina van Drimmelen came to assume duties in the Geneva office. Miss Drimmelen was an ordained pastor in the Netherlands Reformed Church, director of a lay academy for ten years.

The next few years brought additional persons to the staff. Mercy Yamoah came in 1967 as youth secretary to concentrate on the Christian education of teenagers, thirteen to nineteen, her concern being primarily with church-related organizations. Miss Yamoah had been a teacher of religious knowledge in a Ghana school and had received an M.A. from Cambridge. She returned (as Mercy Oduyoye) to Africa in 1970 to join her husband in Nigeria.

Maurice Assad came to take responsibility for administering the Educational Renewal Fund in 1970.[26] Mr. Assad was an Egyptian, educated in part in the United States (he had received a Ph.D. from Columbia University). He was a Coptic Orthodox, the first staff member of the council from an Eastern Oriental church. He was employed jointly by the W.C.C.E. and the W.C.C.

There were staff departures, also, in these last years of the council's life. Donald O. Newby relinquished his youth work responsibilities in December 1965, after five years of service in Africa and Geneva. Miss van Drimmelen left the council's employ in mid-1968 for another position in Vienna, Austria. On January 1, 1969, Rafael Garcia-Mely went to be the academic dean of the New World University in San Juan, Puerto Rico. He was succeeded by Gerson Meyer, a Brazilian, who began his work in February 1969, in the Geneva headquarters. Meyer came from the Evangelical Latin American Commission on Christian Education (C.E.L.A.D.E.C.), where he had served ably for six years as general secretary. He had been well acquainted with the work of the W.C.C.E., having been a member of the Board of Managers, and having attended the institutes and conferences in Belfast, Furingen, and Nairobi.

In the midst of these staff changes, veteran Andrew Wright continued, his term of service having been extended by successive actions of the British committee and the Board of Managers.

"World Christian Education"

During this period the quarterly, *World Christian Education,* continued to be edited in turn by staff members, most frequently by Garcia-Mely and Meyer. The circulation remained about the same as in earlier years. The magazine was terminated after the issue of the first quarter of 1972 and replaced by an educational newsletter from the office of education, World Council of Churches.[27]

Finances

It was clear from the beginning of the period that the council was financially overextended and that fiscal stringencies were even then beginning to appear. At the 1966 meeting of the board in Oslo, the estimated deficit for the preceding year was about $65,000. The imprecision in the report was in part attributable to the lack of complete and adequate financial and auditor's reports for 1965. The consolidation of the finances in the three centers of New York, London, and Geneva was even then incomplete, and some financial statements had been lost.

Other years brought further deficits. The justification for the shortages were the pressing program needs. By the time the council merged into the World Council of Churches, the dowry which it brought to the union was far less than what might have been the case had the W.C.C.E. managed to carry on with a balanced budget during these years.

One financial development which did flourish during this period was the Educational Renewal Fund. It had been called by other names since it was first proposed at the Furingen World Curriculum Conference in 1964. At that meeting Asian and Latin American delegates asked for the creation of a fund, to be administered by the W.C.C.E., designed to meet felt needs, usually educational development projects, in the younger churches' programs of Christian education.

At the meeting of the World Educational Services Committee the next year in Mexico City, the same need was expressed and at once the Board of Managers approved such a creation and named a special committee, headed by Alvin J. Cooper of Canada, to report at the next meeting of the Board. The Oslo meeting (1966) continued the committee.

As a fourth draft was submitted to the Nairobi assembly and the Board of Managers in 1967, the objectives of the program were set forth as follows:

1. To support the effective development of the educational programs and training projects of the congregations to equip all members for engagement in renewal, ministry and mission;
2. To share in the responsibilities of the churches and religious organizations for Christian thought and action about public education . . .
3. To encourage and assist in the development of a leadership strategy in every country through specific training projects . . .
4. To provide adequate consultative and leadership resources . . .[28]

It was thought that mission boards, educational agencies, foundations, and generous individuals might respond to such a program or to one of the specific items included in the fund. The total askings in one year, 1968, totaled over a quarter of a million dollars.

Developing curriculum projects (twelve areas)	$142,000
Strengthening Area Christian Education (six areas)	39,808
Supporting World Youth Work	28,550
Providing Leadership Training Opportunities	23,400
Convening Special Conferences and Consultations	24,310
Grants in Aid	7,749 [29]

Within a five-year period it was hoped to secure $2,800,000 for six geographical areas and for central administrative expenses in Geneva.[30]

After Alvin Cooper relinquished the chairmanship, Bishop Yap Kim Hao of Singapore and Malaysia (Methodist), and later W. Kent Gilbert of the Lutheran Church in America, headed the committee. By 1969 and after much negotiation the program came to be a joint venture of the W.C.C.E. and the W.C.C. and a search for two million dollars for it was authorized.[31] Eventually this amount and more was raised and distributed to over fifty projects around the world.

As has been reported, Maurice Assad was called in 1970 to give executive leadership to the fund in Geneva. After the merger of the two councils, Ralph Mould was continued by the World Council of Churches for this program through the year 1972, and until his retirement on January 30, 1973. In the World Council of Churches administration, the program has been amalgamated with its general program of assistance and interchurch aid. This identification resulted in a significant strengthening of the program because of the utilization of tested procedures in the interchurch aid program of the W.C.C.

The Joint Study Commission

A joint study commission established with the World Council of Churches proved to be an absorbing activity of the W.C.C.E. from 1963 to 1968, and, as it was completed, provided a facilitating experience toward open and responsible conversations about merger.

EARLY AUTHORIZATIONS AND CONVERSATIONS FOR THE JOINT STUDY

The earliest official action which led directly to this joint enterprise was a decision reached at the third assembly of the World Council of Churches at New Delhi in the autumn of 1961. Up until that time the World Council of Churches had no single, comprehensive unit dealing with education as a whole. To be sure, it had educational activities and in abundance. The Ecumenical Institute at the Chateau de Bossey near Geneva was a significant educational institution, and its association with the University of Geneva gave it added prestige. The departments of laity and of the cooperation of men and women were essentially activities in adult education. The youth department for years had been administered in connection with the W.C.C.E. Other basically educational programs could be listed.

It was still true, however, that the W.C.C. had no single, conspicuous place where the concerns of education, in its broadest understanding, could be given specialized attention in an organizational setting comparable to its other concerns: relief, faith and order, mission, and other program activities.

Considerations such as these led the staff of the W.C.C. to propose that there be established an educational unit, authorization for it to be secured from the third assembly. An obvious complication was the W.C.C.E. and its work, and the W.C.C. had no desire to compete with it or to duplicate its work. Francis House, the executive of the Division of Ecumenical Action, openly shared the desires of his council with staff and officers of the W.C.C.E., seeking to describe a place for W.C.C. activity which would supplement the ongoing work of the older council.

When the proper assembly committee met in New Delhi to consider the matter, Reuben H. Mueller, then a vice-chairman of the W.C.C.E., had been appointed secretary of the group and I was present throughout its sessions as a consultant. The resulting action of the assembly asserted that ". . . the Division of Ecumenical Action should also be concerned with *Christian Education as a whole*" . . . that "there is great hunger for *education in general* in the modern world and especially in the areas of rapid social change . . ." The Division of Ecumenical Action recommended that

> the Central Committee consider at the appropriate time the creation of a special unit, in the World Council of Churches dealing with educational issues as a whole. . . . In the meantime it is recommended that there should be conversations with the World Council of Christian Education and Sunday School Association regarding the desirability of closer and more general relationships with the World Council of Churches . . .[32]

In the discussion in the assembly, Kathleen Bliss welcomed the report. She felt that the new definition of the functions of the division aided in crystallizing thought about a direction which had been under consideration for some time. The report was adopted by the assembly, and the World Council of Churches had the needed authorization to begin services in education to the member churches.

The W.C.C. action having been taken, it was clear to the officers of the W.C.C.E. that, even with the best of intentions on both sides, difficulties might arise, and it was seen clearer than ever before that an expanded cooperation and understanding was mandatory. By degrees the idea grew in both circles that a joint study of the field of education, both religious and secular, ought to be undertaken. The timetable of the two agencies was such that it appeared that the Belfast assembly of the W.C.C.E., meeting in the summer of 1962, would provide the quickest and most productive consideration of this germinal idea.

Meanwhile, the North American committee had met and, having given the first consideration to such a proposal, brought this recommendation to the assembly:

> The W.C.C.E.S.S.A. should propose to the W.C.C. that there be appointed a Joint Study Commission to consider the theological basis of the Church's responsibility for education both in and outside the Church, Christian education needs throughout the world, and possible ways and means to achieve a common and unified response to them and to our Lord's Great Commission.[33]

The recommendation was approved by the assembly.[34]

Something of the motivation for the calling for this study may be sensed from this excerpt:

> The W.C.C.E.S.S.A. records its conviction that such a study would symbolize and strengthen the evident marriage of Biblical theology and Christian education in our time. It would underline the world's and the Church's sore needs for a vital Christian education relevant to this age, what educational ministry does and must mean in the total context of Church and mission, and the indispensable role and equipment of the laity to serve, and to witness in this world. The deep meanings of Christian faith related to educational communication of that faith to persons of all ages and conditions must be explored freshly and thoroughly. Difficulties, though real, can be overcome through the loving power that is God, who leads, teaches, and redeems His whole creation in Christ.[35]

From Belfast the trail led to the February 1963 meeting of the executive committee of the W.C.C. It generously supported the overture and made suggestions for the work of such a committee.[36]

Following the action of the Belfast assembly, staff conversations were held in Geneva from the 11th to the 13th of March, 1963. Dr. Kathleen Bliss had been chairman of the Division of Ecumenical Action and was then chairman of the board of the ecumenical institute. This *ad hoc* committee worked on "terms of reference" for the committee, and its draft was referred first to the meeting of the W.C.C.'s central committee meeting in Rochester, N.Y. in late August of that year, and next to the meeting of the Board of Managers, in session in Ottawa the next month.

As finally approved by the two bodies the scope of the study was formulated as follows:

1. To consider in the light of the Christian faith the nature and function of education in our changing societies, to examine the nature of the churches' responsibility in and for education, and to work toward the formulation of a common theological understanding of education.
2. To make recommendations to the two sponsoring bodies on ways of assisting the churches in the fulfillment of their responsibilities in general education and to suggest the priorities to which the organizations should address themselves.
3. To make sample studies of the present practices of the churches in the nurture and training of their members; to ascertain what are the most pressing needs and to suggest how the two organizations might be of assistance to the churches in developing new lines of approach to this task.[37]

By September 1963, nominations for membership were in hand, and Herbert A. Hamilton had been appointed by General Secretary Chappel to take chief responsibility for the study. Father Paul Verghese, executive of the World Council of Churches' Division of Ecumenical Action, had a similar assignment from his council.

MEETINGS

The committee was composed equally of persons appointed by the two bodies and had its first ten-day meeting on the campus of the Johannesstift, Spandau, West Berlin. Of the twenty-five persons invited to be members of the committee, twenty-three accepted, and of them, twenty attended the Berlin meeting. Two were prevented from coming by political restrictions. At the first session Dr. Bliss, who had served as convenor, was unanimously elected chairman.

At this first meeting three working groups were established:

1. What is education and who is the person being educated?
2. What is the contemporary role of Christian Institutions and of the Christian teacher?
3. What are the needs of the churches in their own work of training and sustaining the life and worship of the Christian person? [38]

Working papers had been prepared in advance and were presented and discussed. One expanded the terms of reference while others were "situation papers" dealing with the contemporary educational scene in thirteen nations or areas. Four confessional papers were discussed, dealing with the role of education in conversion-centered churches, in Orthodox churches, in

Lutheran circles, and in the Roman Catholic church. Two additional position papers not written were seen as needed: "What is Happening in Education?" and "Education and the Nature of Man."

To deal with the latter concern a further meeting was held at Glion, Switzerland, composed of some from the joint study commission and some who were not, with the theme before them, "The Views of Man Implied in Some Educational Systems." The resulting report proved to be influential, not only for the work of the joint study commission but also for philosophers of education and other theorists in the educational and religious world. It was published by the World Council of Churches under the title, "Education and the Nature of Man."

By the time the next meeting was held at the Isle of Thorns, Sussex, England, August–September 1965 (another ten-day meeting), a number of developments had come to pass. Ralph Mould was now the general secretary of the W.C.C.E. and attended the sessions, whereas Nelson Chappel had been at Berlin the year before. Regional studies had been carried on through the East Asia Christian Council, the All Africa Christian Council, the World's Student Christian Federation, in the Caribbean, and in Australasia. Studies of Christian institutions, colleges, seminaries, and universities had been developed. A cross-cultural study project on the contribution of family group attitudes to religious attitude formation in the young was authorized, with responsibilities to be carried by Dr. R. J. Goldman of Britain and Dr. Malcolm McAfee of the United States—a project which in time proved impossible to develop.

As before, study papers were read. Topics included contemporary happenings in education; the vocation of the Christian teacher; the future of educational institutions; the church's role in education; the nature of man; and the educational influence of the mass media. These papers had been reviewed earlier in many groups throughout the world, including two in the United States.

Meanwhile, Herbert Hamilton had been asked to transfer to the staff of the W.C.C. as an assistant general secretary, and to compensate for his necessarily diminished attention to the affairs of the joint commission, J. Martin Preston was added to its staff and attended the sessions at the Isle of Thorns. At this meeting he was asked to write a short and popular book based upon the paper and discussions on "What is Happening in Education?" This assignment was never completed, for Mr. Preston soon found the work of the joint commission not to his liking and he resigned.

While there were no more meetings of the full joint commission after the sessions at the Isle of Thorns, interim meetings of smaller bodies were scheduled. A third meeting had been planned for January 1967, but it was not held. Instead, there were staff meetings, editorial and steering committee meetings in June and July of 1966, executive committee meetings in May and July 1967.

Martin Preston was replaced by Theodore A. Gill, who was made the director of the study. Meanwhile, H. A. Hamilton, Ralph Mould, and Father Paul Verghese gave substantial assistance. During the year 1966–67, many consultations were set up to consider the work, and a preliminary report of the joint commission went to various sections of the world: three in the U.S.A., one each in West Germany, Nigeria, the Middle East, the Philippines and Indonesia.

REPORT OF THE JOINT COMMISSION

As the months of 1966 and 1967 passed, Dr. Gill conferred with members of the commission in Geneva, London, New York, and other places. At first he proposed to write an independent book with the tentative title, "What Is Going on in Education?" Staff advice to him indicated that a closer fidelity to the work of the joint study commission would be desirable, and Dr. Gill then began to lean more heavily on the findings of that joint commission.

Between sessions of the Nairobi assembly, Dr. Gill met with available members of the joint commission, and following these conferences he presented his draft report to the assembly. Following those sessions, a report was made to the meeting of the central committee of the W.C.C. at Heraklion, Crete. Revisions were made of his report after discussions and responses at both places.

At Heraklion, as Dr. Bliss introduced the draft report, she expressed appreciation for the services of Father Verghese and Mr. Hamilton. After Dr. Gill presented the report and Mr. Mould supported it, the document was referred to Reference Committee II.[39] That committee reported back in these words:

> We would particularly like to see the WCCE more fully in the work of the Division (Ecumenical Action) whether the above changes take place or not. Contact with the education departments of member churches seems to us a "must" for a division already in contact with their youth, women's, men's, and other departments.

Then followed a reservation which, had it become widely known in W.C.C.E. circles, would have caused consternation on all continents: "We cannot imagine the Division wanting to take on children's work, but that they and under 18-year-old teenagers should never be mentioned among us seems a little odd and is explicable only because of this lack of content." The report continued: "In ecumenical education the interest of the W.C.C.E. are those of the Division." [40] There were seven practical suggestions embodied in the joint study commission report presented at Heraklion. The first two are reproduced here:

> a. That the responsibilities assigned the JSCE for a term now find permanent lodging in the parent bodies, and that basic Council structure be accommodated to meet the continuing needs established by this study.

b. That since these needs are of a magnitude which defies denominational remedies alone and, in an ecumenical age shame any long continuation of such unilateral approaches, the World Council of Christian Education and the World Council of Churches take action with deliberate speed to unite their organizations, including their structures and their programmes.

Other recommendations dealt with W.C.C.E. representation on the D.E.A. committee, with the creation of a permanent commission on education and a listing of suggested responsibilities, with establishing regular contacts with U.N.E.S.C.O., and suggesting that the work of the W.C.C.E.'s World Educational Services Committee be merged with the proposed permanent joint commission.[41] The interim report was received by the central committee with the understanding that the final report of 1968 should go to the fourth assembly in Uppsala.[42]

A final report of the joint commission was made to the meeting of the board of managers in 1968 in Frankfurt and to the fourth assembly of the World Council of Churches at Uppsala that same summer. In the latter place, a half an evening's general session was provided for the report. Kathleen Bliss introduced the statement, and Dr. Gill spoke to it under the subject, "the Great Convergence." The report itself was published in English, German, and French.

The summary report in the Uppsala Report reads:

Tuesday evening, July 9
General Session (in the University Aula)
Dr. D. G. Moses presiding.

32. THE GREAT CONVERGENCE (Education Report)

Dr. Kathleen Bliss spoke to the report of the Joint Study Commission on Education (see Workbook, Appendix VIII, pp. 163ff). . . . The report may be regarded as "the beginning of an agenda" for the reconsideration by the churches of the meaning of education, and especially of Christian education. The structural recommendations which form Part III of the report include proposals by which the World Council of Churches and the World Council of Christian Education might, in a more integral relationship to one another, contribute to action upon such an agenda. The Commission was grateful that both the W.C.C.E. and W.C.C. Structure Committee had welcomed this proposal, which would be brought to the Assembly at a later session in a recommendation from the Policy Reference Committee.

Dr. Theodore A. Gill, speaking to the subject of "The Great Convergence," recalled the forces and circumstances which had led the World Council of Churches and the World Council of Christian Education to embark upon the task which had resulted in the Report of the Joint Study Commission on Education. An education explosion is taking place, not only in the vast "proliferation and diversification" of the formal processes of education, but through "all the elements in common culture" which play their part, whether realized or not, in "forming our personalities, shaping our future, proposing our ideals." Into the situation created by this explosion there has recently broken the world-wide student revolt—"a rough rejection of everything taken for granted by all the elements now moulding people, coercing society and determining the future." These students "defy the system which instructs the new generation in means leading to inhuman ends." What s the role of the Church in all this? What does it mean by "Christian education"? "Although the Church was in early on education, we come late to the current phenomenon." If the World Council of Churches and the World Council of Christian Education in some new alignment with one another now move close to the task, "let it be for specific service: let us ask a few qualified people to do one particular job at a time"

Negotiations for Union

The report was important for the two councils, the church public, and the world of education for its substantive content. An organizational recommendation also stemmed from it, one which was to prove significant for the heretofore informal discussions about the possible uniting of the two organizations.

EARLY OVERTURES AND EFFORTS, 1925–1948

Reference has already been made to the finding of the executive committee of the W.S.S.A. in 1926 that as soon as possible the world office of the association should be in Geneva.[43] Again in 1933 Robert Hopkins advanced a similar idea.[44] Nothing came of either proposal until an office was created in 1936 in the League of Nations building, with Adolf Keller as the occupant.[45] No great developments seem to have come about by this Geneva W.S.S.A. office, and it is not clear just how long it lasted.

As the time for the planning for the creation of a World Council of Churches drew near, Robert Hopkins sensed what must lie ahead:

> As the number of ecumenical organizations increases and in view of the steps being taken to form a World Council of Churches it is apparent that the World's Sunday School Association must in due course give careful attention to the relationship which this organization should assume both to the proposed World Council of Churches and to the various ecumenical organizations.[46]

As the delegates from the churches met in Utrecht in May of 1938 to draw up a constitution for a world church organization, Dr. Weigle was present as a representative of the W.S.S.A. He was given a place on the program to inform the gathering about the association:

> Dr. Luther Weigle (World Sunday School Association) sketched the growth of his organization from its foundation in 1889 and pointed out that its work was much wider than its title would imply. It was a federation of national and international Councils and bodies dealing with the Christian education of children, young people and adults, and covering the whole range of education, with the exception of colleges and universities. Most of the bodies affiliated were interconfessional and varied in the closeness of their relation to the Church. He instanced the International Council of Religious Education in the United States

and Canada, and the National Committee for Christian Education in China. He said that the Association would welcome an invitation to affiliate to the World Council, and in the meantime would go on doing its own work.[47]

In this historic meeting, Weigle was one of seven consultative members. Before he made his statement, he had conferred with J. Ross Stevenson, chairman of the committee which had drafted the proposed constitution of the W.C.C.; with W. A. Visser 't Hooft, destined to be its first general secretary; with William Paton, noted missionary leader; with Henry Smith Leiper, American ecumenical pioneer; and others. All of these influential persons assured Weigle that the W.S.S.A. would be invited to be in consultative affiliation with the W.C.C. and that meant that representatives of the association would be on the proposed central committee and in the general assembly as consultative members.[48]

Reporting to the Board of Managers, Weigle distributed three documents from Utrecht and urged participation as a consultative affiliate on the central committee when formed. He went no further than that: "My judgment is that the maintenance of such a relationship is of the utmost importance, both to the World's Sunday School Association and to the World Council of Churches. I do not propose that there be a closer affiliation." [49]

The late summer of 1939 brought the German invasion of Poland and the beginning of World War II. The W.C.C. continued from Utrecht with the subtitle "in process of formation." Obviously intercouncil relations were not the most pressing concern of either body.

From time to time, however, there appear items which indicate that effective and mutually helpful relations were a continuing interest of the W.S.S.A. At a meeting at Lake Mohonk in 1940 the desirability was affirmed "of a prompt and thorough study of the relationships among the various Christian world organizations with a view to forming an adequate strategy for the whole field of Christian religious education." [50] The concern was approved and referred to the Board of Managers.

James Kelly, in his 1941 report of the British committee, said: "It is anticipated that the World's Sunday School Association will have its place within the World Council of Churches while maintaining its own distinctive work and organization." [51]

A little later (1946), Dr. Knapp declared that Christian education must not in its world-wide expression "separate itself by solid walls of partition from other aspects of the ecumenical movements. There must be strong and concentrated and special emphasis upon Christian education, but as a part of, not isolated from, the stream of the ecumenical movement as a whole." [52]

By 1946 there came a proposal which held promise of work on a significant shared responsibility. Three ecumenical bodies (the *ad interim* committee of the International Missionary Council, the provisional committee for the World Council of Churches, and the Board of Managers of the World's Sunday School Association) approved the creation of a "Joint Commission on

Christian Education." A broad range of subjects was envisioned, e.g., the effect of contemporary social change, Christian education in and through the church, the Christian spirit and heritage in state education, Christian nurture in the home, Christian education and better political, economic, and race relations, curricula, education for Christian service, etc.[53] It was expected that Everett Stowe would "give much or all his time to the work of the commission." The four-page proposal had been signed by officers of three councils: for the W.S.S.A., by Arlo A. Brown, Forrest Knapp, and Luther Weigle. The latter had served as chairman.

By 1948 the membership of the commission had been formed: four from each of the three agencies. From the W.S.S.A., there was James Kelly, Chester Miao, Roy G. Ross, and Luther Weigle.[54] Again, the chairman of the commission was Weigle. Everett Stowe was given staff responsibility for the undertaking, and by 1948 a questionnaire was being readied for use.

By 1949 it was "agreed that the first project to be undertaken would be a study of Church youth work and that the responsibility for this study should center in the New York office of the W.C.C.E." [55] At this meeting it was reported by Dr. Knapp that Dr. Stowe had been working on the study and hoped to present and use it at the Toronto cluster of meetings in 1950.[56]

By the time the Board of Managers met in Toronto in 1950, it was reported that only one project had been undertaken, a study of youth work around the world. Dr. Stowe indicated that "a report of the study would soon be issued." The board then voted "to recommend that the World Council of Christian Education propose to the two other cooperating bodies that the Commission be discontinued." [57]

FORMATION OF THE WORLD COUNCIL OF CHURCHES
AND EARLY RELATIONSHIPS, 1948–1962

By the time the constituting assembly of the W.C.C. approached, it was clear that some kind of a cooperating relationship, as yet undecided, had to be effected. The W.S.S.A. was invited to send an official representative to the first assembly in Amsterdam in 1948, and Forrest Knapp was asked to be that person.[58]

Knapp was invited to appear before Committee II in Amsterdam to interpret the work of the W.C.C.E. and to suggest a relationship. He asked for approval of participation by the W.C.C. in the Joint Commission on Christian Education, for close cooperation in youth work, that a representative of the W.C.C.E. be a consultant to the assembly and the central committee, and that the central committee take early steps to provide consultation between the two bodies on total relationships.

Instead of dealing with Knapp's separate points, Committee II

> expressed admiration for the work of the World Council of Christian Education
> and recommended that the World Council of Churches welcome cooperation

with the World Council of Christian Education in the field of Christian Education, and further recommend that the World Council of Christian Education be included among the organizations invited to send representatives in a consultative capacity to the Assembly.

The assembly approved the committee recommendation and added the words "and to the Central Committee."

The action did not completely satisfy Dr. Knapp and, in correspondence with Dr. Visser 't Hooft, he complained that the specific matter of cooperation in youth work, so long established and already of such proven value, was not mentioned. Visser 't Hooft replied that he was sure this work was meant to be included in the committee action, but to be sure he would bring up the matter at the meeting of the W.C.C.'s executive committee in early 1949. He did so, the executive committee made the specific endorsement and Visser 't Hooft wrote, "In this way no uncertainty remains." [59]

During the years immediately after the Amsterdam assembly, relations were uniformly friendly and the W.C.C.E. proved not to be seriously disadvantaged at the denial of Dr. Knapp's original request. James Turnbull attended the first full meeting of the central committee at Chichester, England, in July 1949, and the cooperation in youth work continued undiminished.

Weigle attended a meeting of the British administrative committee in 1951, and said that he would oppose making the W.C.C.E.S.S.A. a Division of Christian Education in the World Council of Churches. His objection was based on the organizational differences between the two councils; the W.C.C.'s assembly being composed solely of official representatives from the churches, none from councils or boards. [60]

From time to time there was an uneasiness expressed by some British leaders of the W.C.C.E. about closer relationships with the World Council of Churches. In the spring of 1959 the tension appeared again within the British committee.

> Some concern was expressed for a paragraph which appeared in the N.A.C. minutes, in which Dr. A. Dale Fiers was quoted as saying, "There should be an appropriate approach [at] an early date to the IMC and the WCC to open further doors of negotiations so as to receive the maximum cooperation now and in the future." It was the unanimous feeling of the Executive that while in the purpose of God this might be the ultimate object, the time was not opportune for its consideration at present. Its discussion would cause serious division in the constituency. It was agreed that there was a need rather for the Council to give a greater measure of world-wide leadership in the educational work of the Church and to seek to plan world strategy for meeting this need. There should be cooperation wherever possible but the wider issue should not be raised. [61]

In response, the N.A.C. explained that further discussion on November 13, 1958, revealed that the British executive committee had read into Dr. Fiers' observation more than he had intended.

The North American committee did not retreat from its position, however, and recommended an ultimate merger with the W.C.C. and the I.M.C. "if and when we can be reasonably unanimous in the W.C.C.E.S.S.A. for such action." [62]

On January 6 of the next year the British section welcomed the wording of the North American group, pointing out that in many European countries churches did not carry responsibilities for Sunday school and youth work.[63]

As the Future Planning Committee reported to the board in 1961, it recorded its desire to improve cooperation with the W.C.C. without prejudice for the future.[64] An additional urging came that year from the North American committee: "VOTED to accept the recommendation brought to the Committee yesterday by Dr. Knoff: 'To recommend to the Board of Managers that it explore with the World Council of Churches all possible aspects of relationships and cooperation between the two bodies.'" [65]

The W.C.C.E.S.S.A. thus found itself in a divided situation. The North American committee pressed for closer relationships with the World Council of Churches. The British committee was frequently uneasy about the direction matters were taking. At the 1962 assembly held at Queen's University, Belfast, Ireland a decisive step was taken.

FROM BELFAST TO NAIROBI, JOINT STUDY AND MERGER PROPOSALS, 1962–1967

The assembly of the council met after extended meetings of a theological education conference and an institute. In each of these meetings representatives of the World Council of Churches participated, and Kathleen Bliss served as the chairman of the former. Father Paul Verghese, the new executive of the Division of Ecumenical Action, was present at the sessions of the assembly.

The Board of Managers reported to the assembly its support of an action of the Future Planning Committee:

> . . . our desire to explore and improve our procedures for cooperation with and our relationship to the World Council of Churches without prejudice or commitment as to specific measures for the future—and asking the staff to prepare a statement on existing relationships, cooperative activities, and possibly overlapping activities, and on the purpose, structure and work of both the WCC and the WCCESSA, indicating similarities and differences in these matters and this would involve full and frank discussion between the staff members of the two organizations. The Board also asked the Secretaries to prepare a statement setting out the composition of our member units and their relationship to the churches and to other ecumenical bodies.[66]

Staff conversations, indeed, had already been held. On April 5 and 6, 1962, Secretaries Chappel, Cheek, and Wright had met in Geneva, with Roderick French, Norman Goodall, and Francis House of the World Council of Churches staff. The history of youth work was reviewed by Messrs. Cheek and French. The W.C.C. people felt that tensions were so strong they had come to the conclusion that, unless the parent bodies could achieve a better relationship between themselves, the W.C.C. youth department would have to withdraw its close cooperation with the W.C.C.E. work. But the secretaries agreed that "no differences had been found of such a fundamental nature as to justify the giving up of the attempt to work together in the service of the churches." [67]

Practical working relationships between the two bodies could be improved, the North American committee believed, such as more exchange of persons at stated meetings; an annual meeting of the two staffs; increased cooperation on family life; continuing and mutual review of developing programs; more careful exchange of basic documents; and sharing information with constituencies of areas and means of cooperation. Moreover, the North Americans asserted, the W.C.C.E. should soon open a Geneva office. [68]

The recommendations and the proddings took effect. All of the recommendations of the North American committee were substantially approved, including the opening of a Geneva office and the creation of a joint study commission, an action which has already been reported. [69]

Embedded in the recommendations was a disarming statement concerning the council's own organizational life, an affirmation which was to increase in importance in the future quadrennium:

> The W.C.C.E.S.S.A. is not primarily concerned about preserving its present patterns of work and structure in comparison to more effectively meeting the tremendous needs of the world to which God leads us as His servants. Nor does the W.C.C.E.S.S.A. see Christian education, though basic, as anything more than one element of total church life and work. The W.C.C.E.S.S.A. is willing in the context and under the urgency of mission to a world in crisis to modify its organizational life, in whatever degree or ways may appear necessary, in order to render a greater Christian education witness and ministry, to and through all churches, on behalf of the whole world God loves. To know Christ and to make Him known is our plumb line. [70]

Immediately after the conclusion of the Belfast assembly, Nelson Chappel interviewed H. A. Hamilton at his home near Brighton, Sussex, and secured his agreement to take charge of the authorized Geneva office for three years. [71]

With the Geneva office established, and with Hamilton and Newby fitting easily and naturally into the staff world of the W.C.C., closer and closer cooperation developed. The North American committee encouraged these developments. They were not always welcome to the members of the British committee. Evidently fearing that a courtship was proceeding too rapidly, "Members asked to have the Belfast resolution read. It was generally agreed that the resolution itself was of a general character without committing the W.C.C.E. to integration—rather to close cooperation and fellowship." [72] This British action was taken only a few short weeks before the Nairobi assembly convened. It did not come to the surface there.

In presenting his first general secretary's report to the 1967 assembly, Ralph Mould reviewed the many cooperative relationships and programs which were going on between the two councils. He mentioned a study on "Christian Education and Ecumenical Commitment" just completed; the achievement of an integrated structural relationship with the W.C.C. youth department; cooperation with four units in the Division of Ecumenical Action; participation with W.C.C. representatives and Roman Catholics on education; scholarship programs; common efforts with the Division of World Mission and Evangelism; the Office of Church and Society; the Churches' Commission on International Affairs; and the service and supportive offices of the W.C.C.[73]

It was an impressive delineation, and when to this list were added many instances in the field where interests and activities coincided, the question came more insistently to the minds of many, "Do we really need two separate agencies to discharge work so evidently common to both?"

So it was at the Nairobi assembly that the decisive action was taken. The Belfast statement was reaffirmed. The chairman and the general secretary were authorized to appoint a special committee with four responsibilities:

1. Explore steps for integration of program;
2. Propose interim working arrangements including W.C.C.E. representation on W.C.C. Committees of units having to do with education;
3. Consult with W.C.C. Secretariate about a task force on the educational impact and potential of all W.C.C. units;
4. Ensure continuity of traditional concerns of all W.C.C. units.

This committee was to report to the Board of Managers and to the next assembly, and the statement was to go to the general secretariate of the W.C.C. and to its committee on structure.[74] This group was a new and important creation of the World Council of Churches, charged with bringing forth a more unified and simplified structure.

The action of the W.C.C.E. assembly was conveyed to a meeting of the central committee of the W.C.C.E. in Heraklion, Crete, a little later that summer of 1967, and it took a reciprocal action.[75]

The central committee also authorized its Committee of the Division of Ecumenical Action to invite not more than five persons nominated by the W.C.C.E. Board of Managers to sit with the governing committee of the D.E.A.[76] The W.C.C. responded quickly and fully to the Nairobi overture. In a short time, Samuel Amissah, A. W. Andrews, Gerald E. Knoff, Gerson Meyer, and U Kyaw Than were appointed by the chairman, Bishop Mueller.[77] Common understanding was furthered by the presence of these W.C.C.E. representatives, and several of them attended 1969 and 1970 sessions at Canterbury, England, and Loccum, Germany, respectively.

These developments did not emerge automatically or easily. Some of the W.C.C. staff and constituency felt that a union of the two world councils would be unwise and that for many reasons. There were also persons on the W.C.C.E. side who had profound misgivings about unification talks for other reasons. Organizational backgrounds were not easy to transcend. Organizational structures were not identical. Patient diplomacy, participation in common effort, thousands of hours of frank exchange, however, produced affirmative results.

MERGER NEGOTIATIONS, 1967–1971

The W.C.C.E. was now seriously committed to exploring outright merger. It was no longer content with "close cooperation and fellowship." Persons were appointed to a Joint Negotiating Committee with the president, Charles Malik, heading the delegation.[78] Kathleen Bliss, for the W.C.C., served as co-chairman with Dr. Malik.

The two councils determined the personnel to serve on the negotiating committee about the same time. Along with its determinations, the W.C.C. concluded its plans for establishing a Christian education desk. It assured the W.C.C.E. that it would be consulted in the appointment of a person. As a symbol of good will and support, the W.C.C.E. transferred funds to the 1969 budget of the W.C.C. in the amount of one-half of the budgeted expenditures not to exceed $12,500. Half-support, not to exceed 4,000 dollars, was promised for the current year, 1968.[79] The funds were available because of a decision not to appoint a study secretary to replace Miss van Drimmelen.

Chairman Malik, at the Frankfurt board meeting, began fulfilling his responsibilities with earnestness and dispatch. He convened his committee before the board assembled, and set it at work at once in subcommittees, which in turn pressed members of the board into service as they arrived and were needed.

As the board meeting convened in a few days, Chairman Malik reported that five working papers had been considered: financial status of the W.C.C.E., organization and staff, function and programmes, the crisis in education today, and issues and problems in the proposed integration.

Chairman Malik was uneasy lest there be some confusion about the assignment to his committee and at his request the board took the following action: "VOTED: General direction endorsed, this Committee to have SOLE responsibility, asked for further report to next B. of M. [Board of Managers] and to any meeting of the Executive Committee." [80]

This reaffirmation was given in the summer of 1968, but as late as March of that year questions were still being raised about the direction the council was taking. As had been the case in earlier significant decisions, affirmative actions turned out to be accompanied by later nagging questions about the wisdom of the decision. The chairman of the British committee, J. Kenneth Meir,

. . . expressed his very deep concern, since he was the only European on the Committee, and was anxious that the European point of view should be clearly expressed. He wondered whether he could take personal steps to discover the reaction of European member Units. The members shared his anxiety to assess and reflect European convictions on this issue.[81]

Soon after the Frankfurt meeting of the Board of Managers adjourned, the 1968 assembly of the World Council of Churches convened in Uppsala. There it was decided that there would be a W.C.C. office of education with three desks or departments: one on general education, one on Christian education, and one on theological education.[82] This decision was implemented by the spring of 1969, when William B. Kennedy, Paulo Freire, and Werner Simpfendorfer were assembled as the staff of the first W.C.C. Office of Education.

Dr. Malik was unable to be present at the next (1969) meeting of the board, but in his absence, after a presentation had been made of the work done during the past year, it was "VOTED that subject to agreement by W.C.C. bodies, reports of the Negotiating Committee be released to Member units of the W.C.C.E. at the earliest possible dates." [83]

The Geneva meeting did not take precipitate action, nor was it without full background material for its affirmative action. Seven papers were before it, prepared at President Malik's direction, dealing with history, background, present issues and problems, practical concerns, and other matters.[84] A clear rationale for integration was set forth, together with appendices of official documents.

Staff members of the two organizations worked closely together on many matters, including the Educational Renewal Fund, a venture which had the side result of building confidence between the staffs of the two agencies. In 1970 the Board of Managers met on the quiet grounds of the German Evangelical Academy at Loccum, and the board was ready then for its final action in recommending the merger. It was voted:

> That the Board of Managers, consistent with the action of the Belfast Assembly of 1962 onwards, expressing its desire to unify the educational work of the churches on a world basis, recommends to the W.C.C.E. Assembly of 1971, meeting in Huampani, Peru, integration with the World Council of Churches according to the document, "A Plan for the Integration of the World Council of Christian Education with the World Council of Churches, July 1970." [85]

The staff, the committee, and the board had completed their long and difficult work and had made their recommendations. It was now up to the assembly of the World Council of Christian Education to make its decision at Huampani, Peru.

The document, upon which the assembly would be asked to take action, bore the title mentioned in the Board of Managers meeting immediately above. It answered first the basic question: "Why integrate?" It said that in response to the Gospel, answering the new demands of the world of education, and in accordance with the expanding concepts of ecumenical work, the councils should terminate their separate existences. A historical section followed, reviewing briefly many of the developments recounted in this history, particularly those from the New Delhi assembly of the W.C.C. in 1961. A recognition of the work of the structure committee of the W.C.C. was included along with a resumé of the meeting schedule over the nearly two-year period, and a listing of the members of the joint committee.

This recital of official actions does not, of course, reveal the details of the difficult and complicated negotiations. Few church mergers are simple, and these negotiations required careful attention to detail, skillful presentations and interpretations on the part of the W.C.C.E., to ensure as much unanimity as possible.

The difficulties were made the more frustrating, because at the very same time, the World Council of Churches was itself undergoing a radical restructuring process, led by General Secretary Eugene Carson Blake and a committee under the chairmanship of Bishop James Mathews of Boston, Massachusetts. The work of the joint negotiating committee was, therefore, that of adding a program freight car to a train that was being reshuffled in the yards, and no one knew just where it was going.

Kathleen Bliss had been early named the chairman of the World Council of Churches' delegation and she gave vigorous and energetic leadership to the work of the committee, equal to that displayed by Chairman Malik. The two alternated in presiding over meetings. The committee worked diligently at its task according to the following schedule:

1968	June	W.C.C.E. members at Frankfurt Board of Managers meeting
	December	Geneva. First meeting of Joint Negotiating Committee
1969	March	Glion, Switzerland. Second meeting of Committee
	December	Geneva. Meeting of Committee Officers and Staff
1970	April	Geneva. Third Meeting
	June	London. Fourth Meeting

During the sessions, Pauline Webb, vice-chairman of the W.C.C.'s central committee, was a helpful liaison person attending some of the London sessions, and Ralph Mould attended all four sessions of the W.C.C.'s structure committee as an invited consultant.

CONSUMMATION OF THE MERGER, 1971

The work of the negotiating committee completed, there remained the obligation of reporting to the two parent bodies. The first of them, the central committee of the W.C.C., was scheduled to meet in Addis Ababa in January of 1971. It had been hoped that General Secretary Ralph Mould and Charles Malik would represent the W.C.C.E. and interpret its work and program at that meeting, but Dr. Malik was unable to be present. I represented the W.C.C.E. at the deliberative sessions considering that portion of the report of the structure committee dealing with the proposed Unit III, "Education and Communication."

The W.C.C. central committee approved its structure committee report, carrying with it approval of the creation of Unit III, Education and Communication, and the merger of the work of the World Council of Christian Education into the latter unit.[86] The action was unanimous.

With this action of the central committee taken, the next and final action was to be by the W.C.C.E. assembly in Huampani, a conference site near Lima, Peru. Chairman Malik made careful preparation for the consideration of the report, arranging the seating so that only properly elected members of the assembly could sit in the voting area. Admission to this section was by distinctive badges. He prefaced the voting by a careful review of the proceedings leading up to the presentation of the report, dealing not only with the work of the joint negotiating committee but also with the developments which in earlier years had led to its creation.

The aim of the W.C.C. unit on education and communication had already been formulated by the joint negotiating committee and was known to the assembly at Huampani:

> To assist churches, councils and movements through processes of education and communication to enable persons, communities and institutions to participate as fully as possible in the changes that faith in God in Christ called for in them, in churches, and in society.

To fulfill this aim, six functions were enumerated:

1. To develop ways by which persons and groups may be drawn into creative participation in the movement of renewal and by which persons, groups and movements engaged in renewal may be mutually involved and supported for the benefit of the whole people of God.
2. To study practices and theories of renewal, education, communication and processes of social change in the light of Christian experience, of theological thinking and of other relevant disciplines.
3. To assist churches in developing programmes and stimulating informal processes of Christian nurture of children, youth and adults, relevant to life in contemporary society.
4. To improve the processes by which the relationships with and among the constituencies allow their diverse life and experience to contribute to one another, to the ecumenical movement and to the life of the World Council of Churches.
5. To provide information and interpretation of the ecumenical movement and especially the World Council of Churches to the public at large and to the constituencies through inter-personal contacts, improved services of translations, printed materials, electronic media and the arts—with due consideration for the variety of cultures and languages.

6. To develop working relationships, mutual aid and inter-change of information among the churches, their councils and agencies, which deepen their involvement in the determination, implementation and appraisal of ecumenical activity.[87]

The general secretary of the World Council of Churches, Dr. Eugene Carson Blake, was present at Huampani and he spoke on "Tasks and Future Shape of the W.C.C." Questions were raised and answered, regional groups met to consider the proposal and other plenary sessions were devoted to the matter. The vote was set for early Wednesday morning, July 21, 1971, and according to earlier decisions, it was done by written ballot. Dr. Malik made the motion.

The resulting vote was 149 for the merger, seven against it, with two abstentions. It was a resounding and affirmative decision.

Chairman Mueller declared the motion carried, praying "that God would bless and seal what we have just decided." "Dr. Malik expressed his delight and hope that 'God would bless the W.C.C. in its new educational tasks which we now hand over joyously.' " William B. Kennedy, of the office of education, responded for the W.C.C. The doxology was sung. The deed was done.

There remained only formalities and provisions for interim responsibilities. Legal resolutions were approved, the existing Board of Managers was reelected to serve the remainder of the year. From now on, under the general direction of the central committee of the World Council of Churches and its general secretary, and under the immediate direction of its Unit III committee and its staff, the worldwide education tasks of the member churches would be carried out.[88]

The Sunday school association of Belsey and Kelly, of Mackintosh and Rank, of Wanamaker and Heinz; the World Council of Christian Education of Weigle and Knapp, of Chappel and Mueller, of Mould and Malik was gone as an institutional entity of sixty-four years (eighty-two years, reckoning from the first London convention). The spirit and the concern, however, it was hoped, went on into the new educational structure of the World Council of Churches, accompanied by hopes, desires, and earnest prayers for its usefulness in bringing the joyous Gospel of Christ into the lives of boys and girls, youth, and men and women.

In such a mood the delegates at Huampani left the pleasant conference ground for the Lima airport to fly to their homes along all the arms of the compass, trusting that an action taken in a land of the conquistadores might lead to the extension of Christ's reign in that and in all other lands.

World Sunday School Conventions

First	London	1889
Second	St. Louis	1893
Third	London	1898
Fourth	Jerusalem	1904
Fifth	Rome	1907
Sixth	Washington	1910
Seventh	Zurich	1913
Eighth	Tokyo	1920
Ninth	Glasgow	1924
Tenth	Los Angeles	1928
Eleventh	Rio de Janeiro	1932
Twelfth	Oslo	1936
Thirteenth	Toronto	1950
Fourteenth	Tokyo	1958

Notes

1. "Fellowship, Inspiration, and Edification," 1889–1907

1. This and some of the other chapter headings were once formulated by Luther A. Weigle, long-time chairman of the World Sunday School Association (World Council of Christian Education).

2. Quoted by Sidney E. Mead, *The Lively Experiment* (New York: Harper and Row, 1963), p. 55. In America, that is. Both Professors Commager and Mead are writing about the United States.

3. Ibid., p. 118.

4. It was reported to the 1889 world convention that more than 6,350,000 teachers and scholars were in the British Sunday schools, more than twenty-two percent of the population. The number of scholars was said to exceed the number of day scholars by one million, and this even with compulsory day school attendance. In Wales, a center of nonconformity, the picture was even more impressive: thirty percent of the population were enrolled in Sunday schools. *First World Convention* (London: 1889), p. 33.

5. Cf. Cecil Northcott, *For Britain's Children*, pp. 29–40.

6. E. Payson Porter, *First Convention*, pp. 76 and 87.

7. *The Development of the Sunday School, 1780–1905:* The Official Report of the Eleventh International Sunday School Convention, Toronto, Canada, 1905, p. 153.

8. Edward K. Warren, "From Milan to Jerusalem" in *The Development of the Sunday-School 1780–1905*, p. 113.

9. Literally true. The early leaders in both the British and the North American movement were men. Only gradually did women find a place in the national and world movements, and that in children's or primary work.

10. Mr. W. H. Groser, *Third World Convention* (London: 1898), p. 184.

11. *A Religious History of the American People*, p. 860.

12. The terminology is admittedly confusing. But that is the way it was. "International" in this sense came to mean only the United States and Canada. It is a defensible usage, e.g., an international bridge, boundary, or marker, and was continued through the lifetime of the International Sunday School Association and the later International Council of Religious Education. "World," fortunately, had only one meaning, and in time that word came to characterize the World Sunday School

Association and the World Council of Christian Education. Canadian participation was often small, e.g., at the fifth convention held in Baltimore, out of 463 persons only twenty were Canadian.

13. These statistics include figures for Newfoundland and Labrador, not a part of governmental Canada in 1887.

14. Edward K. Warren, op. cit., pp. 113–14. In this action "international" meant "world." It was difficult to change familiar usage.

15. Ibid., p. 114.

16. This sequence of events and the wording of the earliest action might serve as an accurate symbol of much of this history: American initiative, British cooperation, concurrence by others. Other, more desirable patterns might have been devised. But often this is the way things went.

17. Reports of attendance given in various places do not exactly agree. Warren, op. cit., says that of the 873 delegates coming from eighteen countries, 415 were from thirty-three states and provinces of the United States and Canada. The eighth convention reported that in 1889 there were 904 delegates; 429 from the United States and Canada, 440 from Great Britain and Ireland; and thirty-five from other places. Perhaps part-time attendants were included in some enumerations.

18. *First World Convention,* op. cit., pp. 4–13.

19. *Third World Convention,* op. cit., p. 12.

20. Ibid., pp. 8–14.

21. Arthur Black, *Golden Jubilee, 1889–1939,* pp. 9, 10.

22. Charles G. Trumbull, *Pilgrimage to Jerusalem,* p. 13.

23. Ibid., p. 9.

24. Ibid., p. 406.

25. *Fifth World's Sunday School Convention,* pp. 2, 3.

26. Ibid., pp. 20–37.

27. Ibid., pp. 9–20.

28. *First World Convention,* op. cit., p. 195.

29. Ibid., pp. 197, 198.

30. Ibid., p. 206.

31. B. L. Green, of Manchester, ibid., p. 204.

32. Quoted in Constance M. Parker, *Fifty Years of Teacher Training,* p. 15. In collection of Robert Raikes Historical Society, Nutfield, Redhill, Surrey, England.

33. *Third World Convention,* op. cit., p. 67.

34. Ibid., p. 63.

35. Ibid., p. 88.

36. *First World Convention,* op. cit., pp. 375, 376.

37. *Sixth World Convention* (Washington: 1910), p. 83. It is interesting to observe that the New York cable address of the World Council of Christian Education and Sunday School Association, until its dissolution in 1971, was "Daybreak." Could this proclamation have been its origin? No one seems to know.

38. C. D. Meigs, in *Third World Convention,* op. cit., p. 225.

39. *Seventh World Convention* (Zurich: 1913), p. 403.

40. Ibid., p. 42.

41. Thomas Edwards (superintendent of the Continental Mission of the Sunday School Union, London), *Second World Convention* (St. Louis: 1893), p. 280.

42. Charles G. Trumbull, op. cit., pp. 307, 308. Editor Trumbull had in mind, no doubt, Messrs. Wanamaker and Heinz. The name of the third is not so obvious.

43. F. F. Belsey, *Second World Convention* (St. Louis: 1893), p. 288.

44. Address in *First World Convention,* op. cit., p. 245.

45. Address in *Second World Convention,* op. cit., p. 268.

46. Address in *Third World Convention,* op. cit., p. 203.

47. Ibid., p. 26.
48. Closing address by S. H. Blake of Toronto in *Third World Convention,* pp. 282, 283.
49. W. J. Mills, London, *Third World Convention,* op. cit., pp. 154, 155.
50. Charles G. Trumbull, op. cit., pp. 297–98.
51. Bernard A. Weisberger, *They Gathered at the River,* p. 219.
52. Ian Bradley, *The Call to Seriousness,* pp. 52, 53.
53. *First World Convention,* op. cit., p. 195.
54. C. D. Meigs (of Indiana), *Third World Convention,* op. cit., p. 224.
55. Andrew Crawford, *Second World Convention,* op. cit., pp. 316–18.
56. *First World Convention,* op. cit., p. 133.
57. J. G. Fetzer, *Third World Convention,* op. cit., p. 39.
58. Ibid., p. 41.
59. A. Bjureman, in *Second World Convention,* op. cit., p. 306.
60. Op. cit., p. 72.
61. Ann M. Boylan, "The Nursery of the Church: Evangelical Protestant Sunday Schools, 1820–1880" (Ph.D. diss., University of Wisconsin, 1973), pp. 61, 62.
62. Dr. Hall in *First World Convention,* op. cit., pp. 297, 298.
63. G. M. Hitchcock, ibid., p. 352.
64. H. J. Macartney, *Third World Convention,* op. cit., p. 10.
65. Ibid.
66. H. Ussing, *First World Convention,* op. cit., p. 68. When it is remembered that the City Temple spoken of by Mr. Ussing could accommodate 873 delegates, it would appear that a large number of Copenhagen's "higher classes" were being reached.
67. Ibid., p. 298.
68. Constance M. Parker, op. cit., pp. 5, 6.
69. *First World Convention,* op. cit., pp. 297, 298.
70. Ibid., pp. 383–404.
71. *Second World Convention,* op. cit., pp. 447–54.
72. Charles G. Trumbull, op. cit., p. 305.
73. Ibid., p. 286.
74. The presidents, throughout the history of the W.S.S.A./W.C.C.E., were Sir Francis Belsey, B. F. Jacobs, Edward Towers, E. K. Warren, F. B. Meyer, George W. Bailey, Sir Robert Laidlaw, John Wanamaker, W. C. Poole, Sir Harold (later Viscount) Mackintosh, Bishop Shot K. Mondol, Sir Francis Ibiam, and Charles Malik.
75. *Second World Convention,* op. cit., pp. 311, 312.
76. Martin Carnoy, *Education as Cultural Imperialism,* p. 313.
77. Op. cit., p. 135.
78. Alexis de Tocqueville, *Democracy in America,* vol. II, p. 106.
79. *First World Convention,* op. cit., p. 64.
80. Ibid., p. 48.
81. Ibid., p. 68.
82. Ibid., p. 73.
83. Ibid., pp. 31, 67.
84. E. Payson Porter, ibid., p. 76.
85. Ibid., p. 179.
86. Ibid., p. 198.
87. *Third World Convention,* op. cit., pp. 165, 166.
88. *Second World Convention,* op. cit., pp. 354, 355.
89. See "Two Flags Over Two Shoulders," Chapter One.
90. Ibid., p. 433.
91. Ibid., p. 441.

92. Ibid., p. 330.
93. Op. cit., p. 380.
94. *Third World Convention,* op. cit., pp. 76, 77.
95. *Third World Convention,* op. cit., p. 288.
96. Ibid., pp. 159, 160.
97. Samuel E. Morison, *The Oxford History of the American People,* pp. 805–807.
98. *Third World Convention,* op. cit., p. 87.
99. Ibid., pp. 43, 44.
100. Op. cit., p. 45.
101. Ibid., p. 246.
102. Ibid., p. 78.
103. Ibid., p. 160.
104. *First World Convention,* op. cit., p. 23.
105. *Third World Convention,* op. cit., p. 143.
106. Op. cit., p. 374.
107. Op. cit., p. 183.
108. Charles Bieler, ibid., p. 234.
109. Ibid., p. 327.
110. Kenneth Scott Latourette, *A History of the Expansion of Christianity,* vol. IV, p. 415.
111. Charles G. Trumbull, op. cit., p. 289.
112. Fountain J. Hartley, op. cit., p. 33.
113. Ibid., pp. 201–202.
114. A. A. Brown, *A History of Religious Education in Recent Times,* p. 94f.
115. J. Kenneth Meir, *Labour of Love,* p. 29.
116. *Third World Convention,* op. cit., p. 152.
117. Op. cit., pp. 180, 181.
118. Ibid., p. 179.
119. Ibid., p. 199.
120. For a discussion of these developments in Britain see W. Neil, "The Criticism and Theological Use of the Bible, 1700–1950" in S. L. Greenslade, ed. *The Cambridge History of the Bible* (Cambridge, England: Cambridge University Press, 1975), pp. 238–293.
121. Op. cit., pp. 133, 143.
122. Ibid., pp. 119–28.
123. S. G. Green, op. cit., p. 150.
124. *First World Convention,* op. cit., p. 150.
125. Ibid., p. 151.
126. Ibid., p. 152.
127. J. Monro Gibson, in ibid., pp. 131, 132.
128. Op. cit., p. 151.
129. Op. cit., pp. 218–22.
130. Report of the Sunday School Society of the Canton de Vaud, Switzerland, 1893, p. 301.
131. Op. cit., pp. 69, 70, 94, 95, 114.
132. Charles Trumbull, op. cit., p. 288.
133. Op. cit., p. 403.
134. Ibid., pp. 406–12.
135. Op. cit., pp. 75, 76. Edward Ranken was identified as "one of Her Majesty's chief inspectors for education."
136. *Third World Convention,* ibid., p. 110.
137. I. P. Black, in *Third World Convention,* ibid., pp. 103–104.
138. Ibid., p. 119.

139. Op. cit., p. 235.

140. Ibid., p. 235.

141. *First World Convention,* op. cit., p. 234.

142. *First World Convention,* op. cit., p. 367.

143. *Third World Convention,* op. cit., p. 84. Emphasis added. B. F. Jacobs' sexism showed through. Women had a place in the early Sunday school movement and that place was the teaching of little children. The governing of the schools and associations lay in masculine hands.

144. Ibid., p. 84.

145. Jacobs made a mistake with Harper's middle initial but he had the right man in mind, and the story told about him rings true.

146. *First World Convention,* op. cit., p. 367.

147. James Bailey, op. cit., p. 173.

148. *First World Convention,* op. cit., pp. 121–23, 134, 138; *Third World Convention,* op cit., pp. 141–43.

149. P. H. Bristow, in *Third World Convention,* op. cit., pp. 163–65.

150. Benjamin Clarke, op. cit., p. 134.

151. W. H. Groser, ibid., pp. 188–94.

152. By 1898 the committee included in its membership fifteen from the United States and Canada, together with six corresponding members in Great Britain and one each from Australia and India.

153. A. E. Dunning, reporting for the International Lesson Committee, in *Third World Convention,* op. cit., pp. 139, 140.

154. *First World Convention,* op. cit., pp. 281, 282.

155. Op. cit., p. 127.

156. *First World Convention,* op. cit., pp. 211–68.

157. Ibid., p. 227.

158. *First World Convention,* op. cit., p. 188.

159. *First World Convention,* op. cit., p. 183.

160. Ibid., pp. 179, 183.

161. Ibid., pp. 27, 38. One wonders why it was that Sunday liquor *could* be sold if one had journeyed ten miles or more. Were the hardships of travel in the state of Victoria at that time so rigorous that a drink was seen as a justifiable restorative? Research into the matter lies beyond the scope of this history.

162. Constance M. Parker, op. cit., p. 6.

163. Op. cit., pp. 408–12.

164. *First World Convention,* op. cit., pp. 212–13.

165. Ibid., pp. 215, 216.

166. *Second World Convention,* op. cit., p. 289.

167. L. B. Maxwell, op. cit., p. 93.

168. See "Durban," Chapter Three.

169. Op. cit., p. 119.

170. *First World Convention,* op. cit., pp. 55, 339.

171. *Second World Convention,* op. cit., p. 307.

172. Op. cit., pp. 55, 56. The gender used is intriguing. Were most of the teachers in the early Swedish Sunday schools men?

173. A. Bjurman, in *Second World Convention,* op. cit., p. 308.

174. *First World Convention,* op. cit., p. 68. The establishment of a relatively stable dairy industry in rural Denmark was one factor in the smaller emigration, a transition in which the folk schools of Bishop Grundtvig played a significant role.

175. *Second World Convention,* op. cit., pp. 309–10.

176. *Third World Convention,* op. cit., pp. 66, 67.

177. *First World Convention,* op. cit., p. 98.

178. *First World Convention,* op. cit., pp. 312–13.
179. *Third World Convention,* op. cit., pp. 62, 63. (Concerns for some other countries have been recounted earlier in Chapter One, in the section, "Sanctified Common Sense, and Warm-hearted Energy, and Devotion.")

2. Organization and Program Emerge, 1907–1924

1. *Eighth World Convention* (Tokyo: 1920), pp. 24, 25, 29, 30.
2. *Business Committee Minutes,* May 19, 1924, p. 121.
3. *Ninth World Convention* (Glasgow: 1924), pp. 40–43.
4. Op. cit., p. 192.
5. Op. cit., pp. 108–10.
6. Op. cit., p. 84.
7. William T. Ellis, *Earth's Ends Meet, a Report of the Sixth World Convention, Washington, 1910,* p. 90.
8. *Report of Chairman of Executive Committee to Seventh World Convention* (Zurich: 1913), p. 64.
9. Demetrius Kalopothokis, *Fifth Convention,* op. cit., pp. 251, 252.
10. Theodore T. Holway, ibid., p. 211.
11. *Seventh World Convention* (Zurich: 1913), p. 106.
12. *Report of Continental Europe Commission, Seventh Convention,* ibid., p. 112.
13. *Fifth Convention,* op. cit., pp. 202, 203.
14. *Seventh World Convention,* op. cit., p. 118.
15. *Fifth Convention,* op. cit., p. 245.
16. Ibid., p. 204.
17. H. C. Thompson, *Seventh World Convention,* op. cit., p. 276.
18. Ibid., p. 273.
19. *Seventh World Convention,* op. cit., p. 216. If the reference to the Philippines as an American country seems strange to us, it should be explained that in 1913 the islands were just that. Independence came in 1935.
20. *Sixth World Convention,* op. cit., p. 102.
21. *Jerusalem Manual of Worship, Rome Edition.*
22. Op. cit., p. 37.
23. Ibid., pp. 38, 39.
24. Ibid., p. 192.
25. Ibid., p. 47.
26. See "Rome, 1907," Chapter Two.
27. Op. cit., p. 178.
28. Ibid., pp. 207, 208.
29. Ibid., p. 83.
30. *Seventh World Convention,* op. cit., pp. 620–22.
31. Mrs. Layyah Barakat, *Sixth World Convention,* op. cit., p. 366.
32. Read, "The Catholic Church."
33. Ibid., pp. 52, 53. The name of the speaker, Dr. J. W. Butler, gives rise to the suspicion that he was not a Mexican, but a missionary.
34. Ibid., pp. 37, 545–47.
35. *Sixth World Convention,* op. cit., p. 89.
36. Ibid., p. 7.
37. W. H. Ridgway, quoting a Mr. Whifford of Buffalo, *Sixth World Convention,* op. cit., p. 513.

38. John T. Faris, ed. *The Sunday School and World Progress, Eighth World Convention,* op. cit., pp. 1, 2.

39. Ibid., p. 304.

40. *Eighth World Convention,* op. cit., pp. 330, 331.

41. Ibid., p. 296.

42. D. Ebina, in *Eighth World Convention,* op. cit., pp. 301, 302.

43. *Ninth World Convention,* op. cit., p. 205.

44. *Minutes, Executive Committee, W.S.S.A.* (April 24, 1924), p. 157.

45. *Seventh World Convention,* op. cit., p. 513.

46. *Seventh World Convention,* op. cit., pp. 515, 516.

47. J. C. Hartzell, in *Fifth World Convention,* op. cit., pp. 124, 125.

48. Ibid., pp. 289, 290.

49. Robert E. Speer, in *Sixth World Convention,* op. cit., p. 224.

50. *Fifth Convention,* op. cit., pp. 122, 123.

51. Ibid., p. 223.

52. Sanford J. Ungar, "The Intelligence Tangle," in *Atlantic Monthly,* vol. 237, no. 4 (April 1976), p. 32.

53. *World-Wide Sunday School News* (March 1916).

54. Op. cit., p. 134.

55. Op. cit., p. 103.

56. *Ninth World Convention,* op. cit., p. 75.

57. *Minutes, Executive Committee,* April 28, 1921.

58. *Minutes, Executive Committee,* May 22, 1907, p. 6.

59. Op. cit., p. 5.

60. Op. cit., p. 406.

61. Ibid., p. 488. The path of the constructor of curricula has always been hard.

62. Op. cit., pp. 164, 165. The India commission was a subunit of the convention dealing with the needs of the subcontinent, from the very first convention of 1889 of special concern to the Sunday school forces.

63. Ibid., p. 107. She had opened the first of her *case dei bambini* in Rome in 1907. One wonders how many of the Sunday school delegates had direct contact with this home while they were attending the Rome convention.

64. Ibid., p. 540.

65. Ibid., pp. 582, 583.

66. Ibid., pp. 584, 585.

67. Ibid., pp. 460–64.

68. *Minutes, Executive Committee, American Section,* April 25, 1917, p. 10.

69. Ibid., p. 10.

70. *Eighth World Convention,* op. cit., p. 165.

71. Report to British Committee in *Popular Report,* 1922, p. 9.

72. This body soon dropped the words "Sunday school" from its name and became the International Council of Religious Education. It was the cooperative agency for religious education in the United States and Canada. In 1950 it merged with other interchurch bodies into the National Council of Churches and became part of its Division of Christian Education.

73. *Minutes,* Joint Committee, June 11, 1923, p. 5.

74. *Ninth World Convention,* op. cit., pp. 80, 131, 132, 271, 276, 278–80.

75. Ibid., p. 79.

76. *Ninth World Convention,* op. cit., pp. 126–30.

77. Nelson Chappel in *Work Book for Board of Managers,* 1964, Tab. 11.

78. *Sixth World Convention,* op. cit., pp. 111–13.

79. *Minutes, Executive Committee, American Section,* 1919, pp. 84–115.

80. Op. cit., pp. 162, 272–77.

81. Op. cit., pp. 138, 139.

82. *Sixth World Convention,* op. cit., p. 396.

83. *Eighth World Convention,* op. cit., p. 163.

84. *Seventh World Convention,* op. cit., p. 425.

85. *Eighth World Convention,* op. cit., pp. 288–94,. 304, 312–14, 321, 322.

86. *Eighth World Convention,* op. cit., p. 279.

87. *Ninth World Convention,* op. cit., p. 204.

88. *British Committee at Work,* a report to executive committee, American section, 1919, p. 34.

89. Frank L. Brown, *Report to the Executive Committee,* American section, 1919, p. 17. It will be remembered that in 1919, the United States was beginning to experience an intense emotional reaction against Russian Communism. Attorney General A. Mitchell Palmer, succeeded in time by Harry Daugherty, inflamed the populace, prosecuted innocent people, and made the precedents for a later rabble rouser, Senator Joseph McCarthy. Secretary Brown seems to have been taken in by the popular mood.

90. Op. cit., p. 55.

91. Ibid., pp. 311, 312.

92. Ibid., p. 303.

93. Ibid., pp. 166, 167.

94. *Year Book, W.S.S.A.,* 1922, p. 24.

95. *Fifth Convention,* op. cit., pp. 270, 271.

96. *Fifth Convention,* op. cit., p. 275.

97. Ibid., pp. 281, 282.

98. Ibid., pp. 287, 288.

99. *Sixth World Convention,* op. cit., p. 342.

100. *Seventh World Convention,* op. cit., pp. 50, 233. It is interesting to point out that, as plans were made for the Tokyo convention of 1958, Dr. Michio Kozaki was chairman of the National Christian Council of Japan. He served as director of the W.C.C.E.S.S.A. Institute. He was the son of Hiromichi Kosaki.

101. Ibid., p. 242.

102. Ibid., pp. 37, 38.

103. Ibid.

104. Report of Oriental commission, in *Seventh World Convention,* op. cit., p. 218.

105. *Seventh World Convention,* op. cit., pp. 49, 50. The report of this commission undoubtedly was the cause of the unusual interest in things Asian and for the acceptance of the invitation to go to Tokyo for the next meeting.

106. *Fifth Convention,* op. cit., pp. 255, 256.

107. Ibid., p. 226.

108. Ibid., pp. 238, 239.

109. *Report of the Continental Europe Commission,* in *Seventh World Convention,* op. cit., pp. 113, 114.

110. *Fifth Convention,* op. cit., pp. 248, 249.

111. Ibid., p. 244.

112. Ibid., pp. 260, 261.

113. Ibid., p. 307.

114. Ibid., p. 315.

115. Ibid., p. 317.

116. Ibid., pp. 318–21.

117. Ibid., p. 322.

118. Ibid., p. 338.

119. Ibid., pp. 331, 332.

120. *Seventh World Convention,* op. cit., pp. 525, 526.

121. A new development this, as we remember its independent beginnings.

122. *Fifth Convention,* op. cit., pp. 149, 150.

123. Ibid., pp. 370, 371. A comment from Nelson Chappel reports that the ten from other parts did not attend regularly.

124. Cf. Nelson Chappel, op. cit., tab. 11, and ibid., p. 371.

125. *Fifth Convention,* op. cit., p. 342.

126. Ibid., pp. 76, 78.

127. Ibid., pp. 372–75.

128. *Third World Convention,* op. cit., p. 328.

129. *Fifth Convention,* op. cit., p. 50.

130. *Minutes, Executive Committee,* May 24, 1907, p. 9.

131. Robert M. Hopkins, *Twelfth Convention, Oslo, 1936,* p. 168.

132. *Eighth World Convention,* op. cit., p. xii. It appears Mr. Harris did not go.

133. Nelson Chappel, op. cit., tab. 11.

134. *The World's Bible School Convention* reported in *The Christian Standard,* May 28, 1910, p. 8. The comet was Halley's, of course, visible in 1910, the first appearance since 1835.

135. *Minutes, Central Committee,* W.S.S.A., August 1, and September 6, 1911, pp. 1–4.

136. *Minutes, Program Committee,* W.S.S.A., Oct. 19 and 20, 1911, p. 6; and November 22, 1911, p. 1. It was perhaps assumed that listening, French-speaking Swiss also knew German.

137. Cf. Robert C. Albers, *The Good Provider.* A vivid and engaging account of the tour is to be found in this biography of Mr. Heinz.

138. *Eighth World Convention,* op. cit., p. 15.

139. Cf. Frank L. Brown, *A Sunday School Tour of the Orient,* p. 100; and Arthur Black, *Golden Jubilee, 1889–1939,* pp. 9, 10.

140. *Eighth World Convention,* op. cit., pp. xii–xiv. Also Nelson Chappel, op. cit., tab. 11.

141. Nelson Chappel, op. cit., tab. 11.

142. Ibid.

143. The World's Seventh Sunday-school Convention in *The Christian Standard,* Aug. 16, 1913, p. 30.

144. Ibid., pp. 30, 31.

145. *Minutes, Executive Committee, American Section,* June 25, 1914, p. 4. The British section agreed to the proposal the next January.

146. *World Wide Sunday School News,* June 1915.

147. *Minutes, Business Committee* January 13, 1919, p. 26.

148. *Minutes, Executive Committee, American Section,* Oct. 29, 1919, p. 74.

149. Ibid., p. 71. Also *World Wide Sunday School News,* June and October, 1915.

150. *Minutes, Executive Committee,* W.S.S.A., Oct. 12, 1920, p. 791.

151. *World Wide Sunday School News,* November, 1919 and March, 1920.

152. *Minutes, Executive Committee,* October 5, 1920, pp. 79a, 79b.

153. Ibid., October 7, 1920, p. 79e.

154. *Eighth World Convention,* op. cit., p. 126. The discrepancy in the title Viscount or Baron Shibusawa is in the 1920 reports.

155. Nelson Chappel, op. cit., p. 9.

156. *World Wide Sunday School News,* Feb. 1921. Another account reports that $2,000 was given at the doors of the convention hall on the closing night after appeals from J. W. Lowe and Margaret Slattery, and that later tours pledged an additional $7,000. (*Eighth World Convention,* op. cit., pp. 175, 176.)

157. *Year Book, W.S.S.A.,* 1922, p. 12.

158. *Eighth World Convention,* op. cit., p. 15.

159. "Fraternizing to the Point of Compromising" in *The Christian Standard,* Feb. 26, 1921, p. 6.

160. Nelson Chappel, op. cit., p. 10.

161. *Ninth World Convention,* op. cit., pp. 121–25.

162. Convention Yearbooks of 1907 and 1920.

163. *World Wide Sunday School News,* June 1919 and *Minutes, Executive Committee,* October 29, 1919, p. 72.

164. *World Wide Sunday School News,* December 1919.

165. *Sixth World Convention,* op. cit., p. 83.

166. *Minutes, American Section,* July 15, 1913, and January 16, 1914.

167. *Minutes, Business Committee, American Section,* March 31, 1922, p. 73; June 5, p. 80, Oct. 24, p. 84. See also, *W.S.S.A. Yearbook,* 1923, p. 14 and Nelson Chappel, op. cit., p. 9.

168. Nelson Chappel, op. cit., p. 9.

169. Secretary Brown's report is quoted at this length because it needs several comments. California was considering anti-alien land legislation at the time. A formal protest from the Japanese government was sent to the United States, but the bill was, nevertheless, passed and signed by the governor on May 19. The United States government assured the Japanese that existing treaty rights between the two nations were not violated, an assurance which was not altogether convincing to Japan. Further and more far-reaching discriminatory legislation from the United States was to come. The beginnings of the Pearl Harbor attack go a long way back in history.

It would be interesting to know just what was said by way of deploring the action of the state of California, but there is no record of that, save for the general statement above.

The national prejudice, if not racism, of Secretary Brown shines through. Again, it would be interesting, though unproductive, to speculate about what "vastly inferior" people in what Occidental nations he would have shut out ahead of the Japanese. And the touchstone of ninety-eight percent of children in public schools seems not wholly relevant. But enough comment on an effort which did have, after all, laudable purposes—the creation of goodwill in Japan toward America—which had grievously and unnecessarily offended Japan.

170. Frank L. Brown, op. cit., pp. 361–78.

171. *Minutes, Central Committee, W.S.S.A.,* April 23, 1914.

172. *Minutes, Executive Committee, W.S.S.A.,* April 28, 1921, p. 98.

173. Much of the material in this chapter comes from work done by Nelson Chappel, in preparing for the important meeting of the Board of Managers in 1964 in Paris. I acknowledge my indebtedness to him.

174. Nelson Chappel, op. cit.

175. *Minutes, Executive Committee, American Section,* April 25, 1917.

176. *Executive Committee, American Section,* 1919, p. 25.

177. *Executive Committee, American Section,* 1919, pp. 81–84.

178. Ibid., pp. 14–15. Also *Minutes, Business Committee,* October 22, 1917, p. 1.

179. *Minutes, Business Committee,* September 27, 1918.

180. *Minutes, Business Committee,* January 5, 1920, p. 37. In the United States the Interchurch World Movement (1920–1928) was launched, a Protestant cooperative effort to raise a billion dollars. It was a colossal failure, the participating denominations finally assuming its debts. Unified church financing in the United States proved to be an impossible dream.

181. *Minutes, Business Committee,* May 20, 1920, p. 1; and May 11, 1921, p. 55.

182. *Minutes, Business Committee,* January 11, 1922, p. 66; October 28, 1924, p.

127; February 27, 1925, p. 138; and November 26, 1926, p. 173.

183. Nelson Chappel, op. cit., pp. 8, 9.

184. Ibid., p. 5.

185. *Popular Report, British Committee*, 1914, p. 22.

186. It has sometimes been represented that the weakness of the British committee was caused by the vicissitudes of World War I, but actually it began before the war, as is here shown.

187. Nelson Chappel, op. cit.

188. The responsibility involved from $5,500 to $12,000. *Minutes, Business Committee, American Section*, March 29, 1917, p. 1.

189. *Minutes, Executive Committee, American Section*, April 27, 1920, p. 78.

190. *Minutes, Executive Committee, W.S.S.A.*, October 11, 1920, p. 79.

191. Nelson Chappel, op. cit.

192. *Yearbook*, 1923, p. 22.

193. *Yearbook*, 1923, p. 15.

194. *Minutes, Executive Committee, W.S.S.A.*, June 25, 1924, p. 168; and July 10–16, 1928, p. 232.

195. Frank L. Brown, *A Sunday School Tour of the Orient*, pp. xiii, xiv.

196. Nelson Chappel, *Financial Arrangements in the WCCESSA*, Board of Managers minutes, 1957.

3. A Federation of Autonomous Units, 1924–1939

1. *Twelfth World Convention*, op. cit., p. 201.

2. *W.S.S.A. Yearbook*, 1927, p. 59.

3. *Twelfth World Convention*, op. cit., p. 284.

4. James Hoffman Batten, "The Mexican Protestant Outlook," in *Tenth World Convention*, op. cit., p. 159.

5. James Kelly, *Report on His Visits to the Continent*, 1925.

6. Donato G. Golia, *Tenth World Convention*, op. cit., p. 322.

7. C. A. Neff, ibid., p. 229.

8. Ibid., p. 94.

9. Op. cit., pp. 300, 302.

10. *Correspondence Files of the World Council of Churches*, Ecumenical Centre, Geneva. Espy became, in 1963, the general secretary of the National Council of the Churches of Christ in the U.S.A.

11. *Twelfth World Convention*, op. cit., pp. 257–58.

12. *Minutes, Joint Committee on Methods and Materials*, December 4, 1923; March 10, 1924; and October 27, 1926.

13. *W.S.S.A. Yearbook (Addenda)*, 1925, p. 36a.

14. J. W. Robinson, *Tenth Convention*, op. cit., p. 277.

15. Ibid., pp. 217–19.

16. *W.S.S.A. Yearbook*, 1930, p. 71.

17. *Twelfth Convention*, op. cit., p. 272.

18. Op. cit., pp. 274, 275.

19. "Beginning at Jerusalem," in *Tenth Convention*, op. cit., p. 339.

20. Ibid., p. 309.

21. *The Purpose and Plan of the Convention*, op. cit., p. 53.

22. Alexander McLeish, ibid., pp. 255, 256.

23. Ibid., p. 100.

24. Ibid., pp. 149–53.

25. Ibid., pp. 258–61.

26. Ibid., pp. 154–58.

27. Ibid., p. 170.

28. *Minutes, Executive Committee,* 1932.

29. *Twelfth World Convention,* op. cit., p. 58.

30. S. W. Hughes, *The Sunday School, Christian Brotherhood, and World Peace,* ibid., p. 131.

31. Ibid., p. 323.

32. *Twelfth World Convention,* op. cit., p. 121.

33. *Minutes, Business Committee,* April 28, 1937; and June 21, 1937. In the membership of twenty-four persons, were such well known leaders as Roswell P. Barnes, J. Henry Carpenter, Samuel Guy Inman, Leslie B. Moss, Emory Ross, Roy G. Ross, Robert W. Searle, George Stewart, L. J. Shafer, Luther A. Weigle, and others.

34. Cecil Northcutt, *For Britain's Children,* p. 52.

35. James Kelly, *Report of First European Sunday School Convention,* 1931, p. 12.

36. *Bulletin of the British Committee,* June 1933, p. 5.

37. *Eleventh World Convention,* op. cit., p. 86.

38. Ibid., p. 121.

39. Kazuo Kitoku, op. cit., p. 278.

40. *W.S.S.A. Yearbook,* 1930, pp. 74, 75.

41. Edwin R. Brown, op. cit., pp. 155–58.

42. *Tenth World Convention,* op. cit., pp. 56, 57.

43. Report in *The Christian Evangelist,* July 26, 1928, p. 13.

44. Pp. 15, 16.

45. *Minutes, Executive Committee,* July 10–16, 1928, pp. 228, 247. In the end, however, the name was not changed. See "Rio de Janeiro, 1932," Chapter Three.

46. *Tenth World Convention,* op. cit., pp. 79, 80.

47. *World Wide Sunday School News,* September 1929.

48. *Minutes, Committee on Reference and Counsel.*

49. The last item came from the North American section. "The Living Christ," in *Eleventh World Convention,* pp. 206–208.

50. A *Who's Who* of the convention listed ninety-four names. Of these, thirty-six came from the United States, Great Britain, and Canada. Still a heavy percentage, to be sure, but not as overwhelming as in some previous meetings.

51. *Eleventh World Convention, Rio de Janeiro, 1932,* p. 313.

52. "The Living Christ," in *Eleventh World Convention,* p. 3.

53. *World Wide Sunday School News,* April 1931. No list of convention delegates has been found so we don't know if Mr. and Mrs. Gelwick and their two friends made it or not. Let us hope they did.

54. Samuel Guy Inman, "Aggressive, but Patient," in *The Christian Evangelist,* June 22, 1955, p. 7.

55. Nelson Chappel, *Work Book for Paris Meeting Board of Managers,* 1964, tab. 11.

56. *Minutes of the N.A.A.C.,* November 17, 1932, pp. 5, 6.

57. *Eleventh World Convention,* op. cit., p. 36.

58. *Minutes of the N.A.A.C.,* op. cit., p. 11.

59. Samuel Guy Inman, in *Tenth Convention Report,* op. cit., pp. 305–12.

60. *Minutes of the N.A.A.C.,* November 17, 1932, op. cit., p. 3.

61. *Minutes, Board of Managers, 1935,* London, p. 6.

62. *Report of Robert M. Hopkins to the N.A.A.C.,* November 13, 1936.

63. *Minutes, N.A.A.C.,* April 16, 1936.

64. *Twelfth World Convention,* op. cit., facing p. 47.

65. *Minutes, Business Committee* April 6, 1936, p. 5.

66. *Twelfth World Convention,* op. cit., pp. 321, 322.

67. Luther Weigle Papers (Sterling Memorial Library, Yale University, New Haven, Conn.).

68. *Minutes, Business Committee,* September 14, 1936, p. 4.

69. *Minutes, N.A.A.C.,* November 13, 1936, p. 6.

70. *Minutes, Business Committee,* February 19, 1937, pp. 579–81.

71. Ibid., August 5, 1937.

72. *Minutes, N.A.A.C.,* October 6 and 19, 1937.

73. *Minutes, Business Committee,* February 4, 1938, p. 616.

74. *Report of Robert M. Hopkins to the N.A.A.C.,* June 7, 1938.

75. *Minutes, Business Committee,* November 16, 1938; and June 18, 1939. Also *Minutes, N.A.A.C.,* October 10, 1939. See also the efforts of the travel agent for the Oslo convention of 1936, pp. 188, 189.

76. *Tenth World Convention,* op. cit., pp. 115–18, *Twelfth World Convention,* op. cit., pp. 331–35.

77. *Minutes, Board of Managers,* 1938, p. 4.

78. *Popular Report, British Committee,* 1930, p. 1.

79. *Minutes, Executive Committee,* July 10–16, 1928, p. 236.

80. The biographical material here is drawn almost entirely from Viscount Mackintosh's autobiography, *By Faith and Work.* The quotation is from p. 274.

81. Ibid., p. 159.

82. Ibid., p. 167.

83. *Twelfth World Convention,* op. cit., pp. 318, 319, and *World Council, W.S.S.A.,* July 1936, p. 15.

84. Appendix to *Minutes, Business Committee,* June 15, 1936.

85. *Report of the General Secretary to the Board of Managers,* 1965, p. 1.

86. Most of the material in this statement about Luther A. Weigle is to be found in Vergilius Ferm, *Contemporary American Theology,* second series (Round Table Press, 1933). The quotation is on p. 337.

87. *Minutes, Central Committee, W.S.S.A.,* October 20, 1927.

88. *Minutes, Business Committee,* November 16, 1938, pp. 651, 652.

89. *Minutes, N.A.A.C.,* August 1, 1939.

90. *Minutes, W.S.S.A. Council,* 1940, p. 6.

91. *Minutes, N.A.A.C.,* November 17, 1932, pp. 11–13.

92. *Minutes, Business Committee,* July 25, 1938, p. 638.

93. *Minutes, Executive Committee,* October 11 and 12, 1934, p. 3.

94. *Bulletin, British Committee,* October, 1928, p. 2.

95. *Year Book, W.S.S.A.,* 1925, p. 5.

96. Robert M. Hopkins, in *Twelfth World Convention,* op. cit., p. 168; and *British Committee Report,* 1934, pp. 6, 7.

97. Admittedly a subjective judgment, this, and open to challenge.

98. Cf. *Report of Robert M. Hopkins to N.A.A.C.,* April 11, 1935, pp. 6, 7 and *Report of Luther A. Weigle to N.A.A.C.,* same date, same pages.

99. Kuling, China, July 18–27, 1935. *Resolution adopted by the Enlarged Meeting of the National Committee for Christian Religious Education of the National Christian Council in China regarding the visit of Luther A. Weigle in China.*

100. John R. Mott, *Minutes, Business Committee,* June 25, 1935. (Dr. Mott's comments were made on June 24.)

101. James Kelly, *Annual Report,* 1935, p. 6.

102. Nelson Chappel, op cit., p. 12.

103. Ibid., p. 10.

104. *Minutes, Executive Committee,* September 28, 1926, pp. 198–203.

105. *Minutes, Business Committee,* March 12, 1931, p. 310.

106. Forrest L. Knapp, *Suggested Next Steps in Latin America,* p. 48.

107. *Reports of British Section, 1928–1932.*

108. *Year Book, W.S.S.A.,* 1930, p. 27.

109. James Kelly, *Report of the British Section to the Executive Committee,* 1932, pp. 218, 219.

110. James Kelly, *Annual Report of the British Committee, 1933,* pp. 14, 15.

111. James Kelly, *Annual Report of the British Committee, 1936,* p. 13.

112. James Kelly, *Annual Report of the British Committee, 1938,* p. 27.

113. Arthur Black, op. cit., p. 16.

114. *Minutes, Business Committee,* February 11, 1932, pp. 367, 368; and April 28, 1932, p. 383.

115. Nelson Chappel, op. cit., p. 12; and *Work Book, Board of Managers,* 1964, Tab. 11.

116. *Report of North American Section to the Executive Committee, W.S.S.A., The Living Christ,* p. 232.

117. Nelson Chappel, *The Story Behind the World Council of Christian Education and Sunday School Association,* p. 13.

118. Nelson Chappel, *Financial Arrangements in the WCCESSA,* Board of Managers minutes, 1957.

4. Difficulties, Achievements, and Strains, 1939–1953

1. Forrest L. Knapp, *Address to the Council,* Birmingham, 1947, p. 13.

2. *World Christian Education,* April 1947, p. 3.

3. *Minutes, C.W.A.C.,* April 28, 1951. (The Northern Baptist convention had changed its name in the spring of 1950.)

4. Ibid., September 29, 1951.

5. *World Christian Education,* February 1947, p. 6.

6. *Minutes, Board of Managers,* 1946, pp. 8, 9.

7. *Report of British Committee, 1947,* pp. 4, 5. Also *Yearbook, International Council of Religious Education,* 1948, p. 94.

8. *Minutes, the Council,* Birmingham, 1947, pp. 102–104.

9. *Minutes, British Committee,* May 28, 1948, p. 3.

10. *Minutes of the Toronto Assembly, 1950,* pp. 11, 12, also Exhibit I (Eye), p. 76.

11. A. W. Andrews, in *Minutes, British Committee,* June 8, 1951, p. 7.

12. *Minutes, Board of Managers,* p. 4.

13. *Minutes, Board of Managers,* 1953, p. 4, Exhibit E.

14. *Report of Forrest L. Knapp to the North American Administrative Committee,* April 12, 1944, p. 11.

15. *Literature for Christian Education,* an address to the assembly, pp. 18, 19.

16. *Minutes of the Birmingham Assembly,* pp. 107–108.

17. *World Christian Education,* third quarter, 1950, p. 82.

18. Another report gives twenty-seven participants from fifteen countries. Perhaps there were some part-time persons involved.

19. *The Christian College,* 1950.

20. Ibid., pp. 37, 38.

21. *Minutes, N.A.A.C.,* October 9, 1940, p. 3.

22. Ibid., November 21, 1941, pp. 3, 4.

23. *Values for Mexico,* pp. 7–9.

24. Forrest L. Knapp, *Suggested Next Steps in Latin America,* pp. 57–61.

25. *Minutes, Business Committee,* November 22, 1949. It would be most interesting to learn why this action was taken by the British executive committee. But there is no present prospect of ascertaining the background. Perhaps this is as good a place as any to indicate that there is a very unfortunate gap in the documentation for this history—the absence of the records of the executive committee of the British committee for all of its years, save for 1963–64. Diligent search has failed to discover them, and the last British secretary, Andrew Wright, hazards the guess that "they may have been destroyed." If they have been jettisoned, the loss is as regrettable as it is inexplicable.

26. *Official Report,* p. 73.

27. *Who's Who,* Toronto Convention.

28. *Commission Reports, World Institute,* 1950.

29. *World Christian Education,* fourth quarter, 1950, p. 96.

30. *Meeting of the Council,* Birmingham, 1947, p. 94.

31. *Minutes, Toronto Assembly,* pp. 14, 15.

32. Ibid., p. 13.

33. Ibid., Exhibit P, p. 93.

34. *World Christian Education,* fourth quarter, 1950, p. 110.

35. Ibid., p. 17.

36. *Minutes, British Committee,* February 25, 1949, p. 5.

37. Ibid., September 9 and 10, p. 9; and October 12, 1950, p. 4.

38. After his resignation from the W.C.C.E.S.S.A., Dr. Knapp became the general secretary of the Massachusetts Council of Churches. He thus became one who had served a city, a state, a national, and a world council of cooperative Christian work. For many years, and perhaps through the present time, he was the only individual in the United States with this fourfold background.

39. *Report of N.A.A.C. to Toronto Assembly,* 1950, p. 40.

40. *Minutes of the Assembly,* p. 3.

41. *Report of the N.A.A.C. to the Assembly,* 1954, p. 47.

42. *Minutes, Business Committee,* November 4, 1953; and January 29, 1954. Dr. Knapp's resignation and the accompanying factors will be discussed in Chapter Five.

43. Mr. Rank, a British Methodist layman, was much interested in the use of audio-visual materials, including motion pictures, in the service of the church. A worldwide figure in moving picture circles, he devoted large shares of time to his own denomination and to the World Council of Christian Education, putting at their disposal funds, competence and commitment.

44. *Minutes of the British Committee,* February 25, 1949, p. 3; and *Report of the British Committee,* 1949, p. 5.

45. *Report of the British Committee,* 1948, pp. 22, 23.

46. *Report of Adolf Novotny to Birmingham Assembly,* 1947.

47. *Minutes of the Assembly,* Exhibit B, p. 21.

48. *Minutes, Board of Managers,* 1943, p. 1.

49. *Minutes, Business Committee,* December 18, 1942.

50. *Minutes, British Committee,* March 12, 1943, p. 5.

51. *Minutes of Board of Managers,* 1946, p. 6.

52. *Minutes, British Committee,* March 15, 1945.

53. *World Christian Education,* February 1947, p. 19.

54. P. H. Lotz, *Orientation in Religious Education,* pp. 472–74.

55. *Minutes of the N.A.A.C.,* September 8, 1953.

56. *Report of the N.A.A.C. to the Council,* Birmingham, p. 77.

57. *1953 Report.*

58. *Report of N.A.A.C. to Toronto Assembly,* pp. 44–48.

59. *Letters of Forrest Knapp to the "office family,"* August 26 and September 14, 1951.

60. *Goals and Services for 1952 to 1956,* North American Administrative Committee of the World Council of Christian Education and Sunday School Association.

61. *Minutes, N.A.A.C.,* September 8, 1953.

62. *Report of Program Committee to the N.A.A.C.,* September 8, 1953.

63. *Report of British Committee,* 1941, p. 7.

64. *Report of British Committee,* 1942, p. 6.

65. *Report of British Committee to the Assembly,* 1947, p. 74.

66. *Minutes, British Committee,* March 12, 1943, p. 4.

67. *Minutes, British Committee,* February 28, 1950, p. 8; and *Minutes, Board of Managers,* 1950, pp. 5, 6.

68. Cf. Nelson Chappel, op. cit., p. 14, and *Report of Board of Managers to World Council,* 1937, p. 63.

69. *Minutes of the British Committee,* May 11, 1950.

70. *Minutes, Business Committee,* October 1, 1945.

71. *Minutes,* p. 8.

72. *Minutes,* 1947, pp. 96, 97.

73. *Minutes, British Committee,* July 13, and October 5, 1949.

74. Youdell, Edgar S., pp. 23, 24.

75. *World Christian Education,* April 1948, pp. 11, 12.

76. Nelson Chappel, *The Story Behind the World Council of Christian Education and Sunday School Association,* p. 14.

77. Ibid., p. 13.

78. Luther A. Weigle, *Report of Board of Managers to the Council,* 1947, p. 63.

79. *Minutes,* p. 4.

80. *Report of Board of Managers to World Council,* 1947, p. 63.

81. *N.A.A.C.,* October 23, 1940; and February 26, 1942.

82. *Minutes, Business Committee, N.A.A.C.,* April 3, and June 8, 1945 and April 18, 1946.

83. Constant H. Jacquet, Jr., editor.

84. In 1932 this figure was reported as 25,037,836.

85. In 1932, this figure was reported as 30,015,037.

86. The notation for these figures says "admittedly incomplete, especially for Europe."

87. The notation for these figures says for North America, "Estimate: Since the U.S. Census data is not complete, figures are the same as reported to the Ninth Convention, Glasgow, 1924."

88. Or 37,285,000. As early as the Oslo convention of 1936, uneasiness had been felt about the reported statistics from the World Dominion Movement. National units were there invited to review the tentative statistical reports.

89. The figures through 1936 are from *World Christian Education,* April 1948, p. 15. Those for 1950 and 1958 are from the official report of Toronto, and the report to the Tokyo assembly, respectively. Other figures for 1898 give 2,173 delegates.

90. *Assembly Minutes,* p. 10.

5. A Partially Unified Council, 1953–1965

1. See "Zurich, 1913," Chapter Two.

2. Nelson Chappel, *Report to the North American Administrative Committee,* January 22, 1954.

3. *Executive Committee Minutes,* September 28, 1926, pp. 198–203.

4. *Executive Committee Minutes,* June 8 and 9, 1927, pp. 213–15, 227a–d.

5. R. M. Hopkins, *Report to North American Administrative Committee,* May 25, 1933, p. 1.

6. *Minutes of the North American Administrative Committee,* November 13, 1936, p. 4; and October 19, 1937, p. 1. Also *Business Committee Minutes,* December 18, 1936, p. 2; January 15, 1937; and August 28, 1937.

7. *Minutes, N.A.A.C.,* November 20, 1942, p. 11.

8. *Report to the N.A.A.C.,* April 12, 1944, p. 19.

9. May 10, 1945, p. 9.

10. *Looking to the Future,* p. 3.

11. *Address to the Council,* p. 13.

12. *Minutes,* New York City, 1948, p. 9.

13. *Minutes,* August 1949, p. 10.

14. *Assembly Minutes,* Toronto, 1950, Exhibits B, BM-1, BM-2, pp. 21–30. See also "Toronto, 1950," Chapter Four.

15. *Minutes, Board of Managers,* 1950, pp. 9, 10.

16. *Assembly Minutes,* Toronto, 1950, pp. 5, 6.

17. *Minutes, British Administrative Committee,* October 24, 1951, pp. 2–6.

18. *Minutes, N.A.A.C.,* December 20, 1951, pp. 4, 5.

19. *Minutes, Board of Managers,* October 25, 1951, pp. 2, 3; 1952, p. 9; and 1953, p. 3.

20. *Minutes of the British Committee,* 20 June, 1952, p. 11.

21. Nelson Chappel, *Work Book for Board of Managers,* Paris, 1964, Tab. 11.

22. *Minutes of the Board of Managers,* September 9 and 10, 1953.

23. Nelson *Chappel,* June 23, 1977.

24. *Minutes,* October 15, 1952.

25. *Minutes, N.A.A.C.,* January 21, 1953, p. 12.

26. Nelson Chappel, *Minutes, N.A.A.C.,* January 22, 1954.

27. *Minutes of the Assembly.*

28. *Family Album,* p. 35.

29. *Minutes, Program Committee, N.A.A.C.,* September 12, 1945; November 19, 1957; and April 29, 1958.

30. *Minutes, Board of Managers,* 1954, p. 8.

31. *Board of Managers Minutes,* 1955, p. 7.

32. *Minutes, World Educational Services Committee,* 1956, pp. 1, 4.

33. *Report of Special Executive, British Committee,* November 21, 1956; and April 4, 1957.

34. *Report to the Board of Managers,* 1957, p. 11.

35. *Report to the Atami Assembly,* 1958, p. 2.

36. *Minutes, N.A.A.C.,* May 5 and 6, 1959, p. 8.

37. *Board of Managers,* 1959; and *Report to Belfast Assembly,* 1962, pp. 2, 3.

38. *Minutes, Board of Managers,* 1959, p. 8.

39. *Minutes of the World Educational Services Committee,* 1961, pp. 5, 6.

40. *Board of Managers Meeting,* Berlin, 1960; New York, 1961; and *Report of the Board to the Assembly,* Belfast, 1962, p. 4.

41. *Minutes of the WESC,* 1962, p. 1.

42. *Minutes, Board of Managers,* 1961, p. 9, #14, and Exhibit 10.

43. *Report of Future Planning Committee to the Board of Managers,* 1961 Exhibit 10, pp. 5, 6.

44. Nelson Chappel, *Report to the Board of Managers,* 1961, New York, pp. 9, 10.

45. *Staff Recommendations to Board of Managers,* 1963, Ottawa, Work Book, tab.

11, p. 2. "Functional" means here such services as audio-visual programs, youth work, the magazine, etc.

46. Ibid., pp. 3, 4.

47. Ibid., pp. 1–4.

48. Nelson Chappel, *Report to the Board of Managers,* 1965, Mexico City, p. 3.

49. Nelson Chappel, *Report to the Board of Managers,* 1964, Paris, p. 2.

50. *Report of the British Committee to the Board of Managers,* 1964, Paris, pp. 5, 6.

51. Nelson Chappel, *Workbook for the Board of Managers,* 1964, Paris, Tab. 11.

52. *Minutes, Special Meeting of British Committee,* December 2, 1964, in *Workbook for Board of Managers,* 1965, Mexico City, Tab. 12.

53. Nelson Chappel, *Work Book for the Board of Managers,* 1965, Mexico City, Tab. 12.

54. *Report of the General Secretary to the Board of Managers,* 1965, Mexico City, p. 3.

55. *Minutes, Board of Managers,* 1955, Cleveland, Exhibits 11 and 12.

56. *Recommendations of the British Committee to the Board of Managers,* June 23, 1955, pp. 3, 4.

57. *Recommendations of the North American Committee to the Board of Managers,* Exhibit 8, p. 8.

58. In addition, however, and clustered around the convention were other important gatherings:
    1. A world institute held at Seiwa and Kobe Colleges, just prior to the convention, with 260 persons enrolled from fifty-eight countries, a two-week study period;
    2. A seminar on training ministers for a teaching ministry, attended by faculty members from thirty-six seminaries;
    3. A laboratory conference on group life, forty-eight involved;
    4. An institute in the Japanese language, eighty participants;
    5. A Southeast Asia curriculum consultation;
    6. A meeting of the joint W.C.C.E.S.S.A. youth committee;
    7. An Asian youth consultation;
    8. Meeting of the Board of Managers at Atami;
    9. The Quadrennial Assembly, Atami; and
    10. An Asian conference on mass communication.

59. J. M. Macdougall Ferguson, *Tokyo Calling,* pp. 34–36.
    I   The Christian Education of Children.
    II   The Christian Education of Youth.
    III Christian Education in the Home.
    IV   General Christian Education.
    V   The Christian Responsibility of the Layman.

60. Ibid., pp. 38–40.

61. Christian G. Baeta, "Christian Education in a Revolutionary Age," in *Tokyo Calling,* p. 29.

62. *Minutes, Board of Managers,* 1960, p. 8.

63. Randolph Crump Miller, *The Educational Mission of the Church.*

64. Processo Udarbe, and Randolph C. Miller, *The Teaching Ministry of the Church,* pp. 36, 37.

65. Ibid., p. 35.

66. Ibid., p. 34.

67. *World Christian Education,* fourth quarter, 1955.

68. *Minutes, British Committee,* October 24, 1956, p. 4.

69. Nelson Chappel, *Report to the Atami Assembly,* 1958, p. 5.
70. Nelson Chappel, *Report to the Board of Managers,* 1959, Glasgow, pp. 4, 5.
71. Nelson Chappel, *Report to the Board of Managers,* 1960, Berlin, pp. 5–8.
72. Nelson Chappel, *Report to the Board of Managers,* 1961, New York, p. 6.
73. Nelson Chappel, *Report of the Belfast Assembly,* 1962, p. 62.
74. *Work Book, Board of Managers,* 1963, Ottawa, Tab. 10.
75. Nelson Chappel, September 11, 1975.
76. *Minutes, North American Administrative Committee,* November 18, 1955, p. 3.
77. Cf., p. 329.
78. *Minutes, North American Committee,* May 11, 1957, p. 2; November 16, 1957, p. 1; and April 28, 1958.
79. Nelson Chappel, *Report to the Board of Managers,* 1965, Mexico City, pp. 20, 21.
80. *World Christian Education,* second quarter, 1962, p. 78.
81. *Minutes, North American Administrative Committee,* May 13, 1941.
82. *Minutes, Board of Managers,* August 1949, *Report of North American Administrative Committee,* pp. 2, 3.
83. *Report of the North American Administrative Committee to Assembly,* Frankfort, 1954, p. 51.
84. *Report of the North American Committee to Assembly,* 1958, Atami, p. 7.
85. *Report of the North American Committee to Assembly,* 1962, Belfast.
86. *Report of the North American Committee to the Board of Managers,* 1963, Ottawa, p. 2.
87. *Minutes, Children's Work Advisory Section,* North American committee, September 21, 1962.
88. Nelson Chappel, *Report to the Board of Managers,* 1965, Mexico City, p. 19; and *Minutes, Board of Managers,* 1967, Nairobi, p. 8.
89. *Minutes, Children's Work Advisory Committee,* North American committee, May 14–15, 1962, Exhibit G.
90. *Report of the North American Committee to the Board of Managers,* 1963, Ottawa, p. 3.
91. Nelson Chappel, *Report to the Board of Managers,* 1965, Mexico City, Tab. 7.
92. *Report of the North American Committee to the Board of Managers,* 1963, Ottawa, pp. 10–12.
93. Nelson Chappel, *Report to the Board of Managers,* 1965, Mexico City, pp. 19, 20.
94. *World Christian Education,* first quarter, 1966, p. 25.
95. *Minutes, Board of Managers,* 1955, Cleveland, p. 11.
96. *Minutes, Board of Managers,* 1955, Cleveland, Exhibit 13, p. 8.
97. *Minutes, Board of Managers,* 1955, Cleveland, p. 10.
98. *Minutes, Board of Managers,* 1957, Toronto.
99. *Minutes, Board of Managers,* 1961, New York, Exhibits D and E.
100. *Report of the North American Committee to the Board of Managers,* 1961, New York, pp. 4, 5.
101. *Meeting of the WCC/WCCESSA Youth Committee,* St. Andrews, Scotland, 1960, pp. 2, 3.
102. *Minutes, Program Committee of North American Committee,* January 26, 1962, p. 3.
103. *Report of the North American Committee to the Assembly,* 1962, Belfast.
104. *Report of the North American Committee to the Board of Managers,* 1963, Ottawa, p. 6.

105. Nelson Chappel, *Report to the Board of Managers,* 1965, Mexico City, pp. 16, 17.

106. *Report of North American Committee to the Board of Managers,* 1961, p. 8.

107. *Minutes, Adult Work and Family Life Commission,* November 10, 1961, p. 1.

108. Nelson Chappel, *Report to the Board of Managers,* 1955, Cleveland, p. 8; and *Report of the British Administrative Committee,* p. 4.

109. *Report of Andrew Wright to the Board of Managers,* 1960, Berlin, p. 3.

110. Nelson Chappel, *Report to the Board of Managers,* 1965, Mexico City, pp. 17, 18.

111. *Minutes, North American Committee,* November 13, 1958, p. 5.

112. *World Christian Education,* second quarter 1960, p. 57.

113. *World Christian Education,* third quarter, 1960, p. 93. In view of the founding of the W.S.S.A., it is interesting to see that children's work appeared in so low a ranking, and that youth work, so conspicuous an emphasis during this very period, appeared not at all.

114. *World Christian Education,* fourth quarter, 1960, p. 126.

115. *Report of Committee on the Magazine to the Board of Managers,* 1960, Berlin, Exhibit 12.

116. *Report of the North American Committee to the Board of Managers,* 1964, Paris, p. 4.

117. Nelson Chappel, *Report to the Board of Managers,* 1965, Mexico City, p. 7.

118. See "The Quarterly, World Christian Education," Chapter Four.

119. *Interim Report, the Sabbatical Services Project,* 1963–1967, May 1965, pp. 2, 3.

120. Benjamin Guansing is the one exception to the pattern of persons going from older churches to younger churches.

121. Various reports of Nelson Chappel and Ralph N. Mould to Board of Managers, 1958 to 1967.

122. Various reports and articles in *World Christian Education.*

123. Nelson Chappel, *Report to the Assembly,* 1958, Atami.

124. *Printed Report of the British Committee,* 1960, p. 14.

125. *Minutes, Executive Committee, North American Committee,* May 7, 1957, and September 30, 1958.

126. *World Christian Education,* first quarter, 1958, p. 23.

127. *Minutes, British Committee,* October 16, 1958, p. 3; and *Report of the British Committee,* 1958, p. 6.

128. *Report of the British Committee to the Board of Managers,* 1964, Paris, p. 2.

129. *British Committee Report,* 1957, p. 4.

130. *Minutes, Board of Managers,* 1964, Paris, p. 4.

131. *Minutes, Board of Managers,* 1965, Mexico City, p. 1.

132. *London Times* (Dec. 29, 1964).

133. *World Christian Education,* second quarter, 1965, p. 32.

134. *World Christian Education,* second quarter, 1966, p. 40; and *Minutes, Board of Managers,* 1965, Mexico City, p. 2.

135. *World Christian Education,* fourth quarter, 1966, p. 115.

136. *World Christian Education,* third quarter, 1966, p. 86.

137. *Minutes, Board of Managers,* 1953, pp. 2, 3.

138. *Minutes, North American Administrative Committee,* January 20, 1955; *Minutes, Board of Managers,* 1955, Cleveland, pp. 4, 5; *Work Book for Board of Managers,* 1964, Paris, Tab. 11; *The Christian Evangelist,* March 30, 1955, p. 13.

139. *World Christian Education,* third quarter, 1955, p. 87.

140. *Report of the North American Administrative Committee to the Board of Managers,* 1955, Cleveland, Exhibit 8, p. 9.

141. *Minutes, Executive Committee, North American Committee,* May 26, 1959, and Nelson Chappel, *Report to the Board of Managers,* 1959, Glasgow, p. 9.

142. *World Christian Education,* third quarter, 1965, p. 80.

143. *World Christian Education,* third quarter, 1959. She is the youngest daughter of the late Toyohiko Kagawa, Japan's world-famous Christian evangelist.

144. *Minutes, Board of Managers,* 1960, Berlin, pp. 3, 4, and 1961, New York, p. 9.

145. *Minutes, Board of Managers,* 1963, Ottawa, p. 11.

146. *Minutes, Board of Managers,* 1963, Ottawa, pp. 2, 3.

147. Nelson Chappel, *Report to the Board of Managers,* 1965, Mexico City, pp. 6, 7.

148. *Report of the Special Personnel Committee to the Board of Managers,* 1965, Mexico City, pp. 1, 2.

149. Ibid.

150. *World Christian Education,* fourth quarter, 1965, p. 83.

151. *Report of the Special Personnel Committee to the Board of Managers,* 1965, Mexico City, p. 2.

152. Ibid., pp. 2, 3.

153. *World Christian Education,* fourth quarter, 1956, p. 115.

154. *World Christian Education,* second quarter, 1965, p. 42.

155. *Report of the North American Committee to the Board of Managers,* 1963, Ottawa, pp. 5, 6.

156. *Report of the British Committee,* 1956, p. 13.

157. *Report of the British Committee,* 1957, p. 5.

158. Cf. Andrew Wright, *Report to the Assembly,* 1958, Atami, p. 2; and *World Christian Education,* first quarter, 1957, p. 27.

159. Andrew Wright, op. cit., p. 2.

160. *Minutes, British Committee,* October 19, 1961, p. 3.

161. *Report of the British Committee to the Assembly,* 1962, Belfast, pp. 3–8.

162. *Minutes, British Committee,* April 4, 1957, p. 2 of Exhibit, *Report of Special Executive,* November 21, 1956.

163. Andrew Wright, *Report to the Assembly,* 1958, Atami, p. 5.

164. *Minutes, Business Committee,* October 7, 1932, p. 406.

165. Cf. *Minutes, Business Committee,* May 12, 1955; *Minutes of the North American Administrative Committee,* May 25, 1955, p. 3.

166. *Report of NAAC to the Assembly,* 1954, Frankfurt, p. 55.

167. Ibid., p. 53.

168. Report of the North American Committee to the Board of Managers, 1963, Ottawa, p. 3

169. *Work Book, Board of Managers,* 1964, Paris, Tab. 11.

170. *Report of the North American Committee to the Board of Managers,* 1961, New York, p. 8.

171. Nelson Chappel, *Report to the Board of Managers,* 1965, Mexico City, pp. 9, 10.

172. *Minutes, Executive Committee,* N.A.C., September 23, 1960, p. 3.

173. *Year Book,* 1954, pp. 5, 6.

174. Cf. *Minutes, Board of Managers,* 1954, Frankfurt, p. 8; *British Committee Report,* 1955, Cleveland, p. 8; *Report of the Board of Managers to the Assembly,* 1958, Atami, pp. 1, 2.

175. *Report of North American Administrative Committee to the Board of Managers,* 1955, Cleveland, Appendix 8, p. 2.

176. *Report of the Board of Managers to the Assembly,* 1958, Atami, pp. 1, 2.

177. Ibid., pp. 2–5.

178. *London Office Bulletin* No. 3, 1960, p. 2.

179. *Minutes of the 1962 Assembly,* Belfast, p. 4.

180. *World Christian Education,* fourth quarter, 1954.

181. *Minutes of the 1958 Assembly,* Atami.

182. Nelson Chappel, *Work Book for the Board of Managers,* 1964, Paris, Tab. 11.

183. Nelson Chappel, *Work Book for the Board of Managers,* 1964, Paris, Tab. 11.

184. Nelson Chappel, in *Work Book for Board of Managers,* 1964, Paris, Tab. 11.

185. Andrew Wright, *Report of the British Committee to the Board of Managers,* 1961, New York, p. 2.

186. *Report of the North American Committee to the Board of Managers,* 1961, New York, p. 2.

187. A. Wilson Cheek, ibid.

188. Cf. *Reports of the North American Committee to the Board of Managers,* 1963, Ottawa, p. 15; 1964, Paris, p. 5; *Minutes of the Board of Managers,* 1964, Paris, p. 6; and Nelson Chappel, *Report to the Board of Managers,* 1965, Mexico City, pp. 3, 4.

189. Nelson Chappel, *Work Book for the Board of Managers,* 1964, Paris, Tab. 11.

190. *Minutes, Board of Managers,* 1962, Belfast, p. 2.

191. *World Christian Education,* fourth quarter, 1962, p. 144.

192. Nelson Chappel, *Report to the Board of Managers,* 1965, Mexico City, pp. 6, 7.

6. *Common Ecumenical Study and Progress Toward Merger, 1965–1971*

1. *Minutes, Board of Managers,* 1964, Paris, pp. 10, 11.

2. *Report on Institute Preparations, Board of Managers Minutes,* 1965, Mexico City, Exhibit C, p. 1.

3. Randolph C. Miller, "For the Record," in *World Christian Education,* fourth quarter, 1967, pp. 91, 92.

4. Ibid., pp. 94–96.

5. *World Christian Education,* first quarter, 1967, p. 8.

6. *World Christian Education,* fourth quarter, 1967, p. 136.

7. Ralph N. Mould, "Nairobi—Only a Beginning," in *World Christian Education,* fourth quarter, 1967, p. 89.

8. *World Christian Education,* fourth quarter, 1967, p. 161.

9. Carman Hunter, *Encuentro, New Perspectives for Christian Education,* p. 164.

10. Ibid., p. 168.

11. Ibid., p. 258.

12. Ibid., p. 132.

13. *Minutes, Assembly,* 1967, Nairobi, July 30–August 1, 1967, p. 1.

14. *General Secretary's Report to Nairobi Assembly,* 1967, pp. 4, 5.

15. *Minutes, Board of Managers,* 1967, Nairobi, p. 3, and 1968, Frankfurt, p. 4.

16. *Minutes, Board of Managers,* 1969, Geneva, p. 12.

17. *World Christian Education,* first quarter, 1966, p. 25.

18. *World Christian Education,* fourth quarter, 1967, p. 158.

19. *Minutes,* 1967, Nairobi.

20. *Minutes, Board of Managers,* 1967, Nairobi, pp. 1, 2.
21. Sketch of the W.C.C.E.S.S.A.
22. Ibid.
23. *Minutes, N.A.R.C.,* May 6, 1968, p. 15, and of *Board of Managers,* 1968, Frankfurt, p. 3.
24. *World Christian Education,* fourth quarter, 1967, p. 90.
25. *World Christian Education,* first quarter, 1966, p. 26.
26. *Minutes, Board of Managers* 1970, Loccum, Germany, p. 8. For an account of the establishment of the Educational Renewal Fund, see "World Christian Education," Chapter Six.
27. During the years of this period the following emphases were made in the magazine.

Age Groups and Family Education

Youth in the Church's Ministry	Third Quarter, 1966
Youth Work in Crisis	Third Quarter, 1969

Bible, Theology

Interpreting the Bible	First Quarter, 1966

Nature of Christian Education

Christian Education and Ecumenical Commitment	First Quarter, 1968
Renewal in our Educational Ministry	Second Quarter, 1968
Making Relevant our Christian Education Mission	Fourth Quarter, 1968
La Educacion Christiana Latinoamericana	Fourth Quarter, 1966
Our Worldwide Fellowship of the Churches for its Educational Mission	First Quarter, 1969
World Problems	Second Quarter, 1969
Demanding Participation	First Quarter, 1970
International Education Year	Second Quarter, 1970
Education for Development	Third Quarter, 1970
Growing Up in a Revolutionary Society	Fourth Quarter, 1970
What About Sunday School?	Second Quarter, 1971
Church's Role in Education	First Quarter, 1972

Leadership Education

Developing Leadership in Christian Education	Second Quarter, 1966
The Churches and General Education	Third Quarter, 1968
Equipping for Service	Fourth Quarter, 1969

Nairobi and Huampani Meetings

Nairobi, Program, Purposes, Design	First Quarter, 1967
Nairobi Delegates' Workbook for the Institute	Second and Third Quarters, 1967
Report of Fourth World Institute on Christian Education and W.C.C.E. Assembly	Fourth Quarter, 1967
Peru '71 New Perspectives for Christian Education	First Quarter, 1971
Encuentro	Third and Fourth Quarters, 1971

28. *World Christian Education Fund,* July 29, 1967, p. 7.

29. *Projects, 1968*, an eight-page flyer.

30. *Board of Managers Workbook*, 1968, Frankfurt.

31. *Minutes, Board of Managers*, 1969, Frankfurt, pp. 8, 9.

32. *The New Delhi Report*, pp. 198–201.

33. *Report of N.A.C. to the Assembly*, 1962, Belfast, Exhibit E, pp. 5, 6.

34. *Report of the Assembly*, 1962, Exhibit 15, p. 91.

35. Ibid.

36. *Minutes, Board of Managers*, 1963, Ottawa, p. 6.

37. *Minutes, Board of Managers*, 1963, Ottawa, p. 6 and *Workbook, Board of Managers*, 1964, Paris, Tab. 11.

38. *Minutes, Johannesstift Meeting*, p. 1.

39. *Minutes, Central Committee, W.C.C.*, 1967, Heraklion, p. 27.

40. Ibid., Appendix XVII, p. 209.

41. Ibid., pp. 245, 246.

42. *Minutes*, p. 50.

43. Cf., "The North American Administrative Committee," Chapter Three.

44. Cf., "Earlier Attempts at Unifying the Council," Chapter Five.

45. Ibid.

46. *Report of the North American Administrative Committee to the Board of Managers*, 1938, p. 5.

47. *Proceedings of the Conference* (Utrecht), May 1938, p. 20.

48. *Minutes, Board of Managers*, 1938, New York City.

49. Ibid., p. 3.

50. *Minutes, World Council*, May 11, 1940, p. 3.

51. P. 17. There is nothing in the records I have found which substantiates this ambiguous expectation.

52. Forrest L. Knapp, *Looking to the Future*, p. 3. Files of Dr. Knapp.

53. *Meeting of the W.C.C.E. Assembly*, 1947, Birmingham, pp. 128–30.

54. *Minutes, Board of Managers*, 1948, New York, pp. 10, 11.

55. *Minutes, Board of Managers*, 1949, Exhibit IX, p. 1.

56. *Report of North American Administrative Committee to the Board of Managers*, 1949, p. 3.

57. *Minutes, Board of Managers*, 1950, Toronto, p. 8.

58. *Minutes, Board of Managers*, 1947, p. 2.

59. *Correspondence Files of the World Council of Churches* and *Minutes, Board of Managers*, 1949, p. 7. This account from the Board of Managers' minutes does not relate that an earlier desire of Dr. Knapp was turned down by Committee II. He sought to have the W.C.C.E. officially recognized as being in association with the W.C.C., and to have this relationship acknowledged, as was done with the International Missionary Council, on the letterheads and other records of the W.C.C. The Lord Bishop of London, in a private comment, supported the proposal, but the negative observations of President John Mackay of Princeton Seminary proved decisive. He said, in effect, that both the W.C.C. and the I.M.C. dealt with the churches in their total scope and program, while the W.C.C.E. dealt only with one aspect, although an important one, of the churches' mission. Therefore, the status of the I.M.C. and the W.C.C.E. were not the same. This oral report was communicated to me in Amsterdam within an hour or so after Dr. Knapp left the hearing.

60. *Minutes, British Committee*, October 24, 1951, pp. 2, 3. Weigle, at this meeting of the British committee, was seeking to set aside and reverse the sentiment of the British committee to nullify the Toronto assembly actions for an integrated administrative and program structure for the council, and to elect a single general secretary.

As has been reported (see "A New Structure in the Making," Chapter Five), he succeeded in that attempt.

61. *Minutes, North American Committee,* May 5 and 6, 1959, p. 1.

62. *Minutes,* October 13, 1959.

63. *Minutes, W.E.S.C.,* 1961, pp. 5, 6.

64. *Minutes, Board of Managers,* 1961, New York, pp. 10, 11.

65. *Minutes, N.A.C.,* May 24, 1961, pp. 12, 13.

66. *Report of the Board of Managers to the Assembly,* 1962, pp. 7, 8.

67. *Minutes of the Executive Committee of the N.A.C.,* June 25, 1962.

68. *Report of the N.A.C. to the Assembly,* 1962, Belfast, Exhibit E, pp. 4, 5.

69. *Supra.*

70. *Report of the Belfast Assembly,* 1962, Exhibit 155, p. 90.

71. Nelson Chappel, *Report to the Board of Managers,* 1963, Ottawa, p. 3.

72. *Minutes, London Office Advisory Committee,* May 30, 1967, p. 4.

73. Ralph N. Mould, *W.C.C.E. Relations with the W.C.C.,* 1967, Nairobi, pp. 1–6.

74. *Minutes of the Assembly,* 1967, Nairobi.

75. Cf. *supra.*

76. Ralph N. Mould, *Letter to Officers and Members of the W.C.C.E. Board of Managers and Staff,* October 2, 1967.

77. *Minutes, Board of Managers,* 1968, Frankfurt, p. 8.

78. *World Christian Education,* fourth quarter, 1968, p. 118. Serving with Chairman Malik were to be Ralph Mould as vice chairman, Samuel H. Amissah, David Hunter, J. Kenneth Meir, Dean (later Bishop) Federico Pagura, Bishop Kurt Scharf, U Kyaw Than, Randolph C. Miller with Bishop Reuben H. Mueller and Rafael Garcia-Mely *ex officio* and Constable McCracken coopted. Bishop Mueller was unable to attend meetings because of recent surgery and he appointed Gerald E. Knoff as his proxy.

79. *Minutes, Board of Managers,* 1968, Frankfurt, pp. 7, 8.

80. Ibid., p. 11.

81. *Minutes, London Advisory Committee,* March 20, 1968, p. 5. It may be that this informal overture about sounding out European units led to Dr. Malik's request that his committee have *sole* responsibility. Dr. Meir was technically not correct in reporting himself as the only European member of the negotiating committee. Bishop Scharf had also been named. He was not able to attend any of the meetings, however, and functionally it was true that Dr. Meir was the only representative from Britain-Europe.

82. *The Uppsala 68 Report,* pp. 197–99.

83. *Minutes, Board of Managers,* 1969, Geneva, p. 5.

84. *Workbook, Board of Managers,* 1969, Geneva.

85. *Minutes, Board of Managers,* 1970, Loccum, p. 5.

86. Throughout this section the term "merger" has been used as being descriptive of what was proposed and finally done. Attorney Constable MacCracken, treasurer of the council, often pointed out that, technically, a joining of a Swiss association and a United States corporation (the W.C.C. and the W.C.C.E. respectively) could not be called a "merger" in a legally precise use of language. I have used the term, however, in its common and imprecise meaning.

87. *Encuentro,* pp. 226, 227.

88. Ibid., pp. 222–224.

Bibliography

General Historical Background

Robert C. Alberts, *The Good Provider* (Boston: Houghton Mifflin, 1973).

Clarence H. Benson, *A Popular History of Christian Religious Education* (Chicago: Moody Press, 1943).

P. G. Bhagwat, *A Short History of the India Sunday School Union* (1941).

Arthur M. Black, "Sunday Schools and World Evangelism," in *The International Review of Missions,* pp. 255–58, Vol. 28 (London: Oxford Press, April 1939).

W. C. Bower and P. R. Hayward, *Protestantism Faces Its Educational Task Together* (Appleton, Wisconsin: C. C. Nelson Publishing Company, 1949).

W. C. Bower and Roy G. Ross, eds., *The Disciples and Religious Education* (St. Louis: Christian Board of Publication, Bethany Press, 1936).

Anne M. Boylan, "The Nursery of the Church: Evangelical Protestant Sunday Schools, 1820–1880" (an unpublished Ph.D. dissertation, University of Wisconsin, 1973).

Ian Bradley, *The Call to Seriousness: The Evangelical Impact on the Victorians* (New York: MacMillan, 1976).

Arlo A. Brown, *A History of Religious Education in Recent Times* (New York-Cincinnati: Abingdon Press, 1923).

Martin Carnoy, *Education as Cultural Imperialism* (New York: McKay, 1974).

Eldon G. Ernst, *Moment of Truth for Protestant America—Interchurch Campaigns Following World War One* (Missoula, Montana: Scholars' Press, 1972).

Edward D. Grant, "The Sunday School Movement in America" (an unpublished thesis George Peabody College, 1928).

E. N. Green, *The Church of England and the Sunday Schools* (London: Children's Council, Church of England Board of Education, undated).

Hansard, *Parliamentary Debate on Christian Unity,* House of Lords (London: Her Majesty's Stationery Office, 1961).

Robert M. Hopkins, Jr., *Dr. Robert M. Hopkins and International Christianity* (New York: William Frederick Press, 1956).

William Bean Kennedy, *The Shaping of Protestant Education* (New York: Association Press, 1966).

Harold Mackintosh, *By Faith and Work,* A. A. Thomson, ed. (London: Hutchinson and Co., Ltd., 1966).

Sidney E. Mead, *The Lively Experiment, The Shaping of Christianity in America* (New York: Harper and Row, 1963).

J. Kenneth Meir, *Labour of Love* (Nutfield, Redhill, Surrey, England: National Christian Education Council, 1971).

E. D. McCafferty, *Henry J. Heinz, A Biography* (Privately printed, Pittsburgh, 1923).

Cecil Northcutt, *For Britain's Children* (London: National Sunday School Union, 1953).

Constance Parker, *Fifty Years of Teacher Training* (Nutfield, Redhill, Surrey, England: Robert Raikes Historical Society, 1967).

Susan A. Pratt, "Half a Century of Christian Education in Yokohama," in *The Japan Evangelist* (May 1922), pp. 184–185.

Historical Treatments of the World's Sunday School Association, World Council of Christian Education

Arthur Black, *The Golden Jubilee of the World's Sunday School Association* (London: W.S.S.A., 1939).

Frank L. Brown, *A Sunday School Tour of the Orient* (New York: Doubleday, Page & Co., 1916).

Nelson Chappel, mimeographed material from Archives of World Council of Christian Education and Sunday School Association, *Program Administration in the History of the W.C.C.E.S.S.A.*, 1964.

Nelson Chappel, *Sketch of the W.C.C.E.S.S.A.*

Nelson Chappel, *The Story Behind the World Council of Christian Education and Sunday School Association.*

Nelson Chappel, *The World Council of Christian Education and Sunday School Association.*

Forrest L. Knapp, "The World Council of Christian Education," in P. H. Lotz, *Orientation in Religious Education* (New York: Abingdon Press, 1950).

Marion Lawrance, *An Outlined Chronological Table Undertaking to Give Some of the Outstanding Dates in the Development of the Sunday School Work* (London: W.S.S.A., 1923).

Everett M. Stowe, *The Story Behind the World Council of Christian Education.*

Periodicals

The Bulletin, British Committee, W.S.S.A., June 1926 through October 1935.

British Committee Popular Reports, W.S.S.A., 1914 through 1962.

Ladies' Auxiliary for Scotland, British Administrative Committee, World's Sunday School Association, Annual Reports, 1935 through 1959.

W.C.C.E.S.S.A., North American Committee News Bulletin, 1945 through 1964.

World Christian Education, vol. 1, [No. 1], December 1945—vol. 27, first quarter, 1972.

World Wide Sunday School News (mimeographed news releases, 1914–1919; 1921–1934).

Study Guides and Reports of Institutes, Assemblies, and Conferences

(Arranged chronologically)

First European Sunday School Convention, Budapest, 1931.

Havana Conference on Religious Education, 1938.

Christian Education and World Evangelization. Official Report of the International

Congress on Christian Education, Mexico City, D.F., Mexico, 1941.

Reports of Curriculum and Local Church Work Conferences, mostly in Africa, 1949–1956.

The Church College. Report of the Seminar on the Church-related College. Sponsored by the World Council of Christian Education and Sunday School Association and the World's Student Christian Federation, Toronto, 1950.

Commission Reports, World Institute on Christian Education. Toronto, 1950.

Christian Education Around the World Today. The sourcebook for the World Institute on Christian Education, Toronto, 1950.

Report of the West African Conference on Christian Education, 1956.

H. A. Hamilton, *Jesus Christ, the Way, the Truth, and the Life.* A preparatory study guide for the 14th World Convention on Christian Education and the World Institute on Christian Education, Tokyo and Nishinomiya, Japan, 1958.

Everett M. Stowe, *Christian Education in the Present World Situation.* A resource book for the World Institute and the World Convention on Christian Education, 1958.

Report of the World Institute on Christian Education, Nishinomiya, Japan, 1958.

Training Ministers for a Teaching Ministry. Report of seminars on Christian education as a part of the curriculum of the theological seminary, Tokyo, 1958.

The Educational Mission of the Church in Today's World. Report of the Third World Institute, Belfast, 1962.

Randolph Crump Miller, *The Educational Mission of the Church.* A preparatory study guide for the 1962 World Institute on Christian Education, Belfast, 1962.

The Teaching Ministry of the Church. Report of the Second World Theological Education Seminar, Belfast, 1962.

World Consultation on Curriculum, Furingen, Switzerland, 1964.

Christian Education Conference, Oxford, 1964.

Planning Committee Minutes, 1967 World Institute, Nairobi, 1965.

Fourth World Institute on Christian Education, Nairobi, 1967.

Workbook, World Institute on Christian Education, Nairobi, 1967.

C. Ellis Nelson, *Issues Facing Christian Educators.* Report of the fourth World Institute on Christian Education, Nairobi, 1967.

Encuentro, New Perspectives for Christian Education. Report of the 1971 assembly of the World Council of Christian Education.

William B. Kennedy, *Encuentros: A New Ecumenical Learning Experience,* 1971.

Minutes and Records of W.S.S.A., W.C.C.E., W.C.C.E.S.S.A., W.C.C.E. Meetings and Actions

BRITISH SECTION

(Committee, Administrative Committee, European Regional Committee)

Minutes, 1921, 1931, 1932, 1934 to 1953, 1955 to 1971.

Minutes of the Executive Committee, 1963 and 1964.

Minutes of the Sunday School Union, Great Britain, September 18, 1903 to January 19, 1906.

Minutes of the India Sunday School Union, January, 1934–October, 1946.

NORTH AMERICAN SECTION

(Committee, Administrative Committee, North American Regional Committee)

Minutes, July 13, 1928–May 12, 1932, Board of Managers of the North American Section.

Minutes, November, 1932–March, 1971.

Minutes of the Executive Committee, American Section, 1916 to 1920, 1922–1923, 1925–1927, and 1930.

Minutes of the Business Committee (later executive committee), North American Administrative Committee, World's Sunday School Association, 1917–1964.

Minutes of the Advisory Committee to the New York Office, March 1, 1965– September, 1971.

Minutes of other subcommittees of the New York Committee:

Minutes of the Committee on Work in Moslem Lands, 1915–1918.

Minutes of Field Work Committee (Committee on Field Work, Field Committee), American Section, 1916–1925.

Minutes of the Committee on Education, 1916–1927.

Minutes of Committee on Field Program, 1940–1944.

Minutes of the Committee on Curriculum, 1941.

Minutes of the Committee on Interchange of Information through Publications, 1941, 1942.

Minutes of Committee on Education of Workers, 1941–1944.

Minutes of Special (later General) Committee, 1942, 1943.

Minutes of Committee on World Fellowship in Christian Education, 1943, 1944.

Minutes of the Joint Advisory Committee on Methods and Materials for Religious Education on the Foreign Field, 1922–1926.

Minutes of the Adult Work and Family Life Committee, 1959–1964.

Minutes of the Children's Work Advisory Committee, 1951–1966.

Minutes of the Program Committee, 1945–1958, 1960–1963. (No meeting held in 1959.)

Minutes of the Educational Youth Services Committee, 1956–1963.

Minutes of the Sabbatical Services Project and Correspondence to and from Professors, Faculties and Administrative Heads, 1963–1970.

Statement to the Members of the Foreign Missions Conference, 1921.

North American Administrative Committee, W.C.C.E.S.S.A., and Committee on Missionary Personnel, Division of Foreign Missions, National Council of Churches, *The Training of Missionaries and Foreign Students for Christian Education,* 1953.

Workbooks for Meetings of the Board of Managers and for Assembly Sessions

Appendices for Board of Managers meeting, 1955, Cleveland.

Workbook for Board of Managers meeting, 1959, Glasgow.

Workbook for Board of Managers meeting, 1960, Berlin.

Workbook for Board of Managers meeting, 1961, New York.

Workbook for Board of Managers meeting, 1963, Ottawa.

Workbook for Board of Managers meeting, 1964, Paris.

Workbook for Board of Managers meeting, 1965, Mexico City.

Workbook for Board of Managers meeting, 1966, Oslo.

Workbook for Board of Managers meeting, 1969, Geneva.

Workbook for Board of Managers meeting, 1970, Loccum, Germany.

Workbook for Board of Managers meeting, 1971, Huampani, Peru.

Minutes of the Meetings of the Board of Managers and of Its World Educational Services Committee

Minutes of meetings of the Committee of Reference and Counsel (later the Board of Managers), 1928, 1929, and 1931.

Minutes of the meeting of the Board of Managers (first meeting), 1934, New York.

Minutes of the meeting of the Board of Managers, 1935, London.
Minutes of the meeting of the Board of Managers, 1936, Oslo.
Minutes of the meeting of the Board of Managers, 1938, New York. (No meeting in 1937.)
Minutes of the meeting of the Board of Managers, 1940, Lake Mohonk, N.Y. (No meeting in 1939.)
Minutes of the meeting of the Board of Managers, 1943 (unofficial), New York. (There seem to have been no meetings in 1941 or 1942.)
Minutes of the meeting of the Board of Managers, 1946, London. (There seem to have been no meetings from 1943 to 1946.)
Minutes of the meeting of the Board of Managers, 1947, Birmingham.
Minutes of the meeting of the Board of Managers, 1948, New York.
Minutes of the meeting of the Board of Managers, January, 1949 (unofficial).
Minutes of the meeting of the Board of Managers, 1949, London.
Minutes of the meeting of the Board of Managers, 1950, Toronto.
Minutes of the meeting of the Board of Managers, October, 1951 (unofficial), London.
Minutes of the meeting of the Board of Managers, December 1951 (unofficial), New York.
Minutes of the meeting of the Board of Managers, 1952, London.
Minutes of the meeting of the Board of Managers, 1953, New York.
Minutes of the meeting of the Board of Managers, 1954, Frankfurt.
Minutes of the meeting of the Board of Managers, 1955, Cleveland.
Minutes of the meeting of the Board of Managers, 1956, London.
Minutes of the meeting of the Board of Managers, 1957, Toronto.
Minutes of the meeting of the Board of Managers, 1958, Atami, Japan.
Minutes of the meeting of the Board of Managers, 1959, Glasgow.
Minutes of the meeting of the Board of Managers, 1960, Berlin.
Minutes of the meeting of the Board of Managers, 1961, New York.
Minutes of the meeting of the Board of Managers, 1962, Belfast.
Minutes of the meeting of the Board of Managers, 1963, Ottawa.
Minutes of the meeting of the Board of Managers, 1964, Paris.
Minutes of the meeting of the Board of Managers, 1965, Mexico City.
Minutes of the meeting of the Board of Managers, 1966, Oslo.
Minutes of the meeting of the Board of Managers, 1967, Nairobi.
Minutes of the meeting of the Executive Committee, Board of Managers, January, 1968, New York.
Minutes of the meeting of the Board of Managers, 1968, Frankfurt.
Minutes of the meeting of the Executive Committee, Board of Managers, January, 1969, New York.
Minutes of the meeting of the Board of Managers, 1969, Geneva.
Minutes of the meeting of the Board of Managers, 1970, Loccum, Germany.
Minutes of the meeting of the Executive Committee, Board of Managers, 1971, New York.
Minutes of the meeting of the Board of Managers, 1971, Huampani, Peru.
Minutes of the meetings of the World Educational Services Committee, 1956 to 1970.
Reports of the World Educational Services Committee to the Board of Managers, 1956–1967.

Reports and Minutes of the Assemblies

Minutes of the meetings of the Executive Committee, World's Sunday School Association, 1907–1934.

Minutes of the World Council, World's Sunday School Association, 1936, Oslo.

Source Book for the Assembly of the World Council of the World's Sunday School Association (and enlarged North American Administrative Committee), Lake Mohonk, N.Y., 1940.

Minutes of the Assembly of the World Council of the World's Sunday School Association (*and enlarged North American Administrative Committee*), Lake Mohonk, N.Y., 1940.

Work Book for the World Council, World's Sunday School Association, Birmingham, 1947.

World Cooperation in Christian Education, Report of the World Council of the World's Sunday School Association now the World Council of Christian Education, Westhill Training College, Selly Oaks, Birmingham, 1947.

Minutes of the Assembly, World Council of Christian Education (incorporating the World's Sunday School Association), 1950, Toronto.

Minutes of the Assembly, World Council of Christian Education and Sunday School Association, 1953, New York.

Minutes of the Assembly, World Council of Christian Education and Sunday School Association, 1954, Frankfurt.

Minutes of the Assembly, World Council of Christian Education and Sunday School Association, 1958, Atami, Japan.

Report of the General Secretary to the Assembly, World Council of Christian Education and Sunday School Association, 1962, Belfast.

Minutes of the Assembly, World Council of Christian Education and Sunday School Association, 1962, Belfast.

Report of the Assembly, World Council of Christian Education and Sunday School Association, 1962, Belfast.

Minutes of the Assembly, World Council of Christian Education and Sunday School Association, 1967, Nairobi.

Minutes of the Assembly, World Council of Christian Education and Sunday School Association, 1971, Huampani, Peru.

Printed Convention Yearbooks
(Listed chronologically)

The Work Reported, Examined, Improved, Extended, The World's Sunday School Convention, 1889, London (New York and Chicago: Fleming H. Revell, 1889?).

Uniting, Ingathering, Upbuilding, the Second World Convention, 1893, St. Louis, in the Seventh International Convention Yearbook, 1893 (Chicago: Executive Committees of the I.S.S.A and the W.S.S.A., W. B. Jacobs).

The Work Reported, Examined, Extended, The World's Third Sunday School Convention, probably 1898, London (Chicago: W. B. Jacobs).

Mrs. John P. Newman, *Travels in the Orient,* The Fourth World Convention, 1904 (New York: Eaton and Mains, Methodist Book Concern, 1904).

Jerusalem Manual of Worship, Rome edition, 1907.

Short Talks—The Cruise, the Holy Land, the Jerusalem Convention, 1904 (Boston: Central Committee, W.S.S.A., 1904).

Charles Gallaudet Trumbull, *A Pilgrimage to Jerusalem* (Philadelphia: The Sunday School Times, 1905).

Sunday Schools the World Around, the Fifth World Convention, 1907, Rome.

World Wide Sunday School Work, the Sixth World Convention, 1910, Washington.

Four World Tours, 1912.

World Wide Sunday School Work, the Seventh World Convention, 1913, Zurich.

Report on Korea, Commission on the Orient, 1913, Zurich.

A Summary of the Findings of the Six Commissions, 1913, Zurich.

Report of the Commission on Latin-America, 1913, Zurich.

The Sunday School and World Progress, Program Book, the Eighth World Convention, 1920, Tokyo.

The Sunday School and World Progress, Report, the Eighth World Convention, 1920, Tokyo.

H. E. Coleman, "Some Results of the World's Sunday School Convention," in *The Japan Evangelist,* Tokyo, February 1921, pp. 43–45.

Articles in *The Japan Evangelist,* Tokyo, November 1920, pp. 292–315.

The World's Sunday School Convention in *The Chinese Recorder,* December 1920 (Shanghai: Presbyterian Mission Press, pp. 865, 866).

Official Call for the Ninth Convention of the World's Sunday School Association, 1923.

The Sunday School and the Healing of the Nations, the Ninth World Convention, 1924, Glasgow.

Report of Survey Committee, W.S.S.A., 1924.

Thy Kingdom Come, Program Book, the Tenth World Convention, 1928, Los Angeles.

Thy Kingdom Come, Report, the Tenth World Convention, 1928, Los Angeles.

O Cristo Vivo (The Living Christ) the Eleventh World Convention, 1932, Rio de Janeiro (St. Louis: The Bethany Press, 1933).

World's Twelfth Sunday School Convention, Official Handbook, 1936, Oslo.

World's Twelfth Sunday School Convention, Report, 1936, Oslo; Alexander Gammie, compiler.

Christian Education and World Evangelization. Official Report of the International Congress of Christian Education, 1941, Mexico City.

Christian Education Around the World Today. A sourcebook for the World Institute and the World Convention on Christian Education, 1950, Toronto.

Christian Education Today and Tomorrow. A pre-Toronto study guide, 1950, Toronto.

Jesus Christ—Teacher and Lord, official program, the Thirteenth World Convention, 1950, Toronto.

World's Thirteenth Convention, Official Report, 1950, Toronto.

Everett M. Stowe, ed., *Christian Education in the Present World Situation.* A resource book for the world institute and world convention, 1958, Tokyo.

H. A. Hamilton, *Jesus Christ: the Way, the Truth, and the Life.* A preparatory study guide for the Fourteenth World Convention on Christian Education and the World Institute on Christian Education, 1958, Tokyo and Nishinomiya, Japan.

World's Fourteenth Convention, program book, 1958, Tokyo.

J. Macdougall Ferguson, *Tokyo Calling, The Report of the 14th Convention* (London: Religious Education Press, Ltd., 1958).

Relations of the World Council of Christian Education and World Council of Churches

Minutes of the Utrecht Conference, 1938, organizing the World Council of Churches.

Nelson Chappel, *World Council of Christian Education Relations with the World Council of Churches.*

W. A. Visser 't Hooft, ed., *New Delhi Speaks, The New Delhi Report, The Third Assembly of the World Council of Churches,* 1961 (New York: Association Press, 1962).

Minutes of the Working (Planning) Party for the Joint Study Commission on Education, 1964.

Minutes of the Joint Study Commission on Education, Berlin, 1964.

Minutes of the Second Meeting of the Joint Study Commission on Education, Isle of Thorns, Sussex, England, 1965.

Education and the Nature of Man, a document from the Joint Study Commission on education, 1967.

Minutes of the Central Committee, World Council of Churches, 1967, Heraklion, Crete, Greece.

Minutes of the Meeting of the Joint Negotiating Committee, 1968, Geneva.

Minutes of the Second Meeting of the Joint Negotiating Committee, March, 1969, Glion, Switzerland.

Minutes of the Meeting of Officers and Staff, Joint Negotiating Committee, December, 1969, Geneva.

Work Book for Third Meeting of the Joint Negotiating Committee, April, 1970, Geneva.

Minutes of the Fourth Meeting of the Joint Negotiating Committee, June, 1970, London.

Staff Conferences, Studies and Reports

(Arranged in approximate chronological order)

The World's Sunday School Association Moves Forward in These Times: The Conquest of the World Through the Sunday School, 1912.

W. C. Pearce, *Travel Letter,* South America, 1923.

James Kelly, *Report on His Visit to the Continent,* 1925.

Robert M. Hopkins, *The Trip to the Near East.*

——— *What is the World Council of Churches?,* 1947.

Mable Small, and Norman J. Bull, *Oslo Calling, the story of the second World Conference of Christian Youth,* 1947.

Forrest L. Knapp, *Suggested Next Steps in Latin America.*

——— *Looking to the Future,* 1946.

James Kelly, *Religious Conditions in some European Countries and the Near East.*

Forrest L. Knapp, *Forty Eight Leaders from Forty Eight Lands,* 1950.

——— *A Report to Fellow Delegates,* after the World Convention in Toronto, 1950.

——— *Analysis of Present Structure and Work of the World Council of Christian Education,* 1950.

——— *Letters to the "Office Family" from Awka, Nigeria, Port Harcourt, Nigeria, and Kimpese, Belgian Congo,* 1951.

——— *Goals and Services, 1952–1956* (1951).

Christian Education Guides: *Planning the Local Program of Christian Education; Preparation of Curriculum Materials; Preparation for Service in Christian Education; Planning Denominational and Interdenominational Service.*

Edgar G. Youdell, *Research into the Use and Effectiveness of Visual Aids in Christian Education,* 1953.

Wilmina Rowland, and Jean M. Fraser, *National Surveys of Cooperative Church Youth Work,* 1954.

Minutes of Secretarial Conferences, 1955–1971.

Edgar G. Youdell, *A Report of an Investigation into the Use and Effectiveness of Films in Evangelism,* 1957.

World Christian Youth Commission. *The Impact of Secondary Education on Young People,* 1962.

Mildred Proctor, *The Christian Education of Children,* 1962.

World Christian Education Fund, 1967.

Education Renewal Fund.

Index